Entre líneas

Laura Martin
Cleveland State University

Entre líneas

A Strategy for Developing Reading Skills

- Proficiency-based methods
- Authentic readings
- Dictionary skill development
- Culture, culture, culture!

HH Heinle & Heinle Publishers, Inc.
Boston, Massachusetts 02116 U.S.A.

Cover design and illustration: Linda Berg
Text design: Vanessa Piñeiro
Illustrations: Randy Sorenson

Editor-in-Chief: Stanley J. Galek
Production Manager: Erek Smith
Developmental Editor: Janet Dracksdorf
Production Editor: Paula Di Camillo

Manufactured in the United States of America
ISBN 0-8384-1496-6

10 9 8 7 6 5 4 3

CONTENTS

PREFACE

Entre líneas, is different from most other Spanish texts in that it focuses on a single skill: reading. The varied readings, exercises, and other information will help you learn to read better in Spanish.

Another difference is that the goal of this book is to help you read *real* materials, not readings composed just for beginners. All of the reading materials in ***Entre líneas*** have been taken from sources intended for native speakers of Spanish in different countries: magazines, newspapers, signs, brochures, advertisements, and so on. The readings have not been altered; they appear just as they did in the original sources. You can expect to learn about the culture of Spanish speakers as you read these materials.

Each unit in ***Entre líneas*** presents a stage in the *Reading Strategy*, a series of ordered steps and techniques for the development of reading skills. This strategy has been developed in accordance with the ACTFL/ETS Proficiency Guidelines and has been successfully tested with students. Each exercise builds on previous ones and refers to what you learned previously. Each unit also includes a *Dictionary Interlude*, which helps develop dictionary skills, and *Applying the Reading Strategy*, a section that gives you the opportunity to put into practice the skills you are learning.

Entre líneas is intended to be used independently. Because the methods used in the book are new to you and because you are likely to be using them independently, explanations are given in English. However, you will see much more Spanish in ***Entre líneas*** than in most beginning texts because of the large number of reading passages included. You can work through ***Entre líneas*** at your own pace, but you should proceed through the units in order. Where appropriate, exercise answers are included in the Answer Key, and the Appendix provides you with special grammatical guides. Since the goal of ***Entre líneas*** is to have you reading Spanish materials you select yourself, you should think of the passages used here as examples or models of types of passages you can read and of ways to apply the *Reading Strategy*.

Entre líneas uses special symbols to indicate how you are to proceed. It is important that you follow these guidelines.

♟ symbol indicates points at which you are to look at a reading passage. You must not go further in the unit until you have read the material you have been instructed to look at.

◈ symbol marks points where you should pause to complete some reading task, answer questions mentally, or review before going on to a reading exercise. Your success with the *Reading Strategy* depends on taking the time to complete these tasks.

✑ symbol indicates that you will complete a writing task. Be sure to complete and check each written exercise *before* continuing in the unit. If you find an error, always return to the reading passage to check for the correct answer and try to determine why you made an error before you go on.

▬▬▬▬▬ symbol is used to indicate that you can continue on in the unit after completing a reading or writing task. This symbol also indicates a convenient stopping place when you need to put a unit aside for a while. Remember—it is important that you follow the sequence established by the *Reading Strategy*. These symbols will help you do that.

Before beginning your work with ***Entre líneas***, think about the title. Reading is a communication process. Good readers—in any language—do much more than simply look at words on a page. They combine all of their previous experience and their general knowledge with their awareness of the context of the passage they are reading *before* they even begin to read. As they read, they look for the communicative purpose of the passage. When good readers have completed a reading, they think about the connections between what they have read and what they expected from the passage, and they try to respond to the writer's communication. All this mental work takes place "between the lines" of a reading. The strategies and techniques in ***Entre líneas*** were developed by examining how good readers read "between the lines" and applying those habits to Spanish materials.

When you have finished ***Entre líneas***, you may have some suggestions or comments about the readings or the techniques you worked with. If you wish to communicate your reactions, I would be glad to hear from you.

Laura Martin
Department of Modern Languages
Cleveland State University
Cleveland, OH 44115

ACKNOWLEDGEMENTS

A great many people have contributed to the development, design, and production of **Entre líneas**. I was originally encouraged to work on the problem of teaching reading by Bruce A. Beatie whose years of research and experience have been tremendously helpful to me. As the book took shape, several readers provided thoughtful and detailed comments. I am especially grateful to reviewers who examined and evaluated draft versions and whose helpful commentary greatly improved the text and organization:

Bruce A. Beatie
Cleveland State University

David Bedford
Southern Illinois University at Carbondale

Alan Garfinkel
Purdue University

Mark Goldin
George Mason University

Reynaldo L. Jiménez
University of Florida

Carol Klee
University of Minnesota

No author could have hoped for greater encouragement or help than have been provided for me by those associated with Heinle and Heinle Publishers. I owe particular thanks to Editor-in-Chief Stanley J. Galek for his support of the **Entre líneas** project, both early and late, and to Developmental Editor Janet Dracksdorf for her constant good humor and the M & M's® Chocolate Candies. The unusual production requirements of this text have put a special strain on Production Editor Paula Di Camillo, and I have appreciated both her patience and meticulousness. All those unsung heroes of the production process have gone well beyond the call of duty in coping with the design and editing problems created by the uniqueness of this project. Although some people still remain unknown to me, I want to pay special tribute to Copyeditor Jane Wall-Meinike, Text Designer Vanessa Piñeiro, and Cover Designer Linda Berg.

To my colleagues and friends at Cleveland State University—especially to José Labrador, John M. Purcell, Philippa B. Yin, and C. Angel Zorita, among many others—thanks for sharing realia items and information, for clearing away questions and doubts, and for taking up slack while I completed this project. I owe you, as I do all those students who instructed me about the reading process and its applications in the Spanish language classroom. And, finally, particular thanks to Paul Meyer who puts up with a lot.

UNIT

I
Reading with Skill in Spanish

The Reading Strategy

Tactics for readers

You probably have never thought much about what happens when you read. Most of us take our ability to understand written language for granted—that is, until we try to read in a second language! Perhaps because the sounds and structures of the second language are different from English, we conclude that there must be a different way of reading a foreign language as well. Many students decide that they should read along, word by word, mentally translating until they come to one they don't know. They get out a bilingual dictionary and look the word up, then go back to the reading passage and continue in the same way. No wonder students read slowly, and unhappily, in the foreign language!

Fortunately, there is a better way to read in a foreign language, and that's what this book is about. The reading method used in this book is based on recognizing how good readers go about reading in their first language and then applying those techniques to reading Spanish.

In order to accomplish this goal, it is important to recognize some facts about reading. The most significant one is that reading is a *process:* it is accomplished through a series of steps, not by a single action. Second, this reading process is *active:* the reader is not just sitting passively. Not only is reading active, but it is also *interactive:* the writer wants to communicate ideas and the reader wants to understand them. Finally, all the parts of this active and interactive process are mental. That means you have to THINK while you are reading.

Another aspect of reading, one that is often overlooked when learning to read a foreign language, is that one normally reads with a specific *purpose* in mind. Perhaps you have never thought about the different purposes you have for reading, but when you are reading something in Spanish, it is always important to decide first why you are reading it; your reason for reading always affects the way you read. Your purpose may be something as simple as looking for a specific piece of information, such as a date or an address. You probably have this purpose in mind when you read many kinds of materials that aren't books. Before going on, stop and THINK of some examples of this kind of reading. What kinds of materials might you read for such a purpose? ◆

A second common reason for reading is to discover the general idea of a passage, without trying to remember specific details. THINK of a recent occasion when you read with that purpose. What kinds of materials do you often read in that way? ◆

Sometimes we read part of a passage to find out whether or not we want to read any more of it. THINK of the last time you started to read something— a magazine or newspaper article, perhaps—and then decided right away that you didn't really want or need to finish it. ◆

Of course, one of the most common reasons for reading is simply for pleasure. What kinds of materials do you read just for fun? ◆

You will probably find it interesting to discuss your answers to these questions with other students. All of us read many different kinds of things and for many different reasons. In every case, our reading purpose guides the reading process. Let's see how this works.

Exercise A.

Here are several examples of familiar types of reading materials in English. Read each question and then read the appropriate passage to find the answer; write each answer in the space provided. Work as carefully as you need to in order to be confident about your answers. Pay attention to the different ways in which you look at each item to find the information you need. Check your answers in the Answer Key.

1. Look at the television schedule. What program is on Cable Channel 28 at 9:00 a.m.? _____

MONDAY _____ APRIL 7, 1986

CABLEVIEWS MAGAZINE — VIACOM EDITION

AM	USA CABLE 21	ESPN CABLE 22	WAKR CH. 23 CABLE 23	CBN CABLE 24	WOR CABLE 25	CNN CABLE 26	VIACOM Community CABLE 27	WCLQ CH. 61 CABLE 28	MTV CABLE 29	Nickelodeon BET CABLE 31
7 00 15 30 45	Cartoons " " "	Nation's Business Nation's Business	Good Morning America " '' "	Superbook " Flying House "	700 Club Cont'd Straight Talk "	Daybreak " " "		Tranzor " He-Man "	Monkees " VJ: Nina Blackwood	Dennis The Menace Lassie "
8 00 15 30 45	" " " "	Today " SportsCenter "	" " " "	Leo The Lion " Lassie "	" " Romper Room "	" " " "	Kings Korner " The Body Beats	Inspector Gadget Plasticman "	" " " "	Belle And Sebastian Today's Special
9 00 15 30 45	Calliope " " "	PGA Golf Greater Greensboro Open Second	Bruce Forsyth " Morning Stretch	Flying Nun " Hazel "	" " Partridge Family	Daywatch " " "	Viacom's Super Seniors Statewatch "	Dallas " " "	VJ: Nina Blackwood " "	Pinwheel " " "
10 00 15 30 45	Make Me Laugh Gong Show "	Round " " "	700 Club " " "	700 Club " " "	My Favorite Martian My Favorite Martian	" " " "	The Gospel Sounds	Love Boat " " "	" " " "	" " " "
11 00 15 30 45	That Girl " Mr. Merlin "	" " SportsLook "	" " New Love Amer. Style	" " American Baby	Bewitched " I Dream Of Jeannie	" " " "	NASA "	Julia " Addams Family	VJ: Alan Hunter " "	" " " "
12 00 15 30 45	Movie: "The Story Of Vernon And Irene Castle"	Aerobics " Tennis WCT	Ryan's Hope " Loving	Bill Cosby " Doris Day	News " " "	Take Two " " "	Wallpaper "	Movie: "Arizona Bushwackers" "	Monkees " VJ: Alan Hunter	Pinwheel " " "
1 00 15 30 45	" " " "	Championship Final " "	All My Children " "	Farmer's Daughter Patty Duke	Joker's Wild " Tic Tac Dough "	" " " "		" " " "	" " " "	" " " "
2 00 15 30 45	Alive & Well " " "	NHL Hockey Washington Capitals at Philadelphia	One Life To Live " "	Father Knows Best Courtship Of Eddie's Father	Let's Make A Deal Dating Game "	Newsday " " "		Green Acres " Cartoons "	" " " "	Today's Special Belle And Sebastian
3 00 15 30 45	Candid Camera Joker's Wild "	Flyers " " "	General Hospital " "	700 Club " " "	Hawaii Five-0 " " "	International Hour " "		Jetsons " Jayce & The Warriors	" " VJ: Alan Hunter	Adventures Of Black Beauty Danger Mouse "
4 00 15 30 45	Bullseye " Jackpot "	" " " "	Lassie " Lucy Show "	Face The Music Name That Tune	Vega$ " " "	Newsday " " "	Airwaves " Cleveland Rocks	He-Man " She-Ra "	VJ: Martha Quinn " "	You Can't On TV Lassie "

2. Now look at the page from a university course schedule. Suppose you have already registered for PSC 319, Public Opinion. Now you want to add Politics of Urban America to your schedule, but you don't want to have two courses with the same professor. Which sections of PSC 215 can you add?

	COURSE DEPT/NO.	SEC- TION	CALL NO.	COURSE TITLE	PRE REQ	CREDIT HOURS	BLOCK OR HOURS	DAYS	BLDG ROOM LOCATION	INSTRUCTOR	AUTH SIZE
	POLITICAL SCIENCE										
A.	PSC 111	1	1981	AMERICAN GOVT		4	BLOCK 1		RT 219	HOLM	117
	PSC 111	2	1982	AMERICAN GOVT		4	BLOCK 3		RT 212	BUSCH	117
	PSC 111	3	1983	AMERICAN GOVT		4	BLOCK 4		MC 436	HURWITZ	120
	PSC 111	4	1984	AMERICAN GOVT		4	BLOCK 8		RT 218	GOVEA	117
	PSC 214	1	1985	STATE GOVT & POL		4	BLOCK 5		RT 220	FLINN	60
	PSC 215	1	1986	4 POL URBAN AMER		4	BLOCK 7		RT 220	LIESKE	117
	PSC 215	2	1987	4 POL URBAN AMER		4	BLOCK 6		RT 217	KWEDER	117
	PSC 215	3	1988	4 POL URBAN AMER		4	BLOCK 3		RT 220	PLAX	117
	PSC 215	51	1989	4 POL URBAN AMER		4	BLOCK 26		MC 103	CATALDO	60
	PSC 221	1	1990	GOV/POL W EUROPE		4	BLOCK 8		MC 106	HURWITZ	60
	PSC 231	1	1991	INTERNATL POLTC		4	BLOCK 2		RT 339	CHARLICK	60
	PSC 310	51	1992	CON LAW		4	BLOCK 25		MC 103	FLINN	60
	PSC 317	1	1993	POL PARTIES GPS		4	BLOCK 7		RT 317	BUSCH	50
	PSC 318	51	1994	PRES & CONGRESS		4	BLOCK 24		RT 220	CATALDO	50
	PSC 319	1	1995	PUBLIC OPINION		4	BLOCK 3		SH 226	LIESKE	30
	PSC 326	1	1996	POLITICS III WOR		4	BLOCK 6		MC 106	CHARLICK	60
	PSC 332	51	1997	POL MID EAST		4	6:00-10:00	T	MC 421	SEGAL	30
	PSC 341	1	1998	MOD POL THOUGHT		4	BLOCK 4		MC 422	SEGAL	30
B.	PSC 400	1	1999	INDEPENDENT STDY	*	1	TBA		TBA	STAFF	10
B.	PSC 400	2	2000	INDEPENDENT STDY	*	2	TBA		TBA	STAFF	10
B.	PSC 400	3	2001	INDEPENDENT STDY	*	3	TBA		TBA	STAFF	10
B.	PSC 400	4	2002	INDEPENDENT STDY	*	4	TBA		TBA	STAFF	10
C.	PSC 403	1	2003	ADMIN INTERNSHIP	*	12	TBA		TBA	KWEDER	10
D.	PSC 420	1	2004	SEM AMER ELEC		8	BLOCK 3		RT1716	HOLM	20
	PSC 501	51	2005	PA POL PROCESS		4	BLOCK 26		RT 314	KWEDER	50
E.	PSC 599	1	2006	INDIVIDUAL RSRCH	*	1	TBA		TBA	KWEDER	10
E.	PSC 599	2	2007	INDIVIDUAL RSRCH	*	2	TBA		TBA	KWEDER	10
E.	PSC 599	3	2008	INDIVIDUAL RSRCH	*	3	TBA		TBA	KWEDER	10
E.	PSC 599	4	2009	INDIVIDUAL RSRCH	*	4	TBA		TBA	KWEDER	10
	PSC 651	51	2010	RSRCH METHODS		4	BLOCK 24		MC 422	GOVEA	30

A. PSC 111, section 1: Recommended for Freshmen.
B. PSC 400's: Independent Study — Permission of Instructor and Junior standing.
C. PSC 403: Permission of Instructor.
D. PSC 420: Formerly PSC 499, American Elections.
E. PSC 599: Permission of Instructor.

COURSE DEPT/NO.	SEC- TION	CALL NO.	COURSE TITLE	PRE REQ	CREDIT HOURS	BLOCK OR HOURS	DAYS	BLDG ROOM LOCATION	INSTRUCTOR	AUTH SIZE
PSYCHOLOGY										
PSY 121	1	2011	PRIN OF PSYCH		4	BLOCK 6		MC 201	STAFF	232
PSY 121	2	2012	PRIN OF PSYCH		4	BLOCK 3		UC 001	ASHCRAFT	202
PSY 121	3	2013	PRIN OF PSYCH		4	BLOCK 9		MC 202	GRILLY	175
PSY 121	4	2014	PRIN OF PSYCH		4	BLOCK 8		MC 202	BURNS	232
PSY 121	5	2015	PRIN OF PSYCH		4	BLOCK 5		MC 201	REED	232
PSY 121	51	2016	PRIN OF PSYCH		4	BLOCK 25		SR 151	STAFF	150
PSY 222	1	2017	PSY OF PERSON	*	4	BLOCK 5		RT 215	RAKOS	126
PSY 225	1	2018	SOCIAL PSY	*	4	BLOCK 4		SR 151	BLAKE	150
PSY 246	1	2019	CHILD PSYCHOLOGY	*	4	BLOCK 9		MC 440	REED	100
PSY 246	2	2020	CHILD PSYCHOLOGY	*	4	8:00-12:00	S	MC 414	STAFF	50
PSY 260	1	2021	INTRO TO LRNING	*	4	BLOCK 11		MC 102	COLEMAN	95
PSY 260	2	2022	INTRO TO LEARNIN	*	4	BLOCK 7		SH 216	COLEMAN	60
PSY 267	1	2023	GROTH & DEVELPMT	*	4	10:00-11:50	MW	SH 216	STAFF	50

3. According to this bookseller's catalogue, which publisher has the most recent Spanish translation of a book by Frank Herbert?

HAILEY, ARTHUR: El apagón, pap., Barcelona: Bruguera	$7.30
HAILEY, ARTHUR: Hotel, Barcelona: Plaza y Janés	$5.60
HAILEY, ARTHUR: Ruedas, pap., Barcelona: Bruguera	$8.50
HAMMETT, DASHIELL: El halcón maltés, pap., Barcelona: Bruguera	$3.00
HELLER, JOSEPH: Tan bueno como el oro, pap., Barcelona: Bruguera	$7.20
HERBERT, FRANK: Dios emperador de Dune, trans. by Montse Conill, pap., 561 p., Madrid: Ultramar, 1985	$6.90
HERBERT, FRANK: Dune, trans. by Domingo Santos, pap., 702 p., Madrid: Ultramar, 1985	$9.80
HERBERT, FRANK: Herejes de Dune, trans. by Domingo Santos, pap., 565 p., Madrid: Ultramar, 1984	$14.30
HERBERT, FRANK: Hijos de Dune, trans. by Domingo Santos, hardc., 554 p., Barcelona: Acervo, 1981	$16.80
HERBERT, FRANK: El mesías de Dune, trans. by Domingo Santos, hardc., 326 p., Barcelona: Acervo, 1982	$18.10
HERBERT, JAMES: Santuario, Barcelona: Plaza y Janés	$15.00
HIGHSMITH, PATRICIA: Crímenes bestiales, 204 p., Barcelona: Planeta, 1984	$7.80
HIGHSMITH, PATRICIA: Extraños en un tren, Barcelona: Anagrama	$10.30
HIGHSMITH, PATRICIA: El grito de la lechuza, trans. by Joaquín Llinás, 317 p., Barcelona: Noguer, 1984	$9.10

4. Now read a paragraph from a textbook on the American Civil War. According to this author, the South counted on three factors to guarantee its victory.

The belief that the North would not fight wholeheartedly, if it fought at all, was one of the three chief factors that the South had counted on to insure the success of secession. It was a hope that persisted even after the others were gone. One expectation, that of foreign aid, was fading by the end of 1862. After Gettysburg and Vicksburg it had completely disappeared; and also it was by that time no longer possible to hope for a strictly military victory—on the basis of superior leadership, natural fighting qualities, and advantageous geography—against the numbers and resources of the North. The Confederacy was reduced to fighting a stubborn, slowly yielding defensive action that could have but one result—if the North were sufficiently determined upon victory to pay the cost. It may not be too much to say that the last half of the Civil War turned upon this last condition. In the end, of course, the South was herself engulfed in defeatism. . . .[1]

Now list the factors.

_____

_____

_____

5. Read the poem by Lord Byron. Do you think the poet would have protested or supported the Vietnam War? What makes you think so?

When a Man Hath No Freedom to Fight For At Home

When a man hath no freedom to fight for at home,
    Let him combat for that of his neighbors;
Let him think of the glories of Greece and of Rome,
    And get knocked on his head for his labors.
To do good to mankind is the chivalrous plan,
    And is always as nobly requited;
Then battle for freedom wherever you can,
    And, if not shot or hanged, you'll get knighted.[2]

Now, let's review what Exercise A illustrates about the reading process. The first two items concerned similar information: time of day. You probably looked at the times in the TV listings almost as soon as you began, but, in the class schedule, you probably checked the times last. Your reading purpose determined the way you approached the material.

After noting that the third item is a bibliography, you probably did not even look at any entries other than the ones for Frank Herbert, and then looked only at the years of publication and the names of the publishers. You may not even have noticed the title of Herbert's most recent book. There was no reason to do so, since that information wasn't necessary to your reading purpose.

1 Wood Gray. *The Hidden Civil War: The Story of the Copperheads.* (NY: Viking Press, 1964), p. 14. [Compass Books Edition].

2 George Gordon, Lord Byron (1824), from *Norton Anthology of Poetry, Shorter Edition.* (NY: W. W. Norton and Company, 1970) p. 284.

In the prose paragraph, on the other hand, you probably read most of the words, but not all with equal care. The question itself alerted you to the kind of information you were after, just as the other questions had, but the information in this case was a little more difficult to pull out. Were you misled by the three elements of a military victory? Perhaps you had to read some lines more than once, just to be sure you had the right factors. Again, your reason for reading guided the way you examined the material. Finally, you may have read the poem several times, since the question calls for your own interpretation. You shouldn't be surprised to find that other people might not agree with you about the meaning of the poem! Here is where your interaction with the author is most obvious: You are working to understand the meaning the poet wished to convey. Here is also where your own personality and experience have the greatest effect on how you read. In this case, your personal philosophy about war and freedom and your awareness of American history—and even your feelings about reading poetry—may have affected the way you read and interpreted this poem. Each reader brings a different set of experiences to what is read, and, therefore, reads it differently from other people.

Don't be concerned if your own reading processes were not exactly like the ones described here. These differences result in part from your own experiences with this type of reading and possibly from the fact that your reading skills in English are not as highly developed as they could be. If that is the case, you will be glad to know that learning to read Spanish well will help improve your English reading too!

Each of the approaches used in Exercise A represents a series of steps in the reading process, steps we will call the *Reading Strategy*. The goal of this book is to present a strategy for better reading and help you learn to apply it through practice. It is a plan that has been adapted for English speakers who want to learn to read well in Spanish, and it can be applied at the earliest stages in your study of Spanish.

Each of the units in this book builds on the work of preceding ones. The units should, therefore, be completed in order. All the reading materials in a unit relate to a theme. More importantly, all the reading materials included are "real"—that is, they are all intended to be read by native speakers of Spanish. You will read many different kinds of materials in this book. Some of them may not even look like "readings" to you, but all of them are intended to be read in real life. They have not been invented just for students. You will find that many "real" readings are actually easier to understand than the kinds of "reading" that some textbooks include. You will start to see why that is true as soon as you take the first steps in the *Reading Strategy*.

The organization of **Entre líneas** presupposes several things about you. Most likely, you are a native speaker and reader of English. You may be a student, currently enrolled in a Spanish course where you are studying Spanish grammar and working on the skills of speaking and writing. The book does *not* assume that you are using this book in a class or with an instructor, although if you are, you will find suggestions about activities to do in class or with your classmates. The most important assumption in this book is that you will want to use it profitably and that you will therefore use a *Reading Strategy* appropriate to it: You will work through it carefully, from front to back, stopping to do the exercises as they are presented, and THINKING seriously about what you are doing. You should already have looked at **Entre líneas** to see how it is organized and what parts it has, and you should have read the preface for important introductory information. If you have not yet done so, stop here and do it now.

Now, let's begin to be more specific about our *Reading Strategy*. The steps you will follow when reading Spanish take into consideration the value of *guessing*, the relevance of *context*, and the importance of *transferred skills and knowledge*.

The value of guessing. Most of us have probably become convinced that guessing is not as good as knowing. Certainly, random guessing can be pretty risky. A good guess, however, one based on previous experience and knowledge—what one might call a hypothesis—can be almost as good as knowing! One major difference in the way we approach reading in our native language and in a foreign language is how we handle guesses. In a foreign language, we are often afraid to guess. We want to know the "right" meaning of every single word. That's why we seem to spend more time inside our dictionaries than we do with the reading material itself. When we read in our native language, we guess all the time. Good readers are constantly formulating new guesses about the material and checking on previous ones. These guesses are not random; they are hypotheses based on previous experience and knowledge.

Exercise A should have confirmed this fact. When you looked at the TV listing, you guessed that it was organized like similar listings you have seen, with the times presented chronologically and the channels listed in numerical order. When you looked at the the bibliography, you guessed that it was in alphabetical order by author and that the publisher's name would appear toward the end of each listing. In the historical paragraph, you guessed that the factors would be given as some sort of list within the paragraph; you may even have guessed at the meanings of certain words. Certainly, in the poem, you guessed at the possible associations the poet wanted to make to Greece and Rome, and you had to guess whether he was being sarcastic about knighthood.

When you read in Spanish, you must be even more willing to guess. Luckily, many Spanish words are easily guessable by an English speaker, especially when written. These familiar-looking words are called *cognates*. Exercise B will help show you how much cognates can help you when you read. Do the exercise without looking anything up in your dictionary. If you've been in a Spanish class for more than a few days, this exercise may seem very easy to you!

Exercise B.

This exercise lists section titles from a Spanish newspaper and English translations of first lines from articles that might appear in such sections. Match each first line to the section most likely to contain that article. You will not only have to guess the meanings of the words in the headings but also guess what kinds of topics and writing style would be appropriate to each section. Check your answers after you finish.

a. Noticiero científico

b. Guía cinematográfica

c. Correspondencia

d. Opinión editorial

e. Noticias de sociedad

_____ **1.** Congratulations to Dr. Daniel Morales Ruíz and his lovely wife, Teresa, on the happy occasion of their tenth anniversary.

_____ **2.** *Cocoon* (US, 1985), directed by Ron Howard and starring Don Ameche.

     3. To the editors: Your recent article on conditions in the local public housing apartment buildings showed a shocking disregard for fact.

     4. A promising vaccine against leprosy is now being tested in Norway by scientists from several countries.

     5. Of the two candidates for judge, we feel that Julia Pérez Ocampo is by far the more qualified and deserves the support of voters from all parties.

The value of guessing as part of the *Reading Strategy* is hard to overemphasize. Remember that, when reading, you should always pay more attention to what you know or can guess than to what you do not know.

The relevance of context.   In order for your guesses to make sense, you must always pay attention to the context of the reading passage. The photographs you see show what is meant by context.

It is easy to see that the first picture is of a poster advertising the Spanish-language version of a movie that most of us recognize. We can learn something about the movie itself—what actors star in it or who produced it—but beyond that, the context is too limited for us to gather any other information.

The context is larger for the second photograph. We can see that the movie is popular—people are waiting to see it. We can guess the approximate temperature based on the people's clothing. Although there are many things the photo does not tell us (why there are more men than women in line; where the movie theater is located), as our context for the photo grows larger, we gain more information upon which to base guesses and questions. As our context grows smaller, we can focus on greater detail.

In exactly the same way, when we read, the context surrounding reading material provides information that is useful in making good guesses about the content of the reading. A good reader does not think in terms of individual words or sentences; instead, he or she thinks in terms of the appropriate *context unit*, the amount of material needed for and relevant to guessing and comprehension.

The size of an appropriate context unit varies with the type of reading material and the reader's purpose. The size may change at different stages in the reading process. Let's imagine that you are reading the weekly television listings to find out what programs are on at eight o'clock tonight. Your context unit would be just today's listings. If, on the other hand, you wanted to find out the day a particular program is going to be on, your context unit would include the listings for the whole week. Consider a more complex case, a Shakespearean sonnet. The appropriate context unit will be the entire poem, but, as you read, your attention will probably focus on the individual stanzas as units. In longer works, the context unit might be the chapter or the section, but in all pieces of prose, the *immediate* context unit—the important unit for close reading—is always the paragraph.

The importance of transferred skills and knowledge.   Remember that good readers can apply reading skills they use in their native language to reading in a foreign language. Besides specific skills, though, each of us also brings different background knowledge to what we read. For example, read this sentence:

> *Avoid operations that may be restricted by the iAPX286 to assure system integrity, low interrupt latency or low bus request latency (for example, shift/rotate with shift count greater than 31, . . .).*

Specific training or knowledge about computer software programming is what makes a sentence like this one understandable to some readers but not others.

Students of Spanish sometimes forget how much background information they use in understanding what they read in English and that it is just as important when reading Spanish. In order to use this knowledge, you must remember that reading is both *active* and a *process* and that you must always THINK when you read.

One of the specific areas of knowledge that will be most helpful to you when you are reading in Spanish is your knowledge of English vocabulary. Spanish and English share a great many words. An important part of the *Reading Strategy* is to learn to use cognates to help you read in Spanish.

Dictionary Interlude

Selecting and using a bilingual dictionary

Bilingual Spanish-English dictionaries are central to the way many students read. Dictionaries *are* a valuable resource for you as you learn to read in Spanish, but they are most helpful when used efficiently. Any kind of dictionary, including a bilingual one, is intended primarily for use by people who already know a great deal about the language or languages in it. Since most of the bilingual dictionaries sold to Spanish students are not really intended for beginners, these dictionaries are full of pitfalls for a new user. It is best to think of your dictionary as a last resort; it is of limited use, and is only for specific purposes. Using it well requires some specialized training. In this book, each unit contains a Dictionary Interlude that will help you learn to use your Spanish-English dictionary to your best advantage.

Before you can complete Unit I, you will need a bilingual dictionary of your own. Perhaps you already own one, but if not, the following information will help you select a good one. The best bilingual dictionaries have these characteristics:

- They include an ample inventory of words, about 30,000.
- They include several definitions for each entry, not just one or two equivalents. Compare several entries in the dictionaries you are considering and look for the one that contains the most information.

- They indicate the part of speech (noun, verb, and so on) for all entries. They also include other important grammatical information with each entry, such as the gender of nouns and the class of irregular verbs. Make sure the dictionary you are considering includes information of this sort.
- Some dictionaries include a short grammar summary or verb chart as well as a guide to pronunciation. These sections are often useful.
- Some dictionaries designed for students include special sections with lists of common phrases and idiomatic expressions. These are useful if they are well organized, but it is often better to use a dictionary that puts notes about unusual usage right in the entries.
- A good dictionary is legible and its abbreviations and entries are easy to see and to read.

Your instructor may have additional advice about selecting an appropriate dictionary.

Do not continue with this unit until you have a dictionary to use.

Once you have chosen a good bilingual dictionary, you must become familiar with its organization. Exercise C will help you familiarize yourself with your own dictionary.

Exercise C.

Refer to your Spanish-English dictionary and answer the following questions.

1. Where are the Spanish entries in your dictionary—in the front section or in the back?_____

2. Does each section have its own table of contents or is there only one in the dictionary?_____

3. On what page are the abbreviations for the Spanish entries explained?_____

4. If there is a section that includes grammatical description (for example, a list of irregular verbs or a section describing adjective agreement), on what page(s) is it located?_____

5. Is there a preface or a section of advice to the user? If so, locate it and read it.

6. Are there special sections, such as lists of expressions? If so, what kind of material do they include and where will you find them?

_____

_____

_____

Applying the Reading Strategy

In this section, which is found in each unit, the *Reading Strategy* steps developed in the unit are reviewed and then applied to a new set of reading materials. This first unit has introduced some ideas about the reading process itself and has emphasized the importance of knowing your purpose for reading, of knowing the context of your reading, and of guessing on the basis of your previous experience and knowledge. Let's apply those important *Reading Strategy* techniques to a pair of similar passages: weather sections from two newspapers—one from Ohio and one from Spain.

Before even looking at the readings themselves, THINK about the reasons why you might read materials of this type. What kinds of questions do you expect weather maps and charts to answer for you? In other words, what kinds of information are you most likely to look for in that section of a newspaper? What are some of the important words you would expect to see in the weather section of the newspaper in your town? What words might you expect to find in a newspaper from an area of the world that is further north than yours? Further south? What other countries appear in weather maps of the continental United States? What other countries might appear in a weather map in a newspaper from Spain? (If you can't answer this question, stop and locate Spain on the map on page 261 before going on.)

Now you are ready to look at the two weather sections. Look for similarities in the way they are presented (the layout) and in the types of information included in each one. *Do not use your dictionary for this exercise.* (Remember that temperature is measured in Celsius [centigrade] in Europe. You can convert Celsius temperatures to the Fahrenheit system with this formula: multiply the Celsius temperature by 9; divide the result by 5; add 32.)

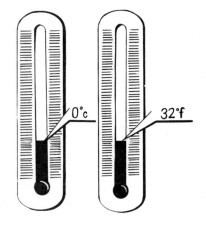

THE WEATHER

A. LOCAL FORECAST

High today 40 (4C). Lake-shore temperature 39 (4C). Low tonight 32 (0C). Damp and raw weather today with chilly temperatures and a bit of rain and snow mixed. Tonight will bring flurries that could whiten the ground in some places. Clouds will give way to a little sun and it will be milder tomorrow. High tomorrow 47.

FIVE-DAY FORECAST

TODAY
Damp and cold with a bit of rain mixed with snow.
HIGH 40   LOW..................32

TOMORROW
Clouds may give way to a little sun.
HIGH 47   LOW..................34

FRIDAY
Partly to mostly sunny, warmer.
HIGH 58   LOW..................38

SATURDAY
Some sun, pleasant.
HIGH 62   LOW..................40

SUNDAY
Increasing clouds with a chance of showers, still mild.
HIGH 58   LOW..................40

B. THE REGION/TODAY'S HIGHS

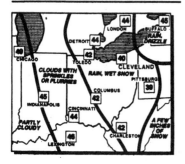

C. REGIONAL FORECASTS

NE OHIO, NW PENNSYLVANIA, WESTERN NEW YORK — Cloudy and cold with rain and wet snow today. Still cloudy and cold tonight. Lows 28-35. Tomorrow will not be as cold but still fairly cloudy. Highs 44-54.

CENTRAL AND SE OHIO, SW PENNSYLVANIA, WESTERN WEST VIRGINIA — Cloudy and cold today and tonight with rain and snow. A small accumulation is possible at night. Highs today 37-45. Lows 30-37. Tomorrow will not be as damp with clouds perhaps giving way to some afternoon sunshine. Highs 45 in Pennsylvania to 55 in Ohio.

NW OHIO, NORTHERN INDIANA, SOUTHERN MICHIGAN, SOUTHERN INDIANA AND THE CHICAGO AREA — Still cloudy and chilly

D.

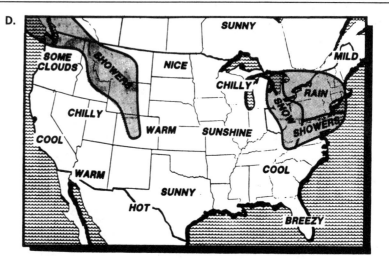

E. METEOROLOGICAL DATA

PROVIDED BY NATIONAL WEATHER SERVICE

Tuesday,

	7 a.m.	1 p.m.	4 p.m.
Barom. (sea level)	29.77	29.78	29.81
Humidity (relative)	89	48	61
High temp......56	Low temp......44	Normal mean......48
High last year 74		Low last year 55
Record high		81 in 1976
Record low		22 in 1935
Precip.		0.37
Snowfall.............zero	Snow depth.............zero

Readings taken between midnight and 4 p.m.

Monday,

High temp.............70	Low temp.............32
Mean temp.............51	Normal mean.............48
Departure for the month	plus 35
Departure for the year	plus 221
Precip. for the day	0.04
Precip. for the month	1.94
Precip. for the year	9.69
Departure for the day	minus 0.07
Departure for the month	plus 0.40
Departure for the year	plus 0.49
Snowfall for the day	zero
Snowfall for the month	0.2
Snowfall for the season	58.3

F. WORLD TEMPERATURES

Acapulco	88/70	s	London	49/42 sh
Amsterdam	48/38	sh	Madrid	58/42 pc
Athens	66/48	s	Manila	95/74 pc
Auckland	65/51	s	Mexico City	82/55 pc
Barbados	82/72	t	Moscow	34/31 r
Beirut	70/55	sh	Nassau	80/66 s
Berlin	45/37	sh	Oslo	36/20 pc
Bermuda	70/60	pc	Paris	50/43 r
Brussels	49/42	sh	Peking	66/44 s
Buenos Aires	70/46	s	Rio de Janeiro	86/74 t
Cairo	90/60	c	Rome	58/42 sh
Copenhagen	40/36	sh	San Juan	88/73 pc
Dublin	45/37	r	Seoul	62/51 s
Edmonton	45/27	pc	Stockholm	35/23 pc
Freeport	81/65	s	Sydney	76/55 pc
Geneva	55/35	c	Tokyo	57/50 sh
Helsinki	34/27	sf	Vancouver	52/46 r
Hong Kong	76/69	sh	Vienna	48/27 s
Jerusalem	69/56	sh	Warsaw	44/26 pc
Lima	74/61	pc	Winnipeg	41/25 pc
Lisbon	58/44	pc		

Numbers are yesterday's high/low temperatures.

The Accu-Weather forecast is aired 60 times daily on WQAL-FM/104.

Numbers are high/low temperatures; letters indicate:		
s:sunny	c:cloudy	pc:partly cloudy
sh:showers	r:rain	t:thunderstorms
i:ice	sn:snow	sf:snow flurries

G. TRAVELERS FORECAST

	Yesterday	Today	Thursday	Friday
Albany	69/31 c	46/39 r	44/37 r	55/32 pc
Albuquerque	74/46 pc	76/45 pc	67/36 pc	67/36 pc
Amarillo	64/32 s	72/50 s	76/54 sh	76/54 sh
Anchorage	37/33 c	40/34 c	42/36 c	42/34 c
Asheville	72/57 pc	54/22 pc	53/32 pc	64/34 s
Aspen	38/22 pc	55/34 sh	43/30 sf	45/22 pc
Atlanta	73/59 pc	58/38 pc	60/35 s	72/41 s
Atlantic City	55/38 c	52/42 r	48/40 r	56/40 pc
Austin	77/53 pc	78/61 t	82/65 sh	80/61 sh
Baltimore	51/40 r	53/40 sh	47/38 r	56/36 pc
Billings	41/17 pc	58/40 sh	55/38 sh	53/36 c
Birmingham	71/53 s	60/40 s	68/49 s	76/54 s
Bismarck	36/20 pc	52/34 s	61/42 pc	44/45 c
Boise	44/44 c	52/36 c	54/38 pc	52/34 pc
Boston	51/42 s	46/40 r	43/37 r	46/35 c
Brownsville	79/73 c	82/70 s	84/72 c	82/70 sh
Buffalo	54/48 r	45/40 r	45/38 sh	55/38 pc
Burlington VT	68/32 c	59/38 pc	59/34 pc	54/31 s
Casper	62/19 pc	62/37 pc	58/37 c	55/35 c
Charleston SC	79/60 pc	68/44 pc	64/44 pc	66/40 pc
Charleston WV	68/56 pc	42/36 r	44/36 sh	57/35 pc
Charlotte NC	78/60 pc	60/39 pc	58/39 pc	68/43 s
Cheyenne	54/20 s	74/27 pc	59/35 c	57/20 s
Chicago	40/31 sn	49/34 c	57/44 pc	65/47 pc
Cincinnati	50/38 c	44/33 c	56/35 pc	67/42 s
Columbia SC	80/62 r	62/38 s	62/36 pc	70/39 pc
Columbus	52/45 r	42/35 sh	52/38 pc	63/44 s
Dal-Ft. Worth	72/44 s	74/55 s	78/61 sh	78/61 sh
Dayton	48/36 sn	39/33 c	53/40 pc	65/45 s
Denver	63/26 s	70/42 pc	61/35 pc	54/30 s
Des Moines	41/29 r	58/40 s	62/42 pc	67/45 sh
Detroit	47/42 c	44/35 sh	53/37 c	62/44 pc
Duluth	50/34 pc	47/33 s	52/38 pc	52/42 c
El Paso	87/52 pc	86/60 s	84/60 pc	82/58 sh
Evansville	49/41 c	50/36 pc	61/41 pc	72/44 s
Fairbanks	42/19 s	34/21 pc	46/25 pc	46/25 c
Fargo	31/24 c	49/37 s	57/42 pc	43/44 c
Flagstaff	59/22 pc	59/32 pc	49/35 sh	57/32 pc
Greensboro	81/56 s	58/34 pc	54/34 pc	63/35 pc
Hartford	68/32 pc	46/42 r	45/38 r	45/33 c
Helena	58/25 pc	54/34 sh	50/33 sh	48/33 c
Hilo	72/67 r	78/66 pc	78/67 pc	78/68 sh
Honolulu	82/70 pc	82/70 pc	84/72 pc	82/72 sh
Houston	78/55 pc	76/64 s	80/67 sh	78/64 sh
Indianapolis	42/35 sn	45/35 c	58/39 s	66/42 s
Jackson MS	74/44 s	73/44 s	75/52 s	79/54 pc
Jacksonville	85/55 pc	73/46 s	70/42 s	70/42 s
Juneau	41/27 r	42/37 c	44/32 c	48/32 s
Kansas City	45/3 c	58/41 s	63/46 pc	70/48 c
Las Vegas	83/47 c	75/49 pc	70/45 pc	75/50 s
Little Rock	65/43 s	68/48 s	72/50 pc	74/52 c
Los Angeles	74/56 pc	70/58 pc	68/55 pc	72/58 pc
Louisville	53/41 c	48/36 pc	59/42 pc	70/44 s
Memphis	62/49 s	62/45 s	70/50 s	78/56 s
Miami	80/61 pc	82/58 pc	77/54 s	77/53 s
Milwaukee	38/33 sn	45/36 pc	50/40 s	62/44 pc
Mobile	81/61 pc	77/58 s	80/63 s	83/69 s
Montreal	62/36 pc	56/34 s	52/34 pc	52/34 pc
Mpls.-St.Paul	52/33 c	50/39 s	60/43 pc	60/43 pc
Nashville	62/40 pc	52/39 pc	66/49 s	76/54 s
New Orleans	80/62 s	75/55 s	77/60 s	80/64 s
New York	63/46 pc	48/42 r	45/39 r	56/42 pc
Norfolk	64/47 c	62/42 c	54/40 sh	58/38 pc
Oklahoma City	64/52 pc	72/52 s	74/52 sh	74/52 sh
Omaha	41/26 c	59/42 s	65/45 pc	65/45 sh
Orlando	86/59 s	78/51 s	74/48 s	76/49 s
Ottawa	61/36 pc	55/34 s	50/32 s	50/32 pc
Philadelphia	57/44 r	51/40 r	44/39 r	56/40 pc
Phoenix	90/64 pc	86/60 s	79/55 pc	84/57 s
Pittsburgh	64/52 pc	39/34 sn	45/34 c	54/35 pc
Portland ME	57/31 pc	52/37 pc	49/35 c	53/32 pc
Portland OR	59/48 pc	53/42 sh	54/46 c	56/44 pc
Providence	63/35 s	44/41 r	46/39 r	48/35 c
Raleigh	79/57 r	61/35 pc	57/35 pc	66/37 pc
Rapid City	46/15 s	68/35 s	68/42 pc	64/40 s
Reno	60/39 pc	54/29 pc	56/32 pc	60/34 s
Richmond	69/48 c	60/41 c	52/37 sh	58/35 pc

EL TIEMPO

Menos estable

José A. MALDONADO

H. 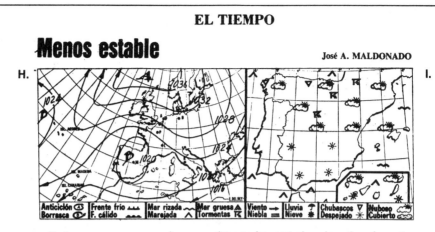 **I.**

| Anticiclón | Frente frío | Mar rizada | Mar gruesa | Viento | Lluvia | Chubascos | Nuboso |
| Borrasca | F. cálido | Marejada | Tormentas | Niebla | Nieve | Despejado | Cubierto |

La borrasca que aparece en el mapa previsto para hoy, centrada encima mismo de nuestra geografía, como también puede apreciarse, es poco profunda y pasaría inadvertida si no fuese porque la situación en los niveles superiores es favorable a la inestabilidad. Con arreglo a lo uno y a lo otro, en el transcurso de las próximas veinticuatro horas lo que podemos esperar son chubascos en buena parte de las regiones septentrionales, así como, de forma más dispersa, en algunas comarcas del Centro. Las temperaturas descenderán ligeramente en el Norte y se mantendrán en el resto de España.

PRONOSTICOS

Area de Madrid.—Aumento de la nubosidad, con riesgo de chubascos por la tarde, que pueden ir acompañados de tormenta. Vientos flojos variables y temperaturas altas.

Cantábrico.—Muy nuboso o cubierto, con chubascos.

Galicia.—Cubierto, con lluvias.

Duero.—Nubosidad variable, generalmente abundante, con riesgo de tormentas, sobre todo por la tarde.

Extremadura.—Algo nuboso en el Norte y poco nuboso o despejado en el Sur.

La Mancha.—Despejado por la mañana y parcialmente cubierto por la tarde.

Andalucía.—Despejado o casi despejado.

Levante.—Poco nuboso o despejado.

Ebro.—Nubosidad variable, con riesgo de tormentas, sobre todo en la cuenca alta.

Cataluña.—Nubosidad variable, con precipitaciones tormentosas en el Pirineo.

Baleares.—Algo nuboso, con riesgo de alguna precipitación débil.

Canarias.—Intervalos nubosos al Norte de las islas y despejado o casi despejado en el Sur.

☐ **Ayer:** Llovió en Galicia, Cantábrico, Alto Ebro y algunos puntos de Aragón, Cataluña y Baleares. Destacaron 32 litros por metro cuadrado en La Coruña, 16 en Vitoria y 12 en Lugo.

Temperaturas extremas: Máxima, 35 grados en Murcia. Mínima, 13 en Salamanca.

☐ **Mañana:** Nuboso con chubascos en el tercio Norte de la Península. Parcialmente cubierto en el Sistema Central, con riesgo de alguna precipitación tormentosa. Poco nuboso o despejado en las demás regiones.

☐ **En Madrid:** Datos meteorológicos.—Temperaturas extremas: Máxima, 32 grados, y mínima, 20. La presión a las veinte horas era de 704 milímetros, tendiendo a descender ligeramente. Los vientos fueron moderados y de dirección variable, llegando a alcanzar una velocidad máxima de 25 kilómetros por hora. La humedad osciló entre el 36 y el 74 por 100.

Temperaturas del agua del mar.—En el litoral español las aguas registraron ayer, aproximadamente, las siguientes temperaturas: Costa Vasca, entre 20 y 21 grados; Costa Verde, entre 18 y 19; Rías Altas, entre 18 y 19; Rías Bajas, entre 17 y 18; Costa de la Luz, entre 20 y 22; Costa del Sol, entre 21 y 23; Costa Blanca, entre 19 y 22; Costa Brava, entre 19 y 21; Baleares, entre 21 y 23, y Canarias, entre 22 y 23.

PARA VIAJEROS

ESPAÑA	M.	m.	X	ESPAÑA	M.	m.	X	EXTRANJERO	M.	m.	X
Albacete	33	19	P	León	27	17	D	Amsterdam	30	14	P
Algeciras	22	16	P	Lérida	34	19	C	Argel	38	19	D
Alicante	31	25	P	Logroño	32	17	P	Atenas	30	23	D
Almería	29	21	D	Lugo	25	15	C	Berlín	25	14	D
Badajoz	28	15	D	Mahón	30	24	D	Bruselas	22	12	D
Barcelona	29	23	P	Málaga	30	18	D	Budapest	29	20	D
Bilbao	26	16	P	Melilla	25	20	D	Buenos Aires	16	6	D
Burgos	30	17	D	Murcia	35	24	D	Caracas	28	20	C
Cáceres	25	15	P	Orense	23	16	C	Casablanca	24	17	D
Cádiz	23	18	D	Oviedo	27	17	Ll	Copenhague	20	15	D
Castellón	32	23	P	Palencia	30	17	D	Dublín	18	10	P
Ceuta	26	17	D	Palma	34	21	D	El Cairo	35	22	D
Ciudad Real	31	20	D	Pamplona	32	16	P	Estocolmo	27	17	D
Córdoba	30	16	D	Pontevedra	22	17	P	Francfort	26	15	P
Cuenca	31	18	P	Salamanca	27	13	D	Ginebra	24	19	D
Gerona	31	16	C	San Sebastián	26	17	C	Lisboa	23	15	P
Gijón	23	13	P	Santander	24	19	P	Londres	24	17	C
Granada	32	17	D	Santiago	18	16	Ll	Luxemburgo	24	15	D
Guadalajara	32	19	D	Segovia	28	18	D	Milán	30	20	P
Huelva	24	17	D	Sevilla	30	15	D	Moscú	22	16	C
Huesca	32	17	D	Soria	29	17	D	Niza	27	21	C
Ibiza	32	25	D	Tarragona	28	21	D	Nueva York	37	26	Ll
Jaén	31	18	P	Tenerife	26	19	P	Oslo	26	14	D
Jerez	26	16	D	Teruel	31	18	P	París	26	16	D
La Coruña	20	17	Ll	Toledo	32	21	D	R. de Janeiro	28	15	Ll
Lanzarote	27	19	D	Valencia	34	21	D	Roma	29	21	P
Las Palmas	23	19	D	Valladolid	32	13	D	Viena	27	17	P

ABREVIATURAS.—M.: Temperatura máxima.—m.: Temperatura mínima.—D.: Despejado.—C.: Cubierto.—Ll.: Lluvias.—P.: Parcialmente nuboso.—T.: Tormentas.—N.: Nieve.—n.: Niebla.—Ch.: Chubascos. (Datos numéricos facilitados por el Instituto Nacional de Meteorología.)

Once you have looked over the two readings, use Exercise D to help you compare them. Remember to THINK! Use everything you know or can guess about the North American weather map to help improve your guesses about the Spanish one.

 Exercise D.

The sections in each of the weather pages can be identified by letters. Match the letters and the sections.

1. Regional maps (the larger context in which the local area is contained)

_____ Continental United States

_____ Western Europe

2. Local maps (the area likely to be most important for readers of these newspapers)

_____ Ohio

_____ Spain

3. Forecasts

_____ Regional US

_____ Local US

_____ Regional Spain

_____ Local Spain (This newspaper is from Madrid.)

4. Meteorological data

_____ Ohio

_____ Madrid

5. Traveler's forecasts

_____ North American newspaper

_____ Spanish newspaper

Now match these symbols used in the Spanish newspaper.

_____ **6.** ☁   a. rain

_____ **7.** ᝰ   b. partly cloudy

_____ **8.** ☂   c. cold front

_____ **9.** ☍   d. area of low pressure

Now look over the weather pages again. THINK about what you know about weather in different seasons of the year.

10. Which of these weather pages was probably published in April?

_____   Which one appeared in July? _____

Now that you are familiar with the organization of these materials, Exercise E will help you find the answers to some typical questions people ask when looking at the weather page. Remember to use what you know about the English material (including vocabulary) to help you guess the meanings of similar Spanish material. Do not look anything up in your dictionary!

Exercise E.

Answer the following questions.

1. What is the weather like in the following cities?

   a. Indianapolis _____

   b. Vancouver _____

   c. Amsterdam in April _____

   d. Amsterdam in July _____

   e. Nueva York _____

2. What is the forecast for these regions?

   a. Texas _____

   b. California _____

   c. Galicia _____

   d. La Mancha _____

Now that you have completed the first step of the *Reading Strategy,* you are probably much more conscious of the way you read in English. Try paying attention to the techniques you use when reading different kinds of materials in English. Your increased awareness will improve your ability to apply those techniques to new materials in Spanish and to benefit from the next unit.

UNIT

2

Looking at
Writing
in Spanish

The Reading Strategy

Prereading: Scanning for format and cognate cues

In Unit 1, you learned about two important aspects of reading: your *purpose* for reading a passage and the *presentation* of the material itself. Different purposes require different approaches to the material, and different layouts give you clues about the way the content is organized. Paying attention to both purpose and presentation help you begin applying the *Reading Strategy*.

During the first stage of the *Reading Strategy*, you prepare to read by using features of presentation to identify the probable content of the material. In this unit, you will become familiar with the way Spanish looks when written. You will learn some helpful facts about the Spanish alphabet and about Spanish names and addresses.

In the next few pages, you will work with written materials extracted from different sources. In each sample, features of the format give you important clues about the source of the sample. All of these samples come from types of writing that are already familiar to English speakers. It will be easy for you to imagine a purpose for reading each of them. Some of the samples use different styles of type to highlight certain information. Others incorporate drawings into the text. Written material is arranged on the page in a different way in each sample. All of these features are aspects of format. It is important to realize how helpful format features are in gathering clues about the content of written material.

To begin, let your eyes run quickly over each sample. Use your knowledge about types of reading materials to identify what type of material each item is. *Do not use your dictionary, and work as quickly as you can.*

Item 1

Cuernavaca Junio 1985   **PEDIDOS 15-33-22**   Campos—Carnicería

[Telephone directory listing — columns of names, addresses, and phone numbers]

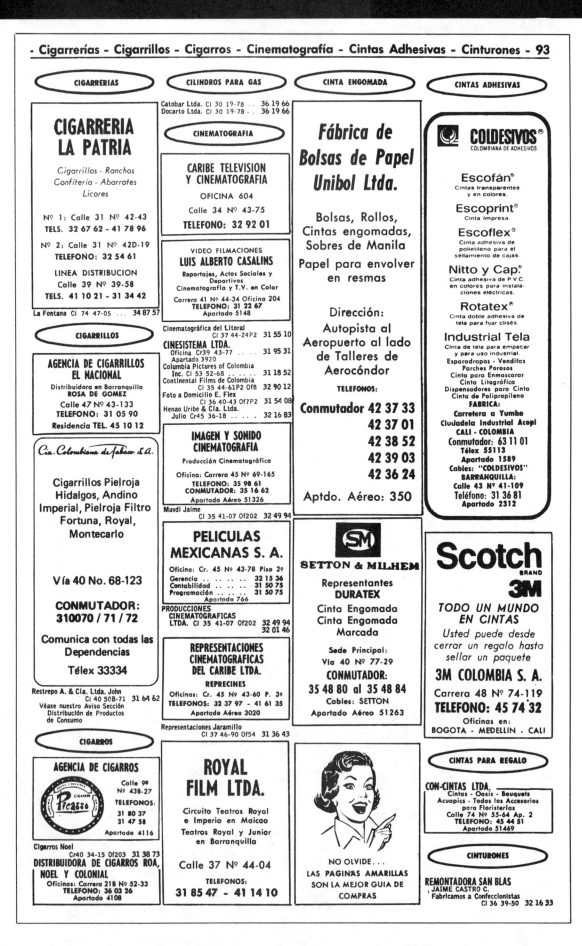

Alejandro Muñoz Alonso
El terrorismo en España

Planeta/Instituto de Estudios Económicos

Item 3

HISTORIA DEL URUGUAY

M. SCHURMANN PACHECO
M. L. COOLIGHAN SANGUINETTI

DESDE LA EPOCA INDIGENA HASTA NUESTROS DIAS

Item 4

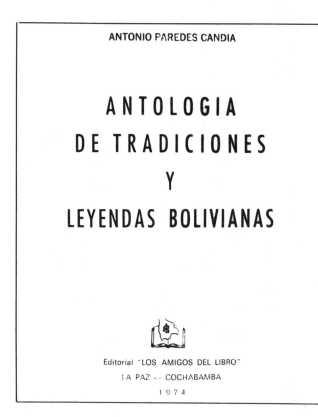

ANTONIO PAREDES CANDIA

ANTOLOGIA DE TRADICIONES Y LEYENDAS BOLIVIANAS

Editorial "LOS AMIGOS DEL LIBRO"
LA PAZ -- COCHABAMBA
1974

INDICE

Item 5

EL PAIS

EDICIÓN INTERNACIONAL

Suscripción a EL PAIS. Edición Internacional (marque con una equis lo que le interese). por un periodo de

☐ 1 año (52 números) 50 $USA ☐ 9 meses (39 números) 39 $USA ☐ 6 meses (26 números) 26 $USA ☐ 3 meses (13 números) 13$USA

NOMBRE Y APELLIDOS

DIRECCIÓN   CIUDAD   D. POSTAL

PROVINCIA, DEPARTAMENTO O ESTADO   PAÍS   EDAD   PROFESIÓN

Forma de pago: Los precios en dólares — o su contravalor en pesetas a la fecha de remisión de este boletín — son iguales para cualquier país del mundo Es imprescindible la recepción del pago para formalizar la suscripción

☐ Por talón bancario o giro postal a la orden de PRISA.(**Miguel Yuste, 40, 28037 Madrid**).

☐ Con cargo a mi tarjeta   **American Express**

                           Visa Internacional

          Master Charge Internacional

                  Fecha de caducidad

FIRMA LA MISMA DE LA TARJETA

Item 9

Dr. Carlos Francisco Riqué Flores.

Médico Veterinario Zootecnista.

Cuauhtémoc No. 18   Teléfono 8-16-91

San Cristóbal de Las Casas, Chiapas.

Item 10

Now write your guesses about what the items are in the blanks. You will check your answers later.

1. _____   6. _____

2. _____   7. _____

3. _____   8. _____

4. _____   9. _____

5. _____   10. _____

Now take a moment to look at each sample again. Pay attention to everything that seems familiar—words as well as format. Try to determine what country each item is from. You may want to revise your first guesses after looking at the samples again. By the way, do not be surprised if you find words that seem to be missing written accents. Accents are often omitted on capital letters.

Now complete Exercise A, which will add to your background knowledge and will help you check your guesses about the items. Check your answers and correct any errors by reexamining the samples to find the proper information.

 ## Exercise A.

Item 1: Residential telephone listings (Mexico)

1. What is the most striking difference between these telephone numbers and yours? _____

2. What two ways of writing telephone numbers are illustrated on this page?_____

Item 2: Business telephone listings (Colombia)

3. What color do you think this page is in the original?   _____

4. Compare this item to the previous one. What are the major differences between them in terms of their formats?

   _____

5. What is the purpose of the heads across the top of the page? How are they ordered? Where do you see them again on the page?

   _____

6. What is the likely meaning of the abbreviation **tels?**   _____

7. **Cinta** refers to various narrow, ribbon-like objects, including packing tape, recording tape, and hair ribbons. What do you think **cinta adhesiva** refers to? _____ What is **cinta para regalo? (Regalo** means "gift.") _____ **Cinta** is also at the root of **cinturón,** *belt).* Can you guess why? _____

Items 3, 4, and 5: Title pages and tables of contents

8. What similar information is found in all three of these items?

_____

9. Which of the items include information about the publishers of the work?

_____

10. What do you think **índice** means? _____

Items 6, 7, 8, 9, and 10: Business materials

11. Which of these materials could have been handed out to passersby on city streets in Spain? _____

12. Match the flyers with the appropriate products.

  a. roll of film   _____

  b. ham sandwich   _____

  c. headache remedy   _____

13. Each of the ads includes an address that mentions its city of origin. Identify the city names. _____

14. Where would you expect to find the items that are *not* ads?

_____

The process that you have just used is called *scanning*. When scanning, we run our eyes quickly over written material to get a general idea of its content and to identify its type. We use the *layout* of the material to help orient our attention. The layout includes the design of the material on the page, any accompanying photographs or drawings, and the way typefaces and titles are used. You probably scan whenever you look through a newspaper or magazine to find the sections you want to read. All good readers scan before they begin to read a passage written in a language they know; however, sometimes they forget to scan when reading a foreign language. Actually, scanning is even more valuable when you are not sure of all the words! The clues from the format of the passage help to offset some of the unknown vocabulary. Scanning also helps bring cognates to your attention, which can help you identify the topic of the material. Once you have scanned a piece of writing, you usually have a general idea about the kind of information it contains. You will also know what other reading techniques will be most productive for that particular piece of material. For these reasons, you should scan all Spanish materials before you actually begin to read. Scanning is a *prereading* technique and the first stage in our *Reading Strategy*.

The materials you have scanned so far in this unit come from different sources, but they all contain similar kinds of information. For instance, they all include proper nouns such as names of people or businesses. Many of them contain place names and addresses as well. Some of them also include alphabetical lists and abbreviations. These features are recognizable because you can see similarities between the materials here and familiar English language materials.

In spite of many similarities, though, there are some differences in the way Spanish and English names, addresses and telephone numbers look. THINK about the differences you noticed in the materials you have been reading.

Hispanic names. Many Spanish speakers use a traditional naming system in which a person has two surnames, known as **apellidos.** The first surname comes from the father's side; the second from the mother's. Originally the two surnames were joined by **y** *(and)*—a way of showing that two families had become linked through marriage. Today, most people omit the **y** and simply write the two names with a space between them. For example, the veterinarian, Dr. Carlos Francisco Riqué Flores, whose business card you read earlier, is the son of a man whose last name is Riqué and a woman whose first (father's) last name is Flores. It is, of course, possible for someone to have two identical surnames. A person may have any number of given, or first, names. Many first names have familiar English cognates. First names are usually referred to as **nombres.** Both first and last names may consist of more than one word. Some two-part surnames are joined by hyphens; others are combined by **de.** These variations are often ignored in alphabetical lists. An especially common pattern in women's first names is the use of **María** with a **de-** phrase, as in **María del Carmen** or **María de Lourdes. María** is often abbreviated **Ma.**

When a woman marries, she usually keeps at least part of her own last name. For example, if Carlos Francisco Riqué Flores marries a woman named Cecilia Cortez Rubio, it would be normal for her to drop her second surname (Rubio) and add her husband's first surname to her own name using the phrase **(señora) de** _____, *([wife] of* _____*)*. She would then be known as Cecilia Cortez de Riqué and might appear with the r's in alphabetical lists. A widow is sometimes indicated by substituting **vda.** (an abbreviation for **viuda** meaning *widow)* in place of **señora.** This practice is especially common when the woman is past middle age, and the husband was a prominent figure.

Look at these death announcements from a Spanish newspaper. Notice the way names reflect kinship and generation.

ANUNCIOS CLASIFICADOS

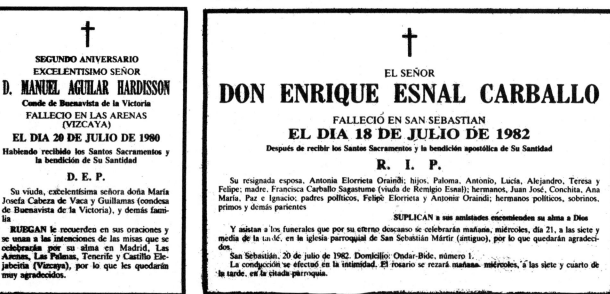

† SEGUNDO ANIVERSARIO
EXCELENTISIMO SEÑOR
D. MANUEL AGUILAR HARDISSON
Conde de Buenavista de la Victoria
FALLECIO EN LAS ARENAS
(VIZCAYA)
EL DIA 20 DE JULIO DE 1980
Habiendo recibido los Santos Sacramentos y la bendición de Su Santidad

D. E. P.

Su viuda, excelentísima señora doña María Josefa Cabeza de Vaca y Guillamas (condesa de Buenavista de la Victoria), y demás familia

RUEGAN le recuerden en sus oraciones y se unan a las intenciones de las misas que se celebrarán por su alma en Madrid, Las Arenas, Las Palmas, Tenerife y Castillo Elejabeitia (Vizcaya), por lo que les quedarán muy agradecidos.

† EL SEÑOR
DON ENRIQUE ESNAL CARBALLO
FALLECIÓ EN SAN SEBASTIAN
EL DIA 18 DE JULIO DE 1982
Después de recibir los Santos Sacramentos y la bendición apostólica de Su Santidad

R. I. P.

Su resignada esposa, Antonia Elorrieta Oraindi; hijos, Paloma, Antonio, Lucía, Alejandro, Teresa y Felipe; madre, Francisca Carballo Sagastume (viuda de Remigio Esnal); hermanos, Juan José, Conchita, Ana María, Paz e Ignacio; padres políticos, Felipe Elorrieta y Antonia Oraindi; hermanos políticos, sobrinos, primos y demás parientes

SUPLICAN a sus amistades encomienden su alma a Dios

Y asistan a los funerales que por su eterno descanso se celebrarán mañana, miércoles, día 21, a las siete y media de la tarde, en la iglesia parroquial de San Sebastián Mártir (antiguo), por lo que quedarán agradecidos.

San Sebastián, 20 de julio de 1982. Domicilio: Ondar-Bide, número 1.

La conducción se efectuó en la intimidad. El rosario se rezará mañana, miércoles, a las siete y cuarto de la tarde, en la citada parroquia.

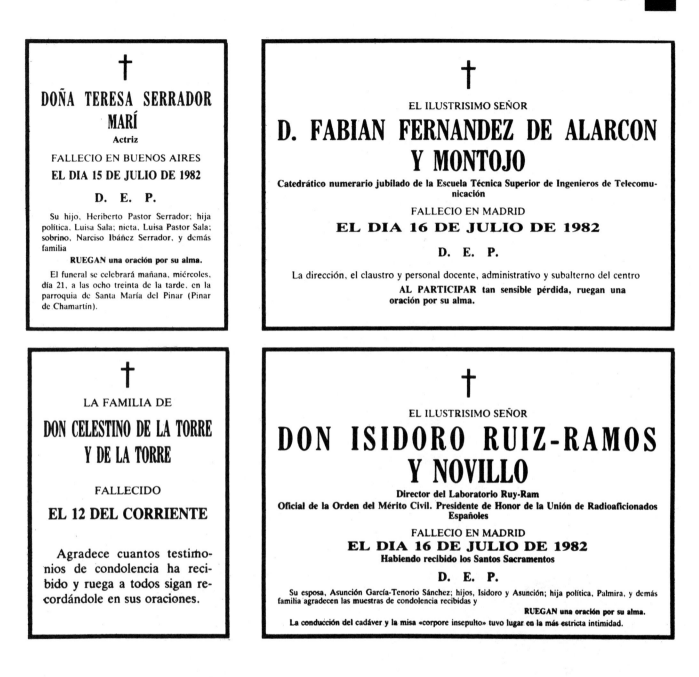

†

DOÑA TERESA SERRADOR MARÍ

Actriz

FALLECIO EN BUENOS AIRES

EL DIA 15 DE JULIO DE 1982

D. E. P.

Su hijo, Heriberto Pastor Serrador; hija política, Luisa Sala; nieta, Luisa Pastor Sala; sobrino, Narciso Ibáñez Serrador, y demás familia

RUEGAN una oración por su alma.

El funeral se celebrará mañana, miércoles, día 21, a las ocho treinta de la tarde, en la parroquia de Santa María del Pinar (Pinar de Chamartín).

†

EL ILUSTRISIMO SEÑOR

D. FABIAN FERNANDEZ DE ALARCON Y MONTOJO

Catedrático numerario jubilado de la Escuela Técnica Superior de Ingenieros de Telecomunicación

FALLECIO EN MADRID

EL DIA 16 DE JULIO DE 1982

D. E. P.

La dirección, el claustro y personal docente, administrativo y subalterno del centro

AL PARTICIPAR tan sensible pérdida, ruegan una oración por su alma.

†

LA FAMILIA DE

DON CELESTINO DE LA TORRE Y DE LA TORRE

FALLECIDO

EL 12 DEL CORRIENTE

Agradece cuantos testimonios de condolencia ha recibido y ruega a todos sigan recordándole en sus oraciones.

†

EL ILUSTRISIMO SEÑOR

DON ISIDORO RUIZ-RAMOS Y NOVILLO

Director del Laboratorio Ruy-Ram

Oficial de la Orden del Mérito Civil. Presidente de Honor de la Unión de Radioaficionados Españoles

FALLECIO EN MADRID

EL DIA 16 DE JULIO DE 1982

Habiendo recibido los Santos Sacramentos

D. E. P.

Su esposa, Asunción García-Tenorio Sánchez; hijos, Isidoro y Asunción; hija política, Palmira, y demás familia agradecen las muestras de condolencia recibidas y

RUEGAN una oración por su alma.

La conducción del cadáver y la misa «corpore insepulto» tuvo lugar en la más estricta intimidad.

Exercise B will help you practice interpreting Hispanic names.

Exercise B.

Refer to the death announcements to answer these questions.

1. What is the full surname of Paloma, one of the daughters of don Enrique Esnal Carballo and his wife Antonia Elorrieta Oraindi?

_____

2. True or False? Narciso Ibáñez Serrador, nephew of doña Teresa Serrador Marí, is her brother's son.

3. Find examples of these types of surnames.
   a. surnames joined with **y**

   _____

   b. surname with two parts joined by **de**

   _____

   c. surname with two parts joined by a hyphen

   _____

Refer to the telephone listing to answer these questions.

4. Locate each of the following names. Using the information provided by its place in the alphabetical list, divide each name into its parts: first name(s), first surname, second surname or husband's name.
   a. María Dolores Cardoso Castrejón
   b. María de la Luz Cárdenas Alvarez
   c. Próspero Cardona Cruz
   d. María Félix Millán de Cardoso
   e. Olga Leticia Santana de Campos
   f. María Luz Castro de Canovas
   g. Nilza Castellanos de Cano
   h. Erasmo Cano del Angel
   i. Constantino Campos Pacheco
   j. María del Carmen Yahuoca vda. de Cano

5. True or False? On the basis of their names, Olga and Constantino might be married.

As you become more familiar with Hispanic names, you will find many variations. For example, shortened forms of the second surname are common, as in Rigoberto Solís L. from Rigoberto Solís Lara. Many people, especially Hispanics in the United States, use only one surname. In such a case, only the father's last name is used. In most parts of the Spanish-speaking world, however, both last names are used. You can see evidence of this expectation on the subscription form: How does it ask for the subscriber's names? ♟

It asks for **apellidos**—in the plural!

Hispanic addresses.   While you have been scanning the various samples of written Spanish, you may also have noticed some differences in the way addresses are written. Look back at the written materials included so far in this unit and find examples of addresses. ♟

Addresses follow the rules of Spanish grammar. The street name is like an adjective and describes the street it names. The number in an address identifies a particular place on the street. Since descriptive adjectives in Spanish

How is an address written in Spanish?

usually follow the nouns they modify, the street name follows the word for the type of street (such as **avenida** or **calle)** and the number comes last. Sometimes a comma is used between the street name and the number, and many house numbers include hyphens. As in English, words such as "avenue" or "street" can be omitted, leaving just the street name and number.

THINK about the street names in your area. Are streets named for famous people or places? Important locations in the area? Geographical features?

Street names in Spanish use all of these sources and more. Many streets are named for important people, but streets in Spanish-speaking countries are also named for important dates and historical events. In the telephone listing, for example, you will see that Otoniel Campos Medina lives at number 109 on **20 de julio de 1969.** Look again at the telephone listing and other materials and find examples of addresses that refer to personal names, important dates or events, and geographical locations. Remember to look for cognates to help you.

Telephone numbers.   As you have seen, Hispanic telephone numbers do not always have the same format as those in the United States. Sometimes there are fewer numbers, and sometimes they are grouped differently.

 Exercise C.

Compare the telephone numbers on the flyers from Spain with the telephone listings from Mexico and Colombia. Based on these samples, identify three different formats for telephone numbers. Then match each format with the country most likely to use it.

1. Spain   _____

2. Mexico   _____

3. Colombia   _____

Differences in punctuation and order are easy to become accustomed to as you read more. Don't let them distract you from the more important clues that help you extract meaning from written materials.

Spanish abbreviations. Many kinds of written materials, especially addresses, include abbreviations. This list of abbreviations commonly found in materials like those in this unit should be a useful reference. Remember that abbreviations of adjectives such as ordinal numbers will indicate the gender of the modified noun, e.g. **3a** for **tercera**. (Use of capital letters may vary.)

What telephone numbers could you call to have something delivered from the pharmacy?

Useful Abbreviations

Addresses

apto. or **apdo.**	apartado *(post office box number)*
A.P.	apartado postal *(post office box number)*
C.P.	Código Postal *(like a zip code)*
No. or **núm.**	número
Avda.	avenida
depto. or **dpto.**	departamento *(means* apartment *in some countries)*
Col.	colonia *(area within a city)*
1° (1ª) or **1er**	primero (primera)
2° (2ª) or **2do**	segundo (segunda)
3° (3ª) or **3er**	tercero (tercera)
Pte.	poniente *(west)* (The other directions are norte, sur, and oriente).
s/n	sin número *(without a number)*
Pza.	plaza
D.F.	Distrito Federal *(capital of Mexico)*
carr.	carretera *(highway)*
km.	kilómetro
Cd.	ciudad *(city)*

Names

Sr.	señor
Sra.	señora
Srta.	señorita
vda.	viuda *(widow)*
lic.	licenciado(a) *(holder of a university degree)*
ing.	ingeniero(a) *(holder of an engineering degree)*
prof.	profesor(a)
Ma.	María

Other useful abbreviations

EEUU or **EE. UU.**	Estados Unidos *(the United States)*
S.A.	Sociedad Anónima *(Spanish equivalent of Inc.)*
Sta.	Santa

On page 32 is a list of people who collect postage stamps or similar items and who hope to correspond with other collectors. When you first look at it, note the way different typefaces are used to distinguish names from addresses and to highlight the list of materials that each person collects. Don't forget to look at the stamps as well! Can you locate all the countries represented? Use the maps in this book to help you.

Now use Exercise D to identify some of the name and address patterns you have been learning about in this unit.

Exercise D.

Fill in the blanks with examples taken from the list of collectors.

1. a person whose two-part surname would be alphabetized under L:

_____

2. a man whose father's name was González:

_____

Roberto A. Flores Osorio. 20 C.P. #57 Col. I.V.U. Santa Ana. El Salvador. *Sellos.*

César Humberto Rodríguez Cabello. Avenida la Paz #70. Maturia. Venezuela 6201. *Sellos y billetes.*

Adriana Chávez Moreno. Jazmines #221. Colonia Reforma. Oaxaca México C.P. 68050. México. *Sellos.*

Hermila Ramírez Romero. Apartado Postal 320 Texcoco. México. *Sellos. postales. billetes y objetos típicos.*

Carlos Ysusi Arias. Magnolia 170 Col. Guerrero 06300. México D.F. México. *Sellos.*

Juan Carlos Aznorez. 9 de Julio 1239 (2700) Pergamino. Buenos Aires. Argentina. *Sellos.*

Manuel Luis Pedreira. Gral. Pacheco. C.P. 1617 Buenos Aires. Argentina. *Sellos y postales*

Juan Manuel González. Bartolomé de las Casas 985 c/s Tobati. Asunción. Paraguay. *Sellos. postales. y monedas.*

Reinaldo López Colmán. Juan del Castillo No. 382 Asunción. Paraguay. *Sellos.*

Carlos Puente Torres. Ave. Prol. Eduardo de Habich 603 Urbanización Ingenieria. Lima 31. Perú. *Sellos.*

Elizabeth L. Jiménez D. Donato Guerra #790 Sector Juarez. Guadalajara. Jalisco. México. *Sellos. monedas y billetes.*

Sergio Teneo. Casilla No. 578 Puerto Montt. *Sellos. postales y billetes.*

Pascual Espósito Cabello. Casilla 323. Arica. Chile. *Sellos.*

Teresa Acuña. Sotomayor 848. Arica. Chile. *Sellos.*

José De La Cruz Díaz León. Apdo. Postal #151 Villahermosa. Tabasco. México. *Postales. monedas y billetes.*

Jesús Domingo Puente Armas. Ave. Obregón y Carr. Costera #3. Escuinthla, Chiapas. 30600. México. *Sellos.*

Vicente Baroccio Mendoza. Valle de Ate Maja C #1086. Col Las Aguilas. Jalisco. México. *Sellos.*

Alvaro López Pardo. Calle 100 No. 9 A 53 (401), Bogotá, Colombia. *Sellos.*

Ramón Granadas Serrano. Patzcuano #1013, Colonia La Pastora. C.P. 67140. Guadalupe. Monterrey Nucuo León, México. *Sellos.*

Georgios Nicolaus Hanschucheim K. Francisco J. Mújica #16. 61420 Tuzpán. Michoacán, México. *Fotos. sellos y postales.*

Marcos D. Villacorta Tocino. "Las Delicias" Apt. 15212, Maracaibo. Edo. Zulia. Venezuela. *Sellos y monedas.*

Carlos y Junior Roque. 187 W. Diamond St. Philadelphia, Pennsylvania, 19122, U.S.A. *Sellos, revistas y periódicos.*

Miguel Angel Vázquez Caña. Ave. 10 de Junio No. 155-2, Piñorate, Urb. Ing. S.M.P. Lima. Perú. *Sellos.*

Eduardo Ortiz González. Apartado aéreo 2141. *Sellos.*

Pedro Navas Bernad. Apartado 16, C.P. 5003-A, Colón, Edo. Táchira, Venezuela. *Estampillas y postales.*

Juan J. López González. Apartado Postal No. 604, Saltillo, Coahuila, México. *Sellos de U.S.A.*

Chang Hoon Lee. "Casa Amiga", General Caballero 633, San Lorenzo, Paraguay. *Sellos, billetes y postales.*

Marcelo D. Ferraris. 531 No. 1342, Dpto. E (1900), La Plata, Argentina. *Sellos.*

Agustina Villarino. Magariños Cervantes 1529, Apto. 3, Montevideo, Uruguay. *Sellos.*

Juan Carlos Muzzio. Laguna 45, 2do. B, 1407 Buenos Aires, Rep. Argentina. *Sellos.*

Gabriel Santos Campo. Luis Aguilar y Canales 4-A, Matamoros, Tamaulipas, México, C.P. 87360. *Postales, billetes, monedas, cajetillas de cigarros y sellos.*

Angel Vieyra. M. Francisco López Rayón No. 421, Ixtlahuca, 50740 Estado de México, México. *Sellos.*

Aldo Alegría Valenzuela. Elena Serrano 274, Santiago, Chile. *Cajetillas de cigarrillos y postales.*

Fabio Arrieta Bustos. La Concepción, Calle 1ra No. 31-18, Cartagena, Colombia. *Monedas, billetes y postales.*

Víctor Hugo Escauriza Dosé. Asunción, Paraguay, Casilla de Correo 1819. *Sellos.*

3. a man whose mother's name was González:

   _____

4. a woman who abbreviates her second surname:

   _____

5. an Argentine resident who uses only one surname:

   _____

6. someone with a post office box (**Casilla**) in Chile:

   _____

7. a street in Uruguay named after a person:

   _____

8. a street in Peru named for a date:

   _____

Dictionary Interlude

Interpreting dictionary entries

One place where you will find many important abbreviations is in a bilingual dictionary. In order to use your dictionary efficiently, you should learn the most important abbreviations. The most useful abbreviations to know at this early stage in your reading are the ones that help you identify the grammatical information about a word. This information includes the part of speech (whether it is a noun or an adjective, for example). If a word is a noun, it is helpful to know its gender. If it is a verb, a good dictionary will indicate whether it is transitive (can take a direct object) or intransitive and if it is irregular. (If these grammatical terms are unfamiliar to you, consult a basic Spanish textbook or your instructor.) Now locate the list of abbreviations used in your own dictionary.

The following exercise will help you understand the abbreviations your dictionary uses.

Exercise E.

Using the list of abbreviations in your dictionary, answer these questions. Write in the blank labeled *a.* the abbreviation from the Spanish-English section.

1. What abbreviation does your dictionary use to indicate that a word is a

   noun?   a. _____   b. _____

2. What marks indicate that a noun is masculine?

   a. _____   b. _____

   Feminine?   a. _____   b. _____

3. What is the abbreviation for a verb?

a. _____ b. _____

4. How do you know if the verb can take a direct object?

a. _____ b. _____

What abbreviation is used for intransitive verbs?

a. _____ b. _____

5. What is the abbreviation for adjectives?

a. _____ b. _____

Now look through your dictionary and find a Spanish entry for each of the abbreviations you filled in above. Write the entry word in the blank labeled *b.*

Now that you are familiar with the entries in your dictionary, you need to become familiar with the differences between the Spanish and English alphabets. The most important difference is a very basic one; it concerns "alphabetical order" in Spanish—something you will surely need to know if you want to look up words! Try it. Use your bilingual dictionary to look up these three words: **chocolate, llama,** and **niña.** Read the complete entry for each one. This exercise is just for dictionary practice, of course—otherwise, you wouldn't look up words you already know or can guess! Don't spend too much time here.

Did you have trouble finding them? In the Spanish alphabet, there are three extra letters: **ch, ll,** and **ñ.** Your dictionary reflects Spanish alphabetical order by having separate sections for words beginning with these letters. They follow the letters **c, l,** and **n. Niña** is listed after all the words which begin with **nin-.** It follows **ninguno** because ñ comes after the letter **n.** Until you become used to these differences in alphabetical order between English and Spanish, you may sometimes think that a word you are looking for is not in your dictionary. Many words are missing from bilingual dictionaries, but before you give up on one, be sure you are looking for it in the proper place in the alphabet. (If you did not find the words discussed here, try again before continuing.)

Did you notice what part of speech **chocolate** is? In Spanish, **chocolate** can *only* be a noun, and not an adjective, as it is in an English phrase like **chocolate ice cream.** Information of this kind is often very useful when you are looking up words in a reading passage. When you looked up **llama,** you may have found two meanings for it. One of them you may already have known (or remembered after you read the entry) but the other one is probably new to you. When you look up a word, always pay attention to the grammatical information in the entry. In later units, you will learn how to use such information to help you read. What is the gender of **llama?**

Besides **ch, ll,** and **ñ,** there is actually a fourth letter in the Spanish alphabet that does not occur in English. This letter is **rr.** When the alphabet is recited, **rr** occurs after **r,** but since no words in Spanish begin with **rr,** there is not a separate section for it in the dictionary. In alphabetical lists, **rr** is treated simply as one **r** followed by another.

Exercise F will help you practice using alphabetical order in locating dictionary entries.

Exercise F.

Answer these questions using your bilingual dictionary.

1. Look up the following words. Read the complete entry for each, checking to be sure you understand any abbreviations. Record the grammatical information you find in the entry.

   a. ñapa _____

   b. dechado _____

   c. callar _____

   d. carnal _____

2. Write these words in Spanish alphabetical order. Then check your order by looking for them in your dictionary.

   a. cartón _____

   b. carrera _____

   c. carácter _____

   d. carnal _____

   e. carpintero _____

   f. carro _____

   g. caro _____

3. According to your dictionary, what important differences are there between the words in the following pairs? Pay attention to grammatical information as well as to meaning.

   a. anejo/añejo _____

   b. ola/olla _____

   c. marchar/marcar _____

4. Why does **galón** come before **gallo?** Why does **garra** come before **garza?**

   _____

5. Write these words in alphabetical order. Check them in your dictionary and circle the ones that are feminine nouns.

   a. calmar _____

   b. calibre _____

   c. calzar _____

   d. calloso _____

   e. cámara _____

   f. cal _____

   g. calar _____

Your skills in using alphabetical order with a dictionary can be easily transfered to other kinds of written material. When you need to find a particular name in an index, a bibliography, or a card catalogue, for example, you must be careful to pay attention to the proper alphabetical order. In reading materials like these, which contain many names, remember that when two **apellidos** are used, they are usually alphabetized as if they were written as a single name.

Exercise G will help you practice these new skills. It uses pages from two of the books whose title pages you read earlier in this unit. Look at them now.

A

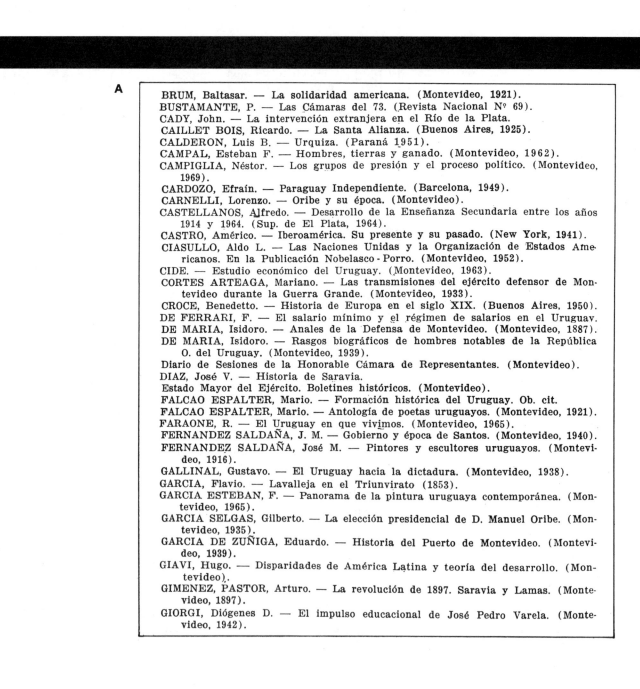

BRUM, Baltasar. — La solidaridad americana. (Montevideo, 1921).
BUSTAMANTE, P. — Las Cámaras del 73. (Revista Nacional Nº 69).
CADY, John. — La intervención extranjera en el Río de la Plata.
CAILLET BOIS, Ricardo. — La Santa Alianza. (Buenos Aires, 1925).
CALDERON, Luis B. — Urquiza. (Paraná 1951).
CAMPAL, Esteban F. — Hombres, tierras y ganado. (Montevideo, 1962).
CAMPIGLIA, Néstor. — Los grupos de presión y el proceso político. (Montevideo, 1969).
CARDOZO, Efraín. — Paraguay Independiente. (Barcelona, 1949).
CARNELLI, Lorenzo. — Oribe y su época. (Montevideo).
CASTELLANOS, Alfredo. — Desarrollo de la Enseñanza Secundaria entre los años 1914 y 1964. (Sup. de El Plata, 1964).
CASTRO, Américo. — Iberoamérica. Su presente y su pasado. (New York, 1941).
CIASULLO, Aldo L. — Las Naciones Unidas y la Organización de Estados Americanos. En la Publicación Nobelasco - Porro. (Montevideo, 1952).
CIDE. — Estudio económico del Uruguay. (Montevideo, 1963).
CORTES ARTEAGA, Mariano. — Las transmisiones del ejército defensor de Montevideo durante la Guerra Grande. (Montevideo, 1933).
CROCE, Benedetto. — Historia de Europa en el siglo XIX. (Buenos Aires, 1950).
DE FERRARI, F. — El salario mínimo y el régimen de salarios en el Uruguay.
DE MARIA, Isidoro. — Anales de la Defensa de Montevideo. (Montevideo, 1887).
DE MARIA, Isidoro. — Rasgos biográficos de hombres notables de la República O. del Uruguay. (Montevideo, 1939).
Diario de Sesiones de la Honorable Cámara de Representantes. (Montevideo).
DIAZ, José V. — Historia de Saravia.
Estado Mayor del Ejército. Boletines históricos. (Montevideo).
FALCAO ESPALTER, Mario. — Formación histórica del Uruguay. Ob. cit.
FALCAO ESPALTER, Mario. — Antología de poetas uruguayos. (Montevideo, 1921).
FARAONE, R. — El Uruguay en que vivimos. (Montevideo, 1965).
FERNANDEZ SALDAÑA, J. M. — Gobierno y época de Santos. (Montevideo, 1940).
FERNANDEZ SALDAÑA, José M. — Pintores y escultores uruguayos. (Montevideo, 1916).
GALLINAL, Gustavo. — El Uruguay hacia la dictadura. (Montevideo, 1938).
GARCIA, Flavio. — Lavalleja en el Triunvirato (1853).
GARCIA ESTEBAN, F. — Panorama de la pintura uruguaya contemporánea. (Montevideo, 1965).
GARCIA SELGAS, Gilberto. — La elección presidencial de D. Manuel Oribe. (Montevideo, 1935).
GARCIA DE ZUÑIGA, Eduardo. — Historia del Puerto de Montevideo. (Montevideo, 1939).
GIAVI, Hugo. — Disparidades de América Latina y teoría del desarrollo. (Montevideo).
GIMENEZ, PASTOR, Arturo. — La revolución de 1897. Saravia y Lamas. (Montevideo, 1897).
GIORGI, Diógenes D. — El impulso educacional de José Pedro Varela. (Montevideo, 1942).

B

Echevarría, alias *Naparra*, José Miguel: 241.
Echevarría Landazábal, Ignacio: 262.
Echeverría, Luis: 44.
Echeverte Aranguren, Eugenio, alias *Antxon*: 271.
Echeveste Arizaren, Eugenio: 255.
Egarra, José Ignacio: 59.
Elbrick, Burke: 200.
Elexpe, Elías: 138.
Elgoroibe, María: 254.
Elias, Isu: 13.
Eliazán Sarasola, Justo: 235.
Elícegui Díez, José: 72.
Elizondo, Luis María: 241.
Elorza, Antonio: 24.
Eneka: 69.
Eriz, Juan Félix: 123.
Escubi, José María: 26, 27.
Escudero del Corral, Ángel: 186.
Espinosa Pardo, José Luis: 108, 117.
Estal, Gladys del: 176.
Estevas Guilman, Alfonso: 130.
Estier, Claude: 259.
Estremiana, Felipe: 228.
Expósito: 42.
Ezquerro Serrano, Julián: 189.

Falcón, Lidia: 32.
Fanjul Sedeño, Juan Manuel: 186.
Feltrinelli: 230, 243.
Ferdig, Dorotea: 183.
Fernández, Antonio: 44.
Fernández, Magín: 261.
Fernández de Castro, Ignacio: 12.
Fernández Cerrá, José: 81.
Fernández Dopico, general: 260.
Fernández Fernández, Benjamín: 271.
Fernández Guaza, José: 80.
Fernández Gutiérrez, Juan Antonio: 35.
Fernández Montes, Diego: 138, 149.
Fernández Palacios: 81.
Fernández Perado, Justino: 256.
Fernández Serrano, Pedro: 162.
Fernández Tovar, Wladimiro: 43.
Ferreiras Simois, Manuel: 185.

Gabirondo, Ignacio María: 226.
Gadafi, Moammar al: 116.
Galarza, Julián: 53.
Galíndez Uría, Félix: 261.
Gamo, Mariano: 37.
Gancedo Ruiz, Luis: 135.
Gandhi, Mohandas Karamchand, llamado el Mahatma: 24.
Garade Bedialauneta, alias *Mamarru*, Isidro María: 255.
Garaicoechea, Carlos: 122, 134, 136, 150, 152, 167, 176, 189, 191, 192, 194, 213, 220, 224, 227, 232, 233, 234, 270.
Garavilla Legaza, José: 225.
Garayalde, alias *Herreka*: 183, 223.
García, Andrés: 168.
García, Juan Bautista: 165.
García Alonso, Félix: 119.
García Cordero, Manuel: 228.
García Díaz, Benigno: 270.
García García, Ignacio: 256.
García García, Jesús: 42, 208.
García González, Alfredo: 72.
García González, Elías: 135.
García Juliá, Carlos: 81.
García Lorente, Juan: 45.
García Mayo, Rafael: 120.
García Payo, Miguel: 155.
García Pellejero, Ricardo: 60.
García Pérez, Ángel: 207.
García Pérez, Juan Carlos: 242.
García Rico: 62.
García Rodríguez, Luis Antonio: 39, 246.
García Sánchez, María José: 261.
García Sánchez, Tomás: 112.
García Sanz, Ramón: 43.
García Serrano, Rafael: 115.
García Vallejo, Celsa: 85.
García-Hoz Rosales, Víctor: 263.
García-Plata Valle, Bartolomé: 45.
Garchitorena, Ricardo: 245.
Gardogui, Miguel: 40, 220.
Garmendía, Imanol: 42, 43, 59.
Garmendía, José Antonio: 94.
Garmendía, José María: 24, 25, 26, 32.
Garrido Caro, Pedro: 139.
Garrido Lázaro, José María: 60.
Garrigues Walker, Joaquín: 178.
Garro Azpiroz, Ildefonso: 108.
Gassent: 62.
Gaulle, Charles de: 184, 212.

Exercise G.

Read over the questions to see what kind of information you will be looking for (your *purpose*). Scan each reading passage before you try to answer the questions, and use *format* clues to help you identify what type of material each item is and to orient yourself to its patterns of organization (the *context*).

1. Part of the context for item A is the larger book that it was taken from. Use the titles in the bibliography to guess which of these books it belongs to.

   a. *El terrorismo en España*
   b. *Historia del Uruguay*
   c. *Antología de tradiciones y leyendas bolivianas*

2. What format feature is used to distinguish the authors' **apellidos** from their **nombres?**_____ Give an example of an entry which is *not* a person's name. _____

3. Examine the authors' names in the bibliography. THINK about what you have learned about personal names. Look at the section of names beginning with **García.** What are the rules for alphabetizing these names?

    _____

    _____

4. Item B is taken from the index for *El terrorismo en España.* Locate the following names in the list.
    a. Angel García Pérez
    b. Andrés García
    c. Víctor García-Hoz Rosales
    d. Félix García Alonso

5. Insert the following new names into the index.
    a. Ramón García Collazo
    b. María García-Conde
    c. Alfredo Garchitorena Díaz

Applying the Reading Strategy

You have learned in this unit that the first stage in the *Reading Strategy* is to *scan.* When you scan, you look over an entire context unit and examine its format: titles, illustrations, typefaces, layout. This first impression is especially important when you are just beginning to read real materials in Spanish. Using what you know about similar materials in English, you can look for clues to the *context* of the passage—what sort of larger piece is it from?—, its *content,*—what is it about? —, and its *organization*—how is the information in it arranged? While scanning a reading passage, you should THINK about it. Formulate a short set of questions that you expect the passage to answer, which can guide you when you read more thoroughly.

Usually when you read materials of the type presented in this unit, you already have a question in mind. For example, you probably read a telephone directory only when you want to look for a specific name or locate a specific service. Each purpose and each type of written material requires some adjustments in the approach you take to it, but the first step in effective reading is always to scan.

Let's apply this first stage of the *Reading Strategy* to a new reading passage, taken from a familiar source. Use the questions in Exercise H to help orient your attention as you scan. Your purpose is to learn as much as you can about the passage, as quickly as you can. *Do not use your dictionary and do not try to read everything on the page.*

Exercise H.

1. What features of the layout indicate that this passage is a contents page?

    _____

2. How does this contents page differ from others you have seen in this unit? (Concentrate on format features.) _____

    _____

3. What is the probable source of a contents page that looks like this one? How do you know that it is not from a book such as ***Historia del Uruguay?***

    _____

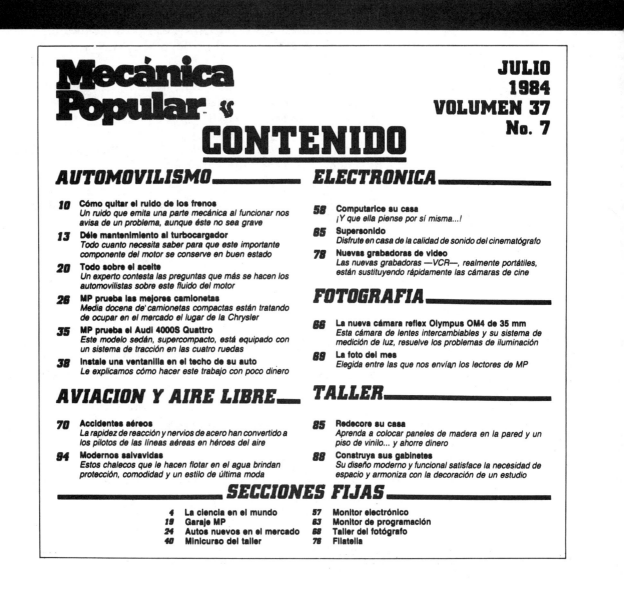

Mecánica Popular 🜂

JULIO 1984 VOLUMEN 37 No. 7

CONTENIDO

4. How are different sizes of type used to indicate the relative importance of different sections? What are the relationships among the various titles?_____

5. What do the various numbers indicate? Why are they not in order? (HINT: Some factor other than numerical order is used to organize the main headings on this page. What is it?) _____

While you were scanning this contents page from the Mexican edition of the magazine ***Mecánica Popular,*** you probably paid special attention to the section headings. The use of bold type and small capital letters makes these words look particularly important. And they are: knowing the meanings of the various headings helps in understanding the organization of the contents. Most of the section headings are easily understandable, because they are close cognates and because you can guess what kinds of articles would occur in ***Mecánica Popular.***

You may not have recognized the word **taller,** however. Look at that section more closely. Can you THINK of a possible meaning for **taller** based on some of the words used in the titles of the articles in that section?

If you had the entire magazine in front of you, you could look at the articles and see if their format features might give you some clues about the kind of section **taller** might be. That would be easier—and more helpful—than using your dictionary, but let's say you decide you want to look it up. Locate the entry for **taller** in your bilingual dictionary. What part of speech is it? What is its gender? Read the entry carefully.

Look again at the contents page. What is the most likely meaning for *taller* in this context?

Taller is a masculine noun and of its various meanings—studio, laboratory, factory, workshop—the last is the most appropriate one for a magazine devoted to mechanics!

Now look at the heading **secciones fijas.** You probably recognize **secciones,** but are you sure what **fijas** means? You can guess its part of speech from the fact that it follows **secciones.** (Remember that in Spanish descriptive adjectives are likely to follow nouns.) You can also use what you know about the typical features and overall organization of magazines to guess the purpose of this section. For many reading purposes, these guesses would allow you to continue to read without using your dictionary. For now, suppose you want to check them to be sure. Look for **fijas** in your dictionary.

Don't worry if you couldn't find it! Dictionaries only list the primary entry for a word. Many words in Spanish have multiple forms, so it is important to know how to identify the *primary entry*. The primary entry for a verb is the infinitive. For a noun it is the singular form, and for an adjective, it is the masculine singular form. **Fijas** is feminine and plural. Do you know the masculine singular form of **fijas**?

The correct answer is **fijo**.

Now look up **fijo** in your dictionary and select the best meaning for the phrase **secciones fijas** in a magazine contents list.

In this unit, you have scanned several different types of writing, and you have used form and layout to help you identify what type of information each piece contains. You have used your guessing skills in combination with your growing knowledge of Spanish and your general knowledge.

As a final opportunity to discover how much information you can gather through scanning and guessing, complete this review exercise. It consists of typical questions a reader might ask about some of the materials you have seen in this unit. You will find that you can answer rather detailed questions without knowing very much Spanish. Of course, knowledge of vocabulary, grammar, and cultural information are all very important to good reading, but the techniques good readers use to answer questions like the ones in this exercise work in Spanish just as they do in English. As you work through the rest of this book, you will learn to develop your ability to apply all these techniques to reading in Spanish.

Exercise I.

Answer these questions without using a dictionary.

1. What is the address of Mr. José Arturo Carbajal Zúñiga of Cuernavaca, Mexico? _____

2. To what address should I write if I want to discuss a film project with the cinematographer Luis A. Casalins? _____
    In what Colombian cities are there offices of the 3M company?

    _____

3. Who are the authors of a book on the history of Uruguay?

    _____

4. Which is the shortest of the Bolivian legends written by Nicanor Mallo?

    _____

    Which author has written a story for the same book which is probably about exciting occurrences which took place at night?   _____

    _____

5. Where would I be most likely to find the Church of St. Catherine in Valencia?_____

6. How long does it take to get photos developed at **Foto Sistema?**
    _____ Besides speed, what are some other reasons for going to **Foto Sistema?** _____

7. Is *El País* a daily, weekly, or monthly publication?   _____

8. Where could I read a review of the new Olympus OM4 camera?

_____

9. What anniversary is commemorated on the stamp from the Dominican Republic? _____

10. In what section of **Mecánica Popular** did the list of stamp collectors probably appear? THINK! _____

This unit has introduced you to the first stages in the *Reading Strategy*. By applying them, you have been able to read and comprehend a great deal of material intended for fluent readers of Spanish. A large part of the strategy has been the process of returning again and again to the reading, each time seeing it in a different way and each time finding new information. As you become a more capable reader in Spanish, you will learn to gather greater amounts of information on each pass, just as you now do in English.

THINK about the ways in which you have worked with the various kinds of material in Unit 2. You used the process of scanning in order to see what kind of writing was involved for each one. You have guessed what kinds of information they might contain. You have then looked at each one more carefully, still not reading every word, but trying to identify their parts and looking for the important information or main idea contained in each one. You have used what you know about advertisements, telephone books, magazines, and other items to help you understand meanings and relationships. You have used your knowledge of Spanish and English to guess the meanings of unfamiliar words. You thought about the connections among the samples and other information. That is, you used *guessing, context,* and *transferred skills.*

Now look back over the materials we have used in this unit one last time and see how fluent a reader you already are!

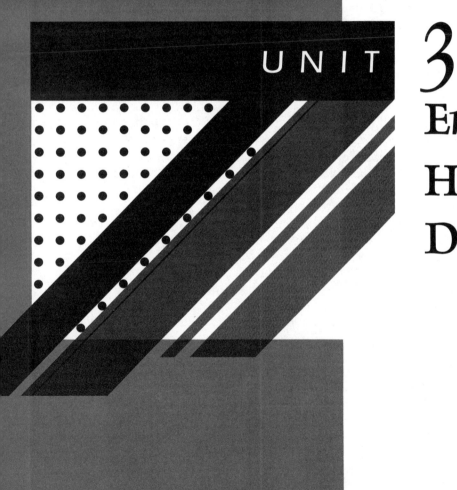

UNIT

3
Encountering
Human
Diversity

The Reading Strategy

Prereading: Scanning for organizational cues

In Unit 3 we will continue to emphasize the importance of format when reading, but we will also begin to focus more on the individual words in a passage. The reading materials in this unit all concern human qualities and characteristics. The materials are easily identifiable by their forms, and they share vocabulary as well. The techniques used to read them are illustrated in detail and can be easily applied to other similar reading passages.

As you learned in Unit 1, a cognate is a Spanish word that resembles a word in English in both spelling and meaning. Many cognates exist because of the historical relationship between Spanish and English. Learning to recognize and use cognates effectively when reading is an important skill. Unit 3 will expand your ability to do so.

In Unit 3 we will also take a look at *agreement* of subjects and verbs and agreement of adjectives with nouns. The rules of agreement are one of the most obvious differences between Spanish and English grammar. Understanding agreement can help make you a more efficient reader. To understand agreement, you must first distinguish the *stem* of a word—which conveys the basic meaning of the word and usually does not change—from the *ending*—the part that usually provides grammatical information and does change. Unit 3 will teach you some techniques for distinguishing stems from endings and for using the agreement system to assist you in your reading.

Another important concept discussed in Unit 3 is the distinction between *content* words and *function* words. Generally speaking, content words are words that convey meaning; they refer to people, things, qualities, actions, or ideas—and it is usually easy to say what they mean.

Function words, on the other hand, are usually short words that occur in the language very frequently, but are difficult to define exactly. There are a limited number of function words in any language, and they usually convey grammatical meaning. Their "function" is to show relationships among the content words of a sentence. In Spanish and in English, function words include definite articles, prepositions (such as *in, to,* and *for* in English, and **a, de,** or **para** in Spanish), and conjunctions (words like *and* or *but;* **y** or **pero).** Unit 3 provides practice in distinguishing content words from function words and using what you know about their differences when you read.

Remember that all reading techniques work best when you preread the passage. Before reading a new passage, it is best to scan it and THINK about its topic. You should THINK about words that are likely to be related to the topic and about ideas likely to be associated with it. If you formulate some questions you expect the passage to answer, you can improve your ability to recognize important information contained in it. Let's review this process with a familiar type of material—an advertisement. This ad was prepared for Spanish speakers in the United States. Begin by scanning the ad. The appropriate context unit for scanning is the entire passage. Pay attention to the format. Note the importance of the art, the way various typefaces are used, and the fact that the ad contains a coupon. THINK about the probable topic of the ad. What is this ad about?

The topic of this ad is soap. You may have recognized the brand. If not, did the illustrations offer any clue to the topic?

Exercise A.

On the basis of what you already know about ads for soap, which of the following sentences best describes the probable message of this ad?

1. Soap is good for you.
2. Camay soap is good for you; try it.
3. Camay soap is good for you; use this coupon to try it.

Before returning to the ad itself, THINK again about the product and about similar ads you have seen. What specific words would you expect to find in an ad like this one?

Exercise B.

Here is a list of content words that might occur in an ad for soap. Select the three words you think would be the most important in an advertisement for a brand of face soap.

1. skin
2. water
3. clean

4. Camay
5. free
6. body

It is often possible to guess some of the meaning in a reading passage by paying special attention to content words on the basis of their importance within the passage. In materials with many format cues, the most important words are often highlighted and tend to be repeated. Paying attention to the patterns of repetition in a passage is an important technique in the *Reading Strategy*. We can illustrate the technique by examining the soap ad again more carefully.

 Exercise C.

Make a list of the content words that occur more than once in the ad and record the number of times each one is repeated. Be sure to check the Answer Key when you have finished.

It is never surprising to find a brand name repeated in an advertisement; it is certainly an important word from the advertiser's point of view! The pattern of the other repetitions suggests that **piel** is also an important word. Knowing its meaning would help us make further guesses about the content of the ad. Unfortunately, **piel** is not an easily recognizable cognate. Its form does not give us many clues to its meaning. If you did not already know this word, you would probably want to look it up. But first, THINK back to your earlier predictions about the words most likely to be found in a soap ad of this type. ◆

It shouldn't surprise you to learn that **piel** means "skin." This knowledge lets us expand what we already knew from format cues: the ad is intended to sell soap, and in order to do so, it says a lot about skin. Now you are ready to read the ad again. As you do so, you should pay more attention to individual phrases and words. Exercise D will help you concentrate on them.

Exercise D.

1. List (or underline) all the content words in the ad whose meanings you already know or which are recognizable cognates.
2. Here are lists of the most easily recognizable cognates. Check these words against your own list to see how many you found. If you overlooked some, go back to find them in the passage and try to guess their meanings.

gratis
personalizado
programa
dividirse

fórmulas
contiene
cosmética
reducir

tipo	natural
normal	suave
intensos	emolientes
necesita	válido

3. In order to fully comprehend the content of this ad, it is helpful to note the arrangement of information within it. Identify three different aspects of the ad that suggest that Camay comes in three types.

Now that you have guessed as much of the meaning as you can using frequency and format cues, you are ready to read the ad again for real comprehension. Exercise E will help you.

Exercise E.

Read all the questions first; they will guide the way you read. Then read the ad again. *Do not use your dictionary*. Remember that knowing an easy answer often helps you guess a harder one.

1. According to the ad, which of the following are types of skin?

   a. grasienta
   b. personalizado
   c. normal
   d. seca
   e. natural
   f. suave

2. Match each skin type to the special soap ingredient it requires, according to the ad.

   _____ 1. piel grasienta   a. strong emolients

   _____ 2. piel seca   b. cosmetic clay

   _____ 3. piel normal   c. natural moisturizer

3. Match each ingredient to its effects.

   _____ 1. intensos   a. reduces shine caused by oil
             emolientes

   _____ 2. humedecedor   b. makes skin feel soft
             natural

   _____ 3. arcilla cosmética   c. cleans gently

4. According to the ad, which of the following is the best reason for trying Camay?

   a. It's very inexpensive.
   b. It's personalized to your skin type.
   c. You can get a bar of Camay free.

5. True or False? The coupon allows you to get three bars of soap free.

While you were working on Exercise E and looking for recognizable words you were probably concentrating on stems, not endings, since stems carry the meaning. In your early examination of a new piece of reading material, the content word stems help most in establishing a quick impression of the topic. Endings, however, like function words, are also important because they give you clues to the relationships among the content words. The system of adjective endings, for example, makes it easy to see which noun is modified by which adjective. Use Exercise F to see how this system works.

Exercise F.

This list contains important nouns from the soap ad. Information about gender is provided by the endings of the adjectives or articles that modify them in the reading. *Without using a dictionary*, determine whether each noun is masculine or feminine. If you think you already know the gender, use the information contained in the passage to confirm your guess.

1. piel	3. fórmula	5. humedecedor
2. programa	4. tipo	6. limpieza

Because adjectives agree with the nouns they modify, they may be separated from the noun or even occur without the noun and still allow a reader to keep track of which noun is referred to. In the next reading passage, knowing which nouns are referred to and the relationships among them is very important.

This reading consists of a set of personal ads by people advertising for pen pals or, in some cases, spouses. The ads are from a Mexican magazine column called the **Club de la Amistad** *(Friendship Club)*. They are generally grouped according to the Mexican state in which the advertiser lives, although there is section called **Especiales** which contains ads from various places. Four states are mentioned: Hidalgo, Chiapas, Chihuahua, and Durango. Locate them on the map of Mexico before going on.

You have probably read ads like these in English. Before you read these Spanish ones, THINK: What kind of information do ads of this kind usually include?

Exercise G.

Here is a list of several types of personal information. Mark the ones you would *not* expect to find in personal ads.

1. age	6. number of credit cards
2. race	7. physical descriptions
3. annual income	8. astrological sign
4. occupation	9. telephone number
5. religion	10. marital status

Now look over several ads and determine the usual format for an ad in this magazine column. Skip any words you do not know; simply try to identify the organization. What kinds of information are always included?

Club de la Amistad

Por: LEONOR MONTIEL

*¿Té gusta coleccionar postales, llaveros, pósters, etc.
Y también objetos de países lejanos?
Aquí encontrarás los nombres y direcciones de muchos
jóvenes que comparten tu ideal.*

HIDALGO

Apolonio de la Cruz.— 62 B.1, Zimapan, Hgo.— "Tengo 25 años, soy un joven decente, sin vicios ni problemas familiares. Deseo tener correspondencia con damitas de 16 a 28 años con fines amistosos o sentimentales. Prometo contestar y enviar fotografía".

Lucy y amigas.— Argentina No. 102-A, Col. Maestranza 42060, Pachuca, Hgo.— "Somos tres chicas de 14 y 15 años, simpáticas y no mal parecidas. Quisiéramos que nos escribieran chicos de todo el mundo, con fines amistosos o sentimentales. Los esperamos, foto".

M. Esperanza.— Lista de Correos, Progreso de O. Hgo.— "Deseo me escriban chicas y chicos de todo el mundo, para iniciar una linda amistad y poder intercambiar todo tipo de objetos, no importa raza, religión ni nada. Soy una chica estudiante de 17 años".

Yeison Valencia.— Lista de Correos, Villa de Tezontepec, Hgo.— Desea tener correspondencia con chicas del Edo. de Hidalgo con fines amistosos o sentimentales, enviar fotografía. Seriedad".

R.V.T.— Leona Vicario No. 105, Pachuca, Hgo.— "Dama de 48 años, decente, sin hijos, divorciada, de buenos sentimientos. Desea tener correspondencia con caballero de edad apropiada a la suya con fines matrimoniales en corto plazo. Enviar fotografía".

Liliana Jiménez.— Sec. Tollan, Tula de Allende, Hgo.— "Quisiera iniciar una bonita amistad con muchachos y muchachas de todo el mundo, sin importar edad ni nada, podremos hablar de nuestras alegrías y penas e intercambiar todo lo que quieran. Te espero".

Ignacio V.— Estación de Ferrocarriles, Apulco, Hgo.— "Soltero de 42 años, sin vicios, trabajador y responsable. Desea encontrar a damita cariñosa, sincera y hogareña, para formar un hogar estable en corto plazo, e iniciar una vida de felicidad. Foto".

Rosa M. O.— Av. 21 de Marzo, Sur No. 107, Tulancingo, Hgo.— "Odontóloga de 50 años, dulce, cariñosa, de buenas costumbres, sencilla, hogareña y sin problemas. Desea le escriba caballero honesto de cualquier nacionalidad con fines matrimoniales, foto".

CHIAPAS

Margarita Capdepont.— Av. 20 de Nov. No. 36, Palenque, Chis.— "Niña alegre, simpática y de buenos sentimientos, de 15 años, estudiante de secundaria. Quisiera conocer a chicos y chicas de todo el mundo, con fines amistosos, no se arrepentirán".

Ariel Alfaro.— Apdo. Postal No. 365, Tuxtla, Chis.— "Soy un chico Aries de 16 años, estudiante, alegre y simpático. Me gustaría conocer a jóvenes de ambos sexos, de todo el mundo, con fines amistosos y para intercambiar todo lo que quieran".

Tere García.— Lista de Correos, Tuxtla, Chis.— "Deseo me escriban muchachas y muchachos de cualquier lugar del mundo, para intercambiar postales, timbres y fotografías e iniciar una sólida amistad, en la que reine la sencilléz, confianza, etc".

José Alfredo Aguilar.— 2a. Calle Sur Poniente, No. 69, Comitán, Chis.— "Con fines sentimentales deseo conocer a señorita de 18 a 20 años, profesionista, de 1.70 m. de estatura. Soy un caballero profesionista de 23 años. Seriedad y foto".

Octavio Arreola.— 5a. Norte y 2a. Poniente S/N Pijijiapan, Chis.— "Tengo 34 años, soy una persona que se siente muy sola y necesita de gente buena que le quiera, sin pensar en los defectos físicos. Busco amistad sincera, prometo contestarles".

Gabriela Domínguez.— 9a. Pte. Sur No. 543, Tuxtla Gutiérrez, Chis.— "Me gustaría entablar una bonita amistad por correspondencia con jóvenes mexicanos y de todo el mundo, para poder conversar sobre política, literatura, etc. Tengo 16 años".

CHIAPAS

Flora y Francisco.— Chilón 29940, Chis.— "Nos gustaría iniciar una bonita y duradera amistad con chicas y chicos de todo el mundo, sin importar raza, religión ni posición económica. Somos dos jóvenes que gustan del baile y de coleccionar de todo".

P.M. y A.O.— 4a. Ote Nte. 514, Tuxtla Gutiérrez, Chis.— "Buscamos con fines sentimentales a dos damitas de 18 a 24 años, rubias de ojos verdes, cultas y decentes. Somos dos amigos, trabajadores, de buenos sentimientos. Seriedad, foto".

Jorge Méndez A.— 9a. Poniente Sur 451, Tuxtla, Chis.— "Quisiera relacionarme con fines amistosos con chicas de 17 a 21 años, dulces y de buenos sentimientos. Soy un muchacho de 21 años, rubio, esbelto, con ojos muy bellos. Prometo contestar".

Elizabeth Zebadúa.— 8a. Norte Pte. No. 763, Tuxtla Gutiérrez.— "Tengo 16 años, soy una chica alegre y sincera, de buenos sentimientos. Quisiera conocer sin importar raza, religión e ideología a chicas y chicos de todo el mundo y de México. Foto".

Alberto Martín.— Mueblería Gutiérrez, Mapastepec, Chis.— "Niño de 8 años, alegre, simpático, que gusta del deporte y todas las diversiones. Quisiera relacionarse con fines amistosos con niñas y niños de toda la República Mexicana. Escribe".

CHIHUAHUA

Elia Morales A.— Calle 18 y Sonora No. 1894, Cd. Cuauhtémoc, Chih.— "Quisiera conocer a joven simpático y educado, sin vicios ni defectos físicos, sincero y comprensivo, con fines sentimentales. Soy chica alegre que promete contestar. Foto".

Rafael Chávez.— Apdo. Postal F-94, Chihuahua, Chih.— "Tengo 48 años, soy un joven delgado, de 1.73 m. de estatura, alegre y decente. Deseo relacionarme con fines sentimentales serios con dama de edad apropiada a la mía. Escribe pronto".

Olivia y Eloisa.— Ave. Hidalgo No. 413, N.C.G., Chih.— "Somos dos chicas alegres y sinceras de 19 y 17 años de edad. Deseamos entablar amistad con caballeros sinceros y serios de 20 a 30 años, podremos hablar sobre nuestras alegrías y penas".

G.M.— Pedro Vargas No. 7706, Col. Churubusco, Infonavit Norte, Chihuahua, Chih.— "Dama de 26 años, sóltera, romántica y de buenos sentimientos. Desea relacionarse con caballero de 27 a 35 años, sin vicios, soltero y trabajador. Seriedad".

Celia y Rosy.— Aldama No. 1423, Cd. Meoqui, Chih.— "Somos dos hermanas, sinceras, no mal parecidas, cristianas, de posición económica desahogada, alegre, de 18 a 21 años. Deseamos que nos escriban chicos de 19 a 29 años, no mal parecidos".

Juan Puerta R.— Apartado Postal No. 715, Chihuahua, Chih.— "Caballero soltero de 29 años, rubio, de ojos verdes, de 1.75 m. de estatura y 75 k. de peso. Desea encontrar con fines matrimoniales a damita morena clara de 20 a 25 años, cariñosa".

Alma Delia S.— Dom. Conocido, Col. Lázaro Cárdenas, Meoqui, Chih.— "Solicito correspondencia con caballero católico, soltero o viudo, serio y sin vicios de 25 a 27 años, con fines matrimoniales en corto plazo. Soy dama hogareña de 20 años. Foto".

Isabel Cristina.— Privada de Balderrama No. 104, Unidad Colina, Col. Infonavit, Cd. Camargo, Chih.— "Chica de 13 años, alegre, estudiante de Secundaria, dulce y simpática. Quisiera recibir correspondencia de chicos y chicas de todo el mundo".

A. Herrero.— Fco. Márquez No. 1339, Melchor Ocampo, Cd. Juárez, Chih.— "Tengo 19 años, soy un chico alto, de cabello y ojos castaños, estudiante alegre y sincero. Deseo tener correspondencia con chicas y chicos de Argentina, Brasil y Canadá".

Ana María R.— Fco. Sarabia No. 108, Cd. Camargo, Chih.— "Tauro de 16 años, dulce, y de buenos sentimientos. Quisiera tener correspondencia con muchachas y muchachos de todo el mundo, sin importar raza, religión ni posición económica, foto".

E.M.G.J.— Río Conchos No. 2301, Fracc. Junta de los Ríos Chihuahua, Chih.— "Chica de 20 años, alegre, estudiosa, simpática y de buenos sentimientos. Desea iniciar una linda amistad con todos los chicos del mundo, que quieran escribirle".

Rita M.M.— Calle Segunda No. 2606, Col. Sta. Rosa, Chihuahua, Chih.— "Soltera de 33 años, blanca, delgada, de pelo castaño, 1.58 m. de estatura. Desea le escriba con fines sentimentales caballero profesionista no mal parecido de 33 a 40 años".

María González.— Cd. Madera, Chih. Méx. Calle Mina, Chih.— "Me gustaría recibir correspondencia de chicas y chicos de todo el mundo, sin importar raza, religión ni posición económica. Soy una chica alegre y amistosa de 14 años, admiro a Menudo".

J. Porfirio G.— Calle Arteaga No. 620 Sur, B, Alto, Cd. Juárez, Chih.— "Deseo tener correspondencia con chicas sinceras de 15 a 20 años, con fines amistosos o sentimentales. Soy un muchacho de 19 años, bajo de estatura, estudioso. Foto".

Mary García.— Apartado Postal No. 139, Chihuahua, Chih.— "Maestra normalista soltera de 28 años, de 1.58 m. de estatura y tez morena clara. Me encantaría conocer a caballero profesionista, católico, serio y responsable de 30 a 33 años".

DURANGO

Sandra Quintana.— Estación Chinicates, La Campana, Dgo.— "Chica romántica, de 17 años, caballo largo, ojos castaños y tez blanca. Desea conocer a chico de cualquier lugar del mundo con fines sentimentales. Escribe pronto, no te arrepentirás".

Rosa Vela.— Calle 10 No. 205, Col. San Isidro, Cd. Lerdo, Dgo.— "Tengo 16 años, soy una chica alta, morena clara, romántica, de signo Virgo muy sincera. Quisiera ser amiga de todos los chicos de este continente, sin importar posición económica".

B.R.G.— Cuauhtémoc No. 515 int. Altos, Sur, Durango, Dgo.— "Con fines matrimoniales en corto plazo deseo conocer a caballero serio, responsable de 50 a 70 años, sea norteamericano y hable español. Soy dama divorciada de 51 años. Seriedad".

Martina Hernández.— Domicilio Conocido, Estación Rosario, Dgo.— "Libra de 17 años, alta, morena de cabello negro y ojos cafés. Desea le escriban jóvenes de 18 a 20 años, de buenos sentimientos para iniciar una linda amistad o algo más. Foto".

Alejandra Marín.— Mercado Fermín Revueltas Local No. 1, Santiago Papasquiaro, Dgo.— "Me gustaría recibir correspondencia de muchachos de ambos sexos de edad adecuada a la mía, con fines amistosos. Soy una chica de 17 años, alegre y muy simpática".

Gloria López.— Prof. Rafael Ramírez No. 220, Col. Fovissste Gómez Palacio, Dgo. "Anhelo tener amigos sinceros en chicos y chicas de todo el universo, podremos intercambiar postales, timbres y monedas. Soy muchacha morena de 16 años. Escriban".

Félix Flores.— Dom. Conocido, Estación Rosario, Dgo.— "Géminis moreno claro, bien parecido, simpático y alegre de 16 años. Desea le escriban damitas de 14 a 18 años, agradables, dulces y simpáticas con fines amistosos o sentimentales. Foto".

ESPECIALES

Isabel Sánchez.— Ret. 4 de Manuel Rivera Cambas, Edif. 26 Entrada "A", depto. 1, Col. Jardín Balbuena C.—. 15900.— "Soy viuda provinciana, de 42 años, sin problemas económicos, con cuatro hijos medianos, alegre, sincera, gordita. Deseo tener correspondencia con caballero de 45 a 50 años, serio, comprensivo y sincero, con solvencia económica, si tiene hijos no importa. Enviar foto en su primera carta".

Jesús Perfecto.— Calle López Cotilla No. 24, Tenamastlán, Jal. C.P. 48570.— "Deseo comunicarme con señorita de 26 años, morena clara, de ojos grandes, boca regular, de 40 a 50 kilos. Más datos en comunicación directa. Seriedad absoluta".

Víctor M. Díaz M.— Ave. Tlaleoligia No. 45, Col. Tlaleoligia, Tlalpan C.P. 14430.— "Anhelo comunicación con chicas del estado de Jalisco, de preferencia de los Altos, blanca, ojos verdes, bonita de 20 a 30 años. Fines matrimoniales. Tengo 30 años y no soy feo. Más datos en comunicación directa".

D.S.V.— Apdo. Postal No. 102, Jojutla, Mor., C.P. 62900.— "Anhelo relacionarme con señorita morena clara o blanca, cariñosa y quiera ayudarme a tener algo para los dos, que tenga por lo menos primaria de 18 a 26 años, de preferencia del Estado de Morelos o D.F. Tengo 35 años, moreno, cariñoso, romántico. Escriban.

Sebu S.M.— Tabasco No. 298-D, Col. Roma, México, D.F.— "Anhelo y deseo relacionarme con muchacha simpática, sencilla y alegre que desee formar un hogar, sin problemas familiares. Soy moreno, delgado, deportista, de buen carácter. Más datos en comunicación directa. Seriedad".

Javier Zendejas.— Apdo. Postal No. 844, Veracruz, Ver. 91700.— "Para damita de 25 a 43 años. Vengo hacia tí ofreciéndote amor apoyado, por necesidad y razones justas, en la conciencia de fidelidad. ¿Puedes expresarme tu amor en los mismos términos? Formaremos un hogar a corto plazo, al cual cada día retornaré para amarte siempre con ternura. Escribe luego. Seriedad".

Luis R. Sánchez.— Apdo. Postal No. 116-032, C.P. 01130, Deleg. Alvaro Obregón.— "Anhelo tener correspondencia con Japonesa o Americana de 18 a 22 años, si radica en el D.F., mejor. Soy caballero de 27 años, moreno claro, sin defectos físicos, con trabajo estable. Fines matrimoniales en corto tiempo. Seriedad absoluta".

Maricela Trujillo Flores.— Calle 16-A No. 11, Col. Santa Rosa C.P. 07620.— "Soy señorita de 29 años, profesionista sincera y atractiva. Desea entablar correspondencia con caballero profesionista con solvencia moral y económica. Enviar fotografía reciente en su primera carta. Fines matrimoniales".

E.M.G.— P.O. Box 424, King City CA 93930.— "Anhelo me escriban caballeros de 50 a 55 años, trabajador, sin vicios, de preferencia de las Islas Marías, si tiene hijos no importa. Soy señora de 46 años, residente legal en E.U. Fines serios."

Tami Hernández.— Oriente 2 B.A. No. 143, Atitalaquia, Hgo. C.P. 42970.— "Tengo 27 años, sin vicios, soltero, de clase media, moreno. Deseo relacionarme con chica de 16 a 22 años, blanca o rubia, que desee casarse en el mes de Agosto. Enviar foto reciente en su primera carta. Seriedad absoluta".

A.F.— Valle de Bravo No. 602, Col. Sánchez, Toluca, Edo. de México, C.P. 50040.— "Caballero de 36 años, delgado, deportista, sin vicios, soltero, moreno, cariñoso, comprensivo, con un pequeño defecto de no poder hablar fuerte. Deseo me escriba dama de 20 a 40 años, sin hijos, soltera o viuda, humilde, comprensiva no me importa su pasado. Matrimonio en corto tiempo. Seriedad.

An essential element in an ad for a pen pal is an address, and each of these ads includes one. (Review the abbreviation chart in Unit 2 if you need to.) In addition, each of these ads also contains a name (sometimes abbreviated) and a personal note, set off by quotation marks. This personal message includes information about the advertiser and describes what kind of pen pal (or spouse) he or she wants. Some ads are from people who want to exchange souvenirs, such as stamps **(timbres)**, post cards **(postales)**, or other objects. Many advertisers request a photo. Most just want to correspond, but others have romantic intentions.

Exercise H.

Match the advertisers with the descriptions provided in their ads.

_____	**1. Ignacio V., Hidalgo**	A. slender 21-year-old with beautiful eyes
_____	**2. Jorge Méndez A., Chiapas**	B. decent young man of 25
_____	**3. Alberto Martín, Chiapas**	C. responsible, hardworking man of 42
_____	**4. Apolonio de la Cruz, Hidalgo**	D. tall, romantic Virgo, 16 years old
_____	**5. Rosa Vela, Durango**	E. Aries, 16 years old and a student
_____	**6. _____**	F. cheerful 8-year-old, likes sports

Who fits the extra description? HINT: The quickest information to locate is the age, because numbers are more noticeable than letters.

Like the soap ad, these ads include many descriptive adjectives. People describe themselves, or their desired pen pal, with adjectives that relate to their physical or psychological characteristics or define the type of relationship they want to have. Many of these adjectives are cognates, and you should be able to read them easily. Remember, their endings help you determine whether they refer to a male or female.

To see how this information helps you read with more comprehension, note that most ads include some description about the advertiser (Person A) and some about a potential respondent (Person B). Look carefully at the following ad and notice how the forms of the adjectives indicate whether the adjective applies to person A or B.

> **C. Hernández.** —Oriente 2, Barrio A. No. 143, Atitalaquia, Hgo.—"Propongo matrimonio a damita **decente rubia, blanca,** sin importar si tiene un hijo. Soy caballero de 26 años, **alto, cariñoso,** sin vicios y muy **trabajador.** Más datos en comunicación directa, foto."

This ad has three parts: a description of the lady Mr. Hernández would like to marry (indicated by **matrimonio)**, a description of himself introduced by **soy,** and a reference to further communication. It contains only two important personal nouns: **damita** *(lady)* and **caballero** *(gentleman).* Each one is modified by both adjectives and phrases. Even if you cannot guess the meanings of adjectives such as **rubia** or **trabajador,** their endings and their positions tell you which person is referred to and help you keep track of various parts of the ad.

As you will see later in the *Dictionary Interlude,* being able to distinguish endings from stems helps you locate a word more easily if you decide to look it up. Of even more importance, however, is that being able to recognize the same stem when it recurs with different endings sometimes helps you avoid having to look it up at all.

Consider an example from the ad by Ignacio V. from the Hidalgo section. Look at that ad and find the stem **hogar** which occurs in the phrase **formar un hogar estable** and as part of the adjective **hogareña,** a characteristic Ignacio is looking for in a lady. Find other examples of this stem in ads from Alma Delia S. from Chihuahua, Rosa M. O. of Hidalgo, and Javier Zendejas in the **Especiales** section.

Its frequency suggests that the **hogar** stem might be a helpful one to know for understanding these ads, but it is not an easily recognizable cognate. You might decide on that basis to look for it in your dictionary. First, THINK for a moment. Can you guess what **hogar** might mean on the basis of the information you have so far? Remember that many of these people have marriage in mind.

Hogareña only occurs as a description for women and an **hogar** is something two people form. Make a guess and see if your meaning fits the contexts. To confirm your guess, look up **hogar.** Be sure to read the entries for any words that share the same stem.

In addition to repeated noun and adjective stems, these ads also display many recurring verb stems. Although the endings—the markers of subject and tense—may change from ad to ad, several verb stems are repeated. Exercise I will help you identify some useful ones.

Exercise I.

This list contains some important verb stems from the ads. They are given in their *infinitive* form (the form that ends in *-r* and does not identify a subject). Some of these stems are cognates. For this and other verb exercises, ignore any variations you may observe in the vowels of the stem. *Do not use your dictionary.*

1. Mark the verb stems in this list whose meanings you know or can guess.

   a. escribir
   b. intercambiar
   c. importar
   d. desear
   e. enviar

   f. iniciar
   g. contestar
   h. conocer
   i. relacionar
   j. tener

2. For each verb you marked, find at least two ads that contain some form of it. Is your guess about its meaning confirmed by its contexts?

3. For verbs which you could not guess (or are no longer certain of), find as many examples as you can in the ads. Look carefully at the contexts for additional clues about meaning.

4. Record a final meaning for each stem before checking your answers in the Answer Key.

Now read through all the ads again quickly. Try to understand as much as possible using the following techniques: pay special attention to stems that appear in several ads; use adjective endings to help keep track of which nouns are referred to; spend more time on words you know or can guess than on unfamiliar ones; and, most important, keep THINKING!

Now you can try some matchmaking of your own!

Exercise J.

Match each person on the left with the most appropriate pen pal listed on the right.

_____ **1.** Yeison Valencia, Hidalgo   A. M. Esperanza, Hidalgo

_____ **2.** Celia y Rosy, Chihuahua   B. Alma Delia S., Chihuahua

_____ **3.** Tere García, Chiapas   C. Jesús Perfecto, Especiales

_____ **4.** G. M., Chihuahua   D. Lucy y amigas, Hidalgo

_____ **5.** Tami Hernández, Especiales   E. P. M. y A. O., Chiapas

What you have done with these personal ads has allowed you to comprehend a great deal of written Spanish. For most reading purposes appropriate to material of this sort, you can conclude that you have successfully read it all. In fact, by now you should be so familiar with the structure and vocabulary of personal ads in Spanish, that you could compose one for yourself! You may enjoy exchanging ads with some of your classmates.

Dictionary Interlude

Identifying roots and endings

Good readers try to understand as much as they can of a passage before they look up any new words. So far in this unit, you have been able to understand a great deal of information by concentrating on format cues, by predicting the content of familiar material, and by guessing the meaning of stems. Nevertheless, it is obvious that you cannot guess the meaning of every stem in Spanish. You will need to use your dictionary some of the time, although you should try to use it as little as possible.

A technique good readers use to increase their dictionary efficiency is to look up only those words that are essential for understanding the passage at just the level their reading purpose requires. The most frequent words are likely to provide information that will help you continue guessing and reading. **Piel** in the soap advertisement is a good example. **Piel** occurred so often in the passage that knowing what it meant was essential. Once **piel** was known, though, it was easier to guess the meaning of other items. Frequency is not always a sign of importance, —some essential words may occur only once—but it is often a clue. Another sign of importance is appearance in a title or caption. It is always important to understand the meanings of words in a title or heading. The title **Club de la Amistad** is a good example of the usefulness of titles. Not only did the title help identify the general topic of the reading, but it also presented a word—**amistad** *(friendship)*—that occured frequently in the ads and was an important key to overall meaning.

In general, during early stages of reading you should concentrate on understanding nouns, verbs, and adjectives—content words. A prominent or repeated content word, which you cannot guess, is a good candidate for the dictionary. However, as you have seen, many content words can have more than one form in Spanish. Since a dictionary lists only the primary form of any stem, it is essential to be able to distinguish stems from endings in order to use a dictionary efficiently. You learned to find adjectives by looking for the masculine singular form. In this *Dictionary Interlude*, you will work on identifying the primary stem of other kinds of words, especially verbs. You will also learn more about the important distinctions between content and function words.

Let's begin by examining a new reading that includes many references to personal characteristics and uses many adjectives. It also includes many verbs that describe everyday activities. You have no doubt often read passages of this sort in English. Look at the reading and identify its type as quickly as you can.

HOROSCOPO

Por Daniel Fernández

ARIES
(marzo 21/abril 19)

Los sectores más favorecidos en este ciclo serán el de las amistades y la vida social, hasta el 18; y el de las cuestiones ocultas o espirituales, a partir de esa fecha. El día 20 se inicia para usted un ciclo de un año en el que Júpiter favorecerá todas las actividades secretas. Recibirá ayuda indirecta, y su intuición se verá muy exaltada. La Luna llena del 24 augura un triunfo laboral.

LEO
(julio 23/agosto 22)

Las relaciones con sus asociados y con su cónyuge ocuparán su mente hasta el 18. Después serán las cuestiones legales o burocráticas las que ganarán su interés. A partir del 20, Júpiter favorecerá esas actividades por un período de un año. Aproveche para firmar contratos y resolver pleitos o herencias. Si no se ha casado, evite discutir con su pareja. La Luna llena del 24 indica ganancias.

SAGITARIO
(noviembre 22/diciembre 21)

La comunicación y los viajes deberán ocupar el centro de su atención hasta el 18; después será su vida familiar la que reclamará su interés. A partir del 20 Júpiter favorecerá durante todo un año las actividades familiares y las operaciones con bienes raíces. La Luna llena del 24 indica un triunfo profesional. Aproveche ese día para solicitar ayuda de superiores, maestros y personas de nivel.

TAURO
(abril 20/mayo 20)

Hasta el 18 los astros le favorecen en su profesión o sus estudios. Aproveche esos días para solicitar ayuda de sus superiores. A partir del 20, se inicia para usted un ciclo de un año en el que su vida social se intensificará, y tendrá oportunidad de conocer nuevas amistades que le serán de mucha utilidad en el futuro. La Luna llena del 24 podría indicar una conquista amorosa.

VIRGO
(agosto 23/septiembre 21)

Hasta el 18 será su trabajo el campo en el que cosechará mejores triunfos; pero a partir de esa fecha deberá prestar mayor atención a sus relaciones con su cónyuge y sus asociados. El 20 se inicia un ciclo de un año en el que Júpiter favorecerá esas relaciones y las ganancias a través de éstas. La Luna llena del 24 augura un triunfo personal. Evite las discusiones con sus familiares.

CAPRICORNIO
(diciembre 22/enero 19)

Disfrutará de oportunidades de aumentar sus ganancias hasta el 18. A partir de esa fecha debe prepararse para expandir su campo de acción, pues Júpiter iniciará el día 20 un ciclo de un año en el que favorecerá sus comunicaciones y los viajes. Las actividades intelectuales también se verán bien aspectadas. La Luna llena del 24 podría significar un viaje largo.

GEMINIS
(mayo 21/junio 21)

Los viajes continuarán siendo el foco central de su agenda hasta el 18. A partir de esa fecha es necesario que dirija su atención a su profesión y sus estudios, pues el día 20 se iniciará un ciclo en el que Júpiter le favorecerá en esas actividades por todo un año. Aproveche para solicitar ayuda de personas de influencia. La Luna llena del 24 favorece actividades domésticas y familiares.

LIBRA
(septiembre 22/octubre 22)

Su vida sentimental continuará siendo muy armoniosa hasta el 18; después deberá prestar mayor interés a su sector del trabajo. A partir del 20 Júpiter favorecerá las actividades laborales y su salud durante un ciclo de un año. La Luna llena del 24 podría indicar la culminación de un proyecto que se ha venido desarrollando en secreto. Preste atención a sus sueños.

ACUARIO
(enero 20/febrero 19)

Antes de que Júpiter salga de su signo, el 20, le aportará un golpe de suerte que le beneficiará en muchos sentidos. A partir de esa fecha será específicamente su sector de las ganancias el que se verá favorecido. Sin embargo, debe continuar observando su dieta, pues tendrá tendencia a aumentar de peso. La Luna llena del 24 indica éxito en cuestiones legales o burocráticas.

CANCER
(junio 22/julio 22)

Los contratos y las cuestiones legales o burocráticas seguirán favorecidas hasta el 18. A partir de esa fecha serán los viajes lo que tomará el primer lugar en su agenda. Júpiter iniciará el día 20 un ciclo de un año que le aportará viajes y favorecerá sus relaciones con el extranjero y las actividades religiosas. La Luna llena del 24 podría significar el inicio o culminación de un viaje.

ESCORPION
(octubre 23/noviembre 21)

Las actividades realizadas en familia y las transacciones con bienes raíces continuarán bien aspectadas hasta el 18. A partir de esa fecha será su vida romántica lo que contará con el favor de los astros. Júpiter iniciará un ciclo de un año el día 20 que le aportará romances, alegría, creatividad e hijos. La Luna llena del 24 indica nuevas amistades y algún éxito en su vida social.

PISCIS
(febrero 20/marzo 20)

Este ciclo le pertenece, pues Venus, el Sol y Júpiter ingresarán en Piscis los días 13, 18 y 20 respectivamente. Esto indica que su magnetismo personal aumentará, que recibirá manifestaciones de afecto, y que durante un año, gracias a Júpiter, la suerte le sonreirá, aunque tendrá tendencia a engordar. La Luna llena del 24 indica éxito en actividades realizadas con su cónyuge o asociados.

This passage is a horoscope, taken from a magazine popular in Central America. Naturally, your ability to recognize parts of a horoscope depends partly on your familiarity with astrology and the signs of the zodiac. Before working with your dictionary, familiarize yourself with the reading by completing Exercises K and L.

Exercise K.

Use format cues to identify the following customary sections of a horoscope.

1. What is the title? _____

2. Who is the author? _____

3. Each zodiac sign has a symbol. What is the zodiac symbol associated with

   the following signs? Leo _____

   Cáncer _____   Piscis _____

4. Each astrological sign has a name. What are the Spanish versions of these

   English astrological signs? Saggitarius _____

   Scorpio _____   Aquarius _____

5. Each astrological sign is associated with a particular period of the year.
   What months are associated with these signs?

   Libra _____   Aries _____

6. Each horoscope provides a prediction. What are the first three words of

   the prediction for Taurus? _____

7. The months for each astrological period are all cognates and easy to recognize. What do you think the numbers found in some predictions might

   refer to? _____

The core of each horoscope entry is the prediction. Before you go on, THINK about the kinds of predictions often found in horoscopes. What areas of life are most likely to be mentioned?

Exercise L will prepare you to understand the predictions.

Exercise L.

1. Which item on this list is *least* likely to be mentioned in a horoscope?
   a. romance and social life   d. work
   b. health   e. money
   c. pets   f. family

2. Scan two or three predictions and use cognates to check the topics of the predictions. For each of the following areas, find an astrological sign with a prediction related to that area. These phrases may not occur in exactly this way in the predictions. THINK and use cognates.

   a. relaciones con la familia _____

   b. actividades sociales o románticas _____

   c. cuestiones profesionales _____

    d. asuntos financieros y legales _____

    e. viajes _____

3. Identify your own astrological sign and read your prediction carefully. Identify which fields listed on page 57 are treated in your particular prediction. _____

Earlier in this unit, you learned that all languages have both *function* and *content* words. Content words contain most of the meaning and function words relate the content words to each other. Because there are relatively few function words in any language, most have various uses. Because they convey primarily grammatical meaning, they are sometimes hard to translate or define. Your dictionary is always more helpful for content words than for function words. Fortunately, even if you have studied Spanish for only a few days, you have probably learned something about the most common function words already, and you can expect to learn about the rest of them soon.

At this early stage in your reading, however, content words are still more important, and verbs are important content words. Most verb forms consist of a *stem*, a *theme vowel* (which designates its class), and an *ending*. The endings of verbs tell such information as the subject and the tense, or aspect, of the verb action. The *infinitive* is the form of the verb that ends in **-r**; an infinitive is not marked for a particular subject or tense.

Infinitives are the verb forms found in a dictionary. Any word ending in **-r** preceded by **a, e,** or **i** is very likely to be an infinitive. Most Spanish verbs belong to one of three classes, named on the basis of their theme vowels: **-ar** verbs, **-er** verbs, and **-ir** verbs. **-Er** and **-ir** verbs have many similarities. If a verb is not used in the infinitive form, it will have some other ending. Most verb endings include the theme vowel, and you can use the ending to help identify the class of a verb—and know what its infinitive would be. (Note that some verb forms, known as *subjunctives,* use the "opposite" theme vowel: **-ar** verbs take **e** in their subjunctive endings and **-er** and **-ir** verbs take **a.** If you cannot find an infinitive you think should be in your dictionary, try looking for it under a different theme vowel.)

When reading horoscopes, you really only need to get the general idea of the passage. Your reading purpose does not require you to understand all the details of tense and person conveyed by the endings. (And you certainly do not need to know how to form or use the verbs yourself!) For example, because horoscopes contain predictions about the future, many of the verbs appear in the future tense, which may be unfamiliar to you. However, future-tense verb forms are easy to spot because of two features: the endings are attached to the infinitive (or a readily recognizable version of it) and they have written accents. Just because you do not know how to form future verbs right now does not mean that you cannot recognize them in a reading. Once you recognize them, it is simple to figure out what stem to look up if you need to know the meaning of a particular verb.

In general, the ending on a Spanish verb is no more than one or two syllables in length. Until you have mastered most of the Spanish tenses, there may be endings that you don't recognize, but you should be able to locate stems fairly easily. Simply knowing the meaning of a verb stem, along with your ability to identify the subject, is enough for most of your reading purposes at this stage. Here is an exercise to help you practice stem identification.

Exercise M.

1. Here is a list of verbs and verb phrases taken from the horoscopes you have been reading. The main verb stem in each phrase is underlined. For each underlined verb stem, use the ending to help you identify its probable class and infinitive: **-ar, -er,** or **-ir.** Write the probable infinitive in the blank.

    a. se <u>inicia</u>   _____

    b. deberá <u>prestar</u>   _____

    c. <u>favorecerá</u>   _____

    d. <u>aproveche</u>   _____

    e. podría <u>significar</u>   _____

    f. <u>tendrá</u>   _____

    g. debe <u>prepararse</u>   _____

    h. <u>intensificará</u>   _____

    i. debe continuar <u>observando</u>   _____

    j. se ha venido <u>desarrollando</u>   _____

2. Using the infinitive forms you just identified, look up any verbs you do not know. If you cannot find the infinitive you are looking for right away, make sure you are looking in the right place and then scan the nearby words to locate a similar infinitive with a meaning that seems to fit the kind of material you are reading. Correct your initial guesses about the form of the infinitive if necessary and record the meaning next to the infinitive.

Do not be concerned if you cannot understand everything you read. If you find yourself lost in a passage that contains many unrecognizable words and few cognates or format cues, the passage may be beyond your abilities at this stage. But good readers are able to tolerate a certain amount of uncertainty as they read, and you should keep this fact in mind when reading Spanish.

Now, read your own horoscope again and see if there are one or two other words you would like to know in order to fully understand what is being predicted for you. If so, identify the stems, determine the infinitives if they are verbs, and look them up. Do not look up more than *three* additional words. (HINT: You may need to know that **éxito** is misleading. It means *success*, not *exit.)*

Does your future look good? Now read this prediction, which applies to every student using this book, regardless of your astrological sign!

Antes de terminar de estudiar este texto, cada estudiante podrá leer muchos materiales de diferentes tipos escritos en español—y con buena comprensión. ¡Trabajar y PENSAR son las actividades que más facilitarán su éxito!

SICOLOGIA

Tiene en su mesa las fotos de su esposa e hijos.
Es un hombre responsable que se preocupa por su familia.

Su escritorio está repleto de papeles
Se nota que es persona ocupada, siempre trabajando.

Está conversando con sus compañeros de trabajo.
Están discutiendo los nuevos proyectos.

No está en su despacho.
Debe estar en una reunión de ejecutivos.

No está en la oficina.
Estará visitando a los clientes.

Salió a almorzar con el jefe.
Su prestigio está aumentando.

El jefe lo criticó.
El mejorará su actuación.

Hizo un mal negocio.
¿Estaba muy disgustado?

Le gritó a un empleado que no cumplió sus órdenes.
Tiene carácter. Sabe imponer orden.

Se va a casar.
Eso lo hará más estable.

Va a ser padre.
Necesitará un aumento.

Va a hacer un viaje de negocios.
Es conveniente para su carrera.

Se va. Tiene un trabajo mejor.
Hace bien en aprovechar la oportunidad.

Faltó al trabajo por enfermedad.
Debe estar muy mal.

Así suelen calificarlo a él en la oficina

HOMBRE Y MUJER:

Tiene en su mesa el retrato de su esposo e hijos.
¡Ummm! Su familia tiene prioridad sobre su carrera.

Su escritorio está repleto de papeles.
No tiene orden, es una chiflada.

Conversa con sus compañeras de trabajo.
Deben estar chismeando.

No está en su despacho.
Seguro que está en el tocador.

No está en la oficina.
Debe haberse ido a las tiendas.

Fue a almorzar con el jefe.
Deben tener un "affair".

El jefe la criticó.
Debe estar furiosa.

Ella hizo un mal negocio.
¿Se echó a llorar?

Le gritó a un empleado que no cumplió sus órdenes.
Está histérica.

Se va a casar.
Pronto quedará embarazada y dejará el trabajo.

Va a tener un bebé.
Le costará a la compañía la maternidad y los beneficios.

Va a hacer un viaje de negocios.
¿Qué dice el marido?

Se va. Ha conseguido un trabajo mejor.
No se puede confiar en las mujeres.

Faltó por enfermedad.
Debe tener un catarrito.

FOTO: George Chinsee

En cambio, vea lo que ocurre con ella

Cuando de trabajo se trata

Applying the Reading Strategy

In this unit you have expanded your ability to use format cues and cognates and you have learned how to be selective in using your dictionary. Now let's apply these techniques of the second stage of the *Reading Strategy* to the new reading on pages 60 and 61. It is a semi-serious article from a contemporary women's magazine called **Vanidades,** which is popular throughout Spanish America. Begin by prereading; do not try to understand the content yet. Simply allow your eyes to run over the material and note the layout, particularly the use of different typefaces, and the titles.

On the basis of your prereading, complete Exercise N.

Exercise N.

Refer to the article as necessary to answer the questions below.

1. This article contains three different types of titles. Which one identifies

    the magazine section in which the article occurs. _____

2. Of these topics found in a women's magazine, which is the most likely
    topic of an article in the **Sicología** section?
    a.   health care and exercise
    b.   nutrition and recipes
    c.   social behavior
    d.   fashion for working women

3. This article presents a series of contrasts. Based on the photographs, the
    layout of the writing, and the titles, which of the following do you think
    best identifies what is being contrasted?
    a.   behavior at work vs. behavior at home
    b.   married people vs. single people
    c.   people employed in office vs. people employed at home
    d.   working men vs. working women

4. The layout of this article features two parallel columns. What similarities
    within the two columns suggest that the content is organized in a parallel

    fashion as well? _____

This article deals with situations in which both women and men working in offices might find themselves. The situations are similar or identical for both men and women and are described in either the present or past tense. Many words are repeated in the paired descriptions. Each situation is followed by a comment, indicated by the use of italics. These comments are presumably made by co-workers, and they differ, depending on whether the worker is male or female. According to the subtitle, these comments evaluate **(calificar)** the workers differently.

The best way to read passages like this one is to read the related material as a unit. In this case, you would read the situation and accompanying comment (in italics) for the man, and then the corresponding sentences for the woman.

Read through the entire article quickly. Don't worry about words or verb endings you do not know. Concentrate on stems you do know or can guess. Try to identify each situation that is described. Pay attention to the way gender marks reflect the fact that men and women are being compared. *Do not use your dictionary.*

Often, you can use a cognate or known word in one part of these paired descriptions to help you guess an unknown word in the other part. For example, in the first situation, you may not know the word **retrato.** By comparing the situations described, however, you might assume that **retrato** is another way of saying **foto.** If you know the word **hijos** *(children)* but not the words **esposo** or **esposa,** you might be able to guess their meaning by reasoning in this way: The situation is about photos in the office; the photos include pictures of the children; who else might appear in such a photo and be male in the woman's case and female in the man's case? (**Esposo** and **esposa** mean "spouse." Can you recognize them as cognates now?) This reasoning is even easier if you use all available information, such as the recognizable word **familia,** contained in the comments.

Now read the first pair of situations and their comments carefully. The style and approach used in them is characteristic of all the others. Would you say that the comments on the woman's side are intended to be more negative than those on the man's side?

Let's see how you can use what you know about Spanish grammar to add to your comprehension. There are three kinds of verbs (or verb phrases) used in this article: **ser** to describe qualities or characteristics (such as **responsable** and **estable**), **estar** to describe locations or conditions (such as **en su despacho** or **furiosa),** and action verbs that describe what people do. In sentences with **ser** or **estar,** the nouns or adjectives carry the bulk of the meaning. In sentences with action verbs, the verbs are almost always very important. In verb phrases, the last verb stem usually carries the most important content. In this article, there are many verb phrases with helping verbs such as **estar, ir** *(go),* and **deber** *(to have to).* Many different verb endings are used, including the future. Exercise O will help you use this grammatical information to comprehend more of the article.

Exercise O.

Look back at the article to complete the following tasks.

1. Underline at least two sentences that use a form of **ser** as the main verb. Try to understand as much as you can about the situations or reactions the sentences describe.

2. Underline at least two sentences that use a form of **estar** as the main verb. Try to understand as much as you can about the situations or reactions the sentences describe.

3. Underline at least two sentences that have action verbs as the main verbs. Try to understand as much as you can about the situations or reactions the sentences describe.

4. Select a situation with each kind of verb that seems especially interesting, but which you are not sure that you understand completely. Pay special attention to the verb stems. Look up no more than three new content stems you think will help you.

Remember, your reading purpose for an article like this one is to understand enough of the content to get the author's point. You do not have to be able to understand every detail in it or to translate it into English. Materials of this sort are meant to be read for pleasure. By using your awareness of the social setting referred to in the article and your guessing skills, together with judicious use of your dictionary, you can understand everything that is important in this article, which was intended for educated Latin Americans. Use the following review exercise to guide you through the article one more time. Refer back to the article whenever you need to. You should guess as much as you can, but you may find that you need to look up one or two more words to be sure of your answers. Do not look up more than two—choose them carefully!

Exercise P.

Match the situations on the left to the commments that might be made about a woman employee, according to the article.

_____	**1. Va a tener un bebé.**	a.	They're having an affair.
_____	**2. Faltó por enfermedad.**	b.	They're just gossiping.
_____	**3. Almorzó con el jefe.**	c.	She'll cost the company in maternity benefits.
_____	**4. El jefe la criticó.**	d.	She's just got a cold.
_____	**5. Conversa con sus compañeras.**	e.	She's probably really upset.

Match the comments on the left to the situations in which a male employee might find himself, according to the article.

_____	**6. Están discutiendo nuevos proyectos.**	f.	He's going on a business trip.
_____	**7. Sabe imponer orden.**	g.	He's going to be a father.
_____	**8. Necesitará aumento.**	h.	He's talking with his coworkers.
_____	**9. No está en su despacho.**	i.	He yelled at an employee who didn't obey orders.
_____	**10. Es bueno para su carrera.**	j.	He's visiting clients.

Perhaps you are ready to make up some situations for an article of your own!

The reading process you have used in this unit and the preceding one may seem somewhat cumbersome to you. In these units, the prereading process has been presented very slowly. When it becomes natural, however, you will find that it takes much less time than the "look up every other word" method that most beginning students use. Look for additional readings similar to the one you have been reading here so that you can practice the *Reading Strategy* on your own.

UNIT

4
Planning
for Travel

The Reading Strategy

Prereading: Skimming for information

In Unit 4, we will practice a reading technique that will help you locate detailed information in longer reading passages. All the readings in the unit contain information a traveler might need, and you will recognize the kinds of information they contain by examining their formats. Most of them contain numbers in one form or another, and the unit should help improve your ability to interpret numbers in Spanish materials. You will also learn more about an important class of function words—prepositions—and you will learn how to cross-check dictionary entries to improve your accuracy.

We'll begin with several items that you might encounter if you were traveling in a Spanish-speaking country.

Scan the ten items on pages 67 and 68. As quickly as you can identify what kind of item each one is.

Look at the items again and THINK about the circumstances in which you might come across each of them. Then go on to Exercise A.

Exercise A.

Classify each item according to the following categories: ticket; advertisement; bill or receipt (for either goods or services).

1. _____   6. _____

2. _____   7. _____

3. _____   8. _____

4. _____   9. _____

5. _____   10. _____

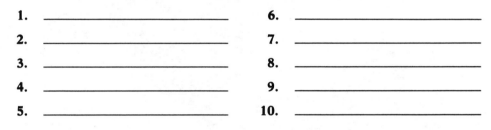

These items all contain one or more of the following types of information: addresses, dates, times, and prices. Information of this type almost always includes numbers. Reading such material is made easier if you are aware of certain differences in the ways numbers are written in English and in Spanish.

Let's begin with dates. The first major difference between English and Spanish concerns order. Ordinarily, we write dates in English with the month followed by the day: e.g., August 18, 1988. In Spanish, in nearly all contexts, the day is placed before the month: **18 agosto 1988.** Dates appear in this order whether they are written only in numbers or in both words and numbers. This order results from the typical spoken way of referring to dates in Spanish: **el** (number of the day) **de** (name of month) **de** (number of year) as in **el veinte de abril de mil novecientos ochenta y siete.** Many of the documents reproduced here include a space for the **fecha** *(date)*, and the requested order is always **día, mes, año.**

Another common feature of Spanish dates is the use of Roman numerals to indicate the months. In such a system, March, the third month, would be written as III and August, the eighth month, would be written as VIII.

Item 1

53 V 85

METRO

112 - 5

SENCILLO

UTILIZACION SEGUN TARIFAS

CONSERVESE HASTA LA SALIDA

48020

Item 2

C. T. N. E.
DPT.° DE TRAFICO

SERIE: № 0411

CENTRO: ....
FECHA: 8 MAYO 1985
HORA: 11'25
SOLICITANTE: /

El importe de la comunicación automática interurbana celebrada por Teletax, en la cabina n.° 40 asciende a ptas. 60 -

Talón Recaud. Cobro Teletax Cód. 171212

Item 4

NEWSTUDIES LANGUAGES CORPORATION
C/. Carretas 33, 3.°
Tel. 269 62 75
28012-MADRD

INGLES

ALEMAN - FRANCES
ESPAÑOL PARA EXTRANJEROS
DESDE

4.350 Ptas./mes

NUEVO TEL 4692232

- CURSOS GENERALES
- CURSOS INTENSIVOS
- CURSOS COMERCIALES
- GRUPOS - MAXIMO 8 ALUMNOS
- METODO DIRECTO
- NIVELES HOMOGENEOS
- CURSOS DE PERFECCIONAMIENTO EN GRAN BRETAÑA Y ESTADOS UNIDOS
- SERVICIO A EMPRESAS

CENTRO PROFESIONAL

—PLAZAS LIMITADAS—

¡INFORMESE!

Item 3

OPORTUNIDADES
REMIS

PRECIOS DE FABRICA:

Pantalón caballero verano desde	1.190,-
Camisa bambula	2.850,-
Vaquero lavado	1.790,-
Faldas verano moda desde	1.690,-
Camisas unisex moda desde	490,-
Sueters señora lino	1.690,-

GRAN SURTIDO PRENDAS SEÑORA Y CABALLERO

MONTERA 34-2ª PLANTA

Item 6

Cafetería Bonampak

Dr. Belisario Domínguez, No. 180
Tuxtla Gutiérrez, Chis
R F C LEE0451003 001

№ 51085

23/11/85 | No. Mesa: 7 | Mesero: 2

No. Comanda	No. Personas	No. Folio	Firma Recep.

Cant.	CONCEPTO	Importe
2	limonada c/p.	320 -
2	tortas pollo	680 -
2	Ensaladas f	720 -

PAGADO

SUMA	1720
IVA $	258 -
SubTotal $	1978 -
% Serv. $	
TOTAL $	

Firma huésped

No. Habitación

Item 5

R F C
ZEBJ-570101

PAPELERIA NUEVA
GRAL. UTRILLA No. 9 TEL. 8-10-91
SAN CRISTOBAL DE LAS CASAS, CHIAPAS.

NOMBRE | DIRECCION

CANT.	DESCRIPCION	PRECIO	IMPORTE	C.I.
11	postales	35 -	385	00
4	postales	30 -	120	00
5	Folder T/C	18 -	90	00
12	Sobres T/C	9 -	108	00
1	Blok T/C		280	00
1	Caja de clips		205	00

DIA / MES / AÑO: 19

VENDEDOR

$ 1,188.00

SUB TOTAL
IVA 15%
IMPORTE TOTAL 1,188.00

GRACIAS POR SU COMPRA

D 012401

1-03617-4 FTE. 1 Y 2

Item 7

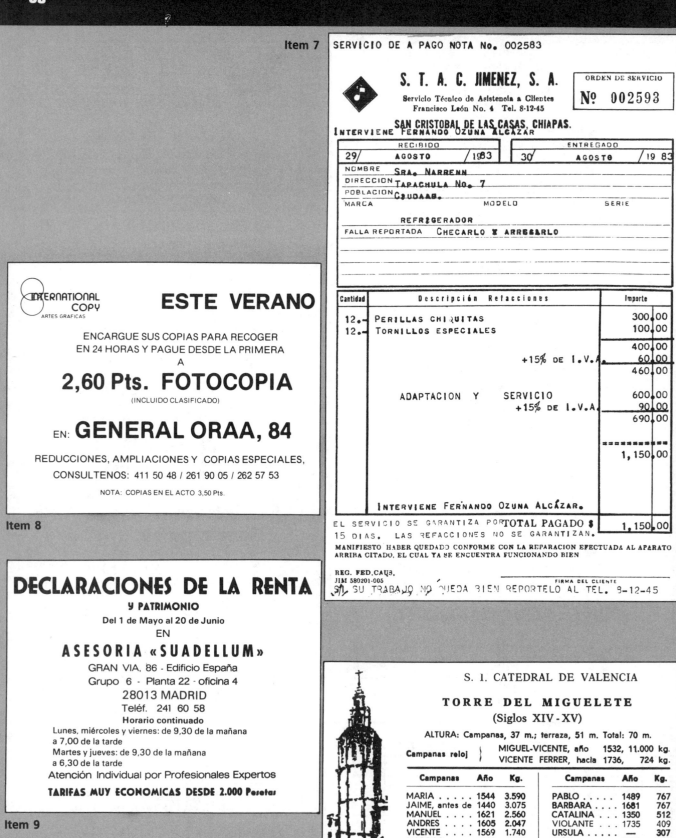
Item 8

Item 9

Item 10

Exercise B.

Answer the following questions based on the items from Exercise A.

1. Which of the following types of materials typically provide space for a date?
   a. tickets
   b. sales receipts
   c. restaurant receipts
   d. service receipts
   e. ads

2. Based on these items, which of the following is *least* likely to have the date filled in?
   a. tickets
   b. service receipts
   c. sales receipts
   d. restaurant receipts

3. Which item illustrates the use of Roman numerals in dates?

   _____

4. Which items illustrate the "day-month-year" order when using all numbers? _____

Some of the items you have seen include times as well. In many parts of the Spanish-speaking world, the twenty-four-hour clock is used, especially for official business. In the twenty-four-hour clock system, the hours begin with one A.M. and continue on through 2400 hours (midnight). 1:00 P.M. is 1300 hours and 5:00 P.M. is 1700 hours. With a twenty-four-hour clock, it is unnecessary to specify A.M. or P.M., since the hour itself makes that information clear. One thing to keep in mind when reading times in Spanish is that there is more variation in the way the times are written than we find in English. Where we almost always use a colon to separate the hours and minutes, for example, Spanish speakers may use a comma, an apostrophe, or a period, as well as a colon.

Most of the materials you have been reading also include some references to prices. Being able to read prices is, of course, a valuable skill for any traveler. The first thing to remember about prices is that they are given in the currency of the country. Each country has its own monetary unit. Often the name of the unit is abbreviated or indicated by a symbol. For example, prices in Mexico are often given with the notation **M.N.**, which stands for **moneda nacional** (*national currency*) or with a symbol that looks like a dollar sign but has only one vertical bar: **$**. In Spain, the abbreviation **pta(s)** is often seen; it stands for **pesetas**, the Spanish national currency. You can see several kinds of currency represented in the photo on page 70.

In order to know how much a price is equal to in US dollars, you must convert the price according to the current rate of exchange. (Rates of exchange are generally posted in banks and listed in newspapers.) For example, if the **peseta** is at 133 to the dollar, then the price for services at the **Asesoría Suadellum** would cost about $15 in US dollars (2000 **pesetas** divided by 133). (Your instructor may be able to help you find a listing of current exchange rates so that you can convert the other prices you see throughout this unit.)

How many different Spanish speaking countries are represented here?

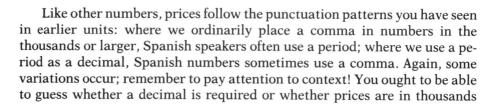

Another aspect of many of the prices you see here is the "value-added tax" or VAT. The VAT is a special tax, usually about 15%, which is added to the price of certain goods and services. It is common in many Spanish-speaking countries (as well as elsewhere throughout the world.) The equivalent acronym in Spanish is **IVA**. THINK: Can you identify the Spanish phrase it stands for?

Like other numbers, prices follow the punctuation patterns you have seen in earlier units: where we ordinarily place a comma in numbers in the thousands or larger, Spanish speakers often use a period; where we use a period as a decimal, Spanish numbers sometimes use a comma. Again, some variations occur; remember to pay attention to context! You ought to be able to guess whether a decimal is required or whether prices are in thousands simply by knowing what product is for sale and what currency is in use. Notice that unlike most prices in the United States, prices in Spanish-speaking countries tend to be expressed in whole numbers. You may have noticed that handwritten numbers have some distinguishing features too. The most obvious example is the number seven, which is almost always written as **7**. This practice helps distinguish seven from the numeral one, which is often written with a little tail in front of it: **1**. Look at the C. T. N. E. receipt for an example.

Be sure to remember that Spanish-speaking countries use the metric system and often abbreviate metric measures such as **kilómetro, metro,** and **kilogramo.**

Exercise C.

Look at the materials again, concentrating on prices, then answer the following questions.

1. What is the monthly rate for language lessons at the Centro Profesional of the Newstudies Languages Corporation in Madrid? _____

2. What is the difference between the **precio** and the **importe** at the Papelería Nueva? _____

3. What is the *total* amount of **IVA** charged by S. T. A. C. Jiménez on the August 29th bill? _____

4. If a **peseta** is made up of 100 **centavos**, what is the price in **centavos** of a single photocopy at International Copy's Artes Gráficas department?

    _____

5. What item includes an example of the use of periods to divide thousands in a number that is *not* a price? _____

The questions you have just answered are typical of questions that require *skimming*. Skimming is a reading technique that combines some aspects of scanning with some of the techniques used for close reading. We use skimming when reading materials known to contain specific information or details that we need, surrounded by information of less interest. Skimming is the physical process of allowing your eyes to move quickly over written material (as you do in scanning), but with your attention focused so as to notice a particular word or phrase or type of material. You have used skimming for review exercises in earlier units. In those cases, you skimmed materials that were already familiar in order to locate particular information. Skimming is just as useful as a primary reading technique for materials that you do not want to read closely but from which you must extract certain specific information. In such a case, you may first *scan* to see what kind of information a piece of writing actually contains, then *skim* to locate the particular detail of interest. Schedules of any kind are perfect for skimming. While schedules often pack a great deal of information into a small space, there is usually only one piece of it that is of interest to any particular reader at any particular time. Consider the photograph of people in an airport in Spain on page 72. Examine the sign in it carefully, using what you know about airports and cognates to help you identify the types of information presented there.

This airport sign presents information of interest to departing passengers. THINK about what you see in the sign. Did you see that the general "title" of the sign is **Salidas Nacionales** and that information about the time of the **salida** is given for each flight? How do you interpret the word **puerta?** If you cannot be sure of the meaning of **embarque**, what help can you get from the times? Specifically, what is the probable meaning of **embarque** given that **embarque** seems to always take place about twenty minutes before **salida?**

The next exercise helps you practice skimming with a set of questions airplane passengers typically ask. As you answer each one, pay very careful attention to the way in which you locate the different types of information. Your eyes should skim the sign until you locate the detail you require and then read more closely. Try it!

 Exercise D.

1. You are on flight 583. Where are you going? _____

2. You are on flight 597. What time does it leave? _____

3. You are on flight 413. What gate does it leave from? _____

4. You are going to Málaga. The time is 16.00. Is your flight already boarding? _____

5. You are at gate 7. What flight are you on? _____

6. What two flights leave at 16.20? _____

7. How many flights are going to Madrid? _____

Here is a more complex piece of material aimed at Spaniards interested in a healthful vacation at a spa featuring mineral waters. (**Balneario** means "spa".)

    Begin by scanning the brochure found below and on page 74. Use format cues and cognates to identify its important sections.

HOTEL-BALNEARIO VALLFOGONA
3 ESTRELLAS - TARRAGONA

AGUAS:

Cloruro-sódico-sulfatadas. Variedad bromo yodaduras isotónicas. Altamente radioactivas.

ESPECIALMENTE RECOMENDADAS PARA:

Reumatismos, ciáticas, lumbagos, artrosis, artritis.
Eczemas, psoriasis, dermatosis.
Estreñimiento, dispepsia, gastritis, hígado y riñón.
Obesidad, diabetes.
Afecciones bronquiales y laringorespiratorias.
Afecciones cardiovasculares.
Afecciones de las vías urinarias.

HOTEL-BALNEARIO

El Hotel Balneario de Vallfogona de Riucorp se encuentra situado en la provincia de Tarragona a unos 70 Kms. de la ciudad de Tarragona y unos 100 Kms. de la de Barcelona, y tan solo a unos 30 Kms. de la autopista Barcelona-Zaragoza, enclavado en la pequeña localidad del mismo nombre se abre ante los ojos del espectador un frondoso paisaje de bosques en el que se sitúa el Hotel-Balneario de 3 estrellas dotado de las más modernas comodidades, ascensores de subida y bajada, grandes salones, bar, TV., cine, salón de juegos, solarium, piscina, pista de tenis, campo de fútbol, parque infantil y un extenso jardín donde se sitúa la capilla y el garaje. Las habitaciones están dotadas de baño completo, con baño o ducha, calefacción y agua caliente.

En la planta baja del hotel se encuentra el balneario, con acceso directo de las habitaciones y componen sus instalaciones los baños, duchas a presión, pulverizaciones, masajes sistema Trautwein, sala de inhalaciones y sauna finlandesa.

NO LO DUDE, LE ESPERAMOS EN VALLFOGONA

VIAJES CEMO S.A.
G.A.T. 419

Génova, 1   28004 **MADRID**
Tels.: (91) 419 33 89/419 37 26
(Metro Alonso Martínez). Télex: 45.582

¡UNICA OPORTUNIDAD!

***
Hotel - Balneario VALLFOGONA
Provincia de Tarragona
PRECIO POR PERSONA: 27.950 Pts.

INCLUYE:
Autocar + Pensión Completa, incluído vino + Asistencia guías + Reconocimiento médico + Consultas médicas + Tratamiento balneoterápico + Programa de Animación.

SALIDA: 28 DE JULIO
REGRESO: 8 DE AGOSTO

P R O G R A M A

DIA 1.º: Salida. Trayecto en autocar. Cena y alojamiento en el Hotel-Balneario.

DIA 2.º al 11.º: Estancia en Pensión Completa con vino en el Hotel-Balneario incluyendo tratamiento balneoterápico.

DIA 12.º: Desayuno en el hotel. Trayecto en autocar.

— Reconocimiento médico a la entrada, no olviden llevar la CARTILLA médica de desplazados.

— Asistencia de un guía especializado toda la estancia, música, bailes, cine, concursos y excursiones con precios especiales.

VIAJES CEMO S.A
G.A.T. 419

GENOVA, 1 - METRO ALONSO MARTINEZ
Telfs. 419 33 89 - 419 37 26 - 419 26 97
Télex 45582 - 280 4 MADRID

Scan again to answer the questions in Exercise E.

Exercise E.

1. What is the name of the spa? _____

2. What is the name of the province in Spain where the spa is located?

   _____

3. What travel agency is responsible for arranging the vacations?

   _____

4. What is the title of the section containing a description of the facilities offered by the spa? _____

5. Name at least one ailment for which a spa vacation might be helpful, according to the brochure. _____

6. How much does a spa vacation cost? _____

7. What do DIA 1º, DIA 2º, and so on refer to? _____

Use Exercise F to guide you as you skim the brochure.

 Exercise F.

Skim the brochure in order to answer the following questions about the vacation package at the Hotel-Balneario Vallfogona.

1. How many days (total) is the vacation package for? _____

2. At which Metro stop is the travel agent located? _____

3. Which of the following is *not* included in the package price?
   a. transportation by bus to and from the spa
   b. guide service
   c. special clothing
   d. medical consultation

4. True or False? Diabetics should consider a spa vacation.

While these questions require specific details as answers, they concern general features of the program described in the brochure. Locating the answers is made easier by using format cues. For example, information such as the length of the vacation, the price, the location of the travel agent, and so on is contained in clearly identified sections of the brochure. Once you have successfully located (by scanning) the list of ailments treated by the spa waters, you merely have to skim the list to locate a reference to diabetics. But skimming is possible, and just as useful, for material with few format cues. Look quickly at the section of this brochure that includes two paragraphs describing the **hotel-balneario** itself. ♠

There are no illustrations or obvious format cues in this part of the passage. Nevertheless, skimming can help you identify the type(s) of information contained in the two paragraphs, and decide whether or not it is worthwhile to read the paragraphs more closely.

Prose material is not totally without format cues. Paragraph divisions themselves are a kind of formatting. Punctuation, such as a series of commas that indicate a list, and the use of special characters, such as numbers or capital letters, can be clues to content. Since Spanish prose is often characterized by the use of extremely long sentences, the format cues of prose are valuable aids to help orient you within a long sentence. One of the characteristics of long sentences is that they usually contain many prepositional phrases—phrases introduced by function words known as prepositions. In general, the function of prepositions is to show how nouns that are neither subjects nor objects of verbs are related to the verbs in a sentence. You have undoubtedly already learned some important Spanish prepositions such as **en, de**, and **a**.

Spanish and English prepositions are used in different ways, however, and it can take a good deal of experience to use them properly when you speak or write. Using prepositions when you read is not as difficult, and they can be especially helpful in interpreting long sentences. An important early technique is to separate prepositional phrases from core verb phrases. For that reason, you should begin now to be aware of the presence of prepositions in your reading.

Now let's practice the *Reading Strategy* techniques you have learned so far on the short piece of prose in the Vallfogona brochure. First, scan the two paragraphs of prose. Let your eyes slide quickly over the material, collecting information about the probable content of the piece as a whole. *Do not attempt to read closely.*

Without returning to the passage, complete the next exercise.

Exercise G.

1. True or False? The passage contains detailed information about the location of the Hotel-Balneario.

2. True or False? The passage includes one or more lists.

3. Select the best short title for this passage.
   a. Finding the Hotel-Balneario Vallfogona
   b. Activities at the Hotel-Balneario Vallfogona
   c. Location and Facilities of the Hotel-Balneario Vallfogona

Did you notice that the two paragraphs of prose contain only three sentences? The first of these is quite long and contains many prepositional phrases. Format cues and punctuation can help you identify its basic subdivisions: the location of the Hotel-Balneario in relation to important cities and highways; the physical setting of the Hotel-Balneario; and the list of modern features of the spa. The second sentence (end of paragraph one) describes the rooms at the spa; and the last paragraph-sentence describes the spa facilities.

Exercise H contains several questions a person interested in a spa vacation might ask. Read over the questions and then skim the two paragraphs to locate the answers as quickly as you can. Use format cues and cognates, and guess as much as possible. Do not use your dictionary. Remember, when you scan material, you are trying to discover what it contains. When you skim, you are trying to find particular details that you already expect it to contain.

Exercise H.

1. Exactly how far is the Hotel-Balneario from Barcelona?   _____
2. True or False? There are facilities for playing tennis at the spa.
3. True or False? You can watch television at the spa.
4. True or False? You can get a room with a private bath.
5. True or False? There is a sauna at the spa.

Now let's use these two paragraphs to work with prepositions.

 Exercise I.

Locate three prepositional phrases for each of the prepositions below.
Write the phrases in the spaces provided.

1. en   _____

    _____

    _____

2. de   _____

    _____

    _____

3. a   _____

    _____

    _____

4. con   _____

    _____

    _____

THINK about the relationship of the noun in the prepositional phrase to the
rest of the sentence. If you have trouble with this exercise, consult the Answer
Key.

Before going on to the *Dictionary Interlude*, go back over the **Vallfogona**
brochure and read it from beginnning to end, seeing how much new information you can discover. Mark any words you do not know but that seem especially important to the passage. If you were really a potential spa vacationer,
you would probably want to look those words up in your dictionary.

Dictionary Interlude

Selecting among multiple entries

A major difficulty in using bilingual dictionaries is that they provide translation equivalents, not true meanings. A dictionary entry does not tell you what a word means; it simply provides a list of the words in the other language that can be used to translate that word. Generally, bilingual dictionaries do not provide much direct help in selecting from among the several possible equivalents for any particular word. For a skilled user, however—one who THINKS while using the dictionary—there is some assistance available in the dictionary. In this *Dictionary Interlude*, we will illustrate some techniques that can increase your ability to select the proper equivalent for the word you need. You should (1) know the part of speech; (2) read the entire entry; (3) pay attention to related entries; and (4) cross-check. Let's see how these techniques work with some specific examples.

Identifying the appropriate equivalent for a word is often easy if you *know the part of speech*. Identifying the part of speech depends partly on the context in which the word is used and partly on its form. In English, form sometimes gives almost no information about part of speech, as this pair of sentences illustrates.

I think I heard a *knock* at the door.

I don't want to *knock* on her door at this late hour.

In these example sentences, *knock* has the same form. In the first case, the presence of an indefinite article, *a*, before the word is a signal that *knock* is a noun. So is the fact that *knock* seems to be closely related to the verb phrase *heard—knock* is its object, a grammatical role filled only by nouns, noun phrases, or noun clauses. In the second sentence, the use of the infinitive marker *to* indicates that *knock* is a verb. In other contexts, form changes might establish more clearly that it is a verb. In the sentence, "He *knocked* at the door for more than an hour," the past tense marker *-ed* indicates the part of speech.

In Spanish, because of the agreement patterns of nouns and adjectives and because verbs take endings that specify the subject, determining the part of speech of a word is sometimes a little easier than in English. For example, **golpe** is one translation equivalent for *knock*; it is a noun. A related word is **golpear**, whose infinitive **-r** shows that it is a verb. Their forms reflect their part of speech. Once you know the part of speech, you can use the abbreviations in a dictionary entry to guide you to the most appropriate class of translation equivalents. Look up **golpe** and **golpear** in your dictionary.

What are the abbreviations your dictionary uses to indicate their parts of speech?

golpe _____   golpear _____

The **golpe** entry should offer several translation equivalents. (It may also include a series of phrases using **golpe**, but for now, concentrate on the single-word translations.) When you use a dictionary to help you read, it is often sufficient for your reading purpose to recognize the common idea shared by several translation equivalents in order to make sense of the word you have looked up. In order to understand a sentence such as **Al entrar en la sala, Lilia recibió un golpe fuerte en la cabeza,** you only have to recognize the common feature in the various meanings of **golpe**—a strong contact between two objects—to be able to guess that Lilia got a bump. (The prepositional phrase tells you where: on her head.)

Except when your reading purpose is to produce a direct translation, you do not need to be able to translate every word in a passage. You simply have to be able to extract the important sense of the passage. Trying to translate just slows down your reading process and makes reading more difficult.

Sometimes, though, when you find multiple meanings in your dictionary, you may need to select a specific one. Often only one meaning is appropriate for the context you are reading, and you must choose from several possible entries. The first thing to do with an entry with several translation equivalents is to *read the entire entry* carefully. This practice is helpful in three ways. First, it will help you identify the common semantic ideas, or meanings, the items in the entry may share. It will also help you locate the group of items from the appropriate grammatical class for the context you have. Finally, reading the entire entry can alert you to related cognate words that may appear as synomyns elsewhere in the context and save you the time of looking up the additional words later.

A related technique, which only takes a moment, is to *pay attention to related entries*. This practice serves the same purposes as those described above for reading the entire entry and can also help expand the possible semantic associations for the word you have looked up. By looking up **golpear**, for example, you would also have seen **golpe** and a series of related words with the same root. Since, as you know, important roots recur in reading passages, it is always useful to have an idea of the possible variations of a root you have looked up. Many people find it useful to pencil a small dot next to words as they look them up. If you find that you are looking up the same word (or related ones) a second or third time, you can conclude that the word is a common one and worth remembering.

The last technique is related to the fact that your dictionary is bilingual. You can *cross-check* your chosen equivalent by looking it up in the English-Spanish section and using the infomation contained there to help you judge the appropriateness of your choice.

Now let's try some dictionary work to illustrate these techniques. Your dictionary may not include the exact information referred to here, but it should be similar enough to let you follow the illustration. If your dictionary seems to include very few of the translation equivalents used here, perhaps you need a more complete one. Remember, though, that no bilingual dictionary can include every possible word in either language and that technical terms are especially hard to find.

Sometimes, even if you think you recognize a word, you may not be able to fit the meaning you know for it to the context in which it occurs. If it is a frequent or highlighted word in the reading passage, you will probably need to look it up. Such a situation might occur with the word **pieza** which should look familiar to you. Here are some possible contexts in which you might come across **pieza.**

Mi amigo vive en un apartamento de cuatro **piezas.**

Esta **pieza** de equipaje es nueva.

Hoy presentan una **pieza** de tres actos.

These contexts provide the grammatical information that **pieza** is a noun (it can be modified by adjectives and preceded by indefinite articles, and it can be the subject, direct object, or object of a preposition). The last two sentences tell you that **pieza** is feminine (its adjectives are marked for feminine agreement). Cognates elsewhere in the sentences make it possible for you to guess at the meaning of **pieza** in most of these contexts, but let's say you want to look it up to be sure. Look it up now and remember to read the entire entry carefully.

Pieza has several possible translation equivalents. Your dictionary may have included some of the following: *piece, part, room, coin.* Did you already suspect that **pieza** might be a cognate of the English word *piece?* The list given here provides all the information necessary to determine the meaning of **pieza** in the first two sentences, but it is less helpful for the third: **Hoy presentan una pieza de tres actos.** THINK: What kinds of things are presented and have three acts?

Play would fit the sentence, and some bilingual dictionaries include it among the entries for **pieza.** If yours does not, you could confirm your guess by using the cross-checking technique. Look up *play* in the English-Spanish section of your dictionary.

The entry for *play* is probably quite long, since *play* has various meanings in English, but in the noun section you should have found Spanish equivalents such as **drama, comedia,** and **pieza.** These cognates confirm that **pieza** as a noun can mean *play* in the theatrical sense, and that is the best translation equivalent for the third example sentence.

Cross-checking is most helpful when you have no particular way to choose from among several translation equivalents that differ substantially in meaning. You do not need to cross-check everything: that would be too time-consuming. However, it is more practical to cross-check an important word than to misinterpret it. As you gain more reading experience, you will gain confidence and use cross-checking less, but, for now, it is an extremely helpful technique.

Here is a reading passage that contains important information for air travelers. We will apply these dictionary techniques to new words in it. First, scan the reading and discover as quickly as possible what sort of information it contains. Remember, at the scanning stage of the *Reading Strategy,* you should read only the material contained in headings, titles, and special illustrations.

AEROLINEAS ARGENTINAS

FRANQUICIA DE EQUIPAJE DESDE LOS ESTADOS UNIDOS

PASAJEROS DE PRIMERA CLASE:

1. — Dos (2) piezas de equipaje en bodega. La suma de las dimensiones (largo, ancho, profundidad) de cada pieza no debe exceder las 62 pulgadas **Y** el peso de cada pieza debe limitarse a 35 kgs. (77 lbs.)

2. — Una ó más piezas de equipaje de mano para ser llevado por el pasajero en la aeronave. Deberá caber en el espacio provisto debajo del asiento, no debiendo exceder su **peso total** los 35 kgs. (77 lbs.)

PASAJEROS DE CLASE TURISTA/ECONOMICA:

1. — Dos (2) piezas de equipaje en bodega. La suma de las dimensiones de las dos piezas en conjunto, (largo, ancho, profundidad) no debe exceder las 106 pulgadas **Y** a condición de que la suma de las dimensiones de ninguna pieza exceda 62 pulgadas. El peso de cada pieza debe limitarse a 35 kgs. (77 lbs.)

2. — Una ó más piezas de equipaje de mano para ser llevado por el pasajero en la aeronave. Deberá caber en el espacio provisto debajo del asiento, no debiendo exceder su **peso total** los 35 kgs. (77 lbs.)

FRANQUICIA DE EQUIPAJE PERMITIDA A NIÑOS E INFANTES:

1. — A los infantes que abonan el 10% de la tarifa normal de adultos se les permite UNA pieza de equipaje en bodega. La suma de las dimensiones de la misma (largo, ancho, profundidad), no debe exceder las 39 pulgadas **Y** el peso debe limitarse a 35 kgs. (77 lbs.) Además, se permite un cochecito o silla de paseo plegable para infantes.

2. — A los niños que abonan el 50% o más de la tarifa normal de adultos se les permite la misma franquicia otorgada a pasajeros que pagan la tarifa de adultos.

> **IMPORTANTE: FRANQUICIAS DE EQUIPAJE Y CARGOS POR EXCESO DE EQUIPAJE PARA PASAJEROS QUE CONTINUAN Y/O REGRESAN SERAN DETERMINADAS POR LAS LEYES Y REGULACIONES LOCALES APLICABLES.**

CARGOS POR EXCESO DE EQUIPAJE DESDE LOS ESTADOS UNIDOS

Los cargos por exceso de equipaje serán fijados como sigue:

   a. Por cada pieza que exceda lo permitido en cada una de las categorías (TARIFA BASICA)
   b. Por cada pieza que exceda la suma permitida de las tres dimensiones (largo, ancho, profundidad) hasta 80 pulgadas (TARIFA BASICA)
   c. Por cada pieza que exceda lo permitido en cada una de las categorías **Y** que exceda la suma permitida de las tres dimensiones (largo, ancho, profundidad), hasta 80 pulgadas (TARIFA ESPECIAL)
   d. Por cada pieza de la cual la suma de las tres dimensiones (largo, ancho, profundidad) **exceda las 80 pulgadas y/o cuyo peso exceda los 35 kgs. (77 lbs.)** (TARIFA ESPECIAL)
   e. Por cualquier otro tipo de equipaje no especificado más arriba, se ruega contactar a AEROLINEAS ARGENTINAS.

TARIFAS BASICAS DE EXCESO DE EQUIPAJE:

DESDE: / A:	Miami, Fla.	Otros Puntos en Estados Unidos
ARGENTINA BRAZIL	$45.00	$51.00
COLOMBIA	$20.00	$26.00
ECUADOR	$25.00	$31.00
PERU	$30.00	$36.00

TARIFAS ESPECIALES:

Para información adicional y/o clarificación, se ruega contactar la oficina más cercana de AEROLINEAS ARGENTINAS.

Exercise J.

Answer the following questions by skimming the passage.

1. Which of the following national airlines produced this page?

   a. Bolivia b. Argentina c. Spain

2. The travelers for whom this page is intended are traveling from which of the following countries?

   a. Spain b. Argentina c. United States

3. This page concerns which of the following types of information?

   a. passport and visa restrictions

   b. arrival and departure schedules

   c. baggage and cargo allowances

4. According to the information in the chart, which of the following destinations is *not* served by **Aerolíneas Argentinas**?

   a. Madrid, Spain b. Lima, Peru c. Quito, Ecuador

This passage contains many new words. Scan all the sections of the passage again, paying attention to frequency and highlighting as clues to the importance of certain words. THINK about what you know about similar materials in English.

Exercise K will help you practice the new dictionary techniques with some important words from the passage.

Exercise K.

The words in the list below are important to the passage. Look for them in the passage and choose *at least* four of them to look up, either because you cannot guess their meanings or are not sure of the accuracy of your guesses.

1. franquicia _____
2. bodega _____
3. asiento _____
4. peso _____
5. pulgadas _____
6. equipaje _____

Look up the four you choose, practicing the dictionary techniques presented in this *Dictionary Interlude*. Remember to THINK about each word in its contexts in the passage and relate those contexts to the dictionary information you find. Your goal is to select the most appropriate equivalent. Write the translation equivalent you choose in the space provided.

You may enjoy comparing your choices in Exercise K and your results with those of your classmates. Since each reader has unique resources—experience in air travel, for example, or awareness of different cognates—each person can create a unique set of words to look up. In any case, it is important to remember that you want to use your bilingual dictionary only when necessary and in the most efficient way possible. Once you have decided to look something up, however, you can use these techniques to extract as much useful information as possible and to guarantee the accuracy of the conclusion you draw from it.

Applying the Reading Strategy

This section presents an extended exercise based on several related pieces of material that one might use while planning a trip to the Mexican town of Oaxaca, a favorite destination for many American tourists. It will help you use your new skills with numbers and prepositions as well as your ability to skim for specific information.

Exercise L.

The two charts contain important information about Oaxaca. Use them to answer the questions. Use your dictionary as necessary.

INFORMACION TURISTICA

○ ESCASAS FACILIDADES
● FACILIDADES

	ARQUITECTURA COLONIAL	LUGAR HISTORICO	SITIO ARQUEOLOGICO	BALNEARIO TERMAL	BALNEARIO	ARTESANIAS	CAZA	PESCA	DEPORTES ACUATICOS	HOSPEDAJE	AUXILIO TURISTICO	AEROPUERTO INTERNACIONAL	AEROPUERTO NACIONAL	AEROPUERTO LOCAL	FERROCARRIL	OFICINA DE TURISMO	RESTAURANT
GUELATAO		●															
HUAJUAPAN DE LEON	●	●	●							○	●		●				●
JUCHITAN						●											
MIAHUATLAN						●	○										
MITLA			●								●			○			
MONTE ALBAN			●								●						
OAXACA	●	●	●		○	●				●	●		●		●	●	●
PINOTEPA NACIONAL	●				○	●	○				○		●				○
PUERTO ANGEL									●				●				
PUERTO ESCONDIDO									●								
SALINA CRUZ									●		●				●		●
TELIXTLAHUACA											●						
TEHUANTEPEC		○	●		●						●						●
TLAXIACO	●																
TUXTEPEC																○	
ZAACHILA			●														

TABLA DE DISTANCIAS

Los Números que aparecen arriba son distancias en Kilómetros, los que aparecen abajo son Millas

Ejemplo: entre la Ciudad de México, D. F. y Salina Cruz, Oax. hay una distancia de 775 kms., 481 millas

	HUAJUAPAN DE LEON	OAXACA	PINOTEPA NACIONAL	PUERTO ANGEL	PUERTO ESCONDIDO	SALINA CRUZ	TAPANATEPEC	TEHUANTEPEC	TUXTEPEC
ACAPULCO, GRO.	598 / 372	666 / 414	258 / 160	916 / 569	402 / 250	934 / 560	1047 / 650	916 / 569	877 / 545
CAMPECHE, CAMP.	1109 / 689	1146 / 712	1554 / 966	1396 / 867	1410 / 876	912 / 567	943 / 586	894 / 556	964 / 599
CHETUMAL, Q. ROO	1233 / 766	1272 / 790	jO / 1044	1522 / 946	1536 / 955	1038 / 645	1069 / 664	1020 / 634	1090 / 677
COATZACOALCOS, VER.	493 / 306	535 / 332	943 / 586	785 / 488	799 / 497	303 / 188	330 / 205	285 / 177	348 / 216
CUERNAVACA, MOR.	262 / 163	455 / 283	602 / 374	705 / 438	746 / 463	723 / 449	836 / 569	705 / 438	679 / 422
MERIDA, YUC.	1301 / 808	1338 / 831	1746 / 1085	1588 / 987	1602 / 996	1104 / 686	1135 / 705	1086 / 675	1156 / 718
MEXICO, D. F.	314 / 195	507 / 315	654 / 406	757 / 470	771 / 479	775 / 481	888 / 552	757 / 470	731 / 454
PUEBLA, PUE.	216 / 134	409 / 254	556 / 346	659 / 410	472 / 294	677 / 421	790 / 491	659 / 409	320 / 199
PTO. JUAREZ, Q. ROO	1623 / 1009	1660 / 1032	2068 / 1285	1910 / 1187	1924 / 1196	1426 / 886	1457 / 905	1408 / 875	1478 / 919
QUERETARO, QRO.	525 / 326	718 / 446	865 / 538	968 / 602	982 / .611	888 / 552	1001 / 622	968 / .602	942 / 585
TAPACHULA, CHIS.	868 / 539	675 / 419	1083 / 673	925 / 575	939 / 583	443 / 275	294 / 183	425 / 264	899 / 559
TUXTLA GTZ., CHIS.	735 / 457	542 / 337	950 / 590	792 / 492	806 / 501	308 / 191	159 / 99	290 / 180	766 / 476
VERACRUZ, VER.	337 / 209	530 / 329	677 / 421	780 / 485	794 / 493	798 / 496	911 / .780	780 / 485	201 / 125
VILLAHERMOSA, TAB	895 / 556	702 / 436	1110 / 690	952 / 592	966 / 601	475 / 295	506 / 314	457 / 284	517 / 321

1. Suppose you are interested in the following activities. According to the chart, which are easily available in Oaxaca?

    a. using a spa

    b. touring historic and archeological sites

    c. going fishing

    d. buying crafts

2. Puerto Angel is near Oaxaca. What activity not available in Oaxaca itself would a side trip to Puerto Angel provide? _____

3. How far is Oaxaca from Mexico City? _____

Once you arrive in Oaxaca, you decide to stay at the Hotel Plaza on the corner of **Las Casas** and **Miguel Cabrera**. The desk clerk at the hotel provides you with a tourist map of downtown Oaxaca. This map advertises a local craft store and it shows both the streets of Oaxaca as well as a list of tourist attractions. It is typical of the sort of town maps visitors receive all over Mexico. Your skimming skills are extremely valuable for reading maps, since only some information on the map will be of interest to you.

First scan to orient yourself and to see how information is presented. Once you have scanned the map, you can locate necessary information by skimming. Finally, examine the map closely for specific details such as addresses or route plans. (HINT: As is the case in many Mexican towns, Oaxaca's street system is centered on the **zócalo** or public square. Oaxaca's square is known as the **Plaza de la Constituciòn**. A street north of the square may have a different name after it passes the square going south.) Scan the Oaxaca map before going on.

4. Now you are ready to plan a day of sightseeing. You decide to see these places of interest on your first day:

    a. the town square

    b. the cathedral

    c. the former convent of Santa Catalina

    d. the Rufino Tamayo Museum of Precolombian Art

    e. the Regional Museum of Oaxaca (located in the old convent of Santo Domingo)

Also during the day, you plan to mail a few postcards (at **Correos**, the post office) and pick up some information at the National Tourist Office. Locate all these points of interest on the map and mark the best route to them, starting and ending at your hotel.

5. While you are at the Regional Museum, you realize that you are near the crafts store and decide to visit it. The name of the store is **ARIPO** and it is located at **García Vigil, 809**. Add **ARIPO** to your route.

Since it is now about 1:15—nearly lunchtime in Oaxaca—you decide to have lunch and look more closely at the flyer that details the merchandise you will find in **ARIPO**. You are particularly interested in buying some baskets, a toy for your younger sister, and some earrings for your mother. Over lunch, you read the flyer carefully, checking *no more than five words* in your dictionary; choose them carefully. (Remember your reading purpose! While you are interested in learning about all the craft items available at **ARIPO**, you are especially interested in locating particular ones.) After you have read the flyer, go on to the questions.

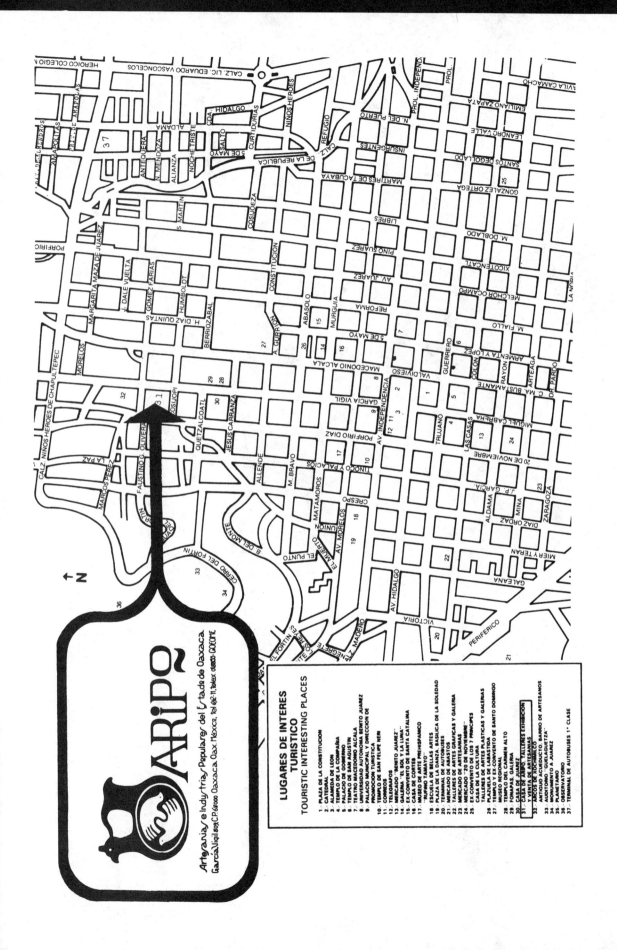

**LUGARES DE INTERES
TURISTICO**

TOURISTIC INTERESTING PLACES

1.- PLAZA DE LA CONSTITUCION
2.- CATEDRAL
3.- ALAMEDA DE LEON
4.- TEMPLO DE LA COMPAÑIA
5.- PALACIO DE GOBIERNO
6.- TEMPLO DE SAN AGUSTIN
7.- TEATRO MACEDONIO ALCALA
8.- UNIVERSIDAD AUTONOMA BENITO JUAREZ
9.- PALACIO MUNICIPAL Y DIRECCION DE
      PROMOCION TURISTICA
10.- TEMPLO DE SAN FELIPE NERI
11.- CORREOS
12.- TELEGRAFOS
13.- MERCADO "BENITO JUAREZ"
14.- GALERIA "EL SOL Y LA LUNA"
15.- EX-CONVENTO DE SANTA CATALINA
16.- CASA DE CORTES
17.- MUSEO DE ARTE PREHISPANICO
       "RUFINO TAMAYO"
18.- ESCUELA DE BELLAS ARTES
19.- PLAZA DE LA DANZA, BASILICA DE LA SOLEDAD
20.- TERMINAL DE AUTOBUSES
21.- MERCADO DE ABASTOS
22.- TALLERES DE ARTES GRAFICAS Y GALERIA
23.- MERCADO DE ARTESANIAS
24.- MERCADO "20 DE NOVIEMBRE"
25.- EX-CONVENTO DE LOS 7 PRINCIPES
       CASA DE LA CULTURA
26.- GALERIAS DE ARTES PLASTICAS Y GALERIAS
27.- PLAZUELA DE LABASTIDA
28.- TEMPLO Y EX-CONVENTO DE SANTO DOMINGO
29.- TEMPLO DEL CARMEN ALTO
30.- CONADAS, GALERIA
31.- CASA DE ARIPO, TALLERES EXHIBICION
       Y VENTA DE ARTESANIAS
32.- ARCOS DE XOCHIMILCO
33.- ANTIGUO ACUEDUCTO, BARRIO DE ARTESANOS
       "GUILLAQUETA"
34.- MONUMENTO A JUAREZ
35.- PLANETARIO
36.- OBSERVATORIO
37.- TERMINAL DE AUTOBUSES 1ª CLASE

ARIPO

Artesanias e Industrias Populares del Estado de Oaxaca.
García Vigil 809 C.P. 68000 Oaxaca, Oax. México, Tel 62-11, telex 018825-GOGOME

EN ARIPO USTED PODRA ENCONTRAR

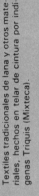

Barro negro, vistosa cerámica de fino acabado. Diseños tradicionales y modernos hecha en el poblado de San Bartolo Coyotepec.

Textiles tradicionales de lana y otros materiales, hechos en telar de cintura por indígenas Triquis (Mixteca).

Molinillos, cucharas y otros artículos de cocina torneados y tallados en madera.

Ropa típica, vestidos, huipiles, camisas y otras prendas tradicionales y modernas, con vistosos bordados.

Máscaras de diversos materiales, decorativas y ceremoniales.

Tenates de palma, tejidos por manos indígenas de la Mixteca con bonitos diseños de grecas y otros.

Canastos con tapa y pizcadores hechos con fuerte carrizo del Valle de Oaxaca.

Cuchillería fina con hoja grabada a mano.

Artículos de piel y gamuza, chamarras, sacos, portafolios, carpetas para escritorio, bolsas, monederos hechos en el valle de Oaxaca.

Juguetería de diversos materiales, trabajada artísticamente en distintos lugares del estado.

Hoja de lata, espejos, candeleros y figuras decorativas hechas por artesanos de la Ciudad de Oaxaca.

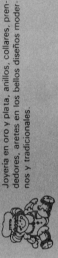

Joyería en oro y plata, anillos, collares, prendedores, aretes en los bellos diseños modernos y tradicionales.

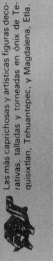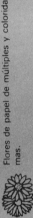

Las más caprichosas y artísticas figuras decorativas, talladas y torneadas en ónix de Tequisixtlan, Tehuantepec, y Magdalena, Etla.

Flores de papel de múltiples y coloridas formas.

Así como una gran selección de artesanías y sobre todo… ¡Buenos Amigos!

Abierto de Lunes a Sábado de 9:00 a 13:00 y de 16:00 a 19:30 Hrs.
Domingos de 9:00 a 13:00 Hrs.

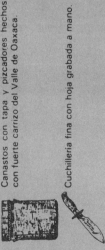

ARIPO

Artesanías e Industrias Populares del Estado de Oaxaca
García Vigil 809, C.P. 68000 Oaxaca, Oax. México.
Tel. 6 12 11, Telex 068805-GOGOME.

6. ARIPO is an acronym. What phrase does it stand for?

_____

7. At what time will **ARIPO** open again after lunch? _____

8. Match the following products with the material they are made of.

_____	flores coloridas	a.	madera
_____	artículos de cocina	b.	palma
_____	aretes	c.	diversos materials
_____	máscaras	d.	oro y plata
_____	tenates	e.	papel

9. You are familiar with the word **piel** from an earlier unit, but the meaning it had in the Camay ad is inappropriate in this context. Guess a more appropriate meaning. _____

10. Match the following products with the place they are made.

_____	candeleros	a.	Valle de Oaxaca
_____	figuras de ónix	b.	San Bartolo Coyctepec
_____	textiles	c.	Tehuantepec
_____	cerámica	d.	La Mixteca
_____	canastos	e.	ciudad de Oaxaca

11. Which craft item in the list below does _not_ incorporate both traditional and modern designs?

a. jewelry   c. onyx figures

b. clay pots   d. dresses and shirts

12. Since you are interested in buying toys, use the drawings to help you guess which descriptive statement pertains to crafts of that kind. In most bilingual dictionaries, the word **juguetería** is not included. Check yours and if the word is not there, find three related words which can help confirm the probable meaning of **juguetería**.

UNIT

5
Focusing on Work and the Economy

The Reading Strategy

Decoding: Reading for main ideas and details

At this stage in your practice, you cannot expect to understand every word in every reading passage you encounter. As you have seen, however, you can still read with considerable comprehension. For many reading purposes, you need only be concerned with the main idea of a passage, and you only have to understand those words that help you grasp the main idea.

All the materials in this unit are related to the general theme of work and the economy. In the beginning of the unit you will still be reading materials with many format cues, but later you will apply the *Reading Strategy* to short prose passages.

One of the most important reasons for reading in any language is that it increases your vocabulary. In the early stages of learning a second language, vocabulary growth is very rapid. In this unit, you will learn how to increase your Spanish vocabulary even more by using word relationships to help you guess the meanings of new words.

We will begin reading with some material of a familiar type. Identify the type of material on pages 90 and 91 as quickly as you can.

This photograph shows a labor protest in Cuzco, Peru. How many of the banners can you read?

Exercise A.

Use cognates and format cues to help you answer these preliminary questions.

1. In what country do you think this material was first published? What information provides the clue for this answer?

   _____

   _____

2. To which of the following categories do the jobs in these ***Ofertas de Empleo*** belong?

   a. skilled manual labor   d. medical professionals

   b. domestic help   e. unskilled manual labor

   c. office/industrial professionals

   What part of each ad gives you the information necessary to answer this question? _____

3. The following information is found in all the ads. Arrange the topics in the order in which they appear in most of the ads.

   _____ a. address for mailing application materials

   _____ b. title of position being advertised

   _____ c. benefits offered

   _____ d. requirements of the position

   _____ e. information about the business advertising the position

4. List no more than six words that are new to you but which, on the basis of what you know about the *Reading Strategy*, seem to be especially important for reading this material. You will have an opportunity to check your words in Exercise B.

   _____   _____

   _____   _____

   _____   _____

These want ads advertise employment opportunities in Spain for people with various kinds of office or industrial skills. Certain words are repeated and form a "core" vocabulary for material of this type. Look at the ads again, and notice the repeated words.

A number of words appear in large or boldface type in many of the ads, suggesting that they could be the most useful in understanding the reading passage. Some of these key words are listed below. Those identified by an * are words whose meanings most beginning readers can guess, although their meanings in this context are not necessarily the same as the first meaning that comes to mind. How many of them are on your own list in Exercise A?

ofrece *	requiere *	empresa	dirección *
jefe	secretaria *	delegado	precisa

Exercise B.

Return to the passage and find the words listed at the bottom of page 92. Then answer the following questions.

1. THINK about the contexts in which these words appear. Why are these particular words most important?

2. Use the dictionary techniques you learned in earlier units to choose a meaning that is appropriate for the context in which each of the listed words occurs.

　a. ofrece　_____

　b. requiere　_____

　c. empresa　_____

　d. dirección　_____

　e. jefe　_____

　f. secretaria　_____

　g. delegado　_____

　h. precisa　_____

3. Now compare this list with your list from Exercise A. If there are any other words from your original list that you need to look up, use good dictionary techniques to choose appropriate translation equivalents for them.

At this point you have probably looked closely only at those portions of the want ads that appear in large or dark type, helping you understand the overall content of the passage. Now you are ready to look more closely at the material. At this stage, an important *Reading Strategy* technique is to THINK of questions that you expect the material you read to answer. Then, as you look over the material more carefully, you can answer your own set of "prereading" questions.

Let's see how this process works for the material we have here. Once you identified this passage as a group of want ads, you immediately formed certain expectations based on your previous experience with such ads. You probably expected each ad to say something about the job available, about the necessary qualifications, and about the application process. The questions you answered in Exercise A are the type of questions you could make up yourself, on the basis of no more information than the fact that this reading passage is composed of job ads.

Scanning the ads probably confirmed your expectations. Then you went on to the next stage, using known words and words whose meanings you could guess together with cognate cues to look for the overall organization of material. You continued scanning to gather additional information about the topic and the general content of the reading passage. You identified important words on the basis of their frequency and highlighting, and you looked up those that seemed most likely to be helpful in interpreting the passage. You paid attention to context and thought carefully about the connections among the parts of the passage.

Now you are ready to examine the passage for details. Naturally, your reading purpose is still important. If you were simply looking at a Spanish newspaper for reading practice, you might not have much reason to select one ad over another. If, on the other hand, you were actually looking for a particular sort of job, you would probably *skim* the ads looking for information that would alert you to a possible one.

Let's assume that you are looking for a job. Here are your credentials: you have five years of experience as a sales representative for a major corporation; you are 28 years old and a long-time resident of Madrid; you love to drive; you speak and write English fluently; you are looking for a job with responsibility and opportunities for advancement. Identify the four ads for which you have the general qualifications. (Be sure to use the available format cues to help you interpret the material.)

These are the four ads you should have selected: Bédaux; TEST; Dinkal, S.A.; and the ad for a photographic supplies importing company. If you selected other ads, reexamine them to see why they may not be appropriate choices.

Now read each of the four ads listed above very closely, paying special attention to the details concerning the job. Look up anything you feel is absolutely essential for understanding the proper level of detail. Then complete Exercise C.

Exercise C.

1. Match each company with the appropriate position.

    _____ Sales agent   a. Bédaux

    _____ Sales representative   b. TEST

    _____ Exhibition representative   c. Dinkal, S.A.

    _____ Store clerk   d. Photographic supplies
                                               importer

2. Which position requires knowledge of English?   _____

3. Which position is specifically looking for women?   _____

4. Which position requires you to own a car?   _____

5. Which position requires specific sales experience in the field of construc-

    tion? _____

6. Now add these facts to your résumé: you are male; your sales experience was with an office machine company. Which two of the four ads describe jobs for which you are not qualified?

    _____

At this stage, most of the important material in these ads should be clear to you. Some, however, may still be unclear. This uncertainty is a normal part of the reading process, even when reading one's native language. THINK about the last time you read a difficult and detailed passage about an unfamiliar subject. The material may have included unfamiliar words or concepts that were not completely clear. How did you react?

Good readers try not to panic when they encounter a passage they do not immediately understand! They keep on reading, trying to find connections within the material, expanding the context, and staying alert to familiar material rather than emphasizing the unfamiliar. You can use these techniques in reading Spanish too.

If an entire passage is thoroughly incomprehensible even with the *Reading Strategy* techniques you have practiced up to now, it may simply be beyond your skills at this stage. If that is the case, turn to something less complex. Remember, the more familiar format cues a passage has, the easier it should be for you to read. In materials with fewer format cues, your background knowledge about the topic is important in determining your ability to comprehend what you read.

From now on, you should get in the habit of *prereading*: using *Reading Strategy* techniques to orient yourself to a passage and prepare a set of mental questions that you expect the passage to answer. Now, when you come to each new reading passage, you will be reminded to apply these techniques, but we will now begin to concentrate on *Reading Strategy* techniques appropriate for close reading, the actual *decoding* of the meaning of a passage.

Decoding is the part of the reading process during which the reader reaches a deeper and more detailed understanding of the reading passage. Most beginning readers in a foreign language want to begin decoding as soon as they see a reading passage. However, as we have seen, the prereading process, which we perform automatically and rapidly in our own language, is an essential first step for reading a foreign language.

At the decoding stage, the reader begins to pay attention to the "small print" in materials with many format cues. In prose materials, certain patterns of organization usually allow the reader to predict where important information is located. In the *Reading Strategy*, those patterns of organization serve the same purpose as format cues.

Up to now, you have been learning to let your eyes skip around a reading passage, allowing your attention to be drawn to material that seemed familiar or important. This ability to see a reading passage as a whole is very valuable, especially in the early reading stage. However, for decoding, your eyes must work in a different way. Now your attention must be drawn to smaller units. The primary context unit when decoding short passages is the sentence; in longer passages, it is the paragraph.

When decoding sentences in Spanish, it is very important to be able to locate the main verb and identify its associated subject. Since Spanish sentences can be quite long, there are usually several verbs, some of which are subordinate to others. Many subordinate clauses in Spanish are introduced by **que** *(that)*. For now, the first important *Reading Strategy* decoding technique is to learn to use whole sentences as context units.

Now you will work with three related pieces of reading material—ads from popular magazines. Apply all the prereading techniques learned so far to the three ads, looking for the features they have in common. (Remember—these materials are included in a unit whose theme is work!)

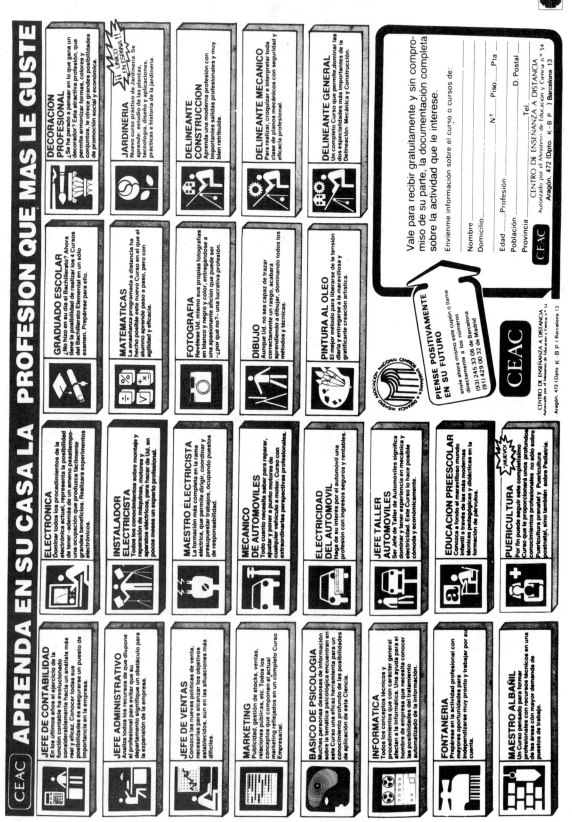

You should be able to answer the questions in Exercise D easily after pre-reading the three ads.

Exercise D.

1. What is the type of product is being advertised in each of these ads?

   _____

2. What method can the reader use to get more information about the product? That is, what is included in each ad for use by the interested reader?

   _____

3. What specific kinds of illustrations are included in each ad?

   _____

The questions in Exercise E require you to skim for details about the correspondence courses advertised.

Exercise E.

1. In the CEAC ad, which courses deal with automobiles?

   _____

2. Which CEAC course is the only one of its kind in Spain?

   _____

3. Which two CEAC courses involve work with young children?

   _____

   _____

4. Besides sending in the coupon, you can also communicate with CEAC by telephone. What is the number to call if you live in Barcelona?

   _____

5. What does the acronym CEAC stand for?

   _____

6. Which National Schools course listed on the coupon is not listed in the first part of the ad? _____

7. According to the National Schools ad, what can a student expect to gain with a job in one of the fields illustrated?

   _____

8. In what country can you take a correspondence course to become a detective? _____

9. In what year was the detective school founded? _____

10. True of False? You must pay to get additional information about being a detective? _____

11. What information requested on both the CEAC and National Schools coupons is not required by the detective school?

    _____

12. Which course offerings available at National Schools are also offered by CEAC? _____

   _____

Before considering these ads in more detail, you should note that they contain many verbs in the imperative (command) form. In general, you can recognize formal commands in Spanish from the fact that they have the "opposite" theme vowel in their endings: **-ar** verbs have **e** in their endings and **-er** and **-ir** verbs have **a**. Your instructor or your textbook can give you more information about commands, but remember, you do not have to be able to *produce* direct commands in order to *read* them!

Now let's consider the CEAC ad on page 96 in more detail and try decoding some of the course descriptions. Since these descriptions are very short—some consist of only one sentence or even a part of a sentence—each one can be treated as a context unit. Begin with the ad for the course in basic psychology. Even though the descriptive sentence is long, there is only one conjugated verb form. Read the sentence carefully, trying to understand the main verb and the most important nouns.

The important nouns in a sentence are usually the ones that are not introduced by a preposition and that are closely associated with the main verb. In this sentence, the first noun **(personas)** is the subject of the main verb **(encuentran)**. The verb refers to an action (finding something), which the subject (people) can do. The verb is one that usually takes an object, so we can expect to find a second important noun in the sentence. This noun should refer to the thing which is found. **Herramienta** is the only other noun in the sentence not introduced by a preposition. Therefore, we can assume that **herramienta** refers to the object and is an key word. If **herramienta** is new to you, look it up.

Each of these course descriptions can only include a little bit of information about the course, but the information could be of several different kinds. For example, a description might mention the economic advantages of the profession, or it might give some details about the actual content of the course. The description might refer to the personal benefits to be gained by knowing about the course's subject. The sentence in the psychology course ad is a long and complex one, but it is fairly easy to understand that what this course offers is primarily information and not job training.

Read the ad for the course titled **Electricidad de Automóvil**. Its description begins with a command verb: **haga**. There is only one noun that can be its object: **profesión**. THINK about the relationship between that verb and that object.

On the basis of what you know so far about this descriptive sentence, which of the following categories do you THINK the **Electricidad de Automóvil** course description is most likely to fall into?

Economic advantages of knowing the course content

Topics covered in the course

Personal benefits of knowing the course content

Your choice is actually a prediction, a hypothesis about the meaning.

Decoding is a process of making, checking, confirming, and revising your hypotheses about meaning. As you practice decoding, you will become more proficient at it.

Read the course description again, very carefully. Try to understand the overall content of the sentence. Do not try to create an English translation for it, but do THINK about the sentence as a complete idea. Is your prediction confirmed by the entire context? If you did not select the best topic—the third—reexamine the context.

 Exercise F.

Here is a list of some other course descriptions. For each one, use the main verb and/or the important nouns to help you match each description with the category that best describes the type of information it contains.

_____ 1. **Pintura al óleo**   a. economic benefits

_____ 2. **Jardinería**   b. course content

_____ 3. **Delineante construcción** c. personal benefits

_____ 4. **Maestro albañil**

_____ 5. **Educación preescolar**

Some course descriptions refer to both professional and personal advantages. The course descriptions for **Electrónica, Decoración Profesional,** and **Fotografía** are of this type. Read these descriptions carefully, looking for the information included in each one. Remember to use your dictionary sparingly. After looking up a word, look again at the context to see whether knowing the new word helps you decode additional meaning. Work on the sentences in these descriptions only until you are able to confirm that they refer to both professional and personal goals.

If any other course descriptions look interesting to you, decode them before you go on.

The ad for the **Primera Escuela Argentina de Detectives** on page 98 provides a great deal of information about its program. Look carefully at the section of the ad that outlines the major advantages of the school. It is introduced by a boldface section that includes the word **ventajas** *(advantages)*.

Format cues (the dark dots) suggest that five advantages are listed. Consider each advantage as a context unit. Read each sentence carefully, paying special attention to the main verbs and nouns. It will help if you circle the main verb in each sentence. (Do not be misled by the peculiar use of capital letters. Ads, in many languages, often break punctuation and spelling rules!)

Exercise G.

From this list, select the five advantages mentioned in the ad.

1. The textbook is simple.
2. No experience is required.
3. The program is inexpensive.
4. The program operates all year.
5. Even if you move, you can keep studying in the program.
6. The professors are pleasant and friendly.
7. The lessons are clear and direct.
8. The program guarantees a good job.

Check your selections in the Answer Key. If you did not make the correct choices, review the passage before going on.

Now let's turn to the National Schools ad on page 97. Much of the vocabulary here should be familiar to you by now. The paragraphs associated with each course title are longer than ones in the CEAC ad and can therefore include more information. Note that the first description is actually for two separate sets of courses, indicated by the function word **o** *(or)*.

Read each description carefully. As you read, pay attention to the type of claims made for each course. Do not stop at the first word you do not recognize—keep reading until you come to the end of the sentence. Remember, *the minimal context unit for decoding is the sentence.* You need to look at an entire sentence before you will know which words in it are the most important ones and in which order to look up any that you absolutely need to know.

Now complete Exercise H, based on your reading.

Exercise H.

1. Which course descriptions mention better pay?

2. According to the descriptions, why are **Refrigeración y Acondicionamiento** promising fields?

3. What kinds of jobs are available to those who speak English?

4. If you want to sell and service sound equipment, which course should you take: **Radio/Televisión** or **Audio Electronica y Communicaciones**?

Dictionary Interlude

Using derivation and word families

As you have just seen, decoding expands many of the reading techniques you have been practicing all along. When decoding, however, you must also focus greater attention on vocabulary since, in decoding, you want to understand as many of the words in a passage as possible. Fortunately, vocabulary building in Spanish is made easier through an understanding of the patterns of roots and affixes. In this *Dictionary Interlude*, you will learn some of these patterns.

Consider the following set of Spanish words.

niño	boy	**niñito**	little boy
niña	girl	**niñita**	little girl
perro	dog	**perrito**	puppy
casa	house	**casita**	cottage
libro	book	**librito**	booklet
copa	goblet	**copita**	a quick drink

The suffix **-ito/-ita** is called a diminutive, and Spanish is rich in words with diminutive endings. Sometimes the noun that results from the addition of a diminutive suffix merely refers to a smaller version of the original noun (as with **perrito**), but sometimes the new meaning implies affection (as with **niñito**) or is even metaphorical (**copita**).

BANOBRAS, like many trade names is a made-up word. It is a compound of two Spanish nouns. Can you figure out what they are?

In English, we often use completely different roots to convey these changes of meaning, as you can see in most of the examples above. In Spanish, though, diminutives and similar suffixes allow us to build many new words from a single root. If we recognize the root, we can often make a guess about the meaning of the derived form. Because the meanings of derived words are often predictable, the derived forms themselves are generally not included in bilingual dictionaries. In most cases, only root words are listed. In many bilingual dictionaries, you can locate the derived Spanish forms only as translation equivalents for English entries. For this reason, it is helpful to know the most common Spanish word-building suffixes and patterns.

Many common Spanish suffixes add information about size, as in the case of the diminutive **-ito/-ita**. A similar suffix is **-illo/-illa**, as in **zapatilla** *(slipper)* from **zapato** *(shoe)* or **casilla** *(post office box)* from **casa** *(house)*. Like **-ito/-ita**, **-illo** adds the notion of smallness to the original noun, but sometimes it also has a slightly negative connotation as well, as in **chiquillo** *(kid; brat)* from **chico** *(boy)*. Other suffixes, such as **-ón/-ona**, add the meaning of "large": **casona** *(mansion)*. There are even suffixes that suggest both large size and a negative attitude by the speaker, such as **-ote/-ota** which changes **libro** *(book)* to **librote** *(a big, old tome)*.

When you are reading, the root of a word is generally the most important part, but the more you pay attention to the uses of derivational suffixes, the more meaning you can get from each word and the larger your vocabulary will be. Sometimes roots undergo a few minor spelling changes when word-building suffixes are added (as in **chiquillo** above), but enough of the root is retained to make it easy to see that the two words are related. Here are some exercises to help you recognize some common Spanish word-building suffixes.

Exercise I.

Use your dictionary as necessary to answer the questions.

1. Here is a group of nouns with a suffix in common. Identify the root of each of these words and write it in the space. (Some of the roots have changed spelling with the addition of the suffix, so check if you are not certain.)

    a. **cartera**   portfolio   _____

    b. **ensaladera**   salad dish   _____

    c. **lechera**   milk pitcher   _____

    d. **papelera**   letter pad, note pad   _____

    e. **ponchera**   punch bowl   _____

    f. **tabaquera**   tobacco pouch   _____

2. What meaning does the suffix **-era** have? _____

3. What part of speech are the roots to which it is added? _____

4. What part of speech are the resulting words? _____

5. What is the gender of a word ending in **-era**? _____

Exercise J.

Look at these pairs of words. Use your dictionary as necessary to answer the questions.

alto/alteza	limpio/limpieza
cierto/certeza	puro/pureza
grande/grandeza	triste/tristeza

1. The first word in each pair above is an adjective. What part of speech is

   the word ending in **-eza?** _____

2. What is the general meaning of the **-eza**? _____

3. Here is another set of adjectives to which **-eza** can be added. Predict the form of the new word that would be created and its meaning.

   a. bello   _____   _____

   b. simple   _____   _____

   c. duro   _____   _____

   Check your answers in your dictionary.

Several Spanish suffixes have the same general meaning and function as **-eza**; these suffixes include **-dad** and **-ura**. Consider these examples: **sucio** *(dirty)* and **suciedad** *(filth)*; **hermoso** *(beautiful)* and **hermosura** *(beauty)*. Remember that, unlike the suffixes that form verbs, word-building suffixes cannot always be added to every possible root. For example, **sucio** cannot take **-eza** or **-ura**; this particular root only takes **-dad**. Some derived words may not be included in your dictionary, and it should not surprise you to find that others simply do not occur at all.

Exercise K presents two more common Spanish word-building suffixes.

 Exercise K.

Listed below are some nouns for articles of commerce. These nouns serve as roots for two kinds of related words: the dealers associated with the articles and the place of business involved. Identify the two suffixes involved in creating these new words by applying these dictionary techniques.

   a. Look at related words that appear near the main root in the Spanish dictionary listing.

   b. Use the English section of your dictionary to locate regular formations not included in the Spanish section. (For instance, look up the translation of *brewery* in order to find an example of the Spanish business suffix.)

   c. Once you have formed a hypothesis about the suffix involved, look up enough additional examples to confirm it. (By the way, the **-eza** on **cerveza** is *not* the word-building suffix.)

cerveza	beer
joya	jewelry
libro	book

pastel	pie, pastry, dessert
reloj	watch, clock
zapato	shoe

1. What is the suffix for dealers? _____

2. What is the suffix for the place of business? _____

Bolsa has several meanings in Spanish, one of them is technical term in economic circles. Can you guess its meaning from information contained in this photograph? Check your dictionary to be sure.

BOLSA DE MADRID

VALORES	ANTERIOR	ACTUAL
B. CENTRAL	323	318.
B. ESPAÑOL DE CREDITO	337	330
B. HISPANO AMERICANO	212	207
B. DE FOMENTO	187	184
FECSA DE 1000	69.12	68.5
HIDRO ESPAÑOLA	75.7	74.2
IBERDUERO	82.2	81.62
SEVILLANA	68.87	68.2
EBRO	550	565
DRAGADOS Y CONST.	158	157.
ESPAÑOLA INVERSIONES	121.	121
GRAL. DE INVERSIONES	122	117
PONFERRADA	34.5	35.
ESPAÑOLA DE PETROLEOS	153.7	157
EXPLOSIVOS RIO TINTO	37.2	37.7
S.E.A.T.		
ESPAÑOLA DEL ZINC	220	220.
MATERIAL Y CONST.	79.5	76.5
C.A.M.P.S.A.	250	257.
TELEFONICA	92.7	92.

Not all word-building processes in Spanish use suffixes. Some new words are formed by adding a prefix to the root. Many new verb roots are formed in this way. **Tener** *(to have)*, for example, is the root for these verbs, all formed with prefixes that have cognates in English: **detener** *(to detain)*; **contener** *(to contain)*; **retener** *(to retain)*; **sostener** *(to sustain)*; **obtener** *(to obtain)*. Once you know a root and can recognize various common prefixes, you can successfully guess the meanings of many new words. Exercise L helps you practice another common prefix.

Exercise L.

1. What is the new meaning of the following verbs when the prefix **des** is added?

   a. **ayunar**   to stop eating, to fast   _____

   b. **cansar**   to tire   _____

   c. **esperar**   to hope   _____

   d. **hacer**   to make   _____

   e. **pegar**   to glue, to stick on   _____

   f. **prender**   to fasten, to grab   _____

2. What is the general meaning of **des-**?   _____

3. Find at least three more examples of words with the prefix **des-**.

   _____

   _____

   _____

4. Identify the verb root for each of the examples you chose and predict its meaning. Then check your answers by looking up the roots.

In addition to adding suffixes and prefixes, Spanish also creates new words by combining two words into a compound word. Compounds are very common in English (e.g. *blackbird*, *rowboat*, or *putdown*.) They are less common in Spanish, but they still occur. The most common Spanish compounds are formed with a third-person verb form and a plural noun, as when **guardar** *(to guard)* combines with **espaldas** *(shoulders; back)* to form **guardaespaldas** *(bodyguard)*. Use your dictionary as necessary to answer the questions about compounds in Exercise M.

Exercise M.

1. Draw a line between the two parts of each of these compounds. Write the English equivalent for each part in the spaces marked a. and b.

el guardafangos   a. _____   b. _____

el salvavidas   a. _____   b. _____

el abrelatas   a. _____   b. _____

el paracaídas   a. _____   b. _____

el tocadiscos   a. _____   b. _____

el lavaplatos   a. _____   b. _____

el parabrisas   a. _____   b. _____

el paraguas   a. _____   b. _____

2. What is the gender of these compounds? _____

3. True or False? These compounds are plural.

The more you read, the more patterns of word building you will be able to recognize and use when making hypotheses about meaning. Whenever you see a word with a familiar affix, THINK about its likely meaning based on other uses you have seen. By using your knowledge of roots and endings, you may be able to guess the meanings of words that are not even in your dictionary.

Applying the Reading Strategy

In this section you will be reading prose material with few format cues. The *Reading Strategy* to be practiced is identifying the main idea of a passage. You are not expected to understand every word in the passages, but you should try to understand the important information. Use your dictionary as necessary, paying special attention to new words based on roots you already know.

These reading passages come from a series of brief reports on economic issues from a national newspaper published in Spain. Each day's report includes an opening sentence in bold type. Each opening sentence provides a very important clue to the main idea contained in the passages. Before you look at the passages, complete Exercise N.

Exercise N.

Read the following list of the opening sentences you will see in the passage; then answer the questions that follow.

La CEPAL analizará la situación del comercio mundial.

La tasa de inflación en la CEE fue en noviembre la más baja de los últimos 12 años.

El INI anuncia el despido de 2.000 trabajadores de los astilleros.

Las reformas económicas húngaras escandalizan a los socialistas ortodoxos.

Acuerdo entre la CEE y EE UU para autolimitar sus exportaciones de acero.

Andorra quiere negociar su futuro directamente con la CEE.

Trabajadores de Astano afirman que tendrán que echarles a tiros del astillero.

El fiscal alemán recomienda la extradición de Ruiz-Mateos.

1. Underline the portion of each opening sentence that identifies the probable topic of the passage.

2. THINK about the topic and about the vocabulary most likely to be associated with it. Make sure you understand the important vocabulary contained in the opening sentence.

3. Based on the opening, make a list of several questions you expect the passages to answer.

4. Based on the opening sentences, which two reports seem to be most closely related? _____

5. Which acronym is likely to be the most useful one to know?

_____

6. Which of the following countries is *least* likely to be mentioned in these particular reports?

    a. the United States   d. Canada

    b. Andorra   e. Spain

    c. Germany   f. Hungry

Review these general decoding guidelines before going on to the passages themselves. Treat each report as a single context unit. All of them are organized in the same way: each one consists of a single paragraph; each contains only a few sentences; the opening sentences are a kind of headline or summary of the entire report. The first sentence in regular type is the real introduction to the report and is likely to contain the most important information. In most paragraphs, the last sentence is the next most useful one. You should begin the decoding process by concentrating on those two sentences.

Decode by locating the main verb and nouns of the first and last sentences. THINK about the probable topic and predict as much of the meaning as you can. Then read the entire paragraph through, sentence by sentence. *Do not attempt to translate the reports.* Read only until you are confident that you know the main information contained in each piece.

Now proceed to the reports using Exercise O to help you as you decode.

Exercise O.

These questions follow the order of the news items. Note that they are like the questions that good readers create for themselves as aids to reading.

1. What does CEE stand for? What is its English equivalent?

2. Is Andorra already a member of the CEE?

3. What was the inflation rate for the CEE? What factors might be influencing it?

4. What are **astilleros?** Why are they being fired? (HINT: This is an ongoing story dealing with incorporation of workers into the national system of workman's compensation. What kind of information would you probably need in order to understand this news brief fully? Remember, part of being a good reader is being able to tell why you do not understand what you read. If it is because of vocabulary or grammar, you can get help. If it is a lack of background or information, the reading may simply be beyond your comprehension, even if you understand all the words.)

5. What limits are being put on steel exports? Why? (Remember, this is a Spanish newspaper. The exports are coming from Europe to the United States, not the other way around!)

6. Who is Ruíz-Mateos? What country wants to extradite him from Germany? Why?

7. How many of the Astano company's workers are resisting their firing?

8. What is CEPAL? How does it plan to conduct its analysis? What aspects of world trade is CEPAL most interested in?

9. What economic reforms have taken place in Hungary? Why does the reporter think they are scandalous?

Jueves 3

Andorra quiere negociar su futuro directamente con la CEE. Josep Pintat, presidente del Gobierno de Andorra, ha manifestado que la negociación directa con la Comunidad Económica Europea, tras la entrada de España, es una exigencia que "no sólo debe ser escuchada, sino admitida y puesta en aplicación". Pintat, que realizó estas afirmaciones en su discurso de año nuevo, señaló que el Principado prevé conseguir una moratoria en el estatuto actual y que se dispondrá de un período transitorio tras la adhesión de España a la CEE.

Viernes 4

Las pérdidas de Rumasa se redujeron un 40% durante 1984. El administrador general de Rumasa, Javier Ruiz Ogarrio, ha manifestado que las pérdidas operativas del grupo durante 1984 han sido reducidas en un 40% como resultado de la gestión llevada a cabo. La revista *Mercado,* en una entrevista con Ruiz Ogarrio aparecida el 28 de diciembre pasado, atribuía unas pérdidas al grupo para el conjunto de 1984, excluidas Galerías Preciados e Hispano Alemana de Construcciones, de 102.988 millones de pesetas. De esa cifra de pérdidas, alrededor de 50.000 millones de pesetas corresponden a pérdidas por ventas de empresas, al haberse adjudicado por debajo de su valor. El resto corresponden a pérdidas de gestión.

La tasa de inflación en la CEE fue en noviembre la más baja de los últimos 12 años. La tasa de inflación anual de la Comunidad Económica Europea (CEE) cayó en noviembre pasado al 6,5%, lo que supone la cifra más baja registrada desde la primera crisis del petróleo, en 1973, según cifras oficiales reveladas ayer en la capital belga. A finales de dicho mes, la tasa de inflación anual española se situaba en el 9,7%.

Sábado 5

El INI anuncia el despido de 2.000 trabajadores de los astilleros. La División Naval del Instituto Nacional de Industria (INI) remitirá, a partir del lunes 7, cartas de despido a cada uno de los más de 2.000 trabajadores excedentes del sector naval que no han querido acogerse a los Fondos de Promoción de Empleo. Aunque el plazo para decidir su integración en dichos fondos finalizó el pasado día 27 de diciembre, el INI admitió una tolerancia en la fecha que concluirá definitivamente el lunes.

Acuerdo entre la CEE y EE UU para autolimitar sus exportaciones de acero. La CEE llegó el viernes 4 a un acuerdo de principio con Washington —faltan aún algunos detalles por concretar la próxima semana— para autolimitar en 1985 y 1986 sus exportaciones de tubos de acero hacia Estados Unidos a un 7,6% del mercado estadounidense. Ésta parece ser una victoria de la Administración de Ronald Reagan, que a finales de noviembre decidió unilateralmente interrumpir las importaciones de tubos comunitarios.

Domingo 6

El fiscal alemán recomienda la extradición de Ruiz-Mateos. El fiscal del Tribunal Supremo del Estado alemán occidental de Hesse ha recomendado formalmente la extradición de José María Ruiz-Mateos, solicitada por el Gobierno español. En sus conclusiones, el fiscal alemán occidental acepta como válidos los argumentos presentados desde Madrid en cuatro de los siete presuntos delitos de los que se acusa en España al fundador de Rumasa. Concretamente estima que Ruiz-Mateos puede tener responsabilidades por delitos fiscales, impago a la Seguridad Social, falsedad de documento mercantil y estafa y falsedad de libros de contabilidad.

Trabajadores de Astano afirman que tendrán que echarles a tiros del astillero. El comité de empresa de Astano informó el sábado 5 que "unos 2.500 trabajadores del astillero ferrolano están dispuestos a resistir hasta que los echen a tiros. No tenemos miedo al despido", añadieron, "y cuando así suceda, Astano será de los trabajadores".

Según informa la agencia Efe, que cita datos de los representantes de los trabajadores, son 2.900 las personas que no han contestado a la requisitoria de la empresa que daba dos alternativas, o acogerse a los fondos de promoción de empleo o cobrar las indemnizaciones.

La CEPAL analizará la situación del comercio mundial. La Comisión Económica para América Latina (CEPAL) celebrará los próximos 28 y 30 de enero, en Río de Janeiro, una reunión de expertos en comercio mundial para estudiar la situación económica internacional y sus perspectivas. Para esta reunión han sido invitados 36 especialistas en comercio exterior procedentes de once países latinoamericanos. El seminario de la CEPAL es previo a las conferencias internacionales que se realizarán en las próximas semanas, con especial énfasis en la del Acuerdo General sobre Tarifas y Aranceles Aduaneros (GATT), con el propósito de preparar una posición común.

Las reformas económicas húngaras escandalizan a los socialistas ortodoxos. En lo que constituye una de las facetas más osadas de la intrépida reforma económica del socialismo magiar, una empresa húngara productora de medias de señora ha emitido a primeros de año acciones de unas 35.000 pesetas (10.000 florines húngaros), a un interés anual del 11% y destinadas a inversionistas particulares. Ya existe en Hungría una bolsa de valores, constituida por acciones vendidas entre empresas o, desde ahora, a particulares que nada tienen que ver con ellas. Esta medida húngara ha vuelto a escandalizar a los sectores más ortodoxos de los demás países socialistas miembros del Comecon, pero se sabe que funcionarios soviéticos, polacos y alemanes del Este se han interesado por el mecanismo de la Bolsa húngara.

Now return to the headline sentences with which you began and reread them. THINK about what you know about the content of the paragraph itself. Are you able to answer the questions you posed in Exercise N? If so, you have read enough to satisfy the reading purpose of this unit!

On the next page there is a similar series of economic news briefs from a later issue of the same newspaper. Use them to practice the *Reading Strategy*. Follow the same steps you used with the earlier news briefs. Try to reach the same level of comprehension.

Lunes 2

Una delegación del grupo Mitsui visita España. Una delegación de ocho empresas del grupo Mitsui —uno de los tres grandes grupos financieros e industriales de Japón, que controla casi 2.000 empresas— visita España con el objetivo de llegar a acuerdos de colaboración tecnológica con determinadas entidades españolas. Ésta es la primera vez que uno de los principales grupos nipones viene a España, donde mantendrá contactos y reuniones con casi una treintena de compañías españolas, con ese propósito.

Martes 3

La dirección de Almaraz reconoce que ha habido escapes en uno de los reactores. La dirección de la central núclear de Almaraz ha reconocido públicamente que el pasado día 25 de noviembre se produjo un escape de gas en uno de los reactores de la planta. Al parecer es la primera vez que los propietarios de Almaraz admiten que se ha producido un escape de gas radiactivo, aunque han restado importancia al hecho.

La Sociedad Italiana del Vidrio Española se constituyó en Valencia. La Società Italiana del Vetro (SIV) constituyó definitivamente, el lunes 2, la Sociedad Italiana del Vidrio Española, SA (SIVESA). La nueva empresa se instalará en Sagunto con un capital social de 1.000 millones de pesetas y una inversión de 5.500 millones, de los cuales 90 son aportados por la Caja de Ahorros de Valencia, 110 por la Caja de Ahorros y Socorros de Sagunto y 1.200 por la Generalitat valenciana.

Miércoles 4

La multinacional japonesa Panasonic fabricará vídeos en España. La multinacional japonesa Panasonic, marca internacional del grupo Matsushita —en Japón comercializa sus productos con la marca National—, podría decidir instalarse en España para fabricar vídeos antes de que finalice el presente mes de diciembre. Las negociaciones entre el Ministerio de Industria —ya que la operación se entroncaría en el marco del Plan Electrónico e Informático Nacional (PEIN)— y la filial española del grupo japonés, Panasonic España, culminaron de forma positiva hace ya algún tiempo y sólo se requiere el visto bueno de la casa matriz en Japón.

El Gobierno canadiense autoriza la compra de De Havilland por Boeing. El Gobierno canadiense ha dado autorización para que Boeing, el mayor fabricante mundial de aviones comerciales, adquiera la compañía De Havilland, controlada por el Estado norteamericano, por un importe de 155 millones de dólares canadienses (18.500 millones de pesetas).

Jueves 5

La renta de los agricultores registró un crecimiento del 45% en el último trienio. Carlos Romero, ministro de Agricultura, Pesca y Alimentación, muestra su satisfacción por la marcha del sector agrario desde que el PSOE está en el Gobierno. Por lo menos esa es la impresión que transmitió el martes 3 en un almuerzo con la Prensa especializada y que se celebró, una vez más, en la cafetería del propio ministerio.

Viernes 6

La Banca acuerda no asumir el recorte de pensiones del Gobierno. Los presidentes de los grandes bancos mantuvieron el jueves 5 su tradicional almuerzo mensual, en el que se habló de la postura que la patronal tiene que mantener ante la negociación colectiva del sector, que se iniciará en los primeros días de enero y cuyo problema fundamental se refiere al mantenimiento o no del complemento de pensiones que las entidades financieras cubren para mantener el ciento por ciento del salario de sus trabajadores jubilados. Los grandes bancos —y, por tanto, el conjunto del sector— mantienen una posición clara de no asumir ellos la rebaja de pensiones decidida por el Gobierno.

El Deutsche Bank compra las 59 compañías del consorcio Flick. Friedrich Karl Flick, el mayor magnate de la industria de la República Federal de Alemania (RFA), ha anunciado la venta de todo su consorcio, compuesto por 59 compañías, al Deutsche Bank. La operación, mantenida en absoluto secreto hasta estar prácticamente ultimada, ha causado gran sensación en medios económicos alemanes.

Nueve regiones españolas recibirán ayuda preferente del Fondo Social Europeo. El Consejo de Ministros de Asuntos Sociales de la CEE llegó el jueves 5 a un acuerdo para que nueve regiones españolas —Andalucía, Canarias, las dos Castillas, Extremadura, Galicia, Murcia, Ceuta y Melilla— sean consideradas como superprioritarias para acceder a las partidas especiales del Fondo Social Europeo. Los *diez* no han querido incluir a Asturias, por el momento, aunque de cualquier forma al ministro de Trabajo, Joaquín Almunia, considera que es un buen resultado.

Italia aprueba el tratado de adhesión de España y Portugal a la Comunidad. Italia aprobó el jueves 5 definitivamente el tratado de adhesión de España y Portugal a la Comunidad Económica Europea, después de que diera el visto bueno la Cámara de Diputados. El Parlamento ratificó el tratado por 383 votos a favor, 27 en contra y ninguna abstención.

Sábado 7

Los barcos españoles no podrán pescar en aguas mauritanas, según 'Onda Pesquera'. Todos los barcos pequeños españoles que faenan en la actualidad en aguas mauritanas no podrán volver a pescar en ellas a partir del próximo primero de enero, informó ayer *Onda Pesquera*. Esta noticia, sin embargo, ha sido desmentida por la Secretaría General de Pesca, aunque según el citado programa radiofónico, fuentes de la Administración mauritana han asegurado que la decisión se hará pública en una conferencia de prensa que se celebrará en los próximos días.

Domingo 8

La OPEP estudia un cambio de estrategia para recuperar su anterior cuota del mercado mundial de petróleo. La Organización de Países Exportadores de Petróleo (OPEP) estudió el sábado 7, en el primer día de su conferencia ministerial de invierno, la adopción de una nueva estrategia en su política de precios, con el fin de recuperar su vieja cuota en el mercado mundial de crudos. El jeque Yamani, ministro de Petróleo de Arabia Saudí, advirtió a los países productores no englobados en la OPEP sobre la inevitabilidad de una guerra de precios, con tarifas por debajo de los 20 dólares por barril, si persisten en mantener una política de precios al margen del consorcio.

El crecimiento español será similar al del Reino Unido en 1990. La firma auditora Coopers & Lybrand afirma en su informe anual sobre la situación económica y empresarial del mundo que las perspectivas económicas y empresariales de España pueden catalogarse de favorables. A juicio de esta firma auditora, España, "gracias a la estrategia de reestructuración de empresas que, a un alto riesgo político, ha abordado el Gobierno, alcanzará un producto interior bruto (PIB) muy próximo al del Reino Unido en 1990".

Exercise P will help you check the success of your decoding progress. Some of the questions concern details that you can discover by skimming; others check your general conprehension of content. Make sure you can tell the difference between the two types of questions. (If you are in a class with other students, you might find it interesting to exchange questions of your own based on your reading of the news briefs.)

Exercise P.

1. Which of the following countries are mentioned in the news reports? (Consult your instructor or textbook if you need help in identifying the Spanish names of countries and nationalities.)

   a. Germany
   b. United Kingdom
   c. Italy
   d. Andorra
   e. Spain

   f. United States
   g. Japan
   h. Canada
   i. Portugal
   j. Saudi Arabia

2. Which reports deal with issues related to the European Common Market?

3. What sort of relationship seems to exist between Spain and Japan? Is this relationship a recent one?

4. According to a recent audit, what seems to be the state of the Spanish economy?

5. Does the release of gas from the Almaraz reactor appear to have been serious?

6. What threat has Sheik Yamani made concerning oil prices? What would would be the purpose of such a move by OPEC?

7. Calculate the worth of the **peseta** against the Canadian dollar at the time of the De Havilland sale.

8. What two countries were seeking admission to the European Common Market at the time of these reports?

9. *(Dictionary question)* Which words in the article about fishing boats are based on the root word **pez** *(fish)*?

10. *(Dictionary question)* In the Thursday news report, the agriculture minister is happy about the increase in **renta**. Use you dictionary to discover why.

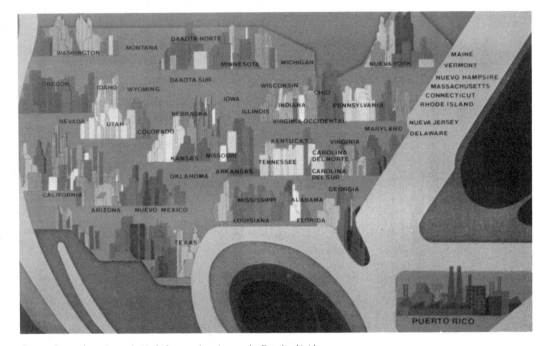
Where would you expect to see an advertisement for a country? This one appeared in a Spanish newspaper. What is the most important economic feature of Puerto Rico, according to the advertisers?

UNIT

6
Examining
the World
of Food

The Reading Strategy

Decoding: Using repetition and grammatical cues

In earlier units, you worked primarily on reading materials with many format cues and on relatively short passages of prose. In Unit 6, you will learn more about applying the *Reading Strategy* to longer prose passages like those found in magazines or newspapers. The theme of this unit is food; the readings examine food from different perspectives. Before you proceed, THINK about the kinds of articles about food that you read in English. What kinds of articles about food would you expect to find in a magazine called *Parents?* In a monthly periodical called *Kitchen and Hearth?* What sort of references to food might be found in a weekly television guide or in a daily newspaper?

In Unit 6 we will read selections in Spanish from these and other sources. At this stage in the *Reading Strategy,* you will begin to concentrate on the individual sentences in a reading passage, learning to decode the contribution that each one makes to overall meaning. While continuing to emphasize repetition as an aid to comprehension, you will also learn to use the grammatical features of Spanish sentences to help you understand the organization of prose passages. In this book, we have emphasized the value of cognates. By now, though, you have probably discovered that some words that appear to be cognates have meanings that are not predictable. These words are known as *false cognates*. In this unit you will learn how to deal with these *false cognates*. You will also find new information about function words that connect sentences to each other.

The purpose of this unit is to illustrate a method for decoding the meaning of reading materials that you select yourself. If you do not already read materials of your own choosing, use the list of reading sources included at the end of this book or consult with your classmates or instructor to find suitable reading materials. You will be surprised at how much you can read!

Remember, as you approach each new piece of writing in Unit 6, first preread it on your own, using the early steps in the *Reading Strategy*. Gather as much information as you can, as quickly as you can. Look up a word or two if essential, but, as always, use your dictionary as a last resort. Brief descriptions of the *Reading Strategy* techniques developed up to this point are listed here as reminders.

Step 1. Scan. Use format cues to identify the type of material and the probable topic of the passage.

Step 2. Look for content vocabulary whose meaning you can guess. Focus on the topic. Formulate preliminary questions about it.

Step 3. Try to understand important content words. Skim for specific information needed for your reading purpose.

Step 4. Look for main ideas. Concentrate on the beginning and end: the first and last sentences or paragraphs.

We'll begin with a short item from a newspaper. This passage comes from a page with the heading **Gente.** English-language newspapers often have sections with equivalent titles. What kinds of information or articles do you expect to find on such a page?

Keeping the context in mind, preread the item.

EL PAIS

*g*ente

Premio nacional de Gastronomía

De Manuel Llano Gorostiza, sus amigos dicen que es la persona que más sabe del vino de Rioja; que lo sabe todo. Manuel Llano Gorostiza, 58 años, natural de una población minera, San Salvador del Valle, en Vizcaya, premio nacional de Gastronomía este año, es mucho·más modesto, dentro de su habitual modestia, y asegura que su único mérito es "insertar el vino dentro de la cultura, porque yo tengo muy claro que existe una cultura del vino". En 1971 el nombre de Llano Gorostia comienza a adquirir relevancia como consecuencia de un libro que hoy día continúa siendo un manual sobre el vino de Rioja. "Fue un compromiso increíble, pero acabé escribiendolo (*Los vinos de Rioja*)". Desde entonces no ha parado de escribir ni de dar conferencias.

Now skim the article to complete Exercise A.

Exercise A.

Answer the questions in the spaces provided and mark the places in the article where you locate each piece of requested information. Do not look up more than three words; choose them carefully!

1. Who is this article about? _____

   What format features help you decide? _____

   _____

2. What has the man received? _____

3. How old is this man? _____

4. Where is he from? _____

5. What is his main area of expertise? _____

Like all prose passages, this item is full of repetition, in spite of its brevity. Good readers pay close attention to patterns of repetition as a guide to decoding. Many of the decoding techniques of the *Reading Strategy* depend on repetitions and help you make the best use of them. Now we will use this paragraph to illustrate some ways to THINK about repetition. Although we will move more slowly through the paragraph than you would if you were reading it for pleasure, the techniques displayed here are among the most important ones to master in order to read complex materials with good comprehension. To begin, see how many of the following ideas were part of your own thinking as you looked at the passage.

Thinking About the Passage

1. The article contains one content word that appears five times, including twice inside quotations. It is a cognate—**vino** *(wine)*—and its number of repetitions suggests that it is probably very important to the topic.

2. The paragraph also has three important repeated phrases. **(Manuel) Llano Gorostiza** appears three times. It is probably a man's name (given the use of capitalization, the familiarity of Manuel, and what you know about Spanish naming patterns). It is likely to be the name of the person in the accompanying photo; he is probably the topic of the paragraph. The article contains personal information about him: his age (58), place of origin (San Salvador del Valle, in Vizcaya) and, possibly, something about his personality **(modesto/ modestia).Vino(s) de Rioja** is repeated three times. **Rioja** looks like a proper name; it could be a type of wine or a place famous for wines. One repetition looks like a book title. **Premio nacional de Gastronomía** appears twice. Its importance is underscored by its use in the title. All words in a title are worth knowing: The meaning of **nacional** can be guessed, and probably the meaning of **gastronomía** as well. (Remember, the article is in a unit about food.) Look up **premio** (if necessary) to discover that it means *prize*. (Note its relationship to *premium* for future reference.)

3. Since this is a "people" page article, includes a photograph, and is very short, it is most likely to be an announcement about the activities of a well-known person. Because of its brevity and because it is taken from a newspaper, the article's first sentence is likely to contain important information about the topic. Even though the subject of the first sentence is **amigos** (the verb, **dicen**, is plural), the topic of the sentence is Manuel Llano Gorostiza; his friends say that he knows about the wine of Rioja.

4. *Conclusion:* Manuel Llano Gorostiza, well-known wine expert and author of a book about the wines of Rioja, received the 1984 National Gastronomic Prize. ◆

Generalmente las frutas pequeñas tienen más sabor.

If you did not notice the repetitions or did not THINK about them in this way, look at the article again. Consider how you approached it originally and THINK about what you would need to do differently in order to extract the information above. Pay attention to the ways in which the format, your background knowledge, the repetitions, and your guesses about vocabulary all work together to provide information about the content. Your main task as a reader is to put that information together in order to discover its meaning.

Es muy peligroso comer setas blandas y de mal aspecto.

If you followed this line of thought, you should have been able to answer the questions in Exercise A easily. Once this kind of thinking is automatic, your comprehension will improve greatly. During the decoding stage of the *Reading Strategy*, you must always remember to THINK! You must pay attention to your reading purpose. For most purposes, especially if you were reading this article for pleasure, you would now know as much as you needed to about the **Premio de Gastronomía** and could go on to another article. However, since you are already familiar with this article, let's use it to demonstrate a technique you need when your reading purpose requires you to understand details. This technique is also helpful if you need to read a passage that is somewhat more complex than you are used to. Under either of these conditions, you will want to do *close reading*, a process that emphasizes decoding sentence by sentence.

In Unit 5, you learned the importance of isolating the main verb of a sentence or clause and of identifying important associated nouns. We call these sets of verbs and their associated subjects and objects the *core* of the sentence; the verb and associated nouns in the main clause form the *main clause core*. A sentence that is actually composed of two or more sentences linked by words such as "and" may include more than one main clause core. In the earlier unit, you worked only on topic sentences, but now you can apply the process of verb core identification to whole passages. Here are some important points to remember when looking for verb cores in Spanish sentences:

1. Spanish sentences may be very long and include several verb cores, either in main clauses that are linked together by words like **y** or **pero** or in subordinate clauses linked by words like **que** and **cuando.**

2. The endings of Spanish verbs indicate the subject. For verbs in the first and second person, singular and plural, subject pronouns are almost never expressed except for emphasis. The subjects of third-person verbs are usually expressed by a noun at the place where the subject is first identified; later in a passage, once the subject is understood, there may be only a pronoun or no word for the subject at all.

3. You can expect to find subject and object nouns close to the verbs they are associated with. Subjects often follow verbs in written Spanish and objects that are indicated by pronouns (e.g., **le, lo, las**) are usually found in front of the verb.

4. The important nouns in a verb phrase (the subject and the object) are those *not* preceded by prepositions. (Don't forget the personal **a,** though! It introduces human direct objects.) The subject is often the topic of the sentence as well, but sometimes the topic may be a noun in a prepositional phrase.

With these points in mind, let's identify the verb cores in the paragraph about Llano Gorostiza. Since you are already familiar with the article, this task will be an easy one for you.

Exercise B.

Locate each verb or verb phrase in the article and circle it. If a subject or object noun or pronoun is stated, underline it. Look up any verb roots you do not recognize and cannot guess. (Remember to distinguish roots carefully.)

This article illustrates some typical characteristics of Spanish prose. It has only five sentences, but there are fourteen conjugated verbs. These numbers suggest that all five sentences are complex, with one or more subordinate clauses in each one. However, the eight main verbs or verb phrases (**dicen, es, asegura, tengo, comienza a adquerir, fue, acabé escribiéndolo,** and **ha parado**) are, for the most part, easily recognizable. If you use your skills at root identification, there is very little that requires looking up, even if you have not yet learned about some of the verb forms. The main difficulty in close reading for a passage like this one is in untangling the long sentences. Look back over the passage quickly to determine which sentences seem to be the most complex.

You probably concluded that sentences two and three are the most difficult to decode. Sentence two, for example, is actually composed of three shorter sentences, and the second and third of these have subordinate clauses as well. The problem in a sentence like this one is grasping the relationships of the various clauses to each other and identifying the contribution that each part makes to the overall meaning.

Once you have found the verb cores, you can begin to unravel the relationships in complex sentences by identifying the type of sentence each verb core represents. There are only a few basic types.

1. *Sentences that state existence.* These sentences report that something exists. Important markers are verbs such as **hay** and **existe.**

2. *Sentences that state equivalence.* These sentences say that "X is Y": "I'm a student." "What is that?" "Mary is a genius." In Spanish, sentences that state equivalence usually have some form of **ser** in them: **Soy estudiante. ¿Qué es eso? María es un genio.**

3. *Sentences that describe conditions.* These sentences tell what something is like: "The soup is cold." "Are you happy?" "We're all tired." Several verbs are used in descriptive sentences in Spanish, but **estar** is one of the most common: **La sopa está fría. ¿Estás contenta? Todos estamos cansados.**

4. *Sentences that tell location.* These sentences tell where something is: "John's in Chile." "My hat's beside the table." They usually include some form of **estar,** often with a preposition such as **en: Juan está en Chile. Mi sombrero está al lado de la mesa.**

5. *Sentences that narrate actions.* Active sentences include verbs of action. They may be *transitive* and require an object, as in "Paul wrote a letter" (**Pablo escribió una carta**), or *intransitive,* with no associated object, as in "They walked slowly." (**Caminaban despacio.**)

Here is sentence two from the article, divided into its three constituent sentences with each verb circled and each subject underlined. Examine it carefully and then go on to Exercise C.

A. Llano Gorostiza, 58 años, natural de una población minera, San Salvador del Valle, en Vizcaya, premio nacional de Gastronomía este año, (es) mucho más modesto, dentro de su habitual modestia,

B. y (asegura) que su único mérito (es) "insertar el vino dentro de la cultura,

C. porque yo (tengo) muy claro que (existe) una cultura del vino."

Los limones de piel delgada suelen ser más jugosos.

Exercise C.

THINK about the grammatical relationships in the sentence as you answer these questions.

1. What type of sentence is part A? _____

2. Which word shows the relationship between parts A and B?

    _____

3. What is the subject of the main verb in B? _____

4. What is the subject of the main verb in C? _____

5. Why has the sentence changed from third person to first person?

    _____

6. What word shows the relationship of B to C? _____

Many beginning readers find such grammatical complexity frustrating. Certainly, most beginners cannot *produce* sentences even remotely like the ones you have been reading. However, the regularities of Spanish sentence grammar make it possible for you to *read* these complex sentences fairly easily, as long as you pay attention to the relationships among the various parts of sentences. Fortunately, once you are in the habit of thinking about sentences in this way, you will find that the process is very swift—you will hardly notice yourself doing it!

Now review the following guide and see how closely it parallels the way you thought about sentence two.

Thinking About the Passage

1. Even though there are many modifying phrases in part A, the presence of **es** is a clue that it is really only a simple "X is Y" statement: Llano Gorostiza is modest. There is a great deal of additional information about Mr. Llano Gorostiza presented in the form of a list, with items separated by commas.

2. Part A is joined with part B by the conjunction **y**; the two parts are of equal importance. They also have the same subject. The subject, Mr. Llano G., is not repeated in part B, but the third-person verb form refers to him.

3. Part B is active. **Asegura** has a subordinate clause introduced by **que** that refers to what Llano G. affirms is his only merit.

4. The punctuation of part B indicates the presence of a quote. The quote contains another clause, C, introduced by **porque.** This third part, the quote, is spoken by Llano Gorostiza, so it has a first-person verb **(tengo)**; the rest of the paragraph is about him and has third-person verbs.

5. Part C is also active; it concerns something Llano G. has. What he has is actually an idea, that a wine culture exists. That information is in a subordinate sentence of existence, also introduced by **que.**

Once this overall structure is clarified, the relationships among the parts are obvious. What is crucial to understanding the overall structure is first to identify the verb cores by eliminating irrelevant modifiers, and second, to pay attention to the ways in which function words like **y, porque,** and **que** relate them.

   Now let's look at a new reading passage. It comes from a summer issue of a Mexican magazine called ***Padres*** and is found in the section called "Cocina." Begin by prereading. What kind of article is it?

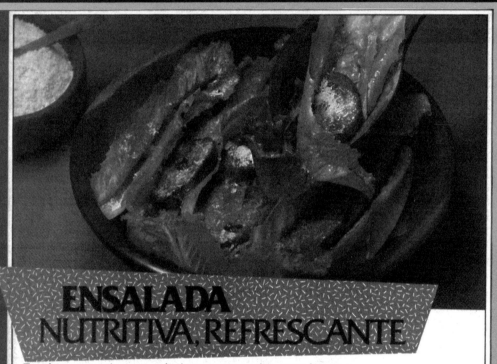

ENSALADA NUTRITIVA, REFRESCANTE

Te ofrecemos algunas prácticas sugerencias para hacer apetitosas y refrescantes ensaladas en estos meses del año tan calurosos.

Las ensaladas son un plato imprescindible en verano: nos aportan las tan necesarias vitaminas que se encuentran de forma abundante en los productos crudos de la huerta. Además, las ensaladas se prestan a un derroche imaginativo por parte del ama de casa. Siempre podremos improvisar una ensalada de nuestra propia «cosecha» creativa y aprovechar por ejemplo, unos restos de pescado o carne molida, o terminar el paquete de garbanzos o alubias que sobró del invierno o utilizar esa fruta demasiado madura que se iba a echar a perder... Las ensaladas son como las sopas, admiten cualquier ingrediente, y el resultado puede ser sorprendentemente bueno.

En los meses más calurosos del año no gustan los platos calientes ni guisos muy pesados de digerir. Es el momento ideal para preparar las refrescantes ensaladas. Se pueden convertir incluso en plato único si les añadimos cualquier alimento con proteínas como trocitos de pescado cocido, atún, unos camarones, o salmón, salchichas o queso, huevo duro, etc.

Podríamos comer todos los días de la semana una ensalada y no aburrirnos nunca, porque cada día le daríamos un toque diferente con tal o cual ingrediente distinto. Y además puede resultar un plato sumamente económico si elegimos los productos más baratos de la estación, tanto de hortalizas como de frutas. Para quienes protestan que se quedan con hambre cuando comen ensalada, podemos agregar a los tradicionales ingredientes, arroz y maíz cocidos, alubias, champiñones, espárragos, pedazos de pan frito, aguacates o nueces... Convirtiendo así a las ensaladas, en una comida deliciosa y sumamente nutritiva.

ENSALADA CESAR

6 rebanadas de tocino su fruta bien picaditas ● 2 copitas de aceite de oliva ● 2 cucharadas soperas de mostaza ● 2 limones, el jugo ● 2 huevos tibios, de un minuto ● 12 pedazos de pan fritos y frotados con ajo ● 1 lechuga orejona lavada y escurrida ● 100 gramos de queso parmesano ● pimienta y sal, al gusto ● jugo Maggi, al gusto.

En una ensaladera ponga el tocino, el aceite, la mostaza y el jugo de limón, los huevos, la pimienta y el jugo Maggi. Mezcle bien. Remoje en este aderezo los pedazos de pan y las hojas de lechuga. Incorpore los ingredientes. Por último espolvoreé el queso y sirva.

COCINA

INED INSTITUTO DE EDUCACION NUTRICIONAL Y SERVICIOS AL CONSUMIDOR

Exercise D will guide you through the decoding sequence.

Exercise D.

THINK about the organization of the passage as you work. Be sure to complete each task in order: stop to read when you are told to and answer all the questions in one section before going on to the next.

1. Reread the titles and subtitle. How many parts does the article have? What are they? _____

    _____

2. Look for recognizable vocabulary. Identify and list the most frequently repeated content words and phrases. _____

    _____

    _____

3. What is the probable topic of this article? _____ What is its probable purpose? _____

4. Read the first and last sentences of the article. How are these sentences related to the title and subtitle? State the article's main idea in a few words. _____

5. Read the first and last sentences of each paragraph. (These are topic sentences.) Using only two or three words, state the probable topic of each paragraph. _____

    _____

    _____

6. Number the paragraphs. Using the topic sentences as your guide, match each of the following statements with the paragraph to which it belongs.

    _____ a. The variations possible with salad ingredients are endless.

    _____ b. The major nutritional advantage of the ordinary garden salad is the vitamin content it possesses.

    _____ c. Salads are especially good in the summer since they are not served hot.

7. Read through each paragraph as a unit. Then match each of these characteristics of salads with the paragraph where it is mentioned. Some of the characteristics in the list are not mentioned in this article. Indicate those with 0.

    _____ a. permit variety in the diet

    _____ b. can serve as an entire meal

    _____ c. use up leftovers

    _____ d. provide fiber in the diet

    _____ e. economical

    _____ f. easy to digest

    _____ g. provide important vitamins

    _____ h. allow the cook to be creative

    _____ i. extra ingredients provide protein

    _____ j. very few people have salad allergies

8. Mark all verb cores, including those in the recipe. THINK about the patterns and similarities among them.

9. Check your answers and correct any errors by returning to the passage.

Here are some important features of the verbs and verb phrases in the salad article. How many of them did you observe?

1. Many third-person verbs use **se** (four examples).

2. Many verbs are in the first-person plural form (seven examples).

3. In the article section, there are many two-part verb phrases, especially with **poder** as the first part (seven examples).

4. The verbs in the recipe are mostly simple commands.

These features tell us some of the characteristics of the article: it is about things and not people (use of **se** verbs); it has a personal tone (use of first-person plural); it offers suggestions about what we can do. The recipe section does *not* offer suggestions; instead, it gives instructions using direct commands. The patterns created by the different verb forms signal important differences in tone. Read through the article again quickly and pay special attention to the verb forms.

Do not be discouraged if you do not always THINK in the way described here. Decoding by using the *Reading Strategy* is not like translating word for word. The techniques we are using in this unit may be new to you, and they require practice to be effective. The more you read on your own, the more quickly the techniques will become natural.

While you have been working on the decoding of these articles, you have reread them several times. Rereading is a technique basic to effective use of the *Reading Strategy.* Each time you go through a reading passage, you should focus on a different aspect, but each rereading has the same goal: to reveal patterns within the passage that will help you decode its meaning. As you have seen, just the examination of verb cores helps orient you to the structure and tone of an article and prepares you to extract further detail from it through close reading.

Close reading is especially valuable for instructional passages, a category that includes recipes. For instance, simply deciding whether or not to use a particular recipe requires reading closely enough to be sure that all the ingredients and utensils are available. Instructions may use specialized vocabulary, some of it probably new to you. Knowing the meanings of all the verbs, and the relationships among them, is essential for understanding instructions. For all these reasons, recipes are appropriate materials to help illustrate some further decoding techniques, especially some that relate to close reading in passages with specialized vocabulary.

Whenever you do close reading, working toward complete comprehension of what you read, you will probably find it necessary to look up words. When you do, remember to apply the dictionary techniques you have practiced in earlier units.

1. Select words by degree of importance to the context.

2. Use your knowledge of roots and endings to make dictionary work go faster.

El perejil, el cilantro, el romero, etc. le durarán más tiempo si los conserva en un lugar fresco y con los tallos sumergidos en agua.

3. Read entire entries.

4. Note nearby related words.

5. Mark the words you look up so that you can keep track of their overall frequency in the type of materials you read.

6. Most important—THINK about the word's meaning in relationship to the larger sentence context.

7. Apply the information gained from each new word to the interpretation of other words and contexts in the passage.

Let's begin with a recipe for **Pechugas a la Potrerillos.** Preread the passage; then use Exercise E to help orient you.

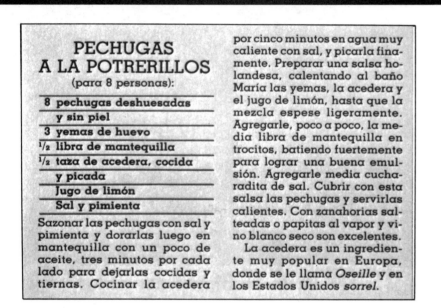

PECHUGAS
A LA POTRERILLOS
(para 8 personas):

8 pechugas deshuesadas
y sin piel
3 yemas de huevo
½ libra de mantequilla
½ taza de acedera, cocida
y picada
Jugo de limón
Sal y pimienta

Sazonar las pechugas con sal y pimienta y dorarlas luego en mantequilla con un poco de aceite, tres minutos por cada lado para dejarlas cocidas y tiernas. Cocinar la acedera por cinco minutos en agua muy caliente con sal, y picarla finamente. Preparar una salsa holandesa, calentando al baño María las yemas, la acedera y el jugo de limón, hasta que la mezcla espese ligeramente. Agregarle, poco a poco, la media libra de mantequilla en trocitos, batiendo fuertemente para lograr una buena emulsión. Agregarle media cucharadita de sal. Cubrir con esta salsa las pechugas y servirlas calientes. Con zanahorias salteadas o papitas al vapor y vino blanco seco son excelentes.

La acedera es un ingrediente muy popular en Europa, donde se le llama *Oseille* y en los Estados Unidos *sorrel*.

 Exercise E.

1. Identify the following elements, typically found in recipes: title; list of ingredients, instructions for preparation; information about the number of servings.

2. What is the most important word in this recipe? _____
   What does it mean? _____

3. What is the root of **deshuesadas?** _____
   What does it mean? _____

4. Which of the following nouns (all followed by **de** phrases) refer to measures? **yemas, libra, taza, jugo** _____

5. THINK about recipes you read in English. Which type of vocabulary do you think varies more from recipe to recipe: nouns or verbs?

The organization and purpose of materials that give instructions control their vocabulary. In recipes, for example, most of the nouns refer to ingredients. Some ingredients occur repeatedly in recipes—flour, sugar, water, and salt, for example—but most are specific to particular recipes. The verbs, on the other hand—beat, chop, stir, cook, and so on—occur over and over again. If you need to read several recipes, it will be more useful in the long run to learn the verbs and depend on your dictionary for help with unfamiliar nouns.

Sentences in recipes are usually short, and they commonly include action verbs that give the reader certain instructions. The subject of verbs in recipes is understood to be you, the reader. However, Spanish has more than one way of presenting instructional verbs. In this particular recipe, infinitives are used for this purpose, so it is easy to identify the roots of core verbs.

Exercise F will help you focus on the grammatical organization of the passage.

 Exercise F.

1. Working sentence by sentence, locate and circle the verb cores in the recipe. Do not overlook compound sentences. Look up any verb root that you cannot be sure of. Assume that the verbs you look up now will be useful in later recipes as well.

2. This recipe contains examples of two important Spanish sentence connectors: **para** and **hasta que.** The verb after **para** is expected to be the result of the action in the previous clause. **Hasta que** links two actions in time. Find the examples of these connectors; then identify and underline the two verb actions each one links.

3. Find three examples of the diminutive suffix **-ito/-ita**. Identify the roots to which they are attached and write them in the spaces.

   _____

   _____

   _____

4. **Baño (a) María** is a specialized cooking term. Even though you may know the meaning of the parts, you probably cannot guess the meaning of the phrase. Check to see if your dictionary includes it. Be sure to look under the most likely entry. What does it mean? _____

Now reread the entire recipe, using your decoding skills to understand the details of preparation. You may need to look up a few more words. After looking up each one, stop to THINK about how you chose it and what you learned by looking it up. Had you already guessed the meaning and were using the dictionary just to check it? Was knowing that particular word helpful in discovering more of the meaning of the passage?

When you understand the recipe thoroughly, go on to Exercise G.

Exercise G.

1. Put these actions into the proper order, based on the instructions in the recipe.

   _____ a. Cook and chop the sorrel.

   _____ b. Brown the chicken breasts in butter and oil.

   _____ c. Cover breasts with sauce.

   _____ d. Prepare hollandaise sauce by combining yolks, sorrel, lemon juice, and butter.

   _____ e. Serve hot with steamed potatoes.

2. How many times is salt added in the recipe? _____

3. When are the carrots added? _____

Here are some new recipes from a popular cookbook. Begin by prereading them.

SOPA DE PUNTAS DE ESPARRAGOS CON LECHE

1 lata de espárragos
4 tazas de caldo de gallina o de huesos, el jugo de los espárragos
2 tazas de leche
2 cucharadas de mantequilla
2 cucharadas de harina
2 cucharadas de cebolla picada

A los espárragos se les cortan las cabezas y la parte gruesa se pone a hervir con el caldo el jugo de los espárragos y las rebanadas de cebolla; ya que esté bien cocido se cuela. Se calienta la mantequilla y se le pone harina moviéndolo con una cuchara; cuando esté bien disuelta se le añade la leche, sal y pimienta en polvo y se deja hervir; en seguida se le incorpora el caldo ya preparado y las cabezas de los espárragos y se le da otro hervor. Se sirve con pedacitos de pan fritos.

SOPA DE CREMA DE ELOTE Y GALLINA

Los 8 elotes grandes se muelen con la cebolla y el ajo y se deshace en un poco de agua, se cuela y se pone a cocer añadiéndoles mantequilla, la crema de leche, sal, pimienta y nuez moscada. Los 6 elotes medianos se salcochan y ya cocidos se desgranan y se ponen a cocer en la leche, y luego se le añaden a lo anterior y también la pechuga de gallina cocida, cortada en cuadritos; se deja hervir por 10 ó 15 minutos y se le pone punto de sal. Se sirve con galletitas saladas.

8 elotes crudos tiernos y grandes
1 cebolla y un diente de ajo
6 elotes tiernos medianos
1¼ litro de leche hervida
1 cucharada grande de mantequilla
1 taza de crema de leche
  sal, pimienta y nuez moscada al gusto
1 pechuga de gallina cocida

SOPA DE PUNTAS DE ESPARRAGOS Y CHICHAROS

1 lata de puntas de espárragos
1 lata de chícharos
1 cebolla
2 cucharadas de mantequilla
  Caldo de gallina o de huesos el necesario
  sal, polvo de pimienta, pedacitos de pan fritos

Se pica la cebolla muy menuda y se fríe en la mantequilla, se le añade la lata de puntas de espárragos y la de chícharos, después el caldo se sazona al gusto con la sal y pimienta y se deja hervir; se sirve con el pan frito en cuadritos.

SOPA DE ZANAHORIAS (SENCILLA)

Se salcochan las zanahorias con sal, luego se muelen y se deshacen en el caldo necesario que quede aguadito. Se pica menudo el tomate, cebolla, chile dulce, se fríe en manteca añadiéndole el caldo ya preparado, sal al gusto, se tapa y se deja hervir unos minutos. Al servirlo se pone la mantequilla y las rebanadas de pan frito.

6 zanahorias grandes
1 cebolla
3 tomates
2 rebanadas de chile dulce
1 cucharada de mantequilla
  caldo el necesario, rebanadas finas de pan francés frito

Para saber si un huevo está en buen estado, póngalo en un recipiente con agua. Si se va al fondo está bien. Si flota, deséchelo.

Did you notice the word **sopa** in the titles? It looks as if it may mean *soap*, but you probably guessed that it means something quite different. (What would soap recipes be doing in a cookbook?) We refer to words like **sopa** as *false cognates*. You will learn more about them in the Dictionary Interlude. For now, make a guess about the meaning of **sopa.** Check your dictionary to be sure. Make sure you know the meanings of all the important words in the name of each dish.

These recipes illustrate another common Spanish device for giving instructions. Instead of infinitives or commands, they use the impersonal **se** construction. All the verbs are conjugated in the third person and are accompanied by the pronoun **se** *(itself/themselves).* This pronoun marks these verbs as reflexives.

In Spanish, the reflexive is often used as an impersonal construction, much as the passive is in English. That is, it indicates that the real subject—the person performing the action—is not known or is not important. What is more important in a reflexive verb is the action itself and the noun it is performed on—the object. For example, the sentence **Se pica la cebolla muy menuda** in the recipe **Sopa de puntas de espárragos y chícharos** means *The onion is chopped very fine.*

In other cases, reflexive verbs used as impersonal constructions treat the real object as if it were the grammatical subject. An example of this construction is found in the opening sentence of the recipe **Sopa de crema de elote y gallina: Los 8 elotes grandes se muelen con la cebolla. . .** This sentence literally says that "eight ears of corn mash themselves with onion"; clearly, though, it is the cook who does the mashing! The reflexive construction is a device for avoiding the repeated mention of a familiar subject.

You may already have studied these constructions; if so, you may wish to review them in your text or with your instructor. If they are new to you, simply think of them as having a kind of passive meaning: "The corn gets (is) mashed together with the onion." In general, these expressions are easy to recognize and easy to read.

Let's work now with the recipe **Sopa de puntas de espárragos con leche,** a soup made of asparagus tips and milk. Like all recipes, this one gives instructions in more or less chronological order, the same order in which the ingredients are listed. Many different actions are mentioned, but there are only three separate sentences. Read through the recipe quickly.

Exercise H.

Underline all the verb cores in this recipe. Remember that **se** and other object pronouns are part of the verb phrase too. THINK about the ways the verbs are related to one another. Check your answers and return to the recipe to correct any errors.

You may have noticed that many of the verb phrases include the object pronouns **le** and **les.** These pronouns identify secondary nouns—objects indirectly related to the verb action. If the noun referred to by the **le** or **les** is

Ni los plátanos ni los aguacates se deben congelar porque se ponen negros.

actually mentioned in the sentence, it will be in a phrase introduced by **a**. In the phrase **se les cortan las cabezas,** for example, **les** refers to **espárragos,** mentioned before the verb phrase. The phrase means "the heads cut themselves off (get cut off) from them (the asparagus)." If no noun is mentioned in a **le(s)** sentence, then the pronoun probably refers to a noun mentioned as part of an earlier verb phrase. For example, in the phrase **se le pone harina,** the **le** refers to **mantequilla,** the subject (no **a**) of the previous verb. The phrase means "flour is put to/with/on it (the butter)." When decoding, it is always important to know which noun is referred to by any indirect object pronoun.

This recipe also illustrates two new sentence connectors: **ya que** and **cuando.** Remember that sentence connectors help the reader keep track of the sequence of actions in a passage. In a recipe, sequencing is especially important, and these particular connectors mean *when* or *as soon as*.

Exercise I.

Reread the recipe **Sopa de puntas de espárragos con leche** to answer these questions.

1. Identify and circle the noun that each use of **le** or **les** refers to. (The same noun may be referred to more than once.)
2. Locate all examples of **ya que** and **cuando.** Identify the two actions that are linked in each case.

Now let's look at some recipes that are organized differently. Preread them. Pay attention to the differences and similarities between these recipes and the ones you have seen earlier in this unit.

Las Super Recetas
de Bertha Zavala:

ENSALADA DE PAPAS

Rebane 1/2 kgs. de papas cocidas y peladas, báñelas con 4 cucharadas de aceite de oliva, 2 cucharadas de vino blanco, 1 cucharada de vinagre, 1 cucharada de perejil picado, 1/2 cucharada de cebolla picada, 3 cucharadas de caldo, una pizca de pimienta y sal, ya bien mezclado sin romper las papas, deje sazonar y enfriar por 2 horas antes de servir.

CARNE FRIA

Muela 2 kgs. de carne maciza de cerdo, con 1/2 kg. de pulpa de res, 25 almendras peladas, 5 rebanadas de jamón, agregue 1 bolillo remojado en leche bien desbaratado, 8 huevos ligeramente batidos, revuelva bien, sazone con sal, pimienta y nuez moscada, cueza a baño María, sírvala acompañada de una ensalada.

ENSALADA DE CAMARONES

Corte en trocitos 1 lata de puntas de espárragos, apartando unos para el adorno, incorpórelos con 1/2 kgs. de camarones cocidos y pelados, 1 taza de mayonesa, coloque en la ensaladera 1 lechuga romanita chica deshojada, y vacíe sobre éstas la mezcla, adorne con los espárragos, 1 pimiento rojo, 1 pimiento verde ambos en rodajas, fondos de alcachofas, 2 huevos cocidos en rodajas y sírvala fría.

Like the **Ensalada cesar** recipe, these recipes use direct commands instead of either infinitives or impersonal verbs. (Remember that the root of a direct command has the opposite theme vowel: an **-e** ending indicates that the infinitive should be an **-ar** form, and an **-a** ending means you should look for an infinitive in either **-er** or **-ir).** In spite of many similarities, these recipes show a major organizational difference when compared to earlier ones: they do not list the ingredients separately. In order to extract an ingredients list, you must decode for detail.

 Exercise J.

1. Begin with the recipe for shrimp salad. Identify all verb cores, looking up roots as you need to. Write the roots in the spaces provided.

   _____ _____ _____

   _____ _____ _____

2. Once you have understood what actions are involved, make a list of all ingredients necessary for this dish.

   _____ _____ _____

   _____ _____ _____

   _____ _____

3. Read the **Ensalada de papas** recipe as quickly as you can for maximum comprehension using the *Reading Strategy*. THINK about how the ingredients or preparation of this recipe differ from your own version of the dish.

4. Here is a recipe from the same source, with the instructions scrambled. Using your knowledge of recipe organization and vocabulary, put these instructions into the most appropriate order. Use your dictionary for new ingredient names only. Pay attention to sequence cues and the way verbs and nouns are cross-referenced.

   Dulce de mandarina

   _____ a. Vacíe en copas para dulce.

   _____ b. Deje enfriar.

   _____ c. Mezcle 2 yemas con 1 taza de azúcar, 1 cucharada de maicena, el jugo de 5 mandarinas, y 1 cucharada de raspadura de mandarina.

   _____ d. Adorne con 1 fresa y sirva bien frío.

   _____ e. Ponga la mezcla a fuego suave, sin dejar de mover, hasta que se vea el fondo del cazo.

   _____ f. Cuando esté bien fría, agregue 2 claras, batidas al punto de turrón, y 2 cucharadas de jerez.

Dictionary Interlude

Handling function words and false cognates

Reading passages about food often include unusual vocabulary. Luckily, they also often have many helpful format cues. Here is a selection with a common format and a great deal of new vocabulary. Identify what type of material it is. What do you think the divisions refer to?

CASA BOTIN

C A R T A
SERVICIO E IMPUESTOS INCLUIDOS

RESTAURANT
3.ª categoría

ENTREMESES Y JUGOS DE FRUTA

Pomelo 1/2	✗
Jugos de Frutas, Tomate, Naranja	150
Entremeses variados	495
Jamón Serrano	1.100
Melón con Jamón	730
Ensalada Riojana	415
Ensalada BOTIN (con pollo y jamón)	495
Ensalada de lechuga y tomate	250
Morcilla de Burgos	210
SALMON AHUMADO	1.100
SURTIDOS DE AHUMADOS	750

SOPAS

Sopa al cuarto de hora (de pescados y mariscos) ..	520
Sopa de Ajo con huevo	295
Caldo de Ave	250
Gazpacho Campero	325

HUEVOS

Huevos revueltos con champiñón	335
Huevos a la Flamenca	335
Tortilla con gambas	335
Tortilla con jamón	335
Tortilla con chorizo	335
Tortilla con espárragos	335
Tortilla con escabeche	335

LEGUMBRES

Espárragos con mahonesa	675
Guisantes con jamón	410
Alcachofas salteadas con jamón	410
Judías verdes con tomate y jamón	410
Champiñón salteado	410
Patatas fritas	150
Patatas asadas	150
Ensalada de endivias	✗

PESCADOS

Ostras de Galicia (6 piezas)	✗
Angulas	2.400
Almejas BOTIN	990
Langostinos con mahonesa	1.560
Cazuela de Pescados a la Marinera	690
Gambas a la plancha	1.100
Merluza rebozada	1.160
Merluza al horno	1.160
Merluza con salsa mahonesa	1.160
Calamares fritos	560
Lenguado frito, al horno o a la plancha (pieza)	1.160
Trucha a la Navarra	530
Chipirones en su tinta (arroz blanco)	555

ASADOS Y PARRILLAS

COCHINILLO ASADO	1.250
CORDERO ASADO	1.375
Pollo asado 1/2	420
Pollo en cacerola 1/2	510
Pechuga «Villeroy»	525
Perdiz estofada (o escabechada) 1/2	820
Chuletas de cerdo adobadas	620
Filete de ternera con patatas	1.050
Escalope de ternera con patatas	975
Ternera asada con guisantes	890
Solomillo con patatas	1.290
Solomillo con champiñón	1.290
Entrecot a la plancha, con guarnición	1.050
Ternera a la Riojana	955

POSTRES

Cuajada	215
Tarta helada	280
Tarta de crema	280
Tarta de manzana	280
Flan	185
Flan con nata	295
Helado de vainilla, chocolate o caramelo	215
Espuma de chocolate	215
Dulce de membrillo	150
Melocotón en almíbar	215
Melocotón con nata	315
Fruta del tiempo	275
Queso	395
Piña en almíbar	175
Piña natural al Dry-Sack	315
Fresón al gusto	✗
Sorbete de limón	275
Sorbete de frambuesa	275
Melón	185

MENU DE LA CASA
(Otoño Invierno)

Precio: 1890 Pesetas

Sopa de Ajo con huevo

Cochinillo asado

Helado

Vino o cerveza o agua mineral

VINOS
Valdepeñas
Tinto y Blanco

Botella	190	Ptas.
1/2 Botella	95	"
Sangría	330	"
1/2 Sangría	180	"
Rosado de Navarra ..	190	"
1/2 Rosado de Navarra	95	"

CAFE 75 – PAN 35 – MANTEQUILLA 50
HORAS DE SERVICIO: ALMUERZO, de 1:00 A 4:00 – CENA, de 8:00 A 12:00   HAY HOJAS DE RECLAMACION
ABIERTO TODOS LOS DIAS

This menu from a small restaurant in Spain offers several luncheons with set prices. Can you identify a category on the Botín menu for each course included in Menu 1? How do these meals differ from your usual midday meal?

Cervezas
EL AGUILA

MENU 1 – GASPACHO GARNICION
MERLUZA SEVILLANA
PAN, POSTRE, VINO ó AGUA M. 550

MENU 2 – ENSALADA DEL TIEMPO
CHULETA DE CERDO 550
PAN, POSTRE, VINO ó AGUA M.

MENU 3 – SALMOREJO GUARNICION
CHAMPIÑON AJILLO 600
PAN, POSTRE, VINO ó AGUA M.

MENU DE LA CASA 550

Many restaurants divide the offerings on their menus into categories. If you know the vocabulary of the categories—even if you do not know the names of particular dishes—you could at least select the courses for a complete meal.

Exercise K.

Use your dictionary as necessary to compose a meal that you would like to eat in a restaurant like this one. Money is no object!

The Wendy's placemat is a different sort of menu. Read the description of each item. Pay special attention to the types of sentences and to the use of command verbs. There are a great many words borrowed from English. Can you guess why?

Throughout the *Reading Strategy* so far, you have depended heavily on the large number of words Spanish and English share and that are easy to guess. The following list includes words from the readings in this unit. They all probably look familiar.

Premio nacional de gastronomía: **compromiso, conferencia**

Ensalada: **crudos, restos, estación**

Wendy's menu: **jamón**

The words in this list, however, are *false cognates*. They do not mean what you expect them to. Sometimes, the obvious guess is one of the meanings of the word, but not the most common one. It is important for you to be aware of the existence of false cognates when you read. If you find yourself in a passage in which you have guessed the meaning of important words, but the passage does not seem to be making sense, suspect a false cognate and use your dictionary to check meanings. Exercise L will help you practice this technique.

Exercise L.

1. Look up each of the false cognates listed on page 133. THINK about the way in which the various meanings you find are related to the meaning you predicted.

2. Locate each word in the reading passage where it occurs. Select the appropriate meaning for that context and write it in the spaces provided.

   a. _____   b. _____   c. _____

   d. _____   e. _____   f. _____

3. Using the English section of your dictionary, look up the meaning you originally predicted for the word. What is the appropriate Spanish equivalent? Is that word related in some way to the false cognate?

As long as you keep the context in mind when you are reading, false cognates shouldn't confuse you very much. But whenever you come across a word that looks familiar but whose meaning does not seem to fit the context, it may be a false cognate. Look it up to be sure.

This is a menu posted in a restaurant in Colombia. Given the context, what do you think **gaseosas** might mean? Can your dictionary help?

```
ESPECIALIDADES
    PARA  HOY

ROBALO  A  LA  PLANCHA  $225
LOMITO  DE  RES          $245
LOMITO  DE  CERDO        $245
CHURRASCO               $225
ARROZ  CON  POLLO       $180
TORTILLA  ESPAÑOLA      $130
HAMBURGUESAS
SANDWICHES

BANDEJA
                        $95

JUGOS   NATURALES       $45
CAPUCHINO
EXPRESS                 $30
AROMATICA               $12
GASEOSAS                $8
KUMIS  CON  BRANDY
CAZUELA  ESPECIAL       $30
                        $75
```

Las verduras nunca deben de lavarse ni cortarse hasta el momento en que se van a usar.

You have learned how to use sentence connectors like **y, porque,** and **pero.** You have also done some work in this unit with **para, ya que, hasta que** and **cuando.** Sentence connectors show the relationships of time, manner, and action that exist among the verbs of complex sentences. An important step in the decoding stage of the *Reading Strategy* is to identify and understand these connectors and their contributions to sentence meaning.

Fortunately, even though sentence connectors are function words, they are relatively easy to locate in a dictionary. Since many of them are phrases, you should look for them in the entry for the most important word in the phrase (usually the longest one). In context, sentence connectors are often followed by **que.** Exercise M illustrates some common connectors you have seen in the readings in this unit.

 ### Exercise M.

THINK about the importance of sentence connectors as you complete these items.

1. In the Llano Gorostiza article, **como consecuencia** occurs. Locate it in the article and read the sentence in which it occurs.

   a. What two verb cores are joined by **como consecuencia** to make one sentence? _____

   b. What kind of relationship exists between the two actions?

   _____

   c. In what order do the actions occur?

   _____

   d. What is the best translation equivalent for **como consecuencia?**

   _____

2. The following connectors are used in the soup recipes. Find an example of each one. Then look up each one in your dictionary and determine which meaning is the appropriate one for the context.

   a. ya (que) _____   b. cuando _____
   c. en seguida _____   d. después _____
   e. luego _____   f. hasta (que) _____
   g. para (que) _____

Al + *infinitive* is an especially useful connector in Spanish that is probably not listed in your dictionary. It means *upon (doing the action indicated by the infinitive).* An example occurs in the last line of the last soup recipe: **Al servirlo. . . ,** which means *Upon serving it , . . .* You will see many examples of **al** + *infinitive* as you read.

In reading these materials, you may have felt that you needed to look up a great many new words. Food vocabulary is somewhat specialized and also quite variable. The same item may have different names in different regions, and the same word may refer to different dishes in different countries. One

What kind of store do you think this is? How many of the items for sale here are part of the Botín menu?

familiar example is **tortilla** which refers to a cornmeal pancake in Central America, but in Spain it is an omelette! Bilingual dictionaries can only provide a certain amount of information about regional variation. What does your dictionary say about **tortilla?**

Dictionaries, as you have learned, also provide only minimal definitions. You should not be surprised if specialized food words are hard to find. For example, **alubia** appears twice in the salad article you read earlier. It is absent from many bilingual dictionaries. Is it in yours?

Even when **alubia** is included, many dictionaries give only *bean*—a vast category—as the translation equivalent. If you do find yourself dealing with ambiguous vocabulary, ask yourself how much detail you really need for the context. Look back at the salad article and locate the contexts for **alubia.** Can you guess enough about the word to read on successfully?

Alubia occurs both times in lists of potential salad ingredients—that's as much as you need to know in order to understand the intent of the passage. It is not necessary to know precisely what kind of bean is referred to. Remember, good readers spend more time in the reading than in their dictionaries. Knowing good dictionary techniques is important, but knowing how to THINK about what you look up is even more valuable.

Applying the Reading Strategy

In this unit, you have practiced new techniques for close reading and have learned some useful new vocabulary items and grammatical structures. Before leaving the unit, practice putting all this new information together by reading an article which is typical of those found in general interest magazines. This is the longest reading you have worked with and you need not attempt to understand everything in it. Use it as an opportunity to explore the effectiveness of the *Reading Strategy* applied to longer passages without many format cues. The following series of exercises will guide you through the article. Be sure to complete each part in order.

El arroz

Originario de Oriente, el arroz, es, con el pan, el alimento más sano, abundante y universalmente conocido. Los pueblos de Asia, Africa y América hacen del mismo una consumición considerable, aunque en algunos países de Europa su consumo sea también importante. En algunos países se hace todavía vino de arroz, de color blanco-ambre y de sabor muy agradable. Esta bebida, el vino, está muy generalizada en China, país en el que el arroz es la base de la nutrición de sus habitantes. España es buena productora de arroz, en sobremanera el país valenciano.

Contrariamente al maíz, que consumimos generalmente en forma de derivados (harinas, sémolas, pan, pastas alimenticias), el arroz se consume bajo su forma natural.

Antes de ser entregado a los mayoristas, el arroz se seca, a fin de que su tasa de humedad no sobrepase los 16 %, tasa por encima de la cual su conservación comienza a resultar difícil. Se eliminan luego del arroz las envolturas externas, y ocasionalmente las harinas adheridas al grano, o se procede a pasarlo por talco o glucosa a fin de obtener una apariencia brillante.

Las clases de arroz que encontramos corriente en los establecimientos especializados son: el de grano redondo, muy rico en almi-

dón, que por norma general ha sido abrillantado. En estos momentos este tipo de arroz aparece también pre-cocido, es decir, cocido al vapor, lo que permite al consumidor prepararlo en mitad del tiempo que se utiliza para hacerlo con el normal. Existe también el arroz de grano largo, más duro, con menos almidón pero con la ventaja de que no se pega a las cazuelas con la facilidad con la que lo hace el de grano redondo. A veces se presenta también pre-cocido o pretratado. Mención también al arroz integral, que consumen en grandes cantidades los naturistas y macribióticos, que no es otra cosa que el grano que ha conservado su envoltura externa, que aprisiona y guarda intactos los cuerpos minerales, vitaminas de rejuvenecimiento de los tejidos que se encuentran en su superficie.

Elegiremos el arroz según dos criterios: su origen, y el uso que queramos hacer del mismo. Ante un arroz de tipo americano, generalmente caro, elegiremos siempre un buen arroz de Valencia o incluso de las zonas catalanas de Pals o San Carlos de la Rápita. Para la elaboración de ensaladas de arroz, arroz con leche, un pastel de arroz, platos que deben quedar «moalleux», se optará por el arroz de grano corriente; para elaborar los «rissotto» o los pilaf y las paellas, así

como para todas aquellas preparaciones en el que al arroz debe quedar suelto, elegiremos el de grano largo que, aunque un poco más caro, tiene la virtud de no pegarse al fondo del recipiente.

Es necesario, pensando en su conservación, preservar el arroz de la humedad, en función de lo cual habrá que proveerse de cajas de metal o potes de cristal, del tipo de los que se utilizan para preparar las conservas.

El arroz aparece en la cultura sistemática aproximadamente algunos milenios después que el trigo y constituye la alimentación de un considerable número de pueblos asiáticos. El arroz pide numerosos cuidados y según sus variedades presenta valores nutritivos desiguales.

Al igual que todos los demás cereales, el arroz tiene un valor calórico elevado y en conjunto, más pobre que el maíz.

Indicaremos, para acabar, que el arroz, cocinado a modo de guisado a la cazuela o paella, el plato barroco por excelencia de nuestra cocina, es una manifestación de la vida comunitaria, ya que en raras ocasiones lo come una persona sola, sino que se reúnen un número considerable para participar tanto de la elaboración del guiso como de su posterior degustación.

Carmen Casas.

Arroz, para todas las comidas.

What's funny about this cartoon?
Would it be equally funny with the
caption translated into English?

Exercise N.

Answer the following questions about **El arroz.**

1. Read the title and the opening sentence.
    a. What is the topic of this article? _____
    b. What vocabulary item do you expect to be the most frequent one in

        this passage? _____

2. Read the first paragraph all the way through. Which of the following
    statements best expresses the main idea of the opening paragraph?
    a. Rice is a very healthful food.
    b. Rice is eaten all over the world.
    c. Rice is a basic element in the Spanish diet.

3. Read the last paragraph all the way through. Which of the following best
    expresses the main idea of the final paragraph?
    a. Eating rice is a baroque experience.
    b. Eating rice is best done alone.
    c. Eating rice is an opportunity to share a communal meal.

4. Note the method used to mark paragraphs in this article. Number the
    paragraphs in order. (You should have nine.) Which paragraphs are likely
    to be the most difficult ones to understand? Why?

Read each paragraph as a whole context unit. Keep reading as long as you feel
that you can understand the general meaning. Do not stop at unknown words.
At the end of each paragraph decide whether a word is important enough to

look up. Look up as few words as possible. THINK about each paragraph as you read through it. Ask yourself how it is related to the previous ones. Remember that you are not reading in order to translate. Your reading purpose at this point is to understand the main ideas and organization of the article.

The next exercise checks your decoding skills.

Exercise O.

Refer to the passage as necessary to answer the following questions.

1. Match each of the following topics with the number of the paragraph it describes.

   _____ a. selecting the proper type of rice

   _____ b. preparation of rice for sale

   _____ c. origin of rice

   _____ d. different classes of rice

   _____ e. preservation of rice

2. Skim for the following information.

   a. The two criteria for selecting rice are _____ and _____.

   b. Before being sold, rice is dried so that it retains only _____% of its humidity.

   c. The region of Spain that produces a great deal of rice is _____.

   d. The major advantage of precooked rice is that it _____

   e. Whole-grain rice is primarily eaten by two groups of people: _____ _____ and _____.

3. Read paragraph four again, very carefully. How many classes of rice are mentioned? List them.

Use your dictionary to help you figure out why this cartoon is funny in Spanish. Can you translate it so that it is funny in English?

Read the article through one last time.

Now complete Exercise P.

Exercise P.

Use these questions to check your overall comprehension.

1. Below is a list of characteristics of rice that might be mentioned in an article about rice. Identify the ones found in this particular article by indicating the number of the paragraph in which each feature is mentioned. If a feature is not mentioned, mark it with 0.

    _____ a. nutritious
    _____ b. available in a variety of forms
    _____ c. inexpensive
    _____ d. universally known
    _____ e. easy to cook

2. Choose the best summary of the content of this article.

    a. Rice is good to eat and good for you.

    b. Rice is an important international product and dietary staple.

    c. Rice is universally available in a variety of forms that lend themselves to different dishes.

Before you go on to Unit 7, be sure to read all the cooking hints scattered in the margins of this unit. You will find them helpful in reviewing some important sentence connectors—and you may learn something useful about food!

UNIT

7 Choosing Leisure Activities

The Reading Strategy

Decoding: Understanding cross-reference and metaphor

In Unit 7, our theme is recreation and leisure activities. You will read materials in several new formats and will practice *Reading Strategy* techniques appropriate for longer prose passages. You will learn about certain grammatical features characteristic of longer passages, and you will learn what to do when you know all the words in a phrase but the result does not seem to make sense. You will also learn the value of summarizing what you read.

Perhaps you have never thought about how much reading is involved in leisure activities. Think about some of the activities people do for fun. Make a list of the activities and think about what kinds of written materials are associated with each one.

On the left is a list of some leisure activities common in Spanish-speaking countries. You will probably find many of them on your own list. On the right is a list of types of written materials. Match the leisure activities with the appropriate reading materials. An activity may have more than one kind of reading material and a reading material may be matched with more than one activity.

_____ 1. attending or participating in sporting events	a.	programs
_____ 2. seeing movies	b.	reviews
_____ 3. going shopping	c.	ticket stubs
_____ 4. listening to music at home or at concerts	d.	album covers
	e.	posters and announcements
_____ 5. going to plays or other performances	f.	lists of regulations
	g.	store directories
_____ 6. going to parks	h.	public signs
	i.	news reports

Note that by thinking about context, you can predict something about the organization and content of written materials related to these activities. In our native language, we bring this awareness to everything we read. The *Reading Strategy* helps you use this awareness for reading in Spanish as well. In this unit, you will have an opportunity to practice reading many of the kinds of written materials listed above.

Let's begin with some simple writing found on the park sign on page 143.

Do you think camping is a traditional activity in Spanish-speaking countries? The fact that the word **camping** is borrowed from English suggests that camping is not a traditional leisure activity for people in Spanish-speaking

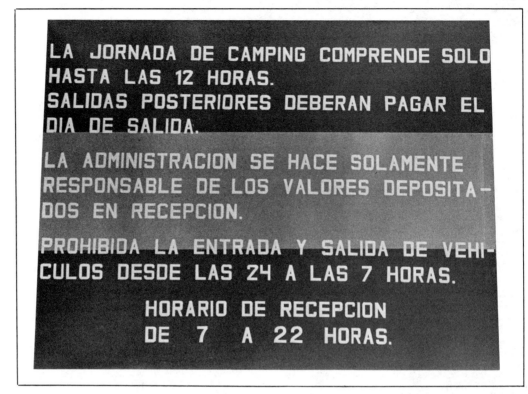

LA JORNADA DE CAMPING COMPRENDE SOLO HASTA LAS 12 HORAS.
SALIDAS POSTERIORES DEBERAN PAGAR EL DIA DE SALIDA.

LA ADMINISTRACION SE HACE SOLAMENTE RESPONSABLE DE LOS VALORES DEPOSITA-DOS EN RECEPCION.

PROHIBIDA LA ENTRADA Y SALIDA DE VEHI-CULOS DESDE LAS 24 A LAS 7 HORAS.

HORARIO DE RECEPCION
DE 7 A 22 HORAS.

countries. It has become popular in recent years, however, and signs like this provide important information for campers. This sign includes several valuable reminders for beginning readers. **Recepción**, for example, is used here in two different senses. Both are related to the meaning of *reception* in English, but neither meaning can be translated by *reception*. Can you guess what **recepción** means in this context? Check you dictionary to make sure.

Did you notice the use of the **se** with a third-person verb in the sign? What is the subject of the sentence?

As used here, **se hace** is a kind of reflexive: the administration makes itself responsible. **Administración** is understood to be the subject of the verb phrase **se hace** because it is nearby, is not introduced by a preposition, and agrees with the verb in number.

Check your understanding of the information on this sign with the following exercise.

Exercise A.

1. According to the sign, what is the latest hour you may arrive and still be admitted to this park? _____

2. What is the latest hour for checking out? _____

3. What is the earliest? _____

Now we'll consider some simple writing related to shopping. If you happened to be a shopper in Madrid, you could go to one of the world's most famous and elaborate department stores, **El Corte Inglés. El Corte Inglés** is so large that it prepares brochures for its customers. Look this one over and make sure you can identify its parts.

PRECIADOS,3 MADRID

MADRID (Preciados, Goya, Castellana,
Princesa y Conde de Peñalver)
BARCELONA (Plaza Cataluña y Diagonal)
SEVILLA - BILBAO
VALENCIA (Pintor Sorolla y Nuevo Centro)
MURCIA - VIGO - LAS PALMAS
MALAGA - ZARAGOZA.

DESGRAVACION FISCAL

SI ES USTED RESIDENTE EN EL
EXTRANJERO y ha realizado compras en nuestros departamentos,
recuerde que puede beneficiarse de
la correspondiente Desgravación
Fiscal de acuerdo con la legislación
vigente.

SOLICITE INFORMACION a cualquiera de nuestros vendedores
antes de iniciar las mismas.

BIENVENIDO A EL CORTE INGLES

Se encuentra Vd. en uno de los
Centros Comerciales, de la primera
cadena de Grandes Almacenes de
España, donde encontrará nume-
rables pequeños detalles que harán
más grata su estancia:

— Amabilidad y profesionalidad en
  la atención de nuestros vende-
  dores.
— Servicios especiales:
  • Agencia de Viajes.
  • Cambio de moneda extranjera
  • Servicio de intérpretes.
  • Cafetería.
  • Restaurante.
  • Aparcamiento.
— Seguridad durante su estancia.
  Instalaciones contra incendios,
  escaleras de emergencia, etc.

— CARTA DE COMPRA. ¡No car-
  gue con sus paquetes! Utilizan-
  do la carta podrá recoger toda
  su mercancía en la CAJA DE
  CARTA DE COMPRAS ¡solicíte-
  la a nuestros vendedores!.

HORARIO COMERCIAL: 10-20 H.

①	PALACIO REAL	⑤	CONGRESO DE LOS DIPUTADOS
②	PLAZA MAYOR	⑥	MUSEO DE LAS DESCALZAS REALES
③	MUSEO DEL PRADO	⑦	TELEFONICA
④	CORREOS Y TELECOMUNICACIONES	⑧	EL CORTE INGLES

ESTE ES EL CORTE INGLES MAS CERCANO A SU HOTEL

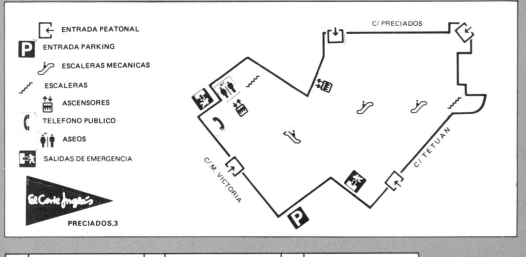

← ENTRADA PEATONAL

P ENTRADA PARKING

ESCALERAS MECANICAS

ESCALERAS

ASCENSORES

TELEFONO PUBLICO

ASEOS

SALIDAS DE EMERGENCIA

El Corte Inglés

PRECIADOS,3

B	**COMPLEMENTOS:** Abanicos. Bisuteria. Bolsos. Cosmética y Perfumeria. Damasquinados de Toledo. Estanco. Fumador. Joyeria. Libreria. Mantillas. Marroquineria. Medias. Pañuelos. Papelería. Relojeria. Sombreros. Souvenirs. Discos.	1	**HOGAR MENAJE:** Artesanía. Accesorios Automovil. Bricolage. Ceramicas. Cristalerias. Cuberterias. Loza. Orfebreria. Porcelanas (Lladró, Capodimonte). Plateria. Regalos. Saneamiento. Vajillas.	4	**CONFECCION SEÑORAS:** Boutique de la piel. Boutiques (Balenciaga, Georges Rech, Guy Laroche, Lasserre, Francisco Delgado, Pedro del Hierro, Pierre Balmain). Lenceria y corseteria. Complementos. Zapateria Peluqueria.
S1	**TEJIDOS:** Mercería. Sedas. Lanas. Fantasia, etc. **ALIMENTACION:** Supermercado. Licores y vinos. **IMAGEN Y SONIDO:** Cassettes. Fotografía. Hi-Fi. Ordenadores. Radio. T.V. Vídeos. Vídeo-Club.	2	**BEBES:** Carroceria. Canastillas. Confección. Regalos bebes. Zapateria Bebes. **NIÑOS/NIÑAS (4 a 10 años):** Confección. Complementos. Boutiques. **CHICOS/CHICAS (11 a 14 años):** Confección. Complementos. Boutiques. **JUGUETERIA. ZAPATERIA:** Señoras, Caballeros, Joven y Niños.	5	**JUVENTUD Y DEPORTES:** Confección Joven El. Confección Joven Ella. Boutiques femeninas (Arco Iris, Carla, Drach, Joly, Zhiva, Tintoretto), Boutique masculina (Peter Lord) Zapateria, Complementos. **DEPORTES:** Golf. Tenis. Caza. Pesca. Montaña, etc. Tiendas Adidas. Ellesse.
S2	**CARTA DE COMPRAS:** Desgravación Fiscal. **PARKING.**			6	**MUEBLES Y DECORACION:** Dormitorios. Salones. Alfombras nacionales-orientales. Lamparas. Mantelerias bordadas. Textiles del Hogar.
S3	**MONTAJE ACCESORIOS AUTOMOVILES. PARKING.**	3	**CONFECCION CABALLEROS:** Ante, piel. Articulos viaje. Boutique. Complementos. Zapateria. Peluqueria. Agencia de viajes. Cambio de moneda. Desgravación fiscal. Oficinas.	7	**OPORTUNIDADES. CAFETERIA.** Restaurante Buffet. Mesón.

Exercise B will guide you through the brochure.

Exercise B.

1. Mark the location of these important subsections on the brochure.

   a. store directory

   b. business hours

   c. credit cards accepted

   d. a list of store branches

   e. map of the store layout

   f. map to locate this branch

2. This branch of **El Corte Inglés** is located on **Calle Preciados.** How many branches are there in Madrid? _____

3. Suppose your hotel is located on **San Agustín,** near the **Plaza de las Cortes.** Use the store location map to plan a route from your hotel to **El Corte Inglés.** Mark your route on the map.

4. The purpose of the section titled **Bienvenido a El Corte Inglés** is to summarize some of the important features of the store. Read it as carefully as you need to in order to understand what four main features are being described. List them. _____

5. It is possible to summarize the **Bienvenido** paragraph even further. Suppose that you were creating a billboard for **El Corte Inglés** and wanted to communicate about the same four features described in the paragraph, but in shorter form. Choose the four words that best describe the features.

   a. conveniente

   b. seguro

   c. barato

   d. amable

   e. completo

   f. exótico

When you are decoding, it is helpful to pause occasionally to summarize what you have read. A summary or paraphrase reduces the content of a written passage to just the main ideas, somewhat like a simple outline. Summaries use words that convey the central meaning of the passage, even if the words themselves have not been used in the passage. In the **Bienvenido a El Corte Inglés** paragraph, the sentence about the attention customers receive from the personnel of **El Corte Inglés** does not include **amable** *(friendly)*, but it can be figured out from the word **amabilidad.** Similarly, the list of special services does not mention completeness as a specific feature of the store, but clearly that is the central idea of the list. It is very useful to be able to recognize or think of synonyms (words that have the same meaning) when reading and summarizing.

Now locate the detailed list of items and services for sale at **El Corte Inglés.** Note that the directory is arranged by floor. In Spain and many other Spanish-speaking countries, floors are called **plantas,** another false cognate. What we ordinarily think of as the first floor is known in Spanish as the **planta baja** and the next highest floor is given the number one. Use Exercise C to help you interpret the store directory.

Exercise C.

1. How many floors are there in **El Corte Inglés?** _____
2. How is **planta baja** abbreviated in this store directory? _____
3. Can you guess what the **S** might stand for in the floor list? Locate a likely translation equivalent in your dictionary. _____

Now look more carefully at the store directory. Each floor listing has a title that summarizes the items and services available on that floor. Among the list of items and services for each floor, you will see some words you recognize and some that are new to you. In general, you can expect the new words to refer to items or services that are related to others on that floor. Perhaps you can guess more than you realize. You will also see that certain types of items (shoes, for example) and services are available on more than one floor. Read the directory, guessing as much as you can. Remember to use the information provided by root words (like **zapato**) when guessing new meanings. *Do not use your dictionary yet!*

Refer to the store directory to complete Exercise D.

Exercise D.

1. Which is the most likely synonym for **complementos** in this context?
   a. cómplices
   b. accesorios
   c. adornos

2. How many floors offer shoes for sale? _____

3. Which floors offer items or services related to automobiles? _____

4. On what floors are these services located (or likely to be located)?
   a. the travel agent _____
   b. the cafeteria and restaurant _____
   c. the interpreters _____
   d. parking _____
   e. the money exchange _____

5. Where can you pick up your purchases when you use the **Carta de Compra?** _____

Suppose that now you have finished shopping and you still have some time on your hands. What else is there to do in a big city like Madrid? Perhaps you could consult a guide to activities. Here is a section from such a guide, a weekly magazine from Madrid called **Guía del Ocio.** Preread it, paying attention to the categories of activities.

para enterarse

CONFERENCIAS

● Monseñor Guerra Campos

Monseñor Guerra Campos, arzobispo de la diócesis de Cuenca, estará presente en el Club Siglo XXI (calle Juan Ramón Jiménez, 8) para hablar sobre «La invariante moral del orden político». Será el jueves, día 29 a las 8 de la tarde.

● Varios temas de actualidad

En diferentes colegios se han organizado conferencias sobre temas de actualidad de gran interés. En el Conde de Romanones (calle Elfo, 143), el lunes 26, hablarán sobre «La enseñanza privada». En el Méjico (avenida de Badajoz, s/n), el día 27, sobre «Las perspectivas económicas». El miércoles 28 se tratará sobre «Asociaciones juveniles» en el colegio Dr. R. Kapur (calle Eduardo Morales, s/n). La última será en el San Juan Bautista (calle Sorzano, s/n), versando sobre «La financiación española». Todas serán a las 8 de la tarde.

● La lírica de Juan Ramón Jiménez

José Gerardo Manrique de Lara, secretario general de la Asociación de Escritores y Artistas, y del Ateneo de Madrid, poeta, crítico, ensayista y novelista, dará una conferencia el miércoles 28, a las 8 de la tarde, con motivo del centenario de nuestro escritor y poeta que lleva por título: «Homenaje lírico a Juan Ramón Jiménez». Tendrá lugar en la sede del Instituto de España (calle San Bernardo, 49).

CONCURSOS

● Traducir a los españoles

Es importante dar a conocer las obras de nuestros grandes autores en los países extranjeros, por ello el Ministerio de Cultura ofrece dos premios de medio millón de pesetas a las mejores traducciones: uno, para los especialistas en autores nacidos con anterioridad a 1800, y otro, para los posteriores. La instancia solicitando concurrir a esta convocatoria deberá presentarse en el Registro General del Ministerio de Cultura antes del 15 de septiembre junto con seis ejemplares de la traducción y el mismo número de ejemplares o copias de la obra original. También se exige un currículum vitae y una memoria explicando las razones por las que se ha seleccionado al autor elegido.

● Literatura infantil

La Fundación Santa María ha convocado la quinta edición de sus premios de literatura infantil Gran Angular y Barco de Vapor, concursos de narración y novela que comparten las mismas bases, excepto la extensión de los trabajos, la dotación de los premios y el plazo de presentación. El primero de ellos está dotado con 500.000 pesetas para trabajos con una extensión entre 130 y 178 folios, que habrán de presentarse antes

del 1 de noviembre. El segundo, con un primer premio de 300.000 pesetas, es para manuscritos de 30 a 50 folios (se entregarán antes del 15 de septiembre).

ARTE

● Inventiva 82

Se inaugura el día 27 y permanecerá abierta hasta el 10 de mayo, en el Centro Cultural de la Villa de Madrid (plaza de Colón). Es ésta una curiosa exposición destinada a recoger todos los descubrimientos de inventores españoles habidos en los últimos años. Hay que reseñar también que durante estas jornadas se celebrarán conferencias coordinadas por el profesor Ting, premio Nobel de Física.

● Realidad soñada

Mario Antolín le definió como un hombre que pinta desde el recuerdo difuminado en rosas y en

azules los perfiles del tiempo. El es Sanz Magallón y estos días presenta sus obras en la Galería de Arte Gavar (calle Almagro, 32). Sus dibujos son ocres, difusos, una especie de niebla envuelve tanto paisajes como figuras consiguiendo transmitir al espectador una sensación de misterio, lejanía y soledad difícilmente superables.

● Templo Mayor de Méjico

Una maqueta de la gran basílica y cientos de esculturas, ollas, máscaras, cuchillos ceremoniales y muchos otros objetos de gran belleza son las piezas recogidas para esta magnífica muestra que se presenta en el Museo Arqueológico Nacional (Serrano, 13). En

la monumental iglesia, construcción matusalénica, se encontraron todas estas piezas que datan del año 1200 al 1500 antes de Cristo. Se clausura el día 30.

● Para los arquitectos

«La vivienda de iniciativa oficial» (1955-1965) es el tema de la exposición que se presenta en el Museo Municipal (Fuencarral, 78), y que recoge planos y fotografías de la época, así como una maqueta a escala real, copia exacta de una vivienda protegida de aquellos años. A todos puede interesar, pero seguro que los que le encontrarán una faceta especial serán los amantes de la arquitectura.

● Un músico alfarero

No es normal encontrar un alfarero que se gane la vida tocando la dulzaina y el tamboril por los pueblos para poder seguir con sus manos modelando el barro, negocio que no resulta excesivamente rentable. Estos días, Alejandro está siendo objeto de una especie de ayuda-homenaje. Sus obras se encuentran expuestas en Adobe (calle Moratín, 42). Acudan si les gusta apreciar el valor de estos cacharros de lujo hechos exactamente igual que los antiguos.

● Panorámica personal

Enrique Fernández Pérez-Serrano, catedrático de Dibujo,

un profesional consagrado en el mundo del arte, presenta sus obras bajo el tema «Panorama de personajes actuales para la Historia», en los salones del Club 24 (calle Claudio Coello, 24). Sus trabajos son impresionantes; el autor prescinde de todo lo accesorio para llegar a la verdadera identidad del objeto o el sujeto reflejado, y lo consigue sin esfuerzo aparente.

TEATRO

● II Festival Internacional de Teatro de Madrid

Si les gusta el arte de Talía, enhorabuena puesto que en esta semana podrán presenciar obras verdaderamente importantes: del 28 al 30 «Garbage» (Basura), por Jango Edwards and Friends Road Show (Holanda-EE.UU.), en el Auditorio del Centro Cultural de la Villa de Madrid. En este espectáculo se toman como punto de partida los pequeños detalles de la vida cotidiana y se los desarrolla hasta el absurdo. El 29 y 30, el grupo checoslovaco Los Cvoci interpretarán «Crac» en la Sala Olimpia (plaza de Lavapiés). Aquí

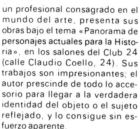

los dos mimos que componen este grupo son una muestra de la más refinada escuela checa en esta especialidad. Se consideran «nietos» de Buster Keaton y Chaplin, de quienes han tomado prestadas algunas de sus técnicas. «La mueca del miedo» será la obra española de la semana, interpretada por el grupo Tábano. Estará en escena en la Sala Cadarso.

FIESTAS Y FERIAS

● Feria de Sevilla

Muy poco hay que decir de estas fiestas de Abril sevillanas que comienzan este año el día 27 para finalizar el domingo 2 de mayo. Por las mañanas el pasear de caballos y carruajes bellamente engalanados, de tarde el repiquete de las palmas en las casetas al son de las sevillanas y bulerías. Alegría sin fin en unos días que ya son famosos en todo el mundo. Preparen sus atavíos andaluces y emprendan el camino, sin olvidar antes reservar alojamiento.

● Patios cordobeses

Comienza el Festival de los Patios Cordobeses el sábado 1 y dura hasta el día 12. La Sultana se viste de gala durante esos días; todas sus calles, sus casas, sus plazas y balcones resplandecientes de un blanco inmaculado se adornan de flores y olor a azahar. Como la copla y como la realidad. La chispa de sus habitantes se desborda durante estas fechas. ¿Los verdaderos protagonistas? Enrejados, tientos... y las guitarras.

● ¡Hurra el ribeiro!

Tiene lugar en Ribadavia (Orense) la Feria-Exposición de Exaltación del Vino de la Zona del Ribeiro. Los del lugar lo celebran del 27 de abril al 2 de mayo, con el resonar de las gaitas y los bailes folklóricos sin que haga falta mencionar, claro está, al caldo gallego más universal, que está presente en todos los momentos.

● Expo-óptica

El primer salón de óptica, optometría y audiometría protésica abrirá sus puertas al público desde el día 30 de abril al 3 de mayo en el Palacio de Exposicio-

MUSICA

nes de IFEMA (Paseo de la Castellana, 257). Por primera vez se celebra en Madrid este tipo de muestra en la cual se exponen toda clase de elementos y novedades relacionados con lentillas, gafas, sonotones, etcétera.

● Canta Carreras

Los días 26 y 28, a las 20,30, aún tendrán ocasión de disfrutar con la ópera de Giuseppe Verdi «La Forza del Destino». Pero si ya la han visto, el domingo 2 se estrena «Carmen», de Georges Bizet, con la participación del tenor José María Carreras, el barítono Justino Díaz y la soprano Alida Ferrarini. El maestro director será Luis A. García Navarro. Ambas se representarán en el Teatro de la Zarzuela.

● Música de cámara y polifonía

Dentro del IV Ciclo de Música de Cámara y Polifonía, en el Teatro Real, el día 27, la Orquesta de Cámara Española, actuando como concertino-director V. Martín, interpretará una sonata de Rossiji, un concierto de Libon y la Sinfonía número 9 de Mendelssohn.

● Sonatas de Mozart

La Fundación Juan March ha organizado un ciclo completo de sonatas para teclado de Mozart. Con tal motivo, el día 28, a las 19,30 horas, podrán escuchar la Sonata en *sol* mayor Kv 283, en *ré* mayor KV 284 (sonata Durnitz), en *do* mayor KV 309 y en *si* bemol mayor Kv 400. Estará interpretada por la pianista Eulalia Solé.

En esta misma entidad, el lunes 26 y dentro de los conciertos del mediodía que tienen lugar a las 12 horas, se ofrece un recital de órgano por Maite Iriarte, con obras de Pachebel, Bach, del Barco y Guridi. La entrada para ambas audiciones es libre.

■ «Las cuatro estaciones»

Esta obra maestra de Antonio Vivaldi se escuchará en el Club Urbis (avenida Menéndez Pelayo, 71) el jueves 29, a las 20 horas. Será una audición musical en alta fidelidad y la entrada es gratuita.

DEPORTES

● Gran Prix de tenis

Del 26 de abril al 2 de mayo se celebra en las instalaciones de la Real Sociedad Hípica Club de Campo el Gran Prix de Madrid de tenis con 200.000 dólares en premios y los mejores jugadores del mundo en tierra batida encabezados por Ivan Lendl, Guillermo Vilas, el francés Noah, José Luis Clerc y otros muchos. También estarán presentes nuestras raquetas más distinguidas, tales como Orantes, Higueras, Luna, Giménez y López Maeso. Todo un acontecimiento para los amantes del tenis con encuentros desde la 1 de la tarde hasta la caída del sol.

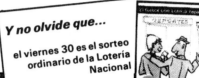

Y no olvide que...
el viernes 30 es el sorteo ordinario de la Lotería Nacional

Ministerio de Cultura
Museo Nacional del Prado

Serie C № 25505

Entrada 400 pesetas

Casón
Guernica

Casón
Salas Siglo XIX

The short paragraphs are brief summaries of activities available to people interested in lectures, art, literary competitions, theater, festivals, music, and sports. A reader would expect such summaries to include information about the dates, times, and locations of the events described—information a reader who already knows about the event might skim for. These summaries also include additional information that might be useful to a reader who does not know much about the topic or the event and wants to find out whether the activity is of personal interest. A reader with that purpose in mind needs to decode.

Let's try decoding some of the summaries. You will see that they contain interesting cultural information and also provide examples of several important grammatical characteristics. We will illustrate the decoding process itself, so it is absolutely essential that you stop to read whenever you are asked to. Respond to all questions and correct your answers before continuing.

Look first at the section titled **Conferencias.** Read the three summaries quickly.

Now use Exercise E to help you decode the summaries in this section.

Exercise E.

1. Did you remember that **conferencia** is a false cognate? It means *lecture,* not *conference.* What is there in the summaries that suggests that *conference* is not the best translation equivalent?

   _____

2. Now look closely at the summary **La lírica.** The first name in the paragraph is the name of the speaker, the subject of **dará la conferencia.** What two positions does José Gerardo Manrique de Lara have?

   _____

3. Circle all the nouns or noun phrases in this paragraph that refer to Mr. Manrique de Lara.

4. What is the occasion being recognized by his lecture? (HINT: Think about the **motivo.**)

   _____

5. Underline the single word which refers to that occasion.

Manrique de Lara's lecture celebrates a centenniel. The grammar makes clear that this centenniel is **de nuestro escritor y poeta.** But who is the writer and poet whose hundredth birthday is being celebrated? Not Manrique de Lara himself, surely! Read the paragraph again and identify the most likely topic of the lecture.

A second name occurs twice in the passage, once in the title and again inside the quotes that give the title of the lecture. Juan Ramón Jiménez, is **nuestro escritor y poeta.** Readers must make the connection between that phrase and the writer's name, by taking into account the entire context of the passage. Cross-referencing in this way is very common in written materials. A writer may refer to a noun some distance away in the passage by means of synonyms—**nuestro escritor** is a kind of synonym for **Juan Ramón Jiménez**—and depends on the reader to make the proper connection. Naturally, the more you know about a culture, the easier it will be for you to make good connections. If you know that Juan Ramón Jiménez is one of Spain's most beloved poets and a Nobel prize winner, recognizing him as **nuestro escritor y poeta** is easier. Remember, the more you read in Spanish using authentic materials, the more you will learn about the cultures of Spanish-speaking people and the more your personal mental context will expand.

The most common example of cross-referencing is in the use of pronouns: all pronouns serve as synonyms for nouns already mentioned or nouns the writer expects the reader to have already identified mentally (by seeing a name used in a title, for example). Possessive adjectives such as **mi** and **su** are also used for cross-referencing.

Other cross-referencing methods are found as well. One common practice in Spanish prose is referring to a noun that has not yet been identified and that the reader may not know, but which will be clarified almost immediately by the context. This characteristic of Spanish writing shows the importance of reading by context unit. If you stop before you get to the noun reference, you will almost surely be confused. If you read on to the end of the sentence (or the whole paragraph if it is short enough), you may be able to clear up any confusion.

Exercise F will help you recognize and practice reading cross-reference patterns of these types.

Exercise F.

1. Read the selection titled **Panorámica Personal. Sus** is used to indicate that the possessor of each newly mentioned noun is the same Enrique Fernández Pérez-Serrano who is mentioned at the beginning of the passage. Underline the noun used as a synonym for Mr. Fernández Pérez-Serrano.

2. Now locate the pronoun **lo** in the verb phrase **lo consigue. Lo** can refer to ideas or events as well as to masculine singular nouns. In this case, **lo** refers to, or is a synonym for, the part of the previous sentence that describes the author's aim. Underline the phrase that **lo** refers to.

3. Read the announcement of the exhibition of inventions called **Inventiva 82.** The opening sentence does not state its subject directly. What is its subject? _____

4. Read the second sentence again, paying particular attention to the use of the word **ésta.** What will the number and gender have to be for any noun to which **ésta** may refer? _____

5. What kind of sentence is the one in which **ésta** appears?
   a. one that tells location
   b. one that shows equivalence
   c. one that states existence
   e. an active sentence
   f. a decriptive sentence

6. What is the noun referent for **ésta?** _____

7. Read the paragraph with the heading **Realidad soñada.** Locate the pronoun **le** in the first sentence. How do you know that Mario Antolín cannot be the referent for this pronoun?
   _____

8. Underline the sentence that identifies the topic of the passage.

9. Circle the noun in the passage that is the correct referent for **le.**

10. Read the description of the artist's works again. Is it likely that Sanz Magallón's drawings will resemble Fernández Pérez-Serrano's or are they in different styles? _____ Underline all the words in each description that determine your answer.

Authors have many ways of referring indirectly to nouns in prose. One of the most common, and most creative, is to use words that are not normally thought of as related to a particular noun in such a way that the reader can see a new relationship. Associations made in this way are said to contain *metaphors* or to be *metaphorical.* Look at the paragraph titled **Patios Cordobeses,** which is full of references of this type. (**Cordobeses** is the adjectival form of Córdoba, a famous city in Spain. Locate Córdoba on the map on page 261.) Read the paragraph carefully. What do you think **La Sultana** refers to?

In this passage, the author refers to the city of Córdoba by its customary nickname, **La Sultana.** While you need some specialized background in order to know this, you can guess from the context that **La Sultana** refers to the topic of the passage, the city itself. This assumption is confirmed throughout the passage, where the writer personalizes the city by using verbs normally associated only with people. Read the passage again to locate examples of such verbs.

Did you identify **se viste** and **se adornan** as verbs with meanings not normally associated with cities? Think about the passage. What does it mean to say that Córdoba "dresses up"?

The phrase **como la copla y como la realidad** is a second indirect reference, this time to the flowers. A **copla** is a popular poem or song. What kind of association do you suppose the author wants you to make among **coplas, realidad** and **flores?** Does it help to know that many **coplas** contain references to flowers and that they are usually written in a romantic, "flowery" style?

Make sure you know what **chispa** and **desbordar** mean. What does the author mean in the sentence **La chispa de sus habitantes se desborda durante estas fechas?** Do the inhabitants of Córdoba really have "sparks"?

You may have to look up the unfamiliar words **enrejados** and **tientos** in order to understand the last line.

Do not be surprised if your bilingual dictionary does not include **tientos** in a meaning that makes sense here. **Tiento** is a technical term and refers to a particular type of short musical composition for stringed instruments. Even if you know that, however, you still have to think in order to understand the sense in which **tientos,** along with balcony gratings and guitars, could be called the "true protagonists" of Córdoba's festival.

The author wants the reader to imagine several kinds of connections among the references to flowers, music, and romance, and also expects his readers to be familiar with certain related customs such as the tradition of singing love songs to young women who listen from behind the iron bars of their balconies. The entire paragraph describes the festival by mentioning objects related to it. The reader must make the necessary connections between the objects and the participants.

Imaginative writing of this kind is fun to read, but only if the reader is aware that the references are not to be taken literally. Metaphorical writing requires that the reader try to share the writer's imagination. It is possible to understand the main idea of this paragraph—there's a festival going on in Córdoba—without understanding every word or making every connection. For some reading purposes, that level of understanding is enough, but a passage like this one is very rich in imagery. Interpreting such imagery is part of the pleasure of reading. The ability to "see" the images created by an author is part of the reward for a careful reader.

After you have practiced reading this type of writing in Spanish, you will find yourself able to react to it as you might in English. An experienced reader, for example, might see the connection in this paragraph between the image of the balcony gratings—vertical bars—and the strings on a guitar. There is also a natural connection between musical compositions and musical instruments. As we now know, there is also an association between music and balconies. But a reader might feel somewhat dissatisfied with the last part of the paragraph. **Tientos** seems to be too technical a term to be used in a passage like this one. You might try rewriting the last sentence to improve it by replacing **tientos** with a different word. Can you think of any other appropriate **protagonistas** that could be included as well?

Exercise G will help you apply decoding skills to other summaries.

Exercise G.

Select six other paragraphs to read on your own. Remember that the more interested you are in the topic and the more you know about it, the easier the reading will be. Decode as much detail as possible in each. Then use the following questions to check your decoding conclusions.

Varios temas de actualidad

1. Are the speakers identified in any way? _____

2. What are the four topics of current interest that will be discussed?

_____

_____

3. Colegios is a false cognate. What is the best translation equivalent for it in this context? _____

Traducir a los españoles

4. How many prizes will be awarded in the translation contest? _____

5. What is the basis for the division between them? _____

6. What four types of materials must a contestant submit to the judging? (HINT: **Memoria** has special meaning here.)

_____

_____

Templo Mayor de Méjico

7. Approximately how old would the **Templo Mayor de Méjico** be now?

_____

8. **Matusalénica** is used in a kind of metaphor. It is based on the proper name **Matúsala**, who lived to great age. What is the best nonmetaphorial translation equivalent for **matusalénica?** _____

Para los arquitectos

9. Why is the exhibit mentioned here of particular interest to architects? (HINT: **Planos** is a false cognate!) _____

_____

Un músico alfarero

10. What is the relationship between the photograph and the opening line?

_____

11. Who is referred to by the pronoun **les** in the last sentence?

_____

Festival Internacional de Teatro en Madrid

12. Three different works are to be presented as part of the festival. What countries are represented among the performing groups?

_____

13. It's easy to see what words make up the expression **enhorabuena,** but its meaning is not as easily determined. Using any translation equivalents you find for it as a guide, identify an appropriate English expression to explain its use in this context. _____

14. Now find an appropriate Spanish synonym for **enhorabuena.**

_____

Feria de Sevilla

15. What are the similarities between Sevilla's festival and the one described for Córdoba?

_____

16. What are the apparent differences between the two festivals?

_____

Expo-óptica

17. What two words in the paragraph have **expo** as their root?

_____

18. Which one is probably the source for the title? _____

Canta Carreras

19. What is Carreras' full name? _____

20. Luis A. García Navarro is not singing at the concert. What is he doing?

_____

Música de cámara y polifonía and **Las cuatro estaciones**

21. What important information mentioned about the Vivaldi concert is not included in the announcement about the chamber music concert?

_____

Gran Prix de ténis

22. What court surface will the tournament be played on?

_____

23. When the writer uses the expression **nuetras raquetas más distinguidas**, **raquetas** is used as a metaphor. What does it stand for?

_____

How many participants are scheduled to appear in the event announced here?

As you have been reading these summaries of various events, you have no doubt noticed the way in which the writers manage to incorporate a great deal of important information in a very short space. Another type of material that uses this technique is the movie review. Here is an example of the briefest possible summary of opinions about a film. It is taken from the same Madrid leisure guide and reflects the movies showing in Madrid during the first week of 1986. Make sure you understand how to interpret the various marks on the chart.

Las estrellas de la guía del ocio

★★★★★ obra maestra ★★★★ muy buena ★★★ buena ★★ interesante ★ regular o mala

ESTRENOS	ANGEL FERNANDEZ SANTOS (El País)	PEDRO CRESPO (ABC)	ANTONIO LARA (Ya)	M. y F. MARINERO M. HIDALGO (Diario 16)	CESAR SANTOS FONTENLA (Cambio 16)	VICENTE MOLINA FOIX (Fotogramas)	CARLOS PUMARES (Antena 3)	ROBERTO OLTRA FELIX CABEZ (COPE)
1. Queen Kelly	★★★★★		★★★★★	★★★★★	★★★★	★★★★★		★★★★
2. Cotton Club	★★★★	★★★★	★★★★★	★★★★★	★★★★★	★★★★	★★★★★	★★★★★
3. La rosa púrpura de El Cairo	★★★★	★★★★★	★★★★★	★★★★★	★★★★★	★★★	★★★★	★★★★
4. Elígeme	★★★	★★★	★★★	★★★★	★★★★	★★★★★		★★★★★
5. Papá está en viaje de negocios	★★★★	★★★	★★★★★	★★★★	★★★	o	★★★	★★★
6. En pleno corazón	★★★	★★★	★★★	★★★	★★★	★★★		★★★
7. Sé infiel y no mires con quién	★★	★★	★★★	★★★★	★★★	★★★		★★★
8. Silverado	★★	★★★	★★★	★★	★★★			★★★★
9. Regreso al futuro		★★★	★★★	★★	★★★	★★		★★★★
10. Buscando a Susan desesperadamente	★★★	★★	★★★	★★★	★★★	★	★★★	★★★★
11. El caballero del dragón		★★★		★★	★★	★★		★★★★
12. La corte de Faraón	★★★	★★★	★★★	★★	★★★	★★	o	★★★★
13. Coronel Redl	★★★	★★		★★★		★		★★
14. Noche de miedo		★★	★★	★	★★		★★★	★★
15. Legend		★★★		★★	★	★		★★★
16. Chico conoce chica		★★			★	★★		★★★
17. Pesadilla en Elm Street	★★	★	★★	★	★★		★★	★★
18. La pasión de China Blue	o	★	★	o	★	★	★	★★★
19. Santa Claus	★	★		o	o			★★

NOTA.—«Las estrellas de la Guía» se confecciona mediante consulta directa y telefónica con los especialistas de los distintos medios de difusión. El orden de las películas se establece según media aritmética entre número de estrellas y número de críticos que han votado.

This chart summarizes the opinions of various movie critics who are identified by name and place of employment (newspapers, television stations, and so on). The opinions are shown with stars.

A section of slightly longer reviews appears on pages 158-159—also a type of summary—that accompany the chart. Read any four entries of interest to you. What specific information do they have in common?

Now read any four additional reviews for films that are on the chart. Is it possible to tell from these summaries what number of stars a film received?

Each of these short reviews includes several pieces of important information for a moviegoer: title (in Spanish and in the original, if necessary); year; production company; length; film category; country of origin; director; cast; plot summary; audience restrictions, where appropriate; and a list of theaters playing the movie. However, the entries do not include critical evaluations. That information has been summarized in the chart. These movie reviews offer a very good way to see how your own knowledge about something affects your comprehension of written material. You may have selected the entries you already read on the basis of your previous knowledge about the movies, since your interest in those movies is understandably greater. In addition, your expectations of understanding plot summaries for those movies are probably higher. Now read four more summaries, but this time be sure to select films you are *not* familiar with.

You may find it interesting at this point to compare your twelve choices with those of your classmates. How much variation is there among you? What patterns are there in your choices and those of other people? Were your selections based on film genre? Stars? Country of origin?

You may have noticed that movie titles are not always translated directly. *Nightmare on Elm Street* and *Desperately Seeking Susan* have straightforward translations, but *Return to Oz* underwent a slight change in its translation, as did *Fletch*. How might these changes affect a reader's ideas about the film?

Translated movie titles are notoriously unreliable, and the foreign-language versions often seem bizarre to speakers of both languages. Your dictionary can help, but you also have to use your background as a moviegoer. Do you recognize these titles?

MAD MAX MÁS ALLÁ DE LA CÚPULA DEL TRUENO

007 EN LA MIRA DE LOS ASESINOS

LOCA ACADEMIA DE POLICÍA 2

TIBURON III

cine

las películas

estrenos que siguen en cartel

ADMIRADORA SECRETA («Secret admirer»). 1985. Lauren. Comedia. USA. Dir.: David Greenwalt. Con C. Thomas Howell, Lori Loughli y Kelly Preston. Un adolescente recibe el último día de curso una apasionada y anónima carta de amor. Comienza a investigar entre sus amigas y las chicas a las que conoce y esto da lugar a numerosos enredos. Mayores 13 años. **Proyecciones y Tivoli.**

BELLS («Llamada mortal»). 1981. 1 h. 33 m. Kalia. Suspense. Canad. Dir.: Michael Anderson. Con Richard Chamberlain, John Houseman y Sara Bostford. A través de una llamada de teléfono comienzan a ser asesinadas una serie de personas. El tutor de una de las víctimas comienza a investigar por su cuenta, ya que la policía cree que las muertes se han producido por un fallo cardíaco. Mayores 18 años. **Azul y Luchana 2.**

BUSCANDO A SUSAN DESESPERADAMENTE («Desesperately seeking Susan».) 1984. 1 h. 45 m. Lauren. Comedia. USA. Dir.: Susan Seidelman. Con Rosanna Arquette, Madonna y Aidan Quinn. Una mujer, atraída por un extraño anuncio en un periódico, decide seguir todo tipo de pistas y correr aventuras tratando de encontrar a la chica desaparecida a la que busca a través del anuncio. Tolerada. **Madrid 1.**

EL CABALLERO DEL DRAGON. 1985. 1 h. 30 m. Warner. Fantástica. Esp. Dir.: Fernando Colomo. Con Klaus Kinski, Fernando Rey y Miguel Bosé. En plena Edad Media, un extraterrestre desciende con su nave a la Tierra y se enamora de una princesa. Su romance tratará de ser impedido por una corte de villanos. Tolerada. **Avenida.**

LA CIUDAD Y LOS PERROS. 1985. 2 h. 5 m. Taurus. Drama. Perú. Dir.: Francisco J. Lombardi. Con Pablo Serra, Gustavo Bueno y Juan Manuel Ochoa. En la Academia militar de Lima se produce la muerte de un joven cadete y las tensiones estallan revelando la corrupción y las humillaciones que se esconden tras las apariencias. Adaptación de la novela de Mario Vargas Llosa. Mayores 18 años. **Madrid 4.**

COCOON. 1985. 1 h. 59 m. Incine. Comedia. USA. Dir.: Ron Howard. Con Don Ameche, Brian Dennehy y Steve Guttenberg. Cuatro alienígenas que han venido a la Tierra para recuperar unas crisálidas devuelven la juventud, la fuerza física y las ganas de vivir a un grupo de ancianos internados en una residencia. Tolerada. **Luna 1 y Minicine Majadahonda** (lunes a jueves).

COMMANDO. 1985. 1 h. 40 m. Incine. Acción. USA. Dir.: Mark L. Lester. Con Arnold Schwarznegger, Rae Dawn Chong y Dan Bdaya. La hija de un jefe de comandos retirado es secuestrada por un viejo enemigo del padre. Ante tal situación éste decide volver al combate. Mayores 18 años. **Bilbao, Consulado, Garden, Liceo, Palacio de la Prensa, Princesa, Vergara, Versalles y Victoria.**

CORONEL REDL. 1985. 2 h. 20 m. Araba. Drama. Hungría. Dir.: Istvan Szabo. Con Klaus María Brandauer, Gudrun Landgrebe y Armin Muller Sthal. La historia de Alfred Redl, de familia humilde, judío y homosexual, que consiguió, gracias a su astucia y falta de escrúpulos, alcanzar los más altos puestos en el ejército del Imperio austrohúngaro. Mayores 13 años. **Narváez y Roxy B.**

LA CORTE DE FARAON. 1985. 1 h. 47 m. Incine. Comedia. Esp. Dir.: José Luis García Sánchez. Con Ana Belén, Fernando Fernán-Gómez y Antonio Banderas. A finales de los años 40 una compañía de aficionados intenta sortear a la censura para poder montar la famosa obra musical «La corte del faraón», que debido a sus atrevimientos políticos, eróticos y religiosos ha sido prohibida. Mayores 13 años. **Castilla** (lunes a miércoles), **Minicine 1 y Multicine Pozuelo.**

COTTON CLUB («The Cotton Club»). 1985. 2 h. 12 m. Filmayer Policiaca. USA. Dir.: Francis Ford Coppola. Con Richard Gere, Diane Lane y Gregory Hines. Retrato y evocación de una época, finales de los años 20 en América, a través del ambiente y los personajes que desfilan por el mítico cabaret de jazz situado en Harlem y conocido como el Cotton Club. Mayores 13 años. **Minicine Majadahonda** (viernes a domingo), **Multicine Pozuelo** (lunes a jueves) **y Peñalver.**

CHICO CONOCE CHICA («Boy meets girl»). 1983. 1 h. 44 m. Musidora. Comedia. Fra. Dir.: Leos Carax. Con Denis Lavant, Mireill Perrier y Carrol Brooks. Un muchacho que aspira a dirigir cine y al que ha abandonado la novia se enamora de otra chica a lo largo de una noche, pero el posible romance acabará mal. **Alphaville 2.**

D.A.R.Y.L. 1985. Filmayer. Aventuras. USA. Dir.: Simon Wincer. Con Mary Beth Hurt, Michael McKean y Kathryn Walker. Un niño con un misterioso pasado es adoptado por una familia y posteriormente es sometido a diversas pruebas científicas. Tolerada. **Juan de Austria y Palacio de la Música 1.**

DOS SUPERPOLICIAS EN MIAMI. 1 h. 51 m. Filmayer. Aventuras. Ita. Dir.: Bruno Corbucci. Con Terence Hill, Bud Spencer y Buffy Dee. Dos policías que actúan con métodos heterodoxos se enfrentan a todo tipo de delincuentes que pululan por Miami. **California, Cid Campeador, La Vaguada M-2, Luna 2 y Minicine 3.**

ELIGEME («Choose me»). 1985. Iberoamericana. Comedia. USA. Dir.: Alan Rudolph. Con Genevieve Bujold, Keith Carradine y Lesley Ann Warren. En un bar pintoresco se da cita todo tipo de gente, desde putas, tipos desquiciados y oyentes de un consultorio radiofónico. Todos buscan amor. **Alphaville 3.**

EN PLENO CORAZON («Mitten in ins herz»). 1983. 1 h. 31 m. Musidora. Drama. Alem. Dir.: Doris Dorrie. Con Beate Jensen, Josef Bierbichler y Gabrielle Litty. A una dependienta de un supermercado que ha sido expulsada de su trabajo, un hombre le propone darle techo, comida y un sueldo mensual a cambio de nada. La extraña relación inicial se va deteriorando progresivamente porque el hombre no se comunica con ella a ningún nivel. **Alphaville 4.**

EXPLORADORES («Explorers»). 1985. 1 h. 50 m. Incine. Aventuras. USA. Dir.: Joe Dante. Con Ethan Hawke, River Phoenix y Jason Presson. Tres niños apasionados de la ciencia-ficción y de las computadoras construyen una nave espacial con chatarra y fracasan en su intento, pero al dormirse su sueño les envía al más fantástico viaje a través de las estrellas. Tolerada. **Conde Duque, Imperial y La Vaguada M-2.**

FLETCH, EL CAMALEON («Fletch»). 1984. 1 h. 35 m. Comedia. CIC. USA. Dir.: Michael Ritchie. Con Chevy Chase, Joe Don Baker y Dana Wheeler Nicholson. A un reportero que acostumbra a adoptar identidades falsas para llevar a cabo sus investigaciones se le ofrece por equivocación una fuerte suma para que cometa un homicidio. A raíz de esta proposición se ve envuelto en una madeja de situaciones misteriosas y aparentemente sin lógica. Mayores 13 años. **Multicine Pozuelo.**

LABERINTO DE PASIONES. 1982. 1 h. 40 m. Musidora. Comedia. Esp. Dir.: Pedro Almodóvar. Con Cecilia Roth, Imanol Arias y Helga Liné. Sexilia, una joven erotómana, encuentra a Riza Niro, el heredero de un derrocado emperador árabe. Su historia de amor es una de las varias que cuenta la película. Mayores 18 años. **Alphaville 4** (viernes y sábado, madrugada).

LEGEND. 1985. 1 h. 36 m. Incine. Fantástica. G. B. Dir.: Ridley Scott. Con Tom Cruise, Mia Sara y Tim Curry. Un muchacho, en compañía de un grupo de enanitos, duendes, unicornios y hadas busca a la princesa a la que ama, que ha sido secuestrada por el Príncipe de las Tinieblas. Tolerada. **La Vaguada M-2, Paz, Real Cinema y Richmond.**

LAS MINAS DEL REY SALOMON («The Salomon's Mines»). 1985. Izaro. Aventuras. USA. Dir.: J. Lee Thompson. Con Richard Chamberlain, Sharon Stone y Herbert Lom. Una nueva versión de la famosa novela de H. Rider Haggard. El aventurero Quatermain es contratado para que encuentre en la jungla africana a un arqueólogo desaparecido, y la búsqueda le llevará a las legendarias minas del rey Salomón. Tolerada. **Callao, Carlos III, Roxy A y Velázquez.**

LA MUJER DE ROJO («The woman in red»). 1984. 1 h. 30 m. Lauren. Comedia. USA. Dir.: Gene Wilder. Con Gene Wilder, Charles Grodin y Joseph Bologna. Un hombre casado se obsesiona con una seductora modelo. Mayores 13 años. **Madrid 3.**

NOCHE DE MIEDO («Fright nights»). 1985. Nueva. Terror. USA. Dir.: Tom Holland. Con Chris Sarandon, William Ragsdale y Amanda Bearse. Un muchacho aficionado a las películas de terror está convencido de que en la casa de al lado vive un vampiro, pero cuando se lo cuenta a su familia, novia y amigos, nadie le cree. Mayores 13 años. **Avenida (Alcobendas)** (viernes a domingo), **La Vaguada M-2 y Rialto.**

OJOS INDISCRETOS. 1984. 1 h. 31 m. Orion. Suspense. Canad. Dir.: William Fruet. Con Kenneth Gilman, Dayle Haddon y Barbara Law. Un joven que pasa las noches contemplando en la oscuridad los juegos eróticos de una vecina descubre un día que ésta ha sido asesinada. A partir de ahí es perseguido al mismo tiempo por el criminal y por la policía. Mayores 18 años. **La Vaguada M-2, Luchana 3 y Rex.**

OLVIDAR MOZART («L'Vergesst Mozart»). 1985. Barcino. Drama. Alem. Dir.: Slavo Luther. Con Armin Muller Sthal y Catarina Raake. En la agonía de Mozart, sus amigos, discípulos y familiares que dudan entre ellos de la posible culpabilidad de alguno en la muerte del genial compositor comienzan a acusarse y la policía interviene. **Bellas Artes.**

cine

OZ, UN MUNDO FANTASTICO («Return to Oz»). 1985. 1 h. 49 m. Fantástica. Filmayer. G. B. Dir.: Walter Murch. Con Nicol Williamson, Jean Marsh y Piper Laurie. Dorothy, la niña que protagonizaba «El mago de Oz», vive innumerables aventuras en la Ciudad Encantada en compañía de El Espantapájaros, El Hombre de Lata, El León Miedoso, El Rey Gnomo y demás legendarios personajes. Tolerada. **Benlliure, Cartago, Infante, Lope de Vega y Novedades.**

PAPA ESTA EN VIAJE DE NEGOCIOS («Otac na sluzbenom putu»). 1985. 2 h. Surf Film. Drama. Yug. Dir.: Emir Kusturica. Con Moreno de Bartolli, Miki Manojlovic y Mirjana Karanovic. A través de la mirada de un niño de seis años cuyo padre ha sido encarcelado se analiza la situación de Yugoslavia durante los 50. **Alphaville 1.**

LA PASION DE CHINA BLUE («Crimes of passion»). 1985. 1 h. 30 m. Lauren. Drama. USA. Dir.: Ken Russell. Con Kathleen Turner, Anthony Perkins y John Laughlin. La historia de una mujer que mantiene doble personalidad. Su trabajo como diseñadora de modas y su existencia tranquila se transforma alternativamente en feroz devoradora de hombres especializada en prácticas sadomasoquistas. Mayores 18 años. **Madrid 2 y Minicine 2.**

PESADILLA EN ELM STREET («Nightmare on Elm street»). 1985. 1 h. 40 m. Paraíso. Fantástica. USA. Dir.: Wes Craven. Con John Saxon, Rones Blakley y Heather Langenkamp. Un grupo de jóvenes descubren repentinamente que les asalta la misma pesadilla. En ella, un hombre con el rostro desfigurado les acosa tan insistentemente que, saliéndose del sueño, acaba asesinando a dos de ellos. Una mujer puede detener la pesadilla si es capaz de despertarse a tiempo. Mayores 18 años. **Torre de Madrid.**

QUEEN KELLY («La reina Kelly»). 1929. 1 h. 30 m. Buho. Drama. USA. Dir.: Erich von Stroheim. Con Gloria Swanson, Seena Owen y Walter Byron. La historia de amor entre un príncipe a punto de casarse con la reina y una chica que está interna en un convento. Una obra maestra del cine mudo. Tolerada. **Rosales.**

REGRESO AL FUTURO («Back to the future»). 1985. 1 h. 50 m. UIP. Fantástica. USA. Dir.: Robert Zemeckis. Con Michael J. Fox, Christopher Lloyd y Lea Thompson. Convencido por un científico excéntrico, un joven se introduce en un coche que le transporta al año 1955 y a la misma ciudad en la que vive. Allí conocerá a sus futuros padres y deberá conseguir que éstos se enamoren para que sea posible su nacimiento y el regreso al presente. Tolerada. **Cristal, El Españoleto, Gran Vía, Multicine Majadahonda, Palafox y Salamanca.**

LA ROSA PURPURA DE EL CAIRO. («The Purple Rose of Cairo».) 1985. 1 h., 22 m. Lauren. Comedia. USA. Dir.: Woody Allen. Con Mia Farrow, Jeff Daniels y Danny Aiello. En la época de la Depresión, una soñadora mujer, que trabaja de camarera y cuyo marido la explota y engaña, encuentra alivio a su desgracia contemplando cine. Un día se produce el milagro: el protagonista de la película sale de la pantalla y se dirige a ella. Tolerada. **Amaya, Gayarre, Pompeya y Sainz de Baranda.**

SANGRE FACIL («Blood simple»). 1984. 1 h. 39 m. Primer Plano. Suspense. USA. Dir.: Joel Coen. Con John Getz, Frances McDormand y Dan Hedaya. El dueño de un bar al que su esposa ha abandonado por otro hombre le encarga a un detective que asesine a ambos. Mayores 18 años. **Alphaville 3 (viernes y sábado sesión de madrugada).**

SANTA CLAUS. 1985. 1 h. 51 m. Incine. Fantástica. G. B. Dir.: Jean Jeannot Szwarc. Con Dudley Moore, John Lithgow y David Huddleston. La historia del mítico Santa Claus, el portador de sueños y regalos que aparece en Navidad para hacer felices a los niños, a través de los tiempos. Tolerada. **Candilejas, Capitol, Carlton, Europa, La Vaguada M-2, Luchana 1 y Urquijo.**

SE INFIEL Y NO MIRES CON QUIEN. 1985. 1 h. 30 m. Iberoamericana. Comedia. Esp. Dir.: Fernando Trueba. Con Ana Belén, Carmen Maura y Antonio Resines. Un enredo enloquecido alrededor de dos socios, sus esposas, sus amantes y su negocio. Basada en la obra teatral del mismo título de Ray Cooney y John Chapman. Tolerada. **Coliseum y La Vaguada.**

SILVERADO. 1985. 2 h. 15 m. Nueva. Oeste. USA. Dir.: Lawrence Kasdan. Con Kevin Kline, Scott Glenn y Rosanna Arquette. Cuatro hombres que se han encontrado en circunstancias peligrosas se hacen amigos y llegan al pueblo donde viven las familias de dos de ellos. Allí deberán enfrentarse a los caciques y pistoleros que tiranizan a la gente. Tolerada. **Palacio de la Música 2.**

TARON Y EL CALDERO MAGICO. 1985. 1 h. 21 m. Filmayer. Fantástica. USA. Dir.: Ted Berman y Richard Rich. Una fantasía épica en dibujos animados que cuenta la saga heroica de un muchacho llamado Taron. Este debe impedir que un malvado rey vikingo se haga dueño del caldero mágico, una misteriosa fuerza capaz de generar un ejército de guerreros sobrenaturales. Tolerada. **Alcalá Palace, Alexandra, Aluche, Aragón, Bulevar, Capri, España Cinema, Excelsior y La Vaguada M-2.**

Do the reviewers agree with the advertizers about the quality of this film? In the capsule review, you will find the word **soñadora.** What word on this poster has the same root?

Some movie titles, like *Legend* and *Cocoon*, are not translated at all. For fun, try your hand at the task of title translation by giving appropriate English or Spanish translations to movie titles that are not translated in the reviews.

Now we'll move on to something slightly longer, but still associated with movies. Remember, you may have to tolerate a certain amount of uncertainty and ambiguity as you read, but the important thing at this stage is to understand as much as possible. Identify the sections that would require more effort if you intended to read for greater detail, and always keep your purpose in mind. For this reading, you want to be able to summarize the reviewer's comments.

If you are not familiar with the movie *Legend*, read or reread the short summary and think about similar movies. If you are familiar with it, read or reread the summary and think about what you already know about the film.

Now think about movie reviews you have read in English and complete Exercise H.

Exercise H.

1. The following are typically found in a film review. Place them in the order in which you would expect them to occur.

   _____ a. plot summary
   _____ b. reviewer's recommendations about seeing the film
   _____ c. comments on direction, scenery, and film techniques
   _____ d. general comments about the film season or industry

2. Are some of these elements less likely to occur than others? Which?

   _____

3. What other elements could you expect to find in a review?

   _____

Now practice the *Reading Strategy* on a review of *Legend*, also from the **Guía del Ocio.** Here is the sequence of *Reading Strategy* steps to follow.

1. Look over the review for helpful format cues and vocabulary that is known or whose meanings can be guessed.
2. Skim to determine the general organization and content.
3. Formulate a set of mental questions that you expect the passage to answer.
4. Read the first sentences of each paragraph to gather additional information about the organization.
5. Think about the topic, the most likely vocabulary to be associated with it, and the probable content. Reread the first and last sentences of each paragraph.
6. Number the paragraphs and begin to decode. Work paragraph by paragraph, identifying verb cores and important nouns and using your dictionary to make sure you understand how they are related to each other. As you work through each paragraph, make a note of the central idea contained in it and think about the overall organization.

crítica

Fernando Méndez-Leite

DEFINITIVAMENTE las Navidades han sustituido al Domingo de Resurrección como fecha clave en la exhibición cinematográfica. Un aluvión de estrenos se precipita en las pantallas madrileñas, y si este material es lo mejor de que disponen las nunca bien ponderadas multinacionales, aviados estamos. ¿Es que ya no va a haber más que películas para niños? ¿Es que ya nunca se estrenarán películas como «Viaggio in Italia», «El buscavidas», «Días de vino y rosas», «Esplendor en la hierba» o «Ma nuit chez Maud»? ¿Es que la vida es tan pobre que sólo nos queda la fantasía más reaccionaria? Parece ser que de ahora en adelante ya nunca podremos ver más que películas de grandes presupuestos, de magníficos efectos especiales, de cuidadísimas ambientaciones, que ocultan el vacío absoluto. Para aquellos que odiamos la ciencia-ficción, las blandenguerías, los buenos sentimientos y las gamberradas de adolescentes ignorantes y neofascistas, sólo quedan los «westerns» y policiacos de la televisión o el reducto verdaderamente ejemplar de los Alphaville, en donde se pueden ver películas tan bonitas como «Corrientes de amor», «Sangre fácil» o «Tierra de nadie».

De entre todas las grandes superproducciones de estas fiestas, «Legend» es el título a priori más atractivo. Su autor, **Ridley Scott**, ha firmado anteriormente tres películas de indiscutible interés. Aunque personalmente sólo admiro la primera de ellas, «Los duelistas», reconozco que «Alien» y «Blade Runner» poseían un ritmo, un clima y un tratamiento visual de extraordinaria originalidad y potencia. «Legend» es una película muy bien hecha, aunque no tan bien contada. Es un cuento infantil ambientado en un mundo fantástico en

Director: Ridley Scott.
Guión: William Hjortsberg.
Fotografía: Alex Thomson.
Música: Jerry Goldsmith.
Producción: Arnold Milchan y Tim Hampton.
Intérpretes: Tom Cruise, Mia Sara, Tim Curry, David Bennent, Alice Playten, Billy Barty y Cork Hubbert.
Locales de estreno: Paz, Real Cinema, Richmond y La Vaguada, sala 3.

«Legend»

el que se enfrentan a muerte las fuerzas del bien, encarnadas en una relamida princesa y un joven y saltarín habitante del bosque, y las fuerzas del mal, capitaneadas por un pintoresco «Señor de las tinieblas», colorado y con gigantescos cuernos, que se da un aire a **Tino Casal**. En ayuda de los primeros acuden un inquietante niño del bosque, una hada ambigua y voladora, a medio camino entre **Campanilla** y **Hanna Schygulla**, y un par de duendes en función de graciosos. Al servicio del Señor de las Tinieblas hay tres monstruosas criaturas que cabalgan por el bosque destruyendo todo lo que encuentran a su paso, y un divertido y repugnante habitante del fondo del lago pantanoso, con el nombre de Señorita Meg, y con voraces intenciones.

Ridley Scott está siempre preocupado por la creación de mundos imaginarios, progresivamente más alejados de la realidad. En esta película hay un exhaustivo trabajo de ambientación, de decoración, de maquillaje, de invención de todo tipo de efectos visuales. Abundan los primeros planos, los continuos juegos entre la luz y las sombras, los ralentís supuestamente embellecedores. Todo es recargado, cursi, blando. Para colmo, hay un par de canciones dobladas al castellano, ahora que entramos en el Mercado Común y no salimos de la OTAN. La pareja protagonista es del género almibarado, se miran tiernamente, se besan y él decide enseñar a su princesa el gran secreto del bosque: los unicornios. Como justo castigo a la transgresión, la primavera, los duendecillos y el polen quedarán congelados para siempre, y en la Tierra reinará la tiranía de la oscuridad. ¿Parábola de la lucha entre dictadura y libertad?, ¿alegoría sobre las consecuencias del pecado carnal?, ¿simple y llana vacuidad esteticista? Vayan ustedes a saber.

Si les gustan las películas que tratan de unicornios, hadas, gnomos, monstruos de todos los tamaños; si les divierten las llamadas películas de evasión, de fantasía, de efectos especiales; si son ustedes inasequibles al desaliento, vayan a ver «Legend», esa película tan bien hecha. Si quieren ver una película buena, repesquen «Cotton Club», «Elígeme» o «La rosa púrpura de El Cairo». Pero, como dice Ana Belén en la «tele», por favor, no se desanimen y vayan al cine.

Check your decoding success with Exercise I.

 Exercise I.

1. The following statements summarize the individual paragraphs of this review. Match them to the number of the paragraph they represent.

    _____ a. If you want to see an escapist fantasy, *Legend* is a well-made one.

    _____ b. The characters of *Legend* are fantastic and supernatural be-ings.

    _____ c. Most movies these days seem to be big-budget spectaculars, intended only for kids.

    _____ d. The good-evil conflict in *Legend* is overshadowed by the di-rector's emphasis on visual effects.

2. Which paragraph(s) contain the material summarized in the capsule re-view you read earlier? _____

3. On the basis of this review, how many stars do you think F. Méndez-Leite assigned to *Legend?* (Refer to the chart you saw earlier for the meaning of the stars.) _____

4. Using the sentences given above in question 1, your notes, and your un-derstanding of the passage, write a brief summary (under fifty words) of the review. You may write in either Spanish or English, according to your teacher's instructions.

At this point in the development of your reading skills, the technique of writ-ing—or at least thinking of—a summary is a very useful one. It helps you see how the parts of a longer passage relate to each other. It provides a compre-hension check as well, since the level of comprehension necessary to construct a good summary is about the same as that required for most reading pur-poses. A summary also serves as a guide for your attention if you do go on to do word-for-word decoding. Your summary can help you formulate a new series of questions to guide your closer reading.

Dictionary Interlude
Dealing with Idioms

You have already learned that even when you know the appropriate mean-ings for all the words in a phrase, the phrase may still not be entirely clear, often because it is intended metaphorically. In order to understand writing that incorporates metaphors and other kinds of nonliteral associations, read-ers must learn to think imaginatively. The more you read, the more easily you will understand writing of this kind. There is a special class of phrases in any language that often originated as metaphorical expressions but have become commonplace. These specialized expressions are called *idioms*. Idioms are fixed phrases of more than one word whose meanings cannot be inferred sim-ply by knowing the meanings of the individual elements. A speaker (and a learner) must know the meaning the whole phrase has when it is used to-gether. When words are used in this way, they are said to be *idiomatic*. An example of an idiom in English—which is rich with them—is the expression "to kick the bucket." The meanings of idioms may be very specialized, and idioms are impossible to translate literally. Idioms may be difficult for a beginning student of a language to understand because, although two languages may both have idioms for the same idea, the metaphors in each idiom are likely to be quite different.

In this Dictionary Interlude, you will work with idioms in both Spanish and English. The purpose of this practice is to help you learn to think about idiomatic expressions and other kinds of metaphorical or imaginative writing. Let's begin with some common English idioms.

Below is a list of English idioms. For each one, think of a nonidiomatic, or literal, expression that conveys the same meaning. Choose one that corresponds precisely, and be sure that your equivalent is not an idiom. For example, the nonidiomatic meaning of "to kick the bucket" is "to die (suddenly);" expressions like "to buy the ranch/farm" or "to croak" are idiomatic equivalents!

1. You took the words right out of my mouth.
2. She really put her foot in her mouth that time!
3. I urged him to make a clean breast of it.
4. Who let the cat out of the bag?
5. The marathon runner hit the wall after eighteen miles.
6. So he finally popped the question!
7. I just can't make up my mind about which course to take.
8. After they sold him down the river, he vowed revenge.

The easiest way to turn an English idiom into a Spanish phrase with an equivalent meaning is to look up a translation of the literal English version. For example, to render "pop the question" in Spanish, you might look up "to propose (marriage)." Good bilingual dictionaries help their users deal with idioms by including some idiomatic expressions, usually in the entry for the key word in the idiom. For example, you might find "sell down the river" listed as a phrase in the English section of your dictionary as part of the entry for "sell" or "river." Often the Spanish version given in such cases is really just a translation equivalent for the nonidomatic version. In the case of "sell down the river," for example, you might find simply **traicionar.**

Many English idioms do have common Spanish idiomatic counterparts. Their origins are often very obscure and, if not overused, they add a pleasing creative dimension to written or spoken communication. In some varieties of Spanish, for instance, the phrase **pelar el ajo** *(peel the garlic)* is used to mean *to die suddenly.* **Anoche Juan peló el ajo** is the equivalent of *John kicked the bucket last night.* Depending on your dictionary, you might be able to find the phrase **pelar el ajo.** Try looking it up.

Exercise J.

The following idioms have Spanish equivalents that are also idioms. Use your bilingual dictionary—both parts!—to help you locate Spanish idioms with the same meanings. Once you have identified the Spanish idiom, translate its parts to get a literal meaning. (Do not be upset if you cannot find everything you are looking for. Just continue working and then check your results with a classmate who has a different dictionary.)

1. to be raining cats and dogs
2. to be in the dark
3. between the devil and the deep blue sea
4. to kill two birds with one stone

It is important to become aware of the frequency of idiomatic language in what you read. Your major task as a reader of Spanish is not the translation of English idioms; it is to be aware of idiomatic language in a passage and its effects on your comprehension. If you can understand all the individual words in a phrase but the combination of meanings does not seem to make any sense, you may be reading an idiom. The best strategy, if you decide that understanding the meaning fully is sufficiently important to the context, is to use your dictionary to try to locate the idiomatic usage and its meaning. Spanish has a great many idioms and the more you read, the more familiar you will become with them.

Exercise K.

For each Spanish idiom below, give its literal meaning and its English meaning, based on the information your dictionary provides.

1. buscar tres pies al gato _____
2. dar calabazas _____
3. meter la cuchara _____
4. sudar la gota gorda _____
5. consultar con la almohada _____
6. poner el grito en el cielo _____
7. quedarse para vestir santos _____
8. no poder ver (a uno) ni en pintura _____

Remember that idioms, and many other common expressions we think of as clichés, are really frozen metaphors. Sometimes you may suspect that you are dealing with an idiomatic or metaphorical expression but your dictionary is of no help at all. Clever writers create novel metaphors all the time and those expressions will not be in any dictionary. In such a case, your only solution may be to ask for help from a native speaker or an instructor. Meanwhile, try to interpret meaning from context as best you can. Above all, expect such problems from time to time and do not let them discourage you from reading. Remember, the more you read, the more you will become familiar with the use of idioms in Spanish and the less difficulty they will cause you.

Applying the Reading Strategy

Many people find that reading is a good way to spend leisure time. In the final section of this unit, you will examine some materials that deal with books. Begin with this store directory from a large bookstore in Madrid.

Exercise L.

On what floor of the bookstore and in which category would you expect to find each of the following books?

_____ 1. *Historia del Uruguay*
_____ 2. *El terrorismo en España*
_____ 3. *Diccionario de la economía*
_____ 4. *Antología de leyendas bolivianas*
_____ 5. *Maravillas naturales del mundo*
_____ 6. *Dragones, dioses y espíritus de la mitología china*
_____ 7. *Los pueblos más bellos de España*
_____ 8. *La obra pictórica completa de Velazquez*
_____ 9. *El Hobbit* (in paperback)
_____ 10. *Entre líneas*

The next reading selection consists of a set of short book reviews (including a review of an issue of a fantasy magazine). First, think about the probable organization and content of such reviews, based on your experience with similar materials in English. Use the *Reading Strategy* to preread and then decode each review. Your goal is to discover basic information about the content of each reviewed item as well as the reviewer's opinion of it. Don't overlook the chart of best-sellers. In which of the two main categories (**Creación** and **Pensamiento**) would each of the books in Exercise L and those in the reviews belong?

The questions in Exercise M are designed to help you check your comprehension of the reviews.

Exercise M.

Mandrágora y el pirata

1. What parts of the review suggest that the reviewer thinks this issue is an improvement over earlier ones? _____

2. According to the reviewer, which four groups of readers will find something to interest them in this issue?

   _____

3. What noun is referred to by **les** in the first line? _____

4. Does the reviewer really like the magazine? _____

El emperador

5. Who is referred to by **sus** in the opening sentence? _____

6. How many stories are contained in the book? _____

7. According to the reviewer, how does the style of **El emperador** differ from that of Forsyth's earlier books? _____

Revistas

«Mandrágora y el pirata». Número 7. 48 páginas. 150 pesetas.

Aunque no les haya gustado ni «Vecinos» ni «Tres por Cuatro», los chicos de estas dos revistas, refundidas hace ya tiempo en una, merecen cierta confianza, especialmente cuando, en la lista de las «películas que nos gustaría ver», incluyen pequeñas maravillas como «Lola Montes», de Max Ophuls; «Vampyr», de Dreyer; «Centauros del desierto», de John Ford, o «Tierra de faraones», de Howard Hawks. Los fanáticos del esteticismo decadente disfrutarán con el editorial dedicado al «Ludwing» de Visconti. Los de las narraciones breves, con el relato «Irene en las afueras». Los cinéfilos, con la historia sobre Melies y el comentario sobre Jean Vigo. Y los adictos a la revista, con el artículo sobre Mandrágora de Tessa Duncan. A subrayar el mejorado aspecto del número, con mejor papel y cuidados colorines en la portada, y una confección menos deslabazada de lo habitual.

Libros

«El emperador», de Frederick Forsyth. Plaza y Janés. 269 páginas.

Quizá aburrido de sus multitudinarios éxitos

(«Chacal», «Odessa», «Los perros de la guerra» y «La alternativa del diablo»), el irlandés Forsyth ha ensayado un nuevo género para él: el relato corto. Porque «El emperador» no es sino una de las ocho historias —de temática muy dispar— que componen el último

libro de este fabricante de «best-sellers». El libro, en su conjunto, tiene menos «pegada» popular que los títulos arriba citados; de hecho será posiblemente una «obra menor» de Forsyth. Sin embargo, «El presidente» y las otras siete historias de este libro están llenas de agudeza y están escritas con un estilo literario bastante más que aceptable. Forsyth, periodista de agencia, demostró talento para fabricar «historias que devorar» y ahora evidencia que también sabe escribir relatos con los que pasar un rato agradable, sencillamente.

«Todos los espejos», de Baltasar Porcel. Colección Austral. Espasa Calpe. 252 páginas.

El mallorquín Baltasar Porcel vuelve a sorprendernos con un libro atractivo, lleno de fuerza y sugerencias. Su última obra es una colección de pequeños relatos, «fugaz sucesión de los instantes», en los que se refleja de manera brillante el microuniverso mítico del autor de «Caballos hacia la noche», «La revolución permanente» y tantos otros libros. En Baltasar Porcel, especialmente en esta obra, no se sabe qué admirar más, si la imaginación sugerente de las historias o el sentido estético de la

narración. El autor se siente subyugado por la palabra, pero no cede a traspasar los límites del clasicismo. Otra cosa es la temática, casi barroca, de sus historias, aunque siempre dulcificada por el espíritu de moderación mediterránea que tanto pesa sobre Porcel. El libro tiene un prólogo relativamente extenso de Jorge Rodríguez Padrón, que es un trabajo excepcional sobre la figura literaria de Baltasar Porcel.

«El terrorismo en España», de Alejandro Muñoz Alonso. Colección Tablero, de Planeta y el Instituto de Estudios Económicos.

La colección Tablero ha empezado a andar con fuerza y está sacando al mercado un título casi por quincena. La obra de Muñoz Alonso lleva como subtítulo «El terror frente a la convivencia pluralista en libertad», que ya explica con claridad cuál es el enfoque al tratar un tema tan variado y con tan múltiples aspectos. Alejandro Muñoz Alonso, a medio camino entre el sociólogo, el historiador y el periodista, ha escrito un libro principalmente desde una óptica política. Hay rigor en la información, ecuanimidad en los planteamientos y brillantez en los juicios. Es una obra de síntesis más que analítica, pero su aportación al conocimiento del tema y su valoración político-social son sumamente estimables.

Libros más vendidos en la semana

Título	Autor	Editor	Puesto anterior	Semanas presente
Creación				
1. El Hobbit	Tolkien	Edhasa/Minotauro	1	4
2. Un día volveré	Marsé	Plaza & Janés	3	7
3. El emperador	Forsythe	Plaza & Janés	2	4
4. Los gozos y las sombras	Torrente Ballester	Alianza/Bruguera	4	2
5. La guerra del fin del mundo	Vargas Llosa	Seix Barral/Plaza & Janés	5	25
Pensamiento				
1. La noche que mataron a Calvo Sotelo	Gibson	Argos-Vergara	2	7
2. Por qué y cómo mataron a Calvo Sotelo	Romero	Planeta	1	4
3. Gárgoris y Habidis	Sánchez Dragó	Argos-Vergara	5	6
4. Nostradamus. Historiador y profeta	Fontbrune	Barcanova	3	19
5. El estado del golpe	Leguineche	Argos-Vergara	—	2

Librerías consultadas:
Antonio Machado (Fernando VI, 17), Aguilar (Serrano, 24), Atlántica (Silva, 32), Casa del Libro (Gran Vía, 29), Corte Inglés (Preciados), Fuentetaja (San Bernardo, 48), Galerías Preciados (Callao), Manzano (Espoz y Mina, 16), Servicio Comercial del Libro (Preciados, 32) y Vips (Velázquez, 84 y 136), de Madrid. Blanco (Villegas, 5), Lázaro (Sierpes, 2) y Sanz (Granada, 2), de Sevilla.

8. What would be a good English equivalent for the expression **historia de devorar?** _____

9. Does the reviewer like this book better than Forsyth's best-sellers? _____

Todos los espejos

10. What two other works by Baltasar Porcel are mentioned by the reviewer? _____

11. What two aspects of this work does the reviewer most admire? _____

12. What contribution is made by the prologue? _____

El terrorismo en España

13. According to the reviewer, what three perspectives does Muñoz Alonso bring to his work? _____

14. What fourth perspective is actually most central to the work? _____

15. What is the major contribution of this work? _____

16. Does the reviewer recommend it? _____

Now practice decoding with a somewhat longer review of a recent novel by Carlos Fuentes, a well-known Mexican writer. **Gringo viejo** is a fictionalized account of the experiences of Ambrose Bierce, an elderly American writer who went to Mexico in 1913 and was never heard from again. Several of Bierce's works are cited by title in the review. According to Fuentes' imagination, Bierce became involved in the Mexican revolution and died by order of the Mexican revolutionary, Pancho Villa. Use Exercise N to guide you through the review.

Exercise N.

1. Preread the review and identify the following information.
   a. the title of the review _____
   b. the author of the review _____
   c. the length of the book _____

2. Examine the review for signs of its organization. Note that there are three short paragraphs and one quite long one. Which paragraph do you expect to contain the meat of the review? _____

3. Read the first line of each paragraph and determine the probable topic of each one. Which two paragraphs seem most likely to contain information about the plot? _____

Suicidio en México

Gringo viejo

Carlos Fuentes. Fondo de Cultura
Económica. Madrid, 1985. 189 páginas.

MARIANO AGUIRRE

En el otoño de 1913, Ambroce Bierce, periodista y narrador norteamericano de 71 años, asmático, cruzó la frontera entre Estados Unidos y México. Llevaba consigo un ejemplar de *El Quijote,* 1.000 dólares en oro, un revólver y un alto grado de cínica desesperanza. Había nacido en Ohio en 1842, luchó en la guerra civil de su país y alternó el periodismo con la narrativa fantástica. (Ver, por ejemplo, *Cuentos de soldados y civiles,* Labor, 1976; *Fábulas de fantasía,* Bosch, 1980, y *Los ojos de la pantera,* Fontamara, 1984.)

Antes de irse a México dejó algunas cartas. A su sobrina le escribió: "Adiós, si oyes que me pusieron contra un muro de piedra mexicano y me despedazaron a tiros, piensa que creo que es una buena manera de dejar la vida (…). Ser un gringo en México ¡eso sí que es eutanasia!". Y a su hija: "En América ya no se puede ir al Este o al Oeste, ni al Norte, la única salida es el Sur".

Carlos Fuentes ya había *dialogado* literariamente con otro escritor norteamericano que también fue a desafiar el infierno en México —Malcolm Lowry— en *La muerte de Artemio Cruz* (como acertadamente señala Juan Lovelock en *Novelistas hispano-americanos hoy,* Taurus, 1976). En su última novela, *Gringo viejo,* repite magistralmente el procedimiento. Fuentes toma tres pilares para construir el libro: lo poco que se sabe de Bierce a partir del cruce de la frontera, varias claves de la obra de este autor norteamericano y las versiones que circularon sobre su asesinato por orden de Pancho Villa. A partir de ahí nace una novela de la que podría-

mos señalar, como mínimo, tres grandes méritos. Primero, es una importante reflexión acerca de la historia, psicología y motivaciones de muchos participantes (simbolizados en el jefe revolucionario Tomás Arroyo) de la revolución mexicana; segundo, como ya es costumbre en su narrativa, maneja hábilmente un lenguaje literario-cinematográfico, siempre innovador y sugerente, que no es un mero juego estilístico, sino la apropiada expresión para una trama que, despejada en las últimas páginas, se nos revela como una gran novela sobre temas universales de la literatura: el amor, la relación del ser humano con la historia y la búsqueda de la propia identidad y el sentido de la vida al confrontarse con un contexto extraño. Y en tercer lugar, una apasionada descripción de los encuentros y desencuentros entre la cultura norteamericana y la mexicana. Todo ello en el contexto doloroso, agobiante de la guerra.

D. Wayne Gunn, en su libro *Escritores norteamericanos y británicos en México* (Fondo de Cultura Económica, Madrid, 1977), contabiliza entre 1805 y 1973 más de 450 novelas, obras de teatro y poemas narrativos, y un número incalculable de cuentos y ensayos sobre México, escritos por ciudadanos de EE UU y el Reino Unido. Malcolm Lowry, **John Reed, Stephen Crane** y **D. H. Lawrence** son algunos de los *grandes* que se vieron impactados por la realidad mexicana. La tesis literaria de Fuentes es que Bierce fue ahí a morir, a buscar, al otro lado del río Grande, el fantasma del protagonista de su cuento *El soldado de caballería en el cielo* que mata a su padre.

The Reading Strategy

Comprehension: Evaluating tone and point of view

Comprehension of what you read is always the goal of the *Reading Strategy*. The early stages of the comprehension process—prereading—taught you to use the cues provided by the layout and context of a passage to guide your search for meaning. The middle stages—the decoding process—taught you to extract even more meaning by paying attention to details of grammar and content. Passages like the ones you have read in earlier units usually convey simple information or convey complex information in simple ways. The comprehension of such information results almost immediately from mastery of the content as you think about prereading cues and the meaning of decoded key clauses.

Skillful reading does not, however, merely mean that you have understood the individual words and phrases in a passage. As we stated in the very first unit, reading is an interactive process, one in which the reader and the writer collaborate in producing the shared meaning. As you move toward reading more complex passages, this collaboration becomes an even more important element in the reading process. In this unit, we will continue to explore aspects of the decoding and comprehension process, using longer passages intended to convey more complex kinds of meaning.

The materials in Unit 8 are of a variety of types, but they share an emphasis on human emotions. You will find that each one exhibits an individual tone and point of view. To fully comprehend the passages, you must be able to identify and evaluate both tone and point of view. Unit 8 will illustrate some techniques to assist you in doing so.

In the course of your work with the *Reading Strategy*, you have become a very proficient dictionary user. In this unit, you will continue to practice dictionary skills and skills to increase your vocabulary. In addition, you will learn some special techniques for handling the language of creative writing.

Our first reading is a questionnaire for psychological self-evaluation taken from a popular Latin American magazine. Such materials have a great many format cues—you have undoubtedly already thought of several likely ones. Before continuing, preread the passage. Do not attempt to decode at this stage, but do remember to use the information contained in titles and subtitles.

Si es usted una persona que verdaderamente posee confianza en sí mismo, no tendrá necesidad de demostrarle nada a su oponente, ni de dejar establecido que es usted quien tiene razón, y si está equivocado.

No se moleste tratando de averiguar cuál es el secreto, la magia, el "don misterioso" que poseen esas mujeres triunfantes: sencillamente, confían en ellas mismas. ¿Y usted...? ¿Posee un alto nivel de autoconfianza, capaz de conducirla al éxito?

Por Jane Clark

En cada multitud hay una... o varias. Esa mujer que es el alma de todas las fiestas; la primera en obtener el puesto que ansía; la primera en conseguir un ascenso. Tiene más admiradores de los que puede atender, y aún así se las arregla para conceder a cada uno un poquito de su tiempo. ¿Qué es lo que posee esta mujer y la hace una triunfadora? Porque tal parece que "eso" es un encanto, una bendición, algo muy misterioso y *especial*...

No se atormente tratando de suponer lo que tiene esa mujer. Es muy sencillo: una gran confianza en ella misma, y ésa es la clave de sus éxitos. ¿Qué tal anda la suya propia? Averigüe por medio de este cuestionario si ¡la importantísima! confianza en usted misma alcanza altos niveles, que la llevarán al éxito, o se encuentra por los suelos... y podría llevarla al desastre.

¿ES ASERTIVA...

PREGUNTAS

1. Se encuentra en una discusión y le consta sin lugar a dudas que usted tiene la razón. Cuando su oponente se resiste a ceder, usted:
a) se marcha y lo deja con la palabra en la boca; no va a conseguir nada insistiendo
b) se aferra a su posición hasta que queda satisfecha
c) admite que quizás usted podría estar equivocada

2. Está citada a las ocho con una amiga para cenar. Ella llega tarde habitualmente y sabe lo mucho que usted detesta esperar. A las ocho y media usted decide:
a) dejarlo pasar y aceptar el hecho de que su amiga no cambiará
b) no esperar más y marcharse
c) cuando su amiga llegue repetirle la forma en que usted siente acerca de esto e insistir en que será la última vez que espera

3. Está en el cine y las personas detrás de usted conversan en voz alta. Usted:
a) se vuelve hacia ellas y las fulmina con la mirada
b) se vuelve y las manda a callar
c) llama al acomodador
d) se marcha y al salir pide que le devuelvan su dinero

4. Acaba de empezar en un trabajo y su jefe la invita a una fiesta de la empresa, esa noche. Usted no se siente bien, así que:
a) ofrece disculpas y se marcha derecho a su casa
b) le pregunta que si es muy importante que usted vaya
c) hace una aparición en la fiesta y se marcha en cuanto considera que es apropiado hacerlo
d) se toma una aspirina y le demuestra a su jefe la resistencia que usted posee, quedándose hasta el final de la fiesta

5. Usted está saliendo con un amigo con quien le interesaría intimar más. ¿Qué haría para averiguar si a él le sucede lo mismo?
a) traer a la conversación el tema de la intimidad y ver cómo piensa
b) explicarle lo que usted siente
c) tratar de aproximársele físicamente y sentir cómo reacciona

6. Al ir a comprar un nuevo equipo estereofónico, usted ve dos modelos de sonido comparable, uno $100 dólares más barato que el otro. El vendedor habla tanto que, en vez de ayudarla, la confunde. Entonces, usted:
a) se guía por su instinto y se compra el más barato
b) busca a alguien más en la tienda que pueda ayudarla
c) va a otra tienda a consultar una opinión enteramente distinta

7. Después de hacer la compra, se mete el vuelto que le han dado en un bolsillo, sin mirar, y cuando llega a su casa descubre que le han dado de menos lo suficiente como para irritarla. Usted:
a) olvida el asunto; no tiene pruebas de lo sucedido y probablemente no recobre su dinero
b) regresa y si es necesario protesta con toda su energía
c) escribe una carta al encargado de la tienda, quejándose

8. Mañana es el gran día: usted va a una entrevista de trabajo o tiene un examen importante. Pero, aunque está convenientemente preparada, no acaba de sentirse tranquila. Por tanto usted debería:
a) irse a la cama temprano, para levantarse despejada y lista
b) ver una película, leer una novela o salir con unos amigos a cenar
c) repasar lo que necesita para mañana hasta que la intranquilidad que siente desaparezca

9. Usted ha cometido un error de apreciación, de esos que todo el mundo comete alguna vez u otra, y entonces usted:
a) le explica a todas las personas involucradas el por qué de su equivocación
b) enseguida que se da cuenta, asume la responsabilidad del error
c) lo deja pasar; eso es algo que le pasa a cualquiera

The format is like that of most questionnaires—a series of situations with several possible responses. On the basis of the answers, the author proposes to evaluate the reader's degree of assertiveness. Also like many questionnaires, this one uses a form of direct address; that is, the author addresses the reader as **usted.** To read such material, you need to interpret third-person personal pronouns (**le, la, se**) as referring to yourself, the addressee. This particular questionnaire comes from a magazine with a large female readership, so most of the pronouns and modifiers are in the feminine form. This stylistic feature requires a similar kind of reader interpretation: the feminine endings are a signal, just like the use of **usted,** of reader identificaton and address. Male readers must reinterpret them to apply them appropriately. Pronouns and patterns of cross-reference provide important cues to the proper interpretation of any material that uses a personal tone.

Now read the article as quickly as you can and respond to the questionnaire. Use your dictionary only as necessary. How assertive are you?

These questions exhibit an important grammatical feature—the subjunctive. Since many of the situations and responses refer to intentions, effects, and probabilities as well as to conditions that may be contrary to fact, they include many verbs in the subjunctive. Subjunctive forms are easily recognized by the "opposite" theme vowel in the ending (the same vowel found in command forms.) If you have already studied the subjunctive, you may want to review its formation and use. If not, the most important thing to remember is that the subjunctive occurs primarily in subordinate clauses in sentences that deal with emotions or with hypothetical or didactic content.

Passages like this questionnaire make greater demands on a reader than strictly factual materials do. They involve a kind of reader response and cooperation not usually required by earlier readings. You must cooperate with the writer by visualizing each scene or situation, placing yourself in it mentally, and imagining your response. The same mental process you follow in reading this questionnaire is required for any kind of creative writing. Later in this unit you will have additional opportunities to experiment with readings of that type.

Now that you have answered the questionnaire, you will be interested in reading the author's explanations of the answers. Read the section titled **Respuestas,** which provides interpretations of the answers. Compare your choices with those the writer believes demonstrate self-confidence.

RESPUESTAS

Compare sus respuestas con las siguientes, que reflejan un alto grado de confianza en una misma.

1. c. Considerar la posibilidad, no de que usted esté equivocada, sino de que *podría* estarlo, con toda seguridad desarma a su oponente. En vez de defender usted *su* posición, lo está obligando a él a defender la suya. Si verdaderamente posee confianza en usted misma, no tendrá necesidad de demostrarle nada a su oponente, ni de dejar establecido que es usted quien tiene razón y él está equivocado.

2. b. A veces la única forma de lidiar con este tipo de personas es hacerles sentir lo mismo. Sobre todo, si no desea establecer como norma de conducta estar tolerando un comportamiento desconsiderado... a costa de su propia tranquilidad mental. La única solución es irse. Este acto demuestra a su amiga que usted posee resolución y firmeza y que sus sentimientos no deben ser tomados a la ligera.

3. b. Un *shhhh* dicho con firmeza, o una frase como: "Perdonen, ¿podrían continuar esa conversación en el vestíbulo?" obran maravillas. Usted no tiene por qué renunciar a su derecho a ver la película.

4. a. Decline amablemente la invitación, váyase a su casa y métase en la cama. Su jefe sabrá que usted tiene suficiente seguridad en lo que hace como para tomar una decisión correcta y llevarla a cabo.

5. c. La voluntad de aceptar riesgos es el componente principal de la seguridad en uno mismo. Así que actúe con firmeza con respecto a sus sentimientos, aunque no con agresividad. Observe la reacción de su amigo y si nota que algo lo detiene o que no se siente cómodo en la situación, ése es el momento de hablar acerca de lo que la preocupa.

6. c. Poseer confianza en uno mismo implica saber con precisión qué es lo que uno no sabe, y estar dispuesto a solicitar el consejo de personas que sí saben. Nadie es experto en todo; no compre el equipo hasta no estar segura de que está recibiendo lo mejor que puede obtener por su dinero.

7. b. Regrese a la tienda. Su presencia —su indignación— probablemente sea más poderosa de lo que usted se imagina. Aun si no le devuelven su dinero, todos los empleados de la tienda sabrán que usted es alguien capaz de defender sus derechos y en lo sucesivo se cuidarán mucho al atenderla.

8. b. Lo mejor que puede hacer es algo que la relaje y le quite de la mente la idea obsesiva de lo que sucederá al día siguiente.

9. b. Admitir las propias equivocaciones o deficiencias es siempre lo mejor. Adueñarse de los errores propios convierte lo negativo en algo definitivamente positivo. Probablemente ésta sea la pregunta más fácil de contestar... ¡y la norma más difícil de llevar a la práctica!

While the situations described in the questions are concrete, the commentary in the answers is abstract. Note that pronouns and cross-reference patterns are used to refer back to the original situations, to the imaginary participants in the situations, and to the presumed responses of the reader. In order to decode the comments, you need to understand the references in each question as you interpret the author's choice of answers. Since you have been working on pronouns and cross-reference, you should not find that part of the passage difficult. Here is an exercise to help you review these important grammatical cues and alert you to their special uses in the comments section.

Exercise A.

Each question below corresponds to the comment (**respuesta**) of the same number.

1. What noun in the first sentence is the referent for **lo, él** and **suya** in the second? _____ Which "incorrect" answer is being denied by the phrase **no tendrá necesidad de demostrarle nada**"? _____

2. The second sentence of the second answer is not complete; it consists only of a subordinate clause introduced by **si**. What phrase in the first sentence is understood to be the idea to which the clause refers?

   _____

3. What is the plural subject to whom the command verb **perdonen** is addressed? _____

4. To whom are the commands **decline, váyase**, and **métase** addressed?
   _____ What noun in the last sentence is the referent for **la** in **llevarla al cabo?** _____

5. Rewrite the last sentence of number five so that the reader is understood to be male and the friend is female. _____

   _____

6. What two verbs are part of the verb phrase that begins with **implica?**

   _____

7. What noun is the subject of **cuidarán?** _____

8. What noun is the subject of **le quite?** _____

9. What is the root of **adueñarse?** _____

The final section of this passage is the **Evaluación**, in which you will discover how your score is evaluated by the author. Total your score according to the instructions and then read the appropriate interpretation (and the others, if you are interested.) Note that the comments are a kind of summary.

EVALUACION
Por cada respuesta correcta a las preguntas 1 a la 8, anótese 6 puntos. La respuesta correcta a la pregunta 9 vale 10 puntos.
Entre 1-12: Usted está consciente de su forma de ser. Sus puntos fuertes son la sensibilidad y la honestidad. También posee una mente abierta a los cambios, pero quizás falta una finalidad a su vida. Una vez que haya logrado concentrar sus deseos y sus aspiraciones en un solo punto... su confianza en usted misma se encargará de lograr que pueda alcanzarlo.

Entre 13-30: La mayoría de las personas se agrupa en este promedio. Hay áreas de su vida acerca de las cuales usted se siente segura, pero otras que requerirían ser mejoradas. La completa autoconfianza está al alcance de su mano ¡sólo necesita apresarla..! y ponerla a trabajar en su propio beneficio.

Entre 31-48: Usted no necesita estímulos exteriores. Sabe lo que quiere y está dispuesta a luchar por conquistarlo. Se siente bien con usted misma y sólo muy de tarde en tarde experimenta alguna insatisfacción. Pero, puesto que es de las personas con confianza propia suficiente para aceptar un pequeño fallo... ¡es al mismo tiempo de las que se anotan los grandes triunfos!

Entre 49-58: El círculo de la seguridad en una misma, que desata en los demás una positiva reacción en cadena... ¡ya está en marcha! Manténgalo funcionando, y atravesará sin esfuerzo cualquier situación que confronte en su vida.

The goal of decoding in the *Reading Strategy* is always to understand the meaning of a passage at a level appropriate for your reading purpose. When your decoding techniques are successful, you achieve sufficient comprehension of a passage that you are able to think about its overall meaning, going beyond the meaning of individual words and phrases. In this passage, for example, your decoding success allows you to relate the situations, the "correct" answers, and the psychological interpretation to each other, and to think about the implications of the author's interpretation. Since your purpose in reading a passage like this one would normally be merely personal interest, you would probably think about it in personal terms. You might find that you disagree with the author's premises, her choice of "correct" answers, or her interpretation of your personality. Your comprehension of the passage invites you to react to the author and to evaluate the passage in the context of your own experiences. That thoughtful interaction—even if you just conclude that psychology questionnaires are not very reliable!—is only possible during the comprehension stage of the *Reading Strategy*. Your ability to undertake it confidently is the sign that you have sucessfully read the passage. How assertive are you as a reader? Answer this question to find out!

> Usted está leyendo un artículo de revista en español pero hay una sección que no sabe interpretar bien. Usted. . .
>
> a. regresa al principio del artículo y lo estudia palabra por palabra, tratando de traducirlo al inglés.
>
> b. regresa al punto donde dejó de comprenderlo y considera todo el contexto, buscando más ayuda de la gramática y la organización.
>
> c. decide que no lo puede compender nunca y deja de leer.

Good readers assume that written material has a context, is organized, and uses repetitions, and is therefore comprehensible. They use mechanical decoding techniques—marking repetitions, identifying verb cores, locating important nouns, looking up vocabulary—to help them through difficult passages, but they never forget that the author's intention is to communicate with them. Guessing, using context, and, above all, thinking are the real keys to successful comprehension of the intended meaning. That's why, in the question above, answer (b) is the mark of a confident reader!

Now let's look at another type of reading material commonly found in magazines and newspapers: an article reporting a recent scientific or medical discovery. Preread it to orient yourself to its topic. Do not look up words from the body of the article at this stage.

¡NO CONTROLES TUS LAGRIMAS! A VECES... LLORAR ES BUENO

POR EL DR. ALFONSO P. FARFANTE

Cuando hablamos de que llorar es saludable, nos referimos al llanto sentimental... ¡ése que nos ayuda a liberar tensiones y a mantener una buena salud física! Sí, porque reprimir el llanto puede producirnos dolores de cabeza, dolores de espalda e hipertensión. De manera que cuando sientas el deseo de llorar... ¡hazlo con toda confianza!

Dale rienda suelta a tus lágrimas... ¡éstas pueden ser el mejor remedio para tu salud mental!

La próxima vez que sientas deseos de llorar... ¡no te reprimas! Está comprobado que el llanto, contrario a ser un símbolo de inmadurez o debilidad, es una respuesta biológica cuando estamos algo tensos. Como es bien sabido, los humanos somos los únicos que lloramos por sentimientos. Esto dio lugar a una investigación donde surge la posibilidad de una relación entre las lágrimas y la eliminación corporal de sustancias peligrosas. El Dr. William H. Frey II, bioquímico y director del Laboratorio de Investigaciones de Siquiatría en Minnesota (Estados Unidos), comparó las lágrimas producidas por el sentimentalismo de una película, con las lágrimas que provienen al cortar una cebolla. En el estudio se descubrió que las lágrimas emocionales contenían más proteínas que las lágrimas causadas por irritaciones en los ojos. Es posible, según revela el informe, que las personas que sufren de problemas emocionales tengan un desbalance bioquímico que se refleja a través de las lágrimas. Aunque todavía no se han podido identificar los componentes químicos de las lágrimas provocadas por la tensión, existen evidencias que indican que la acumulación de lágrimas en el cuerpo afecta tanto la salud mental como la física. Entre otras cosas, contener las lágrimas y no desahogarse puede reflejarse en dolores de cabeza, hipertensión y dolores de espalda. De manera que siempre es mejor llorar que controlarse emocionalmente.

Por otro lado, además de reducir los problemas bioquímicos, el llanto ayuda a relajarse fisiológicamente. Un buen llanto hace que la persona respire más profundo y acelere las palpitaciones del corazón. Luego, cuando cesa el llanto, el diafragma y los músculos de los hombros descansan y la tensión muscular disminuye.

Así como el llanto libera las tensiones causadas por los problemas, llorar también puede contribuir a ver el mundo desde un punto de vista más positivo. Es decir, que cuando una persona está totalmente relajada puede encontrar con más facilidad las soluciones a los problemas. Lamentablemente, los adultos nos negamos a llorar, aun cuando estemos solos. Consideramos que el llanto es cosa de niños, porque es símbolo de debilidad e inmadurez. Pero después de leer este artículo, esperamos que cambies tu opinión. Lógicamente, no se trata de llorar por gusto... ¡sino de hacerlo sólo cuando tu cuerpo o tus sentimientos así te lo exijan!!!

The section title **Medicina** alerts the reader to the general topic, health. The article itself has a title, a subtitle, and a highlighted paragraph. Each of these three elements states the specific topic and summarizes the main idea of the article. (The highlighted paragraph naturally contains the greatest detail since it is the longest.) The article itself, of course, also states the main idea. Reread the title, subtitle, and summary paragraph in that order. Think about the kinds of details likely to be included in an article summarized in these ways.

Now decode the article, using all the techniques of the *Reading Strategy*. Take your time, and try to understand it completely. Remember that the size of a context unit—article, paragraph, or sentence—is related to the amount of detail you can decode.

Exercise B will help you check the success of your decoding techniques and will guide you in drawing out specific information of importance.

Exercise B.

Some of these questions request specific information. Others require you to make connections among pieces of information scattered throughout the article.

1. What was the nature of the experimental research reported in the article?
    a. Who conducted the research? _____
    b. How many kinds of tears were compared? _____
    c. What kinds of tears were compared? _____
    d. How were they produced in the experiment? _____

    _____

    e. What were the findings? _____

2. According to the article, emotional crying produces positive benefits in what two areas? _____

3. List four physical consequences of not crying.

    _____

    _____

    _____

    _____

4. True or False? Scientists know the precise chemical components of emotional tears.

5. How might crying by adults be interpreted by someone who had not read this article, according to the author? _____

    _____

6. Each of the following terms could be applied to this article. Identify one or more features or phrases used in the article that support the choice of each descriptive term.

   a. technical _____

   b. serious _____

   c. reportorial _____

   d. personal _____

7. According to the author, besides reporting a medical finding, what is the purpose of the article?

In working through Exercise B, you deduced the author's intended meaning, not simply by decoding individual sentences or phrases, but also by interpreting connections among various pieces of information, such as that contained in the phrases **la eliminación corporeal de sustancias peligrosas, más proteínas,** and **un desbalance bioquímico.** You cannot comprehend the meaning only by knowing the translation equivalents of these words. You must also understand that excess proteins are an example of **sustancias peligrosas** and that their presence may result in **un desbalance** and that tears are thought to be the mechanism by which the body attempts to eliminate them. This awareness of connections and their implications for overall meaning is a key factor in success at the comprehension stage of the *Reading Strategy.*

Once you have comprehended the passage at that level, you may have reactions to it. Below is a list of questions good readers might think about as they respond to this passage. You might find it interesting to discuss these questions with some other readers of the article.

1. Does the experiment itself seem reliable? What else would be helpful to know about it?

2. Is it a well-known fact that humans are the only creatures to cry from emotion? (In other words, did *you* know it before now?)

3. Do you agree with this statement from the article? **Siempre es mejor llorar que controlarse emocionalmente.**

4. Does the interpretation of adult crying depend on particular circumstances or cultural background? Is crying always interpreted as immature and weak in your culture? What do you know about Spanish-speaking cultures that might be relevant to this issue?

5. Do you agree that emotional crying makes you feel better? In other words, do the claims made in this article correspond to your own experience? If not, what might account for the discrepancy?

6. Does the article change your opinion? If not, what else would you need to know about the topic?

Dictionary Interlude

Interpreting creative vocabulary

As you read materials with more complex themes and more sophisticated vocabulary, you can still apply the dictionary techniques practiced in earlier units. As you have progressed through **Entre líneas,** you have undoubtedly found that reading has added many words to your Spanish vocabulary—words you might never use in your own conversation or writing, but which are understandable when you read. Your reading vocabulary will always be much larger than your speaking vocabulary, just as it is in English. This large reading vocabulary is sometimes called *passive* vocabulary, but the term is inaccurate. Reading is always an active process. You must do a great deal of mental work whenever you are communicating in a foreign language, whether you are producing words or interpreting them.

The types of materials you read will determine whether you will encounter words you already know or many new words. When we read technical articles in fields in which we have considerable prior background, we expect to find very little unrecognizable vocabulary. Familiar topics and context allow for highly successful guessing and transfer of prior knowledge. On the other hand, an article at the same level of technicality on a topic where we have little background knowledge might be much more difficult to read because its content would be less predictable.

Topic alone does not determine the range of vocabulary. Style is important as well. Any writer, no matter what the topic or purpose of the writing, may choose to emphasize the stylistic elements of his or her writing and this decision will affect vocabulary. To a certain extent, the more the writer emphasizes style in a passage, the more he or she expects from the reader in terms of collaboration and response.

One type of written material that usually has unpredictable content and a great deal of new vocabulary, and that requires a high degree of writer-reader interaction is creative writing—poems, stories, plays, or novels. Creative writing is some of the most interesting and entertaining material you can read, and much of what is written in Spanish is accessible to beginning readers with good reading skills. However, creative writers do more with vocabulary than simply arrange it on the page! For example, a poet may select a word because of the way it sounds or because its associations to other words will bring those words to a reader's mind as well. In passages with a literary style, your collaboration with the author must go beyond simply looking for a proper translation equivalent.

The purpose of this Dictionary Interlude is not so much to give you new dictionary skills, but rather to focus your awareness on the creative uses of words and to help you prepare for the special requirements of reading passages in which stylistic considerations are important.

Let's look now at an article that records the results of a survey of some of the Hispanic literary world's best known writers and philosophers. The title and the introductory paragraph that begins **Meses atrás** tell you what the survey was about. The survey results themselves are presented in the form of lists.

Preread the passage to determine its organization and theme.

eses atrás, «El Mercurio», de Santiago de Chile, uno de los diarios más prestigiosos de Hispanoamérica, encargó al profesor español Francisco Javier Bernal una encuesta entre escritores para elegir las diez palabras más bellas de la lengua castellana. Los «Domingos de ABC», que ha obtenido la exclusiva para España de este trabajo, publica esta encuesta durante la semana en que —un año más— el Libro ha celebrado su Día, coincidiendo con el aniversario de la muerte de Cervantes. Las respuestas han sido muy variadas y muchos encuestados han señalado que no pueden seleccionar «las diez más bellas», sino «diez muy bellas». Las palabras resultantes, después de triunfar el criterio semántico sobre el eufónico, son las siguientes: libertad, madre, paz, esperanza, amor, mar, azul, Dios, belleza y amistad.

Las diez palabras más bellas de la lengua castellana

Por Francisco Javier Bernal

ANTONIO GALA:

Amor
Hermandad
Esperanza
Lealtad
Belleza
Alegría
Libertad
Entusiasmo
Paz
Ojalá

CARMEN CONDE:

Dios
Vida
Eternidad
Amor
Madre
Hijos
Poesía
Mar
Lealtad
Tolerancia

ROSA CHACEL:

Paz
Mar
Fe
Alegría
Soledad
Umbría
Esperanza
Olvido
Belleza
Constancia

JORGE LUIS BORGES:

Sándalo
Jacaranda
Penumbra
Sombra
Cristal
Hexámetro
Ambar
Runa
Anhelar
Arena

FERNANDO LAZARO CARRETER:

Libélula
Linfa
Vergel
Libertad
Vida
Madre
Hijo
Aire
Arbol
Mar
Dios
Hermano

¿Con qué criterio se decide la hermosura? ¿La eufonía? Podrían ser libélula, linfa, vergel. ¿Su importancia para la comunidad hablante? Libertad. ¿Para el individuo? Vida, madre, hijo. ¿La belleza física de lo evocado? Aire, árbol, mar. ¿Su belleza moral? Dios, hermano. Salen doce vocablos. Prescindo de las tres eufónicas; y como ahora quedan nueve, repito ésta: libertad.

JULIAN MARIAS:

Estar
Haber
Enamorarse
Ensimismamiento
Convivencia
Sesgo
Gana
Hacienda
Quehacer
Ilusión

Indico diez palabras que me parecen eufónicas, expresivas y que, si no exclusivas, son al menos características del español; es decir, que en la mayoría de las otras lenguas no existen o no en esa forma, o con el sentido pleno que en español tienen.

GREGORIO MARAÑON MOYA:

Patria
Monarquía
Ilusión
Navegar
Nescubrir
Colonizar
Cultura
Religión
Independencia
Hispanidad

Estas palabras compendian todo el proceso americano y español.

CAMILO-JOSE CELA:

Madre
Sangre
Fuente
Simiente
Rosa
Moza
Cielo
Vuelo
Ave
Aire

«Diez muy hermosas, aunque no deba asegurar que sean las más hermosas de todas. En mis preferencias creo que ha pesado no sólo su eufonía, sino también la noción que señalan; a lo mejor existe un parentesco todavía por estudiar entre sonido y concepto.»

MERCEDES SALISACHS ROVIRALTA:

Declive
Costanilla
Linde
Sí
Zaino
Alba
Calmil
Pámpano
Hijuela
Fornecino

ALONSO ZAMORA VICENTE:

Las palabras más bellas de una lengua lo son todas, según su contexto y su circunstancia vital. Incluso su «belleza objetiva» va unida inseparablemente a múltiples cambios, al tiempo en definitiva. Tanto es así que hasta las palabras más pequeñas, vulgares e insípidas tienen en determinadas situaciones una hermosura entrañable, tan llena de afectividad y emoción estética. Como un relámpago deslumbrador. Este tiempo individual, pues, determina lo bello de un término, reflejando una incesante metamorfosis de significados y ropajes. Así descubrimos en nuestro propio uso idiomático preferencias temporales, dependientes del estado psicológico y ambiental, y de la querencia y de los apegos anímicos que nos remueven en cada ocasión. A veces descubrimos palabras nuevas o desenterramos otras viejas, que resuenan con timbre y fuerza desconocida; en esos instantes patéticos, la voz, la palabra, se hacen verso.

Otras veces parece más bien que las palabras adquieren una carga de significado que desborda el suyo original y tienen el efecto de proyectiles semánticos, que son, sin embargo, palabras clave del pensamiento. Tienen unos límites muy difusos. (Piénsese en nuestras «nacionalidades».) Se piensa entonces en el embuste, en el camelo, y se cree que el lenguaje es una trampa y que la vida aparece en él como un muñeco desarticulado, sin alma. Esto es el embeleco. La cuestión estética está presa en este embeleco. Según dijo Matoré, existen palabras-clave y palabras-testigo, y algunas pasan de una cosa a otra con el paso del tiempo.

En una lengua tan vieja como la nuestra, la temporalidad juega y supera cualquier encasillamiento de significado y de belleza eufónica. De hecho encontramos muchos neologismos de sentido, con un valor nuevo y bien distinto del original. **Liberal** significa en los siglos XVI y XVII generoso, opulento, distinguido; en el siglo XIX tiene, sin embargo, un contenido preferentemente político, bien determinado, y hoy, sus connotaciones son ya una calamidad. En tiempos de la Generación del 98, con Pío Baroja y otros, se redescubrió el término **troglodita** y se extendió su uso para hacer referencia a la zafiedad y lo rudo sin límites. Hace algunos años el español blasfemaba mucho aludiendo a toda la corte celestial —porque no respondían debía ser—. Ahora se blasfema menos, a Dios gracias.

¿Encontrar diez palabras bellas? Acaso la belleza de **rosa**, por ejemplo, pueda aislarse de lo que los poetas han escrito..., y que sin ellos no queda más espacio que el de la cursilería. Dejamos, pues, que cada uno encuentre aquí por lo menos diez pautas de belleza, leyendo otras tantas palabras.

En definitiva, el mundo de la lengua, de nuestra lengua vieja, es algo colosal y en el que apenas se puede trazar unos confines, unas líneas: la del cultismo (por ejemplo: **penicilina**...) por arriba, y de lo popular por abajo (**estropajo, cagalera**...), que son los límites mismos que señalan las palabras **esquizofrenia y chaladura**. Por el nivel alto llegamos a la literatura, y por la línea de lo popular, a las lenguas vulgares, a los dialectos. Pero ni eso se debe tomarse como un molde rígido, pues las palabras emigran más allá de esas fronteras, como tránsfugas y duendes, refugiándose en las pequeñas y grandes pasiones del hombre.

MIGUEL DELIBES:

Amor
Libertad
Solidaridad
Justicia
Indulgencia
Comprensión
Fraternidad
Convivencia
Amistad
Corazón

GERARDO DIEGO:

Madre
Azul
Gloria
Susurro
Golondrina
Brisa
Gorjeo
Lámina
Sueño
Mariposa

MARTA PORTAL:

Susurro
Ambito
Acaecer
Júbilo
Ajuar
Pétalo
Culmen
Apacentar
Ocaso
Augurio

LUIS ROSALES:

Luz
Mar
Todavía
Titilación
Nieve
Entinguirillar
Armonía
Ya
Desdolorimiento
Paz

PEDRO SAINZ RODRIGUEZ:

Crepúsculo
Alborear
Susurro
Amapola
Azul
Mariposa
Paloma
Rubor
Enamorado
Gallear

CARMEN BRAVO-VILLASANTE:

Abedul
Voluptuosidad
Extasis
Parsimonia
Garboso
Frivolidad
Predilección
Simbólico
Apasionada
Enamoramiento

«Dejo con pena: nostalgia, anhelo, metamorfosis...»

CARMEN LLORCA:

Aceituna
Alféizar
Carabela
Castillo
Maritornes
Ajonjolí
Mesnada
Alcázar
Encinar
Amapola

RAFAEL LAPESA MELGAR:

Albor
Doncella
Hontanar
Rocío
Asombro
Brío
Entrañable
Huidizo
Mañanero
Vislumbrar

(Las candidaturas serían infinitas: el azar ha designado las de la lista.)

ANTONIO MILLAN PUELLES:

Alba
Centella
Esperanza
Fontana
Luz
Poema
Rumor
Silencio
Torre
Vislumbre

JOSE DONOSO:

Tórtola
Garganta
Maledicencia
Escarpado
Portillo
Milonga
Avatar
Correhuela
Vertical
Alquimia

LUIS MARIA ANSON:

Dios
Amor
Paz
Madre
Mujer
Rey
Navidad
Aria
España
Chile

JOAQUIN CALVO SOTELO:

Alamo
Aljofar
Antaño-hogaño
Bergantín
Extasis
Libélula
Melancolía
Nocturno
Sonata
Tramontana.

ANTONIO GARRIGUES DIAZ-CAÑABATE:

Madre
Amigo
Paz
Inocencia
Luz
Flor
Vida
Armonía
Generosidad
Entrega

JOSE MARIA GIRONELLA:

Vagabundo
Querencia
Embrujo
Igneo
Azabache
Hontanar
Oropéndola
Camposanto
Bienaventuranza
Ajonjolí

TORCUATO LUCA DE TENA:

Anfora
Libélula
Cariátide
Marfil
Rosáceo
Esperanza
Nemoroso
Rumor
Inestable
Nenúfar

JOSE GARCIA NIETO:

Primavera
Alacena
Relámpago
Universo
Estandarte
Oropéndola
Acantilado
Rumoroso
Burbuja
Barlovento

RAMON J. SENDER:

Libertad
Amistad
Tolerancia
Alborozo
Adecuación
Nostalgia
Certidumbre
Voluptuosidad
Firmeza
Misterio

ALFONSO GARCIA VALDECASAS:

Alegría
Estar
Gracia
Hacedor
Jazmín
Querer
Sentido
Sosiego
Ventura
Verdad

FERNANDO CHUECA GOITIA:

Alcalde
Alfarero
Bisagra
Bajel
Cabal
Cárdeno
Castizo
Casamiento
Sosiego
Tacaño

LUIS JIMENEZ MARTOS:

Alba
Aljibe
Azotea
Cardinal
Colibrí
Frijole
Girasol
Melancolía
Misericordia
Yedra

ARTURO USLAR PIETRI:

Amanecer
Almendra
Azul
Esperanza
Ingrimo
Lámpara
Lástima
Pájaro
Ruin
Yermo

JOSE LUIS SAMPEDRO:

Azul
Belleza
Esperanza
Libertad
Melancolía
Música
Mar
Corazón
Paraíso
Esplendor

FEDERICO CARLOS SAINZ DE ROBLES:

Amor
Libertad
Paz
Amistad
Caridad
Espiritualidad
Cultura
Comprensión
Patriotismo
Lealtad

ERNESTO GIMENEZ CABALLERO:

¿Y por qué las diez palabras más hermosas de nuestra lengua y no una veintena? Como son aquellas donde la progenie hispánica se unió a la genuidad americana. ¿A que os estremecen cuando las pronunciamos: Chile, Colombia, Cuba, Paraguay, Perú, Uruguay, Santo Domingo, Ecuador, Bolivia, Méjico, Panamá, Argentina, Puerto Rico, Brasil, Nicaragua, El Salvador, Costa Rica, Honduras, Guatemala y Venezuela? No. No existen vocablos más entrañables en nuestro habla. Porque son nuestra vida misma.

JOSE MARIA DE AREILZA:

Liberalidad
Desasosiego
Difidencia
Lisonjero
Proceloso
Fulgente
Nemoroso
Soñadero
Tornadizo
Yerto.

Now read the introductory paragraph very carefully. Make sure you understand it completely.

Use Exercise C to check your comprehension of the introductory paragraph.

Exercise C.

Find and write the exact words from the introductory paragraph that answer each question most completely.

1. What agent was responsible for the survey?

    _____

2. Who conducted the survey? _____

3. Where did this version of the results appear?

    _____

4. What two anniversaries coincide with the appearance of the survey results? _____

5. What two criteria were important in the survey results?

    _____

The introductory paragraph suggests that most of the writers surveyed selected their ten most beautiful words on the basis of semantic content (the meaning) while a few selected words on the basis of euphony (the sound or beauty of a word, without regard to its meaning). Now turn your attention to the word lists themselves and, as you read them, complete Exercise D. Do not use your dictionary yet.

Exercise D.

1. For each of the following authors, decide which of the two criteria seems to predominate in the list. (It will help if you read the lists aloud.)

    I. *Semantic*   II. *Euphonic*

_____	a.	Antonio Gala	_____ j.	Pedro Sainz Rodríguez
_____	b.	Carmen Conde	_____ k.	Carmen Bravo-Villasante
_____	c.	Rosa Chacel	_____ l.	Carmen Llorca
_____	d.	Jorge Luis Borges	_____ m.	Rafael Lapesa Melgar
_____	e.	Fernando Lázaro Carreter	_____ n.	José Donoso
_____	f.	Julián Marías	_____ o.	Joaquín Calvo Sotelo
_____	g.	Gregorio Marañón Moya	_____ p.	Antonio Garrigues Díaz-Cañabate
_____	h.	Camilo-José Cela	_____ q.	Ramón J. Sender
_____	i.	Miguel Delibes	_____ r.	Federico Carlos Sainz de Robles

2. Which of the two criteria produces a greater number of unfamiliar words? If the lists were given English equivalents, which criterion would produce a list that conveys the reason why each word was chosen?

3. Select three *semantic* lists for which you already recognize the majority of words. Use your dictionary to determine the meaning of any words you do not know. Remember to use all your dictionary techniques. Think about each word. What associations do *you* have with each word? With each group of words? What reaction do you think each writer wants you to have to his or her list? Do the semantic lists have many words or meanings in common?

4. Consider the list by Pedro Sainz Rodríguez. Say the words aloud to yourself as you read them, and use your dictionary as necessary to identify a translation equivalent for each one, even those you think you recognize. (Your dictionary may not include one or two of these words. Be sure to look for related words before giving up.) Think about each word. What associations occur to you? What reaction do you think Sainz Rodríguez wants you to have? Is there a common thread in the list?

5. Consider Calvo Sotelo's list. Use your dictionary to find translation equivalents or related words. When you say the words aloud, note the placement of the accents. Think about the group of words. Do you think the sound of these words is important to this writer? Do the meanings seem to be related in any way?

Some of the writers have commented on their lists or on their reactions to the idea of a list. Read the comments by Lázaro Carreter, Julián Marías, Gregorio Marañon Moya, Camilo-José Cela, Rafael Lapesa Melgar, and Ernesto Giménez Caballero carefully.

When you are sure that you understand each writer's point, go on to Exercise E.

Exercise E.

1. Lázaro Carreter comments specifically on the contrasts of euphony and meaning, but his statement makes it clear which is more important to him. Which?

2. Julián Marías tries to combine the two criteria and adds a third—uniqueness in Spanish. Can you determine good translation equivalents for each word in his list? (Pay attention to the word forms.) Do you agree that the ideas are difficult to render easily and completely in English? Which other writer comments on the attempt to combine criteria in his list?

3. What theme is reflected in Marañón Moya's list? Would you have been able to guess it without the clue given in his comment?

4. What criterion has Ernesto Giménez Caballero used which is neither semantic or euphonic? What reaction do you think he wanted his readers to have to his list?

Now read the short essay by Alonso Zamora Vicente. Be sure to notice how many of the words on other writers' lists are used by Zamora Vicente in his comments.

Use the following exercise to help you identify some of the main ideas in Zamora Vicente's essay.

Exercise F.

1. Why doesn't Zamora Vicente give a list of ten beautiful words?

2. Why does he say (in the opening paragraph) that notions of beauty in words are necessarily idiosyncratic and individual?

3. What does he use the words **liberal** and **troglodita** to explain?

4. What does he use **rosa** to illustrate?

5. What conclusion about language does he express in the last paragraph?

Zamora Vicente suggests that all words can be poetic; their contexts can make them so. Spanish prose offers many opportunities to experience the poetry of the language. Your dictionary is only a small help to you in gaining an appreciation for this aspect of the language. The best way to improve your skill in interpreting the subtlety of style is to read widely and frequently. Try to challenge yourself by selecting materials by serious authors, whether they are essayists, journalists, or creative writers. Spanish language writers pay a great deal of attention to stylistic considerations. In reading such materials, try to go beyond translation equivalents and look for meaning associations that enhance your understanding. Don't forget the role of euphony; poets are not the only writers who seek a pleasant sound in what they write.

Before going on to the next section, return to the lists of the ten most beautiful words in the Spanish language. Many of them are really short poems, whose poetic power resides in the combination of sound, meaning, and associations. Which lists seem the most poetic to you? Could you produce a list of favorite words in Spanish? Could you arrange your words so that they become a poem?

Applying the Reading Strategy

In this section, you will work with two passages. The first is a report of an interview with Jorge Luis Borges, an internationally respected Argentine poet and short-story writer, many of whose works are popular in English translation. The interview took place a few months before Borges' death at the age of 86 in 1986. Before you read the article, think about what you already know about Borges and about Argentina's recent history.

There are several references in the article to important issues in Argentine politics: nationalism; the excesses and violence of the military government (established in 1976) and its opponents; the disappearances of many critics of the government; the popular protests against the government's role in the disappearances, especially those led by a mothers' group known as **Madres de la Plaza de Mayo;** the restoration of democracy through the election of Alfonsín in 1985. It will also be useful for you to know that Borges was blind for much of his life. In this article, many allusions are made to his blindness, especially in the descriptions of his surroundings.

Since this is an interview, you should expect to find quotes from Borges as well as comments from the interviewer. The passage includes many first-person verb forms. However, this interviewer is not simply reporting an encounter; he wants to provide the reader with a feeling for the experience of the interview itself and of his emotions as he listened to Borges talk about his life. The tone is very personal and the style is somewhat poetic. You should expect the use of metaphors as well as new vocabulary.

Read the article carefully. Your reading purpose at this stage is to achieve maximum comprehension, although you do not need to understand every single word or sentence. Certainly, you do not need to be able to translate it. Since this material is somewhat culture-sensitive, do not worry if some of the allusions are difficult to follow; that will not keep you from understanding what you need. Although the article is longer than any you have undertaken so far in this book, it is well within your capabilities if you work carefully, applying the *Reading Strategy*.

EL LUMINOSO ESCRITOR REPOSA EN UN CUARTO OSCURO

El ciudadano Jorge Luis Borges, una de las mentes que con mayor carga de imaginación han transitado por el duro camino de la realidad, vive hoy, en un cuarto doblemente oscuro de Buenos Aires, la tragedia sincopada de su pueblo, cuyo lenguaje conoce y cuya historia ha desmenuzado en versos. Junto con un hermoso poema reciente, Borges cuenta aquí la relación que el autor de *El Aleph* ha tenido con la "verosímil esperanza" del pueblo que acudía a las urnas para ejercer, entre el miedo y el orgullo, el derecho a seguir siendo un país libre.

Jorge Luis Borges vive enfermo los días difíciles de su pueblo

CARLOS ARES, Buenos Aires
El célebre escritor argentino, Jorge Luis Borges, padece nuevamente de un agotamiento físico que ha obligado a su médico personal a recomendarle un estricto reposo. Recibe visitas sólo en determinadas horas del día y ha suspendido los coloquios y conferencias previstos para esta semana. Chasquea la lengua. Orienta el ojo izquierdo extremadamente abierto y, en seguida, su leve voz aletea y se alza desde su extrema debilidad. Sale a través de la ventana del sexto piso de su modesto apartamento en el centro de Buenos Aires y se eleva sobre el tronar de las bombas, el fanático grito de las amenazas telefónicas y el aullido desgarrado de una sociedad harta de violencia. Resuena alta y clara: "nuestro deber es la verosímil esperanza".

Es tarde ya, pero en la agonía de Borges quedan luces encendidas. "Soy un hombre que se sabe incapaz de ofrecer sus soluciones, pero creo poder aceptar las de otros. No entiendo de política, mi vida personal no ha sido otra cosa que una serie de errores. Pero estoy condenado a ello. He tratado de ser un hombre ético, aunque quizá sea imposible serlo en esta sociedad en la que nos ha tocado vivir, ya que todos somos cómplices o víctimas, o ambas cosas. Sin embargo, creo en la ética. La ética pueda salvarnos personalmente y colectivamente también. Yo, como usted, seguramente, estoy en un estado de resignada desesperación. No veo solución a los problemas que nos aquejan. Y no me refiero sólo a nuestro país, porque lo que aquí sucede es, sin duda, menos importante que lo que ocurre en el mundo entero. Creo que Spengler tenía razón cuando habló de la declinación de Occidente. Esa declinación es general…".

Calla. Sigue hablando con los ojos, con alguna voluntad física, pero la falta de aliento suficiente le obliga a retraerse sobre sí mismo en un estertor casi postumo. Fanny, su silenciosa y amante empleada de servicio, le anima con la brutalidad de su origen campesino y él "señor Borges", recibe con placer de heroinómano esa inyección de carne y naturaleza. De pronto, el ordenador se comunica nuevamente con su invisible operador a través de su pantalla ciega.

"Recuerdo que yo estaba en Madison, Wisconsin, hace dos años. Era la noche de Halloween, de las brujas y todos siban disfrazados o con máscaras a la fiesta. Yo estaba invitado a una y me compré una cabeza de lobo que tenía un olor horrible. Entré a la reunión aullando y gritando: *homo homini lupus*, el hombre es el lobo para el hombre. En ese momento siento un tirón en el brazo: era un argentino que me decía 'ha ganado Alfonsín'. Se había producido el doble milagro, el de ese triunfo y el de que yo me disfrazara. Me sentí muy bien entonces porque habíamos salidos de una pesadilla y la confianza de todos era lo que podía salvarnos. Ahora nuestro deber es la esperanza, la probable, la verosímil esperanza".

"Yo descreí de la democracia durante mucho tiempo, pero el pueblo argentino se ha encargado de demostrarme que estaba equivocado. En 1976, cuando los militares dieron el golpe de Estado, yo pensé: al fin vamos a tener un Gobierno de caballeros. Pero ellos mismos me hicieron cambiar de opinión. Aunque tardé en tener noticias de los desaparecidos, los crímenes y las atrocidades que cometieron. Un día vinieron a mi casa las madres de Plaza de Mayo a contarme lo que pasaba. Hace poco estuvo en el juicio y conocí al fiscal, allí recordé la frase de Almafuerte: 'sólo pide justicia, pero será mejor que no pidas nada'. Todo ésto es muy triste y habría que tratar de olvidarlo. El olvido también es una forma de venganza. Fue un período diabólico y hay que tratar de que pertenezca al pasado. Sin embargo, por todo lo que ocurre ahora pienso que hay mucha gente que siente nostalgia por ese pasado. Claro que a mi me resulta fácil de-

Jorge Luis Borges, con Julio César Strassera, fiscal del proceso contra los miembros de las juntas militares que gobernaron Argentina.

cir que debemos olvidar, probablemente si tuviera hijos y hubieran sido secuestrados no pensaría así".

Fanny, secándose las manos en el delantal, acaba de recordar por primera vez que el doctor ha dicho "reposo". Y que él "señor" ya ha estado demasiado tiempo levantado y en el sillón.

"Yo fui comunista, socialista, conservador y ahora soy anarquista. Es decir, yo en el año dieciocho creí en la revolución rusa. Ahora veo que ese es un modo de llegar al imperialismo. Me observo y me veo como a un hombre que cree estar enamorado de una mujer y luego comprueba que ya no lo está. Eso no ha sido una decision mía. Ha sido algo que me fue revelado. He comprobado eso en mí. Ahora yo querría que hubiera un solo Estado, que desaparecieran las diversas naciones, pero se que no estamos maduros para ello. Hay, en este país, algunas circunstancias favorables que se han dado aquí y no en otras repúblicas del Continente. Desearía preguntarme por qué no han sido aprovechadas. Tenemos una fuerte clase media, también es ventajosa la inmigración de muchos países. Creo que el nacionalismo es nuestro mal mayor. No considero a Latinoamérica como núcleo generador de nada y no creo que exista nadie que se considere latinoamericano y sienta eso como algo diferenciador. Ser de un país es una actitud de fe. Yo nunca pienso que soy un mexicano ¿por qué habría de pensarlo, si en realidad soy argentino?. Pero nosotros, los argentinos, insistimos en un nacionalismo y en un latinoamericanismo que es absurdo. Hay pocos países que tengan más próceres y aniversarios que el nuestro".

"Por suerte no es tan excesiva la carga de pasado. Nietzche quería que hubiera buenos europeos y quizá nosotros, los americanos, podemos serlo. Desd eluego estoy seguro que no somos aborígenes. De la violencia actual tienen la culpa las dos grandes guerras europeas. De lo contrario, Europa podría mantener la hegemonía del mundo. Ahora estamos entre dos países que fomentan la violencia, Estados Unidos y la Unión Soviética".

"Mi madre murió a los 99 años y estaba un poco impaciente. Ella podía pedirle a Dios, cada noche, que se la llevara. Yo no, no soy creyente". Vuelve la cabeza con el ojo izquierdo iluminado, alerta. "Siempre uno está solo cuando muere, suspongo. De modo que me he resignado a la vida, que es lo más grave y lo más dificil. Una vez le dijeron a Bernard Shaw que obrar de tal modo era imprudente y él contestó: 'bueno, es imprudente haber nacido, es imprudente seguir viviendo, vivir es cometer imprudencias ¿por qué no agregar una más?'". Fanny impide, con un gesto militar, que alguién más ingrese a la habitación.

"Estoy continuamente pensando en versos. Versos libres, clásicos, sonetos. también en prosa, en cuentos. Tengo que poblar mi soledad con proyectos literarios. Eso no ofrece mayor peligro, sin duda moriré sin haberlos ejecutado. Pero ¿qué otra cosa puedo hacer?".

La puerta se cierra, corta de un tajo el saludo de las manos estrechadas blandamente y retiene sobre ellas la luz que entra por la ventana.

Use Exercise G to check your comprehension of details of the setting of the article. It assumes that you have numbered the paragraphs as part of the decoding stage of the *Reading Strategy*.

 ### Exercise G.

1. How many people are present during the interview? Who are they?

2. What is Borges' physical condition? The interviewer describes it in two different paragraphs. Identify the references.

3. Where does the interview take place? Identify the part of the passage that includes this information.

4. Identify the paragraphs in which Borges discusses the following topics. (Some paragraphs may contain more than one topic.)

   _____ a. religion
   _____ b. the politics of the military government
   _____ c. his personal political history
   _____ d. his reaction to the election of a democratic government
   _____ e. the meaning of death
   _____ f. his poetry
   _____ g. the negative aspects of Latin American nationalism
   _____ h. his description of his current feelings about the world

5. Look at this list of topics. Assign a + or a − to each topic, according to your interpretation of Borges' feelings (generally positive or generally negative) about each one. Underline a quote from Borges that supports each of your interpretations.

   _____ a. religion
   _____ b. politics
   _____ c. Argentina
   _____ d. Western civilization
   _____ e. the United States
   _____ f. Argentina's military government
   _____ g. poetry

While Borges' comments have a generally pessimistic tone, the interviewer's presentation emphasizes a more positive theme. Note the repetition of versions of the quote **Nuestro deber es el verosímil esperanza** (paragraphs 1 and 4 and in the summary that introduces the article). The opening paragraph sets the tone and scene for the entire article and in it, this phrase plays an important role. The quote is set off both physically (in quotes, at the end of the paragraph, and following a colon) and stylistically. Reread the opening paragraph to remind yourself of the imagery the author uses when he describes Borges' voice.

The author has used a metaphor to describe Borges' voice; it resounds over the city of Buenos Aires, drowning out the noises of violence. The author uses this strong image to convey the power of Borges' thinking, and specifically, the power of his idea of hope. The importance of the quote about hope to the overall meaning of the article actually outweighs, or at least matches, the pessimistic tone of the other quotes.

Reread the article, this time paying special attention to its stylistic features. Note, for example, the way the author alternates very short and very long sentences to change the rhythm of the descriptions. Pay attention to the style used to introduce Fanny. Pay careful attention, of course, to Borges' own use of anecdotes, images, and examples in order to convey his ideas.

Use Exercise H to check your comprehension of some important stylistic features in the article.

Exercise H.

Although Borges does not mention the fact that he is blind, the author repeatedly alludes to Borges' blindness. Locate each of the following references, and use their contexts to help you think about the intended meaning of each one. Then answer the questions that follow each reference.

1. "Es tarde ya, pero en la agonía de Borges quedan luces encendidas".
   What does "luces" really refer to? What associations do you suppose the author intends for "tarde"?

2. "Sigue hablando con los ojos. . ."
   How does this image relate to Borges' blindness?

3. "Orienta el ojo izquierdo extremadamente abierto. . ." "Vuelve la cabeza con el ojo izquierdo iluminado, alerta."
   What seems to be the purpose of these references to eyes?

4. "El luminoso escritor reposa en un cuarto oscuro."
   "Oscuro" is intended to be interpreted in at least three ways, two of them literal and one metaphorical. What are they?

Fanny is mentioned at three points; in each case she performs some action. Locate each of the references and reread the contexts. Then answer the questions.

5. What do we learn about Fanny from each of these phrases?
   a. "su silenciosa y amada empleada de servicio" (paragraph 3)
   b. "le anima con la brutalidad de su origen campesino" (paragraph 3)
   c. "secándose las manos en el delantal" (paragraph 6)
   d. "impide, con un gesto militar" (paragraph 9)

6. What is the meaning of the image in the last sentence of Paragaph 3?

7. Why are Fanny's references to Borges always in quotes?

8. In what way is the reference in paragraph 3 to "esa inyección de carne y naturaleza" a synonym for Fanny?

9. In Paragraph 4, Borges tells a story. Read the paragraph.
The wolf's head has both literal and metaphorical meaning. What are the two meanings?

10. Reread the last paragraph. What is the relationship between the image in that paragraph and the earlier images of blindness and darkness?

Now that you understand both the content and the style of the passage, you should be able to respond to its meaning. Use Exercise I to help you think about the passage.

 Exercise I.

1. How does Borges' statement about the importance of personal ethics in paragraph 2 relate to his quotation of Bernard Shaw in paragraph 9? How are these two references related to his comments on poetry? Do you agree with his views on life and death?

2. Borges discusses the evolution of his political views in Paragraph 7. He also comments on some positive and negative aspects of Argentina. Do you agree with his evaluation of the benefits of immigration and the negative effects of excessive nationalism? What else would you need to know about Argentine history in order to understand his implications completely?

3. In paragraphs 7 and 8, Borges comments on the relationship of Latin America and Argentina to the rest of the world. What do you think he means when he suggests that the people of the Americas could be "good Europeans"? Do you think it would be helpful to know more about the original context of reference to Nietzche?

4. What do you think the interviewer's attitude is toward Borges? Toward Fanny?

5. Borges never mentions his blindness. Why do you think the interviewer emphasizes it so much? Do you think that emphasis is primarily a stylistic device or does it have further meaning?

Now that you know something about Jorge Luis Borges and have read some of his own words, you can enjoy his treatment of some of these same themes and feelings in one of his later poems. Before you read it, return to the word lists in the *Dictionary Interlude* and find his. Make sure you know what all the words mean; pay attention to the way they sound. Do you have greater insight into his choice of words because of the interview you read?

This poem, **Elogio de la Sombra,** was written in Borges' old age. It is a very personal reflection on age, death, and the meaning of his existence. The language used in it is quite straightforward, although there are some cultural allusions that may not be immediately clear. It is divided into clearly marked sentences you can treat as context units for the purpose of applying the *Reading Strategy.* Remember, even in poems, the beginning and end tend to convey the most significant meaning. Read the poem carefully, concentrating on comprehending its basic meaning. What is the poet's central theme?

LA VEJEZ (tal es el nombre que los otros le dan)
puede ser el tiempo de nuestra dicha.
El animal ha muerto o casi ha muerto.
Vivo entre formas luminosas y vagas
que no son aún la tiniebla.
Buenos Aires,
que antes se desgarraba en arrabales
hacia la llanura incesante,
ha vuelto a ser la Recoleta, el Retiro,
las borrosas calles del Once
y las precarias casas viejas
que aún llamamos el Sur.
Siempre en mi vida fueron demasiadas las cosas;
Demócrito de Abdera se arrancó los ojos para pensar;
el tiempo ha sido mi Demócrito.
Esta penumbra es lenta y no duele;
fluye por un manso declive
y se parece a la eternidad.
Mis amigos no tienen cara,
las mujeres son lo que fueron hace ya tantos años,
las esquinas pueden ser otras,
no hay letras en las páginas de los libros.
Todo esto debería atemorizarme,
pero es una dulzura, un regreso.
De las generaciones de los textos que hay en la tierra
sólo habré leído unos pocos,
los que sigo leyendo en la memoria,
leyendo y transformando.
Del Sur, del Este, del Oeste, del Norte,
convergen los caminos que me han traído
a mi secreto centro.
Esos caminos fueron ecos y pasos,
mujeres, hombres, agonías, resurrecciones,
días y noches,
entresueños y sueños,
cada ínfimo instante del ayer
y de los ayeres del mundo,
la firme espada del danés y la luna del persa,
los actos de los muertos,
el compartido amor, las palabras,
Emerson y la nieve y tantas cosas.
Ahora puedo olvidarlas. Llego a mi centro,
a mi álgebra y mi clave,
a mi espejo.
Pronto sabré quién soy.

Now read the poem again, this time focussing your attention on the images. How many of them are references to his blindness? Which ones are references to death? Which ones refer to writing? What is the general tone of the poem?

Read the poem a third time, paying careful attention to stylistic features such as the length and rhythm of the sentences and lines. Note the way accents move through the lines and the relationships of various words to each other. Look for groups of related ideas, the use of synonyms, and the repetition of roots or sounds.

Read the poem once more, taking into account everything you have learned from the previous readings, as well as everything you have learned about Borges in this unit. Think about the way this poem relates to his list of beautiful words and to the topics he chose to discuss in his interview.

Use Exercise J to help you check your comprehension. It will also help you articulate your own reactions to the poem.

Exercise J.

1. What does Borges mean by the phrase **el tiempo ha sido mi Demócrito**?
2. The poet suggests that old age is the time of greatest self-knowledge. What images does he use to refer to that kind of knowledge?
3. Is the poet afraid to die? Does his reaction to old age and death as expressed in the poem agree with his comments on those topics in the interview?
4. Borges provides a list of the **caminos** that led him to his **secreto centro.** They are the components of his experience and knowledge. (Note how many of them related to reading and writing.) What do you think he means when he says that now, in his old age, he can forget them?
5. Why does the poet refer to age as a time of happiness and good fortune **(dicha)?** What is the connection between the first and last lines?
6. What is the poet's principal idea in the poem? Do you agree with him?

Before leaving this unit, look back over the readings you have worked on. They are very different from each other, but they were all written with serious purposes and intended for native speakers of Spanish to read, to learn from, and to react to. Because you knew how to approach them and because you read them thoughtfully, you also learned from and responded to them. Through reading, you have engaged in a process of communication, which, as Borges himself suggests, can contribute to your own **álgebra, clave** and **espejo.** And that's the real value of the *Reading Strategy!*

The Reading Strategy

Comprehension: Making inferences

This unit presents the final step in the comprehension stage of the *Reading Strategy*. You will learn to interpret written materials whose purpose is to persuade you or to present a point of view. Such materials include editorials and commentary articles found in newspapers. Passages of this type require that a reader understand not only the main ideas, but also the organization of the ideas and their relationships to each other. Unit 9 gives you some practice in identifying these important aspects of a passage. Persuasive writing exhibits certain typical features that careful readers learn to expect and to rely on when decoding. The Dictionary Interlude of this unit will help you learn about these features and how to use them. You will also continue to practice the important decoding skills to improve comprehension and allow you to respond to an author. The passages in this unit—articles, editorials, political messages and flyers—are specifically intended to produce a response from the reader.

Before beginning the first reading passage, it is important to be reminded that much writing of this kind covers events or issues of local interest. It is expected that the readers will share certain common assumptions as well as specific background information. An article dealing with the outcome of a local election in Mexico, for example, will almost certainly assume a familiarity with the political parties involved, the relevant local issues, and the earlier events in the campaign. Without that background information, you may find that you cannot make much sense of it, even though you may be able to understand every word. If the article comments primarily on the national or international implications of the election, you may have enough background to be able to understand the most important material in the article. If you are totally without background in the current political situation in Mexico, even the international dimension of the article in question may not be enough context to help you interpret it.

What can you do about this problem of cultural context? First, at the beginning, you will have to be selective. Written materials may be too difficult on the basis of their cultural context, even though they are not difficult at all grammatically. Use your prereading skills to identify articles likely to require special background you do not have, and recognize that such material will challenge your skills. Do not give up on reading simply because you have selected a difficult passage. Next, pay attention to global events that are likely to be reflected in the Spanish language materials you like to read. This tactic does not apply only to political issues, of course. A reader interested in reading about the arts in Spanish-language publications should keep up with the names and activities of internationally known artists and writers. A final tactic is to read regularly in similar publications. For example, if you regularly read a Mexican national newspaper, you can follow the development of stories of interest. Although you may find it difficult to follow a story at the beginning, in a short time you will find that you can bring a much wider context and background to each article.

Let's see how you can use headlines to determine what level of background information a passage might require and thus assist you in selecting appropriate readings.

Exercise A.

Look at this series of headlines taken from the front page of the December 26, 1985, issue of **Uno Más Uno,** a Mexican daily newspaper.

    A. En Antropología, el mayor robo a un museo nacional

    B. Vence al mundo la prepotencia, afirma el Papa

    C. Falleció Demetrio Vallejo; fue incansable luchador social: DLM

    D. Pagará deudas el DDF por 340 mil millones

    E. Propone EU a la URSS controles en zonas de pruebas nucleares

    F. 300 mil desocupados, consecuencia de la sequía en Brasil

    G. Creció 89% lo sacado por transnacionales

    H. Aceptó Duarte la tregua navideña

1. Match the following subtitles with the title they are most likely to accompany.

    _____ a. Demanda que haya reducción del hambre y el armamentismo

    _____ b. Viola Washington los acuerdos de Ginebra: Moscú

    _____ c. 31% de su presupuesto

    _____ d. Reconocimiento de PMT y PSUM al ex-dirigente

    _____ e. Creíamos que había seguridad: Florescano

    _____ f. Pérdidas de 4 mil millones de dólares

    _____ g. El ejército la rompió

    _____ h. Cifras de 3 trimestres

2. Categorize each article as either international in scope or of local or national (Mexican) interest.

    I. International   II. National/Local

    _____ A.   _____ C.   _____ E.   _____ G.

    _____ B.   _____ D.   _____ F.   _____ H.

3. Think about your expectations about the content of each article and about the amount of background information likely to be necessary to interpret it. Based on your conclusions, rank the articles from easiest (1) to hardest (8) to read.

    _____ A.   _____ C.   _____ E.   _____ G.

    _____ B.   _____ D.   _____ F.   _____ H.

One of the most important reasons for learning to read well in Spanish is that it opens a whole world of events and commentary to you. Good readers have access to a much wider range of perspectives on current events and international concerns as well as to a larger universe of creative works. Even if you are not able to travel to Spanish-speaking countries or correspond and converse regularly with Spanish-speaking people, you can enjoy communicating with them through what they write. Much of what seems inaccessible at first glance, because of lack of background or cultural context, in time can become comprehensible to you precisely because you continue to challenge yourself by reading widely.

Here's a reading passage that illustrates the way in which familiar content may be treated in an unfamiliar context. It is an article discussing a news story that appeared in many newspapers in the United States. This article appeared in a Mexican magazine of political analysis and opinion. Read it carefully, by following the *Reading Strategy* through the decoding process.

LOS TEXANOS QUIEREN, AUNQUE SEA PRESTADA, LA BANDERA PERDIDA EN EL ALAMO

Desde hace algunos meses, ciudadanos, líderes políticos y medios de comunicación texanos se han enfrascado en una discusión sobre México, su antiguo país. Todo porque el próximo marzo, Texas celebrará el 150 aniversario de su independencia de México y su surgimiento como república.

Abandonados por el centro y azuzados por los ya entonces colonialistas Estados Unidos, los texanos se rebelaron contra el gobierno mexicano y comenzaron a luchar por su independencia como país, que les duró 10 años, ya que en 1845 decidieron adherirse a los Estados Unidos.

En 1835, cuando la rebelión texana comenzó a extenderse, el general y dictador Antonio López de Santa Anna se separó de la Presidencia de la República para ir a combatir a los sublevados. Hubo innumerables batallas y el 2 de marzo de 1836 Texas se declaró formalmente independiente de México.

Sin embargo, cinco días después, el ejército mexicano consiguió una victoria al vencer a los defensores del Fuerte del Alamo en una sangrienta batalla. Cuentan las historias que valientes y patriotas soldados mexicanos murieron tratando —hasta conseguirlo— de arriar la bandera de los defensores del fuerte e izar la mexicana.

López de Santa Anna envió la bandera capturada a la capital de México como evidencia de que filibusteros participaban en la tarea de separar a Texas.

La bandera del Fuerte del Alamo es un estandarte de seda verde, que ha ido palideciendo con el paso del tiempo. Tiene las inscripciones "Primera Compañía de Voluntarios Texanos de Nueva Orleans" y "Dios y Libertad"

La leyenda cuenta que fue hecha por mujeres del este de Texas y presentada a los "Greyss" de Nueva Orleans, soldados voluntarios reclutados en esa ciudad.

Pese al triunfo mexicano en El Alamo, la independencia de Texas se consolidó el 21 de abril de 1836, cuando la fuerza de Sam Houston ganó la batalla de San Jacinto e hizo prisionero a López de Santa Anna, quien logró su libertad a cambio de ordenar el retiro del ejército mexicano y la firma de dos tratados.

La bandera de El Alamo está en manos del Instituto Nacional de Antropología e Historia. Originalmente estuvo expuesta en el Museo de Historia del Castillo de Chapultepec y desde 1981 está en el Museo de las Intervenciones, en el exconvento de Churubusco.

Lo que sucede es que diversos grupos texanos pensaron que una de las formas de celebrar su independencia es rescatar la bandera de El Alamo. La corriente pro-regreso del estandarte está respaldada incluso por legisladores federales de Texas como el senador republicano Phil Gramm y varios diputados. Otros menos ambiciosos han expresado su deseo de que por lo menos les sea prestado.

Se sabe que se hicieron trámites oficiales con las autoridades del INAH, las que han decidido no prestar la bandera, principalmente por el estado de deterioro en que se encuentra. Pero los texanos son obstinados.

El 3 de diciembre, el periódico *Houston Post* intentó poner fin a la polémica, mediante un artículo editorial.

Dijo: "México es un país orgulloso, a pesar de su pobreza, y la bandera del Alamo y la rebelión de Texas son temas muy sensibles ahí. Le recuerdan a este país que la independencia de Texas condujo a la invasión de Estados Unidos y a la pérdida de la mitad del territorio de México que quedó en manos de Estados Unidos en la guerra de 1846-48". La del Alamo —dice el editorialista— es "un símbolo de victoria para ellos" (los mexicanos).

Además, dice, "los texanos ganaron la batalla de San Jacinto que es verdaderamente lo que contó en el resultado de su lucha por la independencia y nosotros tenemos la bandera de San Jacinto. Se encuentra en la Casa de Representantes de Texas.

"Nosotros contamos con nuestro símbolo de la victoria, así que dejemos que ellos guarden el suyo, por lo que representa para ellos. No luchemos contra su orgullo". (**Gerardo Galarza**)

When reading materials that contain opinion, the reader's first important task is to recognize the organization of the author's presentation. The organization of this article is quite straightforward.

Exercise B.

Put the following elements into the order in which they appear in the article by identifying the paragraph(s) containing each one. (Not all paragraphs will be represented.)

_____ **1.** current location of the Alamo battle flag

_____ **2.** statement of the controversy

_____ **3.** account of the events leading up to the Battle of the Alamo

_____ **4.** description and origins of the flag

_____ **5.** description of the battle itself

_____ **6.** outcome of the request to Mexico to lend the flag

_____ **7.** ultimate fate of López de Santa Anna's army

_____ **8.** explanation for the sensitivity of the Mexican government with regard to the flag

_____ **9.** explanation of the timing of the request for the flag

_____ **10.** statement about the importance of the Battle of San Jacinto

Once the overall organization of a passage has been identified, a reader can usually tell whether it contains primarily facts or whether it expresses opinions as well. In reading materials that include opinions, an important task is to distinguish facts from opinions. Exercise C will help you identify fact and opinion in this article.

Exercise C.

1. The following sentences are taken from the article. Identify each one as a fact (F) or an opinion (O).

_____ a. Hubo innumerables batallas y el 2 de marzo de 1836 Texas se declaró formalmente independiente de México.

_____ b. Cuentan las historias que valientes y patriotas soldados mexicanos murieron tratando—hasta conseguirlo—de arriar la bandera de los defensores del fuerte e izar la mexicana.

_____ c. La bandera del Fuerte del Alamo es un estandarte de seda verde, que ha ido palideciendo con el paso del tiempo.

_____ d. Pero los texanos son obstinados.

_____ e. México es un país orgulloso, a pesar de su pobreza, y la bandera del Alamo y la rebelión de Texas son temas muy sensibles ahí.

2. The article contains fifteen paragraphs. Which ones are devoted primarily to the presentation of facts about the history of the disputed flag?

3. Which of the following summaries is the most objective statement of the dispute that gave rise to the article? (Notice how choice of vocabulary reveals a writer's opinion.)

   a. Brave Mexican soldiers won a battle flag during their victorious assault on the Alamo in 1836. Now the descendents of the losing Texans want the flag to use as a symbol in their independence anniversary celebrations. No Mexican who values our heritage would want to give it up.

   b. Mexico won a Texas flag at the battle of the Alamo in 1836. Texans want to have the flag returned in order to display it during the celebration of the anniversary of their independence. Mexico does not want to return it.

   c. Even though the Mexicans ultimately lost the War of Texas Independence, they persist in retaining an important relic of Texas history, namely, the flag they took at the defeat of the Alamo in 1836. The contribution that the flag could make to the state anniversary celebrations is being successfully thwarted by Mexicans who stubbornly refuse even to lend it.

4. Most of the opinions contained in the article are easy to identify because they are those of an editorial writer from the **Houston Post,** quoted at the end of the article. Does the editorialist favor returning the flag?

5. What fact does he use to support his opinion?

6. What supposition does he use to support his opinion?

7. What opinion do you think the author of this article has about the dispute? Why do you think he quotes the Houston journalist without comment?

8. On the basis of this article, do you think that the deterioration in the flag (mentioned in paragraph 11) is the sole reason for not sending it to Texas for the celebration?

The next reading passage is also a newspaper editorial, one which proposes a solution to a problem the author has identified. The author wants to persuade readers that there is a problem and that his solution is the most appropriate one. Apply the *Reading Strategy* to this passage. Pay special attention to understanding the description of the problem and to the characteristics of the institution that is proposed for solving it.

Exercise D will guide you through an analysis of the organization and main ideas of this editorial.

Una Academia para Europa

FRANCESCO ALBERONI

Europa no tiene un sistema universitario unificado como Estados Unidos ni intercambio de profesores ni estudiantes. En su interior no hay ninguna movilidad intelectual. Todos, en cambio, se van a Estados Unidos, como estudiantes o como *visiting professors*. Alcanzada la fama, se quedan como profesores en las universidades más célebres: Harvard, Columbia, Stanford. Europa y EE.UU. no son dos bloques culturales separados y en contacto. Son un único sistema estelar en el que Estados Unidos es el centro y los países europeos los brazos, sin contactos directos entre ellos.

Sólo en el centro está el conocimiento y el poder. Porque sólo el centro conoce el conjunto. Los otros están condenados a tener una visión limitada, regional. Y la diferencia aumenta en desventaja nuestra. Ahora incluso la cultura francesa está perdiendo importancia junto a su lengua. Lo que antes era entre los americanos benévolo desinterés está convirtiéndose en desprecio. Los europeos están perdiendo la fe en sí mismos. Balbucean incluso cuando tienen cosas importantes que decir.

El fraccionamiento y la debilitación de la cultura europea es una catástrofe. No puede haber desarrollo de la ciencia y la tecnología en Europa si no se puede reconstruir un polo de atracción autorizado y digno. No se puede tener conciencia política europea si su elite cultural está continuamente mirando a otra parte y es arrastrada continuamente desde ella. No es posible pensar en una reforma que modifique el sistema universitario. Los estatutos jurídicos son distintos y las retribuciones no son parangonables. Lo que se puede hacer es algo por encima y más allá de la Universidad. Algo completamente nuevo, pensado a escala comunitaria, y que supere de entrada todo lo que es nacional, regional o provincial. La iniciativa debería venir directamente del Parlamento Europeo, con el acuerdo de los Gobiernos, pero debería ser financiada sobre todo con capital privado, con patronazgos y con suministro de servicios. Porque debe estar en estrecha relación con la sociedad real, los intereses económicos y las cosas prácticas.

Una institución de este género, superuniversitaria, de altísimo nivel, existe en todo país, y es la Academia. En Estados Unidos y en la URSS juega un papel importante. En Italia y en Francia ha sufrido un proceso de esclerosis. Pero el principio por el que nació continúa siendo válido. Una Academia Europea de las Ciencias, de las Letras y de las Artes puede ser el lugar en el que converjan todos los grandes estudiosos, todos los grandes artistas sin limitación de sectores. Lo importante es que cada uno haya realizado una contribución original en su campo. Desde la genética hasta el urbanismo, desde el cine hasta la tecnología aeronáutica, desde la economía hasta la pintura. Los ejemplos del Premio Nobel y de la Fundación Balzan nos muestran que es posible encontrar jurados serios y dignos. Para evitar que la Academia se convierta en un geriátrico como la Academia de Francia (y otras), se debería prever una edad de jubilación, por ejemplo a los 70 años. No se debe en ningún modo pensar en una elite restringida. La Comunidad necesita convocar sus mejores competencias e inteligencias. Hoy día los campos de la ciencia, del arte y de la técnica son tantos que una Academia europea está destinada a agrupar millares de personas. Lo importante es que éstas tengan la ocasión de encontrarse, de conocerse, de trabajar juntas, de hacer proyectos avanzados. Lo importante es que la sociedad, los Gobiernos, las regiones, las ciudades, las empresas, las universidades, las utilicen, las pongan a prueba en las tareas más esforzadas, más difíciles, en las que se producen las competencias más elevadas.

Sería catastrófico pensar en esta Academia como una distinción honorífica. Debe ser un centro de pensamiento y un servicio a la patria común europea. Tomar parte en ella significa asumir unos deberes, por lo que sería necesario un compromiso formal de los académicos en este sentido. Por este motivo, la admisión en la Academia debe ser rigurosamente limitada a los ciudadanos de la CEE, sin que sea posible ninguna excepción.

Sé que muchos fruncirán la nariz ante una limitación de este género. Estamos habituados a la retórica de la ciencia que supera las fronteras, que unifica a la humanidad. Pero en realidad nosotros, los europeos, estamos atrapados entre los tremendos nacionalismos americano y soviético, y lacerados por nuestros pequeños y mezquinos nacionalismos interiores. Hoy es preciso tener el coraje de fundar un nacionalismo europeo.

Una Academia europea no debería tener una única sede, salvo una secretaría centralizada por exigencias administrativas. La Europa comunitaria es a un tiempo una y policéntrica, y así debe ser su Academia. Podría, por ejemplo, tener dos o tres sedes en cada país. Pero las sedes no deberían ser un instituto y menos todavía un hotel. Deberían ser, antes que nada, un club, un lugar en que los estudiosos encontraran un despacho, salas donde reunirse y recibir gente, con una secretaría eficiente.

Algo así como el servicio que *American Express* ofrece a los *managers*. Es a estas sedes, conectadas a través de una red, a donde se podrían dirigir todos los que tienen necesidad de expertos.

No hay necesidad de que la Academia organice congresos o investigaciones. No debe ni siquiera sustituir a la Universidad, aunque puede ofrecerle docentes para objetivos especiales. No debe financiar nada, no debe dar su patrocinio a nada. Su objetivo es constituir una comunidad cultural europea, conseguir la masa crítica que haga nuevamente de la Europa comunitaria un centro interesante para sus estudiosos. Debe proporcionar ánimo y dignidad. Debe, al mismo tiempo, exigir la calidad y condenar todo lo que es provinciano y mezquino.

 Exercise D.

1. This editorial contains the following sections. Identify the paragraphs assigned to each section.

_____ a. the character of the proposed institution

_____ b. the statement of the problem and its negative consequences

_____ c. the limitations that should be put on the institution

_____ d. the justification for proposing something completely new to solve the problem

_____ e. the primary objective of the new institution

_____ f. response to criticism of the proposed limitations

_____ g. location of the proposed institution

2. The opening sentence states the problem as the author sees it. The remainder of the opening paragraph presents three negative consequences of the situation. Identify them. (You will have to infer the writer's negative attitude toward the consequences he describes.)

3. The third paragraph presents a justification for establishing a new institution. Its opening sentence claims that the weakening of European culture is a catastrophe. The remainder of the paragraph identifies three aspects of this weakening that require immediate attention. Identify them. (Each one is introduced by a similar grammatical construction.)

4. Paragraph 4 presents some of the characteristics of the new **superuniversidad**, referred to as the **Academia.** What is the name proposed by the editorialist for the new institution?

5. Who will the members of the proposed **Academia** include? Is there to be any restriction as to field?

6. Why is an age limitation proposed?

7. Underline the phrases that identify what the **Academia** members will do.

8. Why is a citizenship limitation proposed?

9. What is required of the meeting places for **Academia** members?

10. Underline the single sentence that states most clearly the purpose of the **Academia**.

In order to comprehend a passage of this type, a reader must often draw inferences from the ideas and organization. Writers do not always state directly the suppositions or judgments on which their opinions are based. In this article, the reader must concentrate on the writer's identity as a European intellectual in order to understand why he might feel that visiting professors who stay in the United States are betraying European culture. Similarly, the author makes repeated references to **nacionalismo** throughout the article. A careful reader must be able to infer the relationship of the author's positive attitude toward the idea of **un nacionalismo europeo** (paragraph 6) to this specific proposal.

This "reading between the lines" is a somewhat advanced reading skill, but it is a very useful one—and crucial when trying to comprehend serious writing about current issues. One way to practice it is to try to adopt the point of view of an author and then predict the reactions such a person would have to specific criticism of his or her claims. Read the passage again, trying to maintain that point of view.

Now go on to Exercise E.

Exercise E.

Imagine that you are a European university professor or writer, concerned about the decline in prestige of European culture, and you agree that Mr. Alberoni's suggestion is a good one. Think about each of the following criticisms of the proposal. What response would you make to each one?

1. An easier solution to the "brain drain" problem would be establishing a law that nationals who go abroad as visiting professors must return within three years or lose their citizenship.

2. While the **Academia** is a good idea, it should not be funded privately because such a restriction would tie it too closely to special economic interests. It should be funded by special government levies.

3. Such an **Academia** will never work because all those important people from such different fields will not have enough in common to be able to work together on anything. Besides, just because someone is a famous author or geneticist does not mean that he or she has any interest in working on major European social problems.

4. Even if an **Academia** could be formed, it wouldn't have much to do, especially if it isn't even going to organize conferences. All the problems alluded to in the article are very general (lack of a European consciousness, for example). There is no evidence that there are any **tareas difíciles** to which such a group could contribute solutions.

The author claims that the model for his proposed **Academia** plays an important role in public life in the United States. He is not referring to a single institution, but to a type of institution. Think about the description he provides for the **Academia**. What kind of American institution does it most resemble? Can you identify the usual name for it in English?

Now read the passage once more, from your own point of view. (Does the **Academia** resemble a *think tank* in some ways?) What criticisms do you have of the proposal? How are your reactions determined by your own experience and background?

The next reading comes from a very different source; it is a street flyer announcing a political demonstration. Like all materials that express opinion, however, it includes some statements of fact, some suppositions, and some opinions. In this case, many of the writer's opinions and suppositions are expressed through the choice of vocabulary. (Remember that the live context of the passage—it was distributed to passersby on a public street—also contributes to a reader's perceptions of the writer's intent.) Read it carefully, paying special attention to the organization of the material and to the presentation of facts and opinions.

Convocatoria

de un acto

por la paz

Muerte a Jomeini — No a la guerra

Condenamos el bombardeo de objetivos civiles y de la población indefensa

Pueblos amantes de la paz:

Para solidarizaros con los movimientos de protesta y las manifestaciones del pueblo y de las fuerzas de resistencia en Irán —organizadas tras el llamamiento del 11 de abril del responsable del Consejo nacional de la Resistencia— y para apoyar el movimiento por la paz y libertad, contra la guerra y represión y contra el régimen anti-humano y reaccionario de Jomeini, participad en las manifestaciones y actos que se celebran en más de 11 ciudades de Europa, Asia y América.
En Madrid tendrá lugar un acto de protesta:

Lugar: el lugar del acto se anunciará posteriormente.
Fecha: el 7 de Mayo de 1985.

Consejo Nacional de Resistencia de Irán

La guerra devastadora Irán-Irak utilizada por el régimen reaccionario y anti-humano de Jomeini como medio para reprimir al pueblo iraní y perpetrar la opresión con vistas a aplazar la caída ineluctable de su régimen inestable, ha tenido como consecuencia:
— *Cerca de un millón de muertos, heridos o inválidos. Sólo en la última ofensiva (Badr) 60.000 personas fueron matadas o heridas.*
— *2 millones de personas sin hogar.*
— *Derrochar la riqueza nacional de nuestra patria, causar espantosos estragos económicos, destruir las ciudades y zonas industriales y edificios históricos que pertenecen al patrimonio cultural del mundo.*

Las más importantes actividades del CNR para conseguir la paz son las siguientes:
— *Denunciar la política belicista de Jomeini en Irán y a través del mundo entero.*
— *Presentar el plan de paz y propagarlo en Irán y a escala mundial.*
— *Conseguir el apoyo de 2.352 movimientos, partidos, organizaciones políticas y personalidades e instancias internacionales.*
— *Obtener el cese de los bombardeos de zonas civiles y de la población indefensa durante una semana el 14 de febrero de 1983.*
— *Organizar actos y semanas de resistencia contra la guerra y por la paz en el interior del país y especialmente dedicar el mes de Osdibehecht (del 21 de abril al 21 de mayo) a este fin.*

Asimismo, el 7 de mayo de 1985 tendrán lugar manifestaciones y actos de protesta, organizados por el CNR, en las ciudades de Madrid, Londres, Washington, Bonn, Estocolmo, Nueva Delhi, Torento, Atenas, Zurich, Copenhague, Viena, Amsterdam y...

In evaluating materials of this type, you must first be sure that you comprehend the writer's point of view and the claims or arguments made in the passage. Only at that point can you properly judge the validity of the claims or respond to the argument. Check your comprehension of this piece with Exercise F.

Exercise F.

1. What is the central issue with which this material is concerned?
2. What organization is responsible for this flyer?
3. When will the demonstration take place? Where?
4. According to the flyer, how many cities will participate in the demonstration?
5. Which of the following is the best statement of the precise purpose of the flyer?
   a. to present facts regarding the Iran-Iraq war
   b. to present opinions regarding the Iranian government
   c. to invite public participation in a demonstration

Sometimes suppositions or opinions are presented as facts. One simple (and common!) way of accomplishing this switch is by carefully choosing words. The opening paragraph of the flyer, presented in the format of a personal letter, illustrates several examples of vocabulary chosen in this way.

Reread this section and note the adjectives used to modify nouns such as **población** and **régimen,** and the form of address that includes a supposition about the political views of potential supporters.

Written materials whose purpose is to persuade readers of something present claims central to that purpose. Some of these claims may be based on facts and others may be statements of the writer's opinion or interpretation of facts not presented in the passage itself. Careful readers always pay attention to these distinctions. You must always think when you read materials that express opinion, since the writer of such materials has a purpose beyond the simple presentation of facts. Your response must be based on an understanding of that other purpose and its potential effect on the presentation of the material. Use Exercise G to help you distinguish opinions from facts in the rest of the CNR flyer.

Exercise G.

1. In the section beginning **La guerra devastadora...**, what motive is attributed to the Iranian government as the basis for the war against Iraq? Is this motive a fact or an opinion of the writer?
2. Three adjectives are used to describe the Iranian regime. Identify them and determine whether they reflect facts or opinions.
3. Three sets of claims about the consequences of the war are given. Identify them and determine which ones are supported by specific examples or details. Does the flyer itself document these claims?
4. What is the purpose of the CNR, according to the section that begins **Las más importantes actividades...?**
5. Five activities are listed. Which of these identify results obtained?

The next passage includes two parts, one of which deals with some of the features of opinion-based discourse. While its focus is on speech, some of its analysis can be applied to writing as well. Examine the entire passage (don't forget titles and photos!), but concentrate on the section titled **Veinte consejos para pedir el voto.**

Hable durante cuarenta horas sin decir absolutamente nada

Método revolucionario para

Normativa clásica

Veinte consejos para pedir el voto

—Pensar en el objeto y finalidad de sus palabras.

—Considerar a fondo la mentalidad del auditorio.

—Pergeñar un borrador con las frases de arranque, el cuerpo y la conclusión, según el patrón ciceroniano.

—Definir exactamente los puntos claves de la disertación.

—Dar pocas ideas fundamentales, pero repetirlas machaconamente con diversas palabras.

—Apoyar los conceptos sobre el sentimiento y la razón.

—Ligar a ciertos individuos con la materia expuesta.

—Citar ejemplos, comparaciones, textos eruditos.

—Aportar experiencias propias.

—Establecer un orden: bien cronológico, bien descriptivo, persuasivo o progresivo (de lo sencillo a lo complejo, de lo conocido a lo desconocido, etc.)

—Evitar tópicos como los de «y como ya no tengo tiempo para más...»

—Presentar un remate altisonante, con las imágenes más gráficas y brillantes.

—Dar coba al público, a la ciudad, a la asociación donde se celebre el acto.

—Atraer la atención del oyente con datos curiosos.

—En cuanto al discurso de salón, es

decir, de ensayo, debe repetirla en solitario de pie, entusiasmado y accionando.

—Ir modificando el esquema original con «morcilllas» que se le vayan ocurriendo sobre la marcha.

—No lea. Sólo debe llevar chuletas de las ideas a exponer.

—Según los expertos de la Universidad de Maxwell (USA) la preparación de una conferencia debe llevarle dos semanas.

—Incluso recomendaban el ensayo en el mismo escenario real horas antes.

—Elegir el marco para el speetch. Con aforo insuficiente, con tarima o estrado alto, con luz conveniente que resalte la actitud del orador...

The **Veinte consejos** present some guidelines for the preparation of a political speech. Many of them apply to political writing as well. Reread the section and make sure that you understand the purpose of each instruction.

Have you ever received similar instructions for preparing oral presentations? Are any of these ideas new to you?

montar un discurso político

¡**N**o les deje a ellos solos! Usted también puede jugar en su casa, con los amigos, en la tertulia, asombre en la oficina. A través de este sistema podrá montar un discurso político de cuarenta horas ininterrumpidas, arengar a las masas sin que éstas desfallezcan cuan diputado radical, cuan jerarca chino ante el plenario del partido. Lo mejor de todo, sin decir absolutamente nada. Para sintonizar mejor con el verdadero espíritu de los profesionales de la casa pública, esa es la gracia del invento.

Que viene nada menos que de la sufrida Polonia, donde un grupo de estudiantes, que conocen el percal, han decidido exportarlo, como broma de oratoria, a Occidente. Un cubo maldito dialéctico, pero mucho más sencillo, titulado «Código universal del discurso político-burocrático para políticos principiantes». La clave reside en ir combinando a su gusto, y sin repetir, las cuarenta frases tipo del cuadro que se adjunta. Por ejemplo, lea la primera fórmula de la primera columna, continúe con la primera de la segunda, únala a la de la tercera y finalice el primer período con la de la cuarta. Prosiga con la misma táctica pero con la segunda y continúe, continúe con desparpajo... hay diez mil combinaciones.

I	II	III	IV
Queridos colegas	la realización de los deberes del programa	nos obliga al análisis	de las condiciones financieras y administrativas existentes
Por otra parte	La complejidad de los estudios de los dirigentes	cumple un rol esencial en la formación	de las directivas de desarrollo para el futuro
Asimismo	el aumento constante, en cantidad y en extensión de nuestra actividad	exige la precisión y la determinación	del sistema de participación general
Sin embargo, no olvidemos que	la estructura actual de la organización	ayuda a la preparación y a la realización	de las actitudes de los miembros de las organizaciones hacia sus deberes
De igual manera	el nuevo modelo de la actividad de la organización	garantiza la participación de un grupo importante en formación	de las nuevas proposiciones
La paradoja de la vida cotidiana prueba que	el desarrollo continuo de distintas formas de actividad	cumple deberes importantes en la determinación	de las direcciones educativas en el sentido del progreso
No es indispensable argumentar el peso y la significación de estos problemas ya que	la garantía constante, nuestra actividad de información y de propaganda	facilita la creación	del sistema de formación de cuadros que corresponda a las necesidades
Las experiencias ricas y diversas	el reforzamiento y desarrollo de las estructuras	obstaculiza la apreciación de la importancia	de las condiciones de las actividades apropiadas
El afán de organización pero sobre todo	la consulta con los numerosos militantes	ofrece un ensayo interesante de verificación	del modelo de desarrollo
Los principios superiores ideológicos así como	el inicio de la acción general de formación de las actitudes	implica el proceso de reestructuración y de modernización	de las formas de acción

Exercise H.

Identify three guidelines given in this passage that seem to have been most important to the writer(s) of the CNR street flyer. For each one you choose, refer to a specific feature of the flyer.

The second part of the article is a satire on politicians and their speeches. In reading satire (remember that satire uses humor and exaggeration to present opinion), it is especially important to be able to identify the underlying intention of the author. In this example, both the title and the subtitle offer some clues that the article is not entirely serious. What two meanings does the word **revolucionario** have in this context? How is exaggeration used in the subtitle?

Now read the introductory paragraph and look for more evidence that the purpose of the article is satirical.

Now go on to Exercise I to check your comprehension.

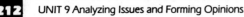

Exercise I.

1. Who is referred to by **les** and **ellos** in the opening sentence?

2. Identify two important exaggerations used for humorous effect in the opening paragraph.

3. Who developed the material in the chart?

4. What is the official title of the chart?

5. What are the instructions for using the chart to produce a political speech?

6. Underline the sentence identifying the target of the satire in the passage.

You will find that the contents of the chart are fairly easy to read because there are a great many cognates. Try composing a few "political statements" of your own. Don't be surprised, though, if, as the Polish students predicted, you can't make much sense out of them!

Dictionary Interlude

Interpreting discourse markers

Although the speech chart was written with a humorous purpose in mind, it does illustrate an important collection of vocabulary items. In earlier units you learned about function words and phrases (such as **y, pero, cuando,** and **hasta que)** that relate individual sentences and sentence parts to each other. A similar set of function words, known as *discourse markers,* have the same role in longer passages; they relate pieces of a narrative to each other.

Discourse markers are clues to the larger organization of a passage and help readers keep track of the progress and direction of the author's presentation. Such words and phrases often carry important semantic content concerning the relationship of the information they introduce to the information that precedes and follows it. They are often located at the beginning of paragraphs and are easy to spot.

You have already learned to pay special attention to some of these markers. In Unit 7, you noticed the importance of words like **primero** and **segundo** in helping you follow a book reviewer's comments.

Structurally, **primero** and **segundo** help readers keep track of the items in a list and also alert them to the semantic fact that the items have something in common. The listed items are part of some larger grouping that is likely to be the writer's real topic. Skillful readers coming across a series like **primero, segundo,** and **finalmente** make sure they know what that larger grouping is as they read the items in the list. The next exercise helps you understand markers of this kind.

This poster announces a public meeting sponsored by the Mexican political group known as OOCR. What are the purposes of the meeting? What does OOCR stand for?

Exercise J.

1. Discourse markers signal several kinds of semantic and logical relationships. This list presents a set of categories and definitions for some of the most important of these relationships. Match each category on the left with the appropriate definition of its function on the right.

   _____ a. additive   A. provides an example

   _____ b. explicative   B. establishes an ordered list

   _____ c. contrastive   C. provides an explanation

   _____ d. illustrative   D. identifies the order in which events occur

   _____ e. enumerative

   _____ f. logical sequence   E. offers new information to be joined to previous material

                                      F. presents opposing information

2. Now match the English discourse markers on the right with their appropriate function categories on the left. For example, *on the other hand* is a contrastive marker. (Some categories include more than one marker.)

   _____ a. additive   A. next   F. finally

   _____ b. explicative   B. moreover   G. however

   _____ c. contrastive   C. namely   H. as a result

   _____ d. illustrative   D. likewise   I. instead

   _____ e. enumerative   E. therefore   J. for example

   _____ f. logical sequence

3. Here is a list of common discourse markers in Spanish. Some are already familiar to you. Use your dictionary as necessary to identify a *discourse* translation equivalent for each one. (Remember, these items are function words. You may have to do some interpretation of the entry to identify the best equivalent.)

a. el siguiente   _____

b. en cambio   _____

c. no obstante   _____

d. además   _____

e. por lo tanto   _____

f. asimismo   _____

g. es decir   _____

h. de igual manera   _____

i. sin embargo   _____

j. en resumen   _____

k. por ejemplo   _____

l. por fin   _____

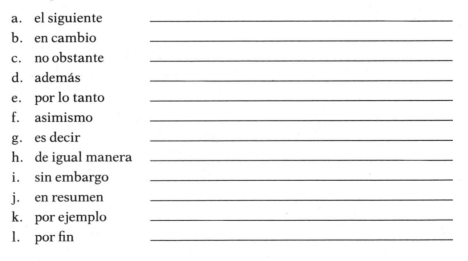

4. Now assign each of the Spanish phrases in the above list one of the following categories on the basis of its semantic and grammatical meanings.

a. additive _____   d. illustrative _____

b. explicative _____   e. enumerative _____

c. contrastive _____   f. logical sequence _____

Writers vary in the degree to which they use discourse markers of these kinds. A technique that beginning readers can use to help them select reading materials is to scan for discourse markers, since such markers make the passage easier to read. A technique for checking your comprehension when you are reading on your own is to try inserting such markers into the passage at the points where they belong. Exercise K reviews the use of discourse markers in the passages you have read so far in this unit. Use your dictionary as necessary.

Exercise K.

1. The article about the Alamo flag contains three important discourse markers: **sin embargo, pese** (a version of **a pesar de**) and **además.** Reread the article to locate them and determine their function in the passage.

2. The author of the editorial about the proposed **Academia** uses very few of these markers. Review the passage and locate these: **en cambio, por ejemplo.** What are their specific functions in context?

3. Return to the third paragraph of the article of the **Academia.** It contains a list of the negative effects of the factionalism of the European intellectual community, along with the introduction to the proposed new **Academia.** Insert the following discourse markers into the paragraph at appropriate places in order to improve the readability of the paragraph: **como consecuencia, de igual manera, además, en cambio, por lo tanto.** (The markers should be inserted in the order they are given here.)

4. In the first column of the chart illustrating the "revolutionary method of political discourse," several discourse markers occur. Classify them according to their discourse marking function:

a. por otra parte _____   d. de igual manera _____

b. asimismo _____   e. junto con _____

c. sin embargo _____   f. así como _____

What metaphor is being exploited in this cartoon.?

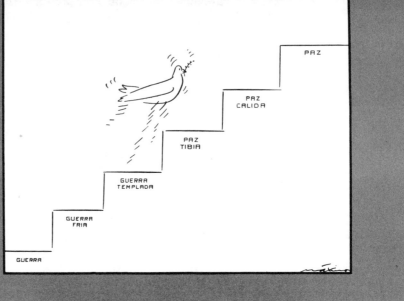

Applying the Reading Strategy

The *Reading Strategy* is now complete. You have progressed through pre-reading, decoding, and comprehension techniques. Although you cannot yet understand everything you read or read everything you see, you can comprehend a great deal of written Spanish intended for native speakers. You are able to select from a wide variety of materials that are well within your skills. Furthermore, you can identify materials that will challenge and improve those skills. The techniques you have learned provide a basis for further practice and development of reading skills in Spanish, and with some modifications, they are applicable to other languages as well.

One of the most important outcomes of your high level of reading skill is that you are now able to enter into a communicative process with writers whose insights into the international situation and the human condition are forever closed off to those who only read in English. You might not always agree with their views, but it is always interesting and provocative to know what they are.

The last reading passage in this unit is an essay written for a Spanish audience; it comments on certain aspects of life and thought in the United States. The essay includes facts as well as opinions. Use the *Reading Strategy* to guide you in reading it. Your goal is to understand the passage so well that you can react to it effectively.

Use Exercise L to check your comprehension of the claims made in the essay. (Remember, you cannot respond until you are sure you know what the writer has said!)

Los jóvenes y sus máquinas

GABRIEL JACKSON

En el curso de las dos semanas siguientes a la triunfante reelección del presidente Reagan realicé mi primera visita a Estados Unidos desde mi jubilación, 20 meses antes, como catedrático de Historia en la Universidad de California. Una de mis hijas es especialista en química del suelo, y la otra, arquitecta paisajista, de manera que pasé la mayor parte del tiempo con jóvenes profesionales y sus familias. Observando sus casas y paseando por los barrios residenciales de Berkeley, me llamó especialmente la atención un rasgo cultural, nada nuevo para mí, pero cuya omnipresencia me resultaba positivamente aterradora: su preocupación por sus casas, sus máquinas y sus jardines. No era algo extraño ver tres coches, o dos coches más una camioneta o un *jeep*, más una motora o un velero, más equipo de esquí o caza, más un congelador, un cortacésped con motor y, en algunos casos, una antena de plato para captar los programas por satélite y los ruidos misteriosos del espacio exterior. Todos estos artículos se encontraban en el garaje o en el patio. Dentro de la casa, naturalmente, había una lavadora, un fregaplatos, una aspiradora y varias herramientas eléctricas.

En el caso de las parejas sin hijos, tanto el marido como la mujer tenían empleos de jornada completa y se preocupaban por sus carreras individuales y por las mejoras salariales. Donde había niños, la mujer tenía un empleo de media jornada, se preocupaba claramente por mantener su posición profesional y, en cualquier caso, no permitía que se le tratase *simplemente* como madre y ama de casa. En la vida interna de la familia reinaba una gran cortesía, había cooperación en las tareas domésticas y en general poca conversación que no estuviera relacionada con el trabajo. Todos colaboraban en el ruido de las máquinas, participaban en la limpieza de la casa, el cuidado de las flores y cortaban el césped.

Otro rasgo sorprendente de esta visita fue el ambiente renovado de prosperidad material. Mis últimos cuatro años de profesor con horario completo y administrador con horario parcial correspondieron con los años de la presidencia de Carter. En esa época, la industria californiana estaba pasando por una fuerte recesión. Resultaba difícil conseguir fondos para la investigación, los sueldos de los profesores iban por detrás del índice de inflación, y los estudiantes se estaban alejando de la rama de ingeniería, ya que parecía ser una carrera con unas salidas laborales muy pobres. Este año, los profesores tendrán unos aumentos del 10% al 12%, hay multitud de empleos en dedicación parcial como consultores, ofrecidos por la industria, y los estudiantes están regresando en masa a los estudios de ingeniería.

Lo que me sorprendió aún más que el ambiente de prosperidad fue la indiferencia (puede que en algunos casos no fuese más que simple ignorancia) respecto a la base de la nueva prosperidad. Si hacen falta ingenieros, si los sueldos de los científicos de investigación aplicada y de los técnicos están subiendo, si corren liberalmente los fondos para la investigación y tareas de consulta, es porque se están invirtiendo miles de millones en una economía de preparación de guerra. *Silicon Valley,* así como todas las industrias de alta tecnología repartidas a lo largo y ancho de Estados Unidos, está produciendo miniordenadores y *chips* especiales para su uso en carros de combate, aviones, carros blindados, submarinos, *jeeps*, satélites de comunicaciones y meteorológicos, misiles, antimisiles y *bombas limpias.* Puede que la *guerra de las galaxias* del presidente Reagan no

sea más que un concepto ilusorio de defensa contra un ataque nuclear masivo, pero entre tanto se están ganando millones en contratos de defensa. Y el enorme gasto militar supone también la prosperidad para una amplia variedad de industrias y servicios civiles: la construcción de viviendas, de carreteras y de todo tipo de instalaciones, guarderías, salones de belleza, centros comerciales, bancos, etcétera.

Pregunté a alguna gente de mi edad y de la edad de mis hijas si se daba cuenta de que el motor principal de su prosperidad era el presupuesto de defensa. Algunos dijeron que sí, pero que era necesaria la *disuasión,* que los soviéticos habían aumentado su capacidad nuclear a gran velocidad durante los años de Carter, que Estados Unidos debía ponerse a su altura y que, en cualquier caso, el armamento de destrucción masiva no se utilizaría más que para negociar desde una posición de fuerza. Otros evadieron la cuestión de la estrategia nuclear y del gasto militar, insistieron en el ciclo comercial acostumbrado, en la expansión tradicional norteamericana y en los componentes de la *industria de servicios,* de carácter civil, de la nueva prosperidad.

De repente me acordé de mi amistad con el desaparecido Herbert Marcuse. Tras recibir un anónimo amenazándole de muerte en 1968, varios colegas, entre los que me encontraba, nos turnábamos para acompañarle a lo largo del recorrido de un kilómetro de su casa a la universidad. Aquellos paseos me dieron la oportunidad de disfrutar de su conversación, siempre animada. Uno de sus temas más frecuentes era la forma en que la cultura industrial avanzada favorecía preferentemente a las clases trabajadoras, anteriormente revolucionarias, y a los elementos *progresistas* de la clase media, tales como estudiantes y profesores de

Universidad. Los trabajadores de la industria automovilística y siderúrgica se habían vuelto conservadores porque defendían sus puestos de trabajo, sus altos salarios y sus futuras pensiones en la industria de defensa. Los profesores universitarios se habían vuelto conservadores porque la hora de trabajo estaba mejor pagada como consultores en la industria y el Gobierno que como profesores. Los estudiantes de ingeniería, que podían esperar ganar más en su primer empleo en la industria que lo que ganaban sus profesores tras 20 años de enseñanza, se harían, como es natural, políticamente conservadores o, por lo menos, políticamente indiferentes, lo cual, a efectos prácticos, significaba ser conservadores.

A raíz de aquella visita de dos semanas a California he pensado mucho en la psicología de los jóvenes profesionales entre los que estuve todo el tiempo. Muestran la ética del trabajo tradicional norteamericana en sus carreras y en la atención que prestan a sus casas. Su afluencia no se traduce en el empleo de la riqueza y el ocio en intereses humanísticos o en la preocupación por el futuro de la raza humana. Emplean el dinero para adquirir posesiones, y su tiempo libre y sus impulsos estéticos son absorbidos por el cuidado de sus casas, sus máquinas y jardines. Muchos van a la iglesia los domingos y se sienten reconfortados pensando que Dios aprueba la economía de guerra que forma la base de su prosperidad.

Prácticamente todos consiguen ignorar o racionalizar las implicaciones destructivas de su *estilo de vida.* ¿Conseguirán despertar a tiempo los dirigentes de los países no ligados a Estados Unidos o a la Unión Soviética para salvarnos a todos de un desastre de *alta tecnología?*

Exercise L.

1. On what personal experience does the author base the essay?

2. What most impressed the author about life in the US?

3. What is the major factor governing the organization of family life in the US, according to the author?

4. What specific contrasts did the author observe at the university during the Carter and Reagan administrations?

5. According to the author's analysis, what is the basis for the improved prosperity of the United States during the Reagan presidency?

6. What three responses did the author receive from Americans to questions about the sources of the new prosperity?

7. According to the author's application of Marcuse's analysis, what explains the political conservatism of automobile workers? Of university professors? Of engineering students?

8. According to the author's observations, what do affluent Americans use their money for? What do they not use it for?

9. What connection does the author make between high technology and the international political situation?

10. Summarize the central idea of this essay in a single sentence.

Now that you understand this author's claims, you are in a position to respond to them. Use the following questions to help you think about the essay. Remember to enjoy the fact that you have achieved the high level of reading skill that permits you to interpret and respond to this writer's opinion.

1. Is the author's description of the number and types of machines in American homes generally accurate? Is it accurate for your own home?

2. Is the description of family life generally accurate? How does it compare to the situation in your own family?

3. Do the author's comparisons of conditions under the two administrations agree with remarks made by American commentators? Do they agree with your own experience?

4. Does the author's explanation of the basis of the new economic prosperity convince you? If you agree, what other examples can you provide? If you disagree, what evidence can you provide for an alternative explanation?

5. If the author had questioned you about this issue, would you have given one of the three types of responses mentioned? Why? If you have a different response, what is it?

6. Do you think the author's explanations of increasing conservatism in various occupational classes are correct? Are there factors the author has overlooked? Do you agree that being politically indifferent is the same as being politically conservative? Why or why not?

7. The author claims that the situation described in the essay results in part from the application of the traditional North American work ethic. Do you agree? If you do agree, do you also agree that the situation is more dangerous than in the past?

8. Is the author's picture of affluent Americans' use of their money an accurate one? Does it describe your own personal priorities? Those of your friends?

This Peruvian political sign has a particular audience in mind. On what basis does it request support from this group?

9. How much do you think that the author's identification with Europe affects the perceptions and analysis presented in the article? How do the author's point of view and cultural background differ from your own? What effects do those differences have on your reaction to the essay?

10. This essay was written in January, 1985. Have any changes occurred since then, either in the United States or internationally, that might cause the author to change some of the content of the essay?

11. Do you think the essay is well written? Are the descriptions clear? Do they create a picture in the reader's mind? Is the argument sound and well defended? (Remember, you do not have to agree with an argument to recognize that it is well constructed!)

12. Do you agree with the author? If you were to write a responding essay of your own, what points would it make?

Congratulations! You are an accomplished user of the *Reading Strategy.* You might find it revealing to go back to the beginning of ***Entre líneas*** and reread the materials that you read only partially at earlier stages. You'll be surprised at how much more information you are able to extract from them now. The final unit of the book includes new reading materials for you to practice on. However, the real test of the *Reading Strategy* is in applying it to materials in Spanish that you select yourself because they contain information you need or want to read. Keep reading and keep THINKING!

UNIT

10
Moving Beyond the Reading Strategy

Applying the Reading Strategy

Vive leyendo

In this final unit, you will have an opportunity to practice the *Reading Strategy* with materials of the type found in popular magazines and newspapers. In fact, Unit 10 is presented in a magazine format with exercises appearing at the end. The reading section is self-contained with its own table of contents and page numbering system. Read the parts of Unit 10 in any order you like. Most of the reading passages are linked to exercises to help you review the various stages and techniques of the *Reading Strategy* and to check your comprehension of the passages. Each reading is identified by a letter keyed to the accompanying exercise, which often provides special hints about the reading. As you have seen, the best approach for materials with accompanying exercises is to proceed through the early decoding stage, read the exercise questions, and then do close reading. Before you turn to the readings, review the stages of the *Reading Strategy*.

Prereading. Examine the entire context unit for format features. Think about its probable purpose, its larger context, and its similarities to passages already familiar to you. Look for known vocabulary and words whose meanings you can guess. Determine the topic. Identify important (repeated) vocabulary. Think about the probable content of the passage. Formulate questions you expect the passage to answer. Skim to extract specific information.

Decoding (first phase). Work by paragraphs. (It helps to number them.) Use the first and last sentences or the first and last paragraphs to help you identify the main idea of the passage. Use good dictionary techniques to help you interpret essential vocabulary that is unfamiliar to you. In longer prose passages, identify the main idea of each paragraph. Think about the overall structure of the passage: its organization; the sequencing of ideas; the relationship of titles, photographs, and captions. Use the questions you originally formulated to revise your predictions about it.

Decoding (second phase). Work by sentences through each paragraph. Identify main verb cores. Concentrate on sequence cues. Beware of false cognates and metaphorical or idiomatic expressions. Think about the entire passage and its meaning. Making a summary helps you clarify the success of your comprehension techniques. Formulate new questions to guide you if you intend to do closer reading.

Comprehension. Reread the passage. Reconsider context and organization. Use your dictionary as necessary to enhance comprehension. Examine problem phrases as possible instances of figurative (nonliteral) language. Pay attention to the author's point of view and to cultural context. When you understand what you have read, think about it. What is your opinion? How would you respond to the writer? What new questions has the passage raised?

Now, enjoy the reading opportunities provided in this unit, but remember that the *Reading Strategy* is only a beginning, an approach. The techniques of the *Reading Strategy* are a key to communication with Spanish speakers of many times and places. The real value of the techniques lies in the pleasure and information to be gained from the writing you apply them to. Use them with confidence!

LÍNEAS

REVISTA PARA LECTORES

Despiértese Cada Mañana con el Nuevo MUNDO LATINO

Desde Miami, Los Angeles, New York, Washington y las capitales del mundo, conozca el mundo de los artistas, el mundo de deportes, el mundo de hoy. SIN, su cadena de televisión, le trae el **Mundo Latino**, en el primer programa matutino de entrevistas.

Mundo Latino combinará noticias, reportajes del tiempo, entrevistas, clases de cocina y ejercicios—todas las cosas que a Ud. le interesan.

No se lo pierda, lunes a viernes, 7:00 a.m.-9:30 a.m./ 6:00 a.m.-8:30 a.m. centro.

SIN Television Network 460 West 42 St. NY 10036

CONTENIDO

DEPARTAMENTOS

ARTÍCULOS

FICCIÓN

LIBROS

Un estudio revela cinco tipos de comportamiento del comprador de libros

BEL CARRASCO, **Barcelona**

Un estudio realizado por la firma Arthur Andersen por encargo de Alianza Editorial clasifica cinco tipos de actitudes de compra en el posible lector: por obligación de estudio o profesión, por intención propia, por influencia de la portada y el hecho de que sea un libro muy vendido o anunciado, para regalo o simple decoración y, por último, las compras de ocasión. Por otra parte, una anterior encuesta realizada en 1978 revela que el 41% de la población española de más de 18 años se puede considerar consumidora de libros.

Sólo el 41% de la población española de más de 18 años se puede considerar consumidora de libros, según un estudio realizado por encargo de la editorial Argos que se publicó en el número 252 de *El Lbro Epañol,* en 1978. Posteriormente se han efectuado diversos análisis que profundizan en la situación del mercado editorial y en las actitudes y hábitos de compra y lectura de los ciudadanos. El más reciente lo llevó a cabo la firma Arthur Andersen por encargo de Alianza Editorial y se presentó en el Congreso de Libreros, celebrado en Palma de Mallorca el pasado mes de mayo y sus resultados han permanecido prácticamente inéditos para el público en general.

Entre otros datos dicha investigación revela que es el título del libro el factor que determina su compra en un 26% de los casos. El 16% de los compradores elige en función del binomio título-autor y un 14% tiene también en cuenta la editorial. Otro 14% se decide según el tema del libro y un 10%, según el nombre del autor. El resto actúa de acuerdo con distintos motivos de índole personal o profesional.

En cuanto a los contenidos, los jóvenes prefieren las obras de autores clásicos y contemporáneos que estimulan la imaginación, libros de poesía, relatos de ficción científica, fantásticos e históricos. Los lectores de edad media muestran preferencia por los manuales, enciclopedias y, en general, las obras de carácter práctico e informativo. Los de más edad retornan a los clásicos y a los ensayos históricos que evocan el pasado.

Este cuadro de preferencias se refleja en la oferta editorial que dedica un 42% de los libros a la literatura y narrativa; un 25% a las ciencias sociales, historia, filosofía, etcétera; un 16% a los temas científicos; un 10% a la poesía y un 7% a los libros de música y arte.

Las condiciones del lector

Las condiciones que el lector-comprador de libros exige en un punto de venta de libros, según el estudio de Arthur Andersen, son las siguientes; en primer lugar, tener posibilidad de tocar y hojear el texto. Además, no sentirse demasiado controlado por el personal y, al mismo tiempo, poder disponer de un consejo o asesoría en caso de requerirla. Las ofertas, descuentos, suministros de novedades y la garantía de encontrar el libro deseado, son otros requisitos que valoran los lectores.

Los jóvenes son los principales alimentadores de la presencia del libro en el hogar a través de la escuela y la Universidad, fundamentalmente. La familia es otro ámbito institucional básico donde se genera y cultiva el hábito de lectura por la propia tradición familiar y el deseo de los padres de no ser superados por el nivel cultural de sus hijos.

La investigación de Andersen clasifica cinco tipos de actitudes de compra en el posible lector: por obligación, razones de estudio o profesión; por intención propia, tanto para tenerlo como para leerlo; por impulso, en el que influye la portada y el hecho de que sea un libro muy vendido o anunciado; como recurso, para regalo o simple decoración y, por último; las compras de ocasión.

—HISTORIA—

Se cumple el segundo centenario del nacimiento del mayor de los hermanos Grimm

FRANCESC ARROYO, **Barcelona**
Han pasado 200 años desde que en la villa de Hanau (actualmente en la República Democrática Alemana, RDA), cerca de la ciudad de Francfort, naciera el mayor de los seis hijos (cinco varones y una hembra) de un abogado apellidado Grimm: Jacob Ludwig Carl Grimm. Era el 4 de enero de 1785. Su hermano Wilhelm Carl Grimm, con el que ha pasado a la historia, nació un año más tarde, el 24 de febrero de 1786, también en Hanau. Para dos entusiastas de las tradiciones populares como ellos, haber pasado a la historia popular debe ser el mejor de los reconocimientos.

La obra más conocida de los hermanos Grimm (Jacob y Wilhelm) es la recopilación de cuentos publicada entre 1812 y 1822, que agrupa un total de 200 narraciones y que fueron tituladas *Kinder und Hausmärchen*. El éxito fue casi instantáneo y, a lo largo del tiempo, han sido traducidas a más de 70 idiomas de todo el mundo. Los hermanos Jacob y Wilhelm Grimm recopilaron en los dos volúmenes de la primera edición —tres en la segunda— una amplia gama de cuentos procedentes en su mayoría de la tradición oral. Cuentos como *Caperucita roja, La cenicienta* o *el sastrecillo valiente*, que forman hoy parte del acervo cultural de todos los niños del mundo y cuyo origen se pierde en la noche de los tiempos y se desvanece en múltiles geografías: Escandinavia, España, Irlanda, Escocia, Finlandia, Inglaterra, Holanda.

Jacob Grimm empezó su carrera como investigador en leyes, tras haber seguido los cursos correspondientes, entre 1802 y 1806, en la Universidad de Marburgo. Allí recibió las influencias de la época

a través de Clemens Brentano, un ferviente admirador de la poesía popular y Friedrich Karl von Savingy, uno de los impulsores de la escuela histórica de jurisprudencia.

Con Savigny Jacob Grimm fue a París, en 1805, para consultar una serie de manuscritos jurídicos medievales. Un año más tarde, ocupó el cargo de bibliotecario, al igual que haría después, en 1814, su hermano Wilhelm.

Pero Jacob y Wilhelm Grimm no fueron sólo eruditos del derecho, la lingüística o las leyendas populares. Dignos hijos de su tiempo, mantuvieron a lo largo de su vida una postura eminentemente liberal que se plasmó, por ejemplo, en el llamado *Manifiesto de los siete,* de 1837. Jacob y Wilhelm Grimm habían aceptado, en 1829, el cargo de bibliotecarios de la Universidad de Göttingen, puesto que llevaba aparejado un trabajo lectivo. Fue allí donde Jacob inició la redacción de *Deustche Mytologye.* Cuando Ernest Augustus accedió al electorado de Hannover, abolió la Constitución de 1833 por considerarla excesivamente liberal. Un grupo de siete profesores de la Universidad de Göttingen, entre los que se encontraban ambos hermanos, dirigieron un escrito al nuevo elector asegurando la lealtad a la anterior carta magna. Ambos fueron apartados inmediatamente de la docencia y Jacob desterrado.

En 1840, Jacob y Wilhelm aceptan la invitación de Federico Guillermo IV de Prusia para residir en Berlín como miembros de la Real Academia de Ciencias. En esta ciudad permanecieron hasta su muerte, el 16 de diciembre de 1859, la de Wilhelm; y el 20 de septiembre de 1863, la de Jacob.

Jacob Grimm, en primer plano, junto a su hermano Wilhelm, según un retrato al óleo de 1855.

El control del tráfico aéreo es una de las áreas en las que empiezan a utilizarse los sistemas expertos.

JOAQUÍN AMESTOY

Llega la inteligencia artificial

El primer centro privado de inteligencia artificial en España se dedicará a los sistemas expertos

MALÉN RUIZ DE ELVIRA, **Madrid**
Las prospecciones geológicas o petrolíferas, el control del tráfico aéreo, la optimización de las líneas de una compañía aérea, el diagnóstico médico o la utilización de ordenadores para descubrir fallos en los propios ordenadores son algunos de los campos en los que ha empezado ya a actuar la inteligencia artificial (IA), ese campo de la informática que trata de acercarse al modo de razonar humano.

En las próximas semanas se pondrá en marcha el primer centro de inteligencia artificial privado de España, que se centrará en la investigación y desarrollo de sistemas expertos. La creación del centro está prevista en el protocolo firmado por la empresa norteamericana Sperry con el Gobierno español para incorporarse al Plan Electrónico e Informático Nacional (PEIN).

Los sistemas expertos constituyen el sector más desarrollado, junto con la robótica, en el aspecto comercial de la IA. Estados Unidos mantiene el liderazgo en la puesta a punto de estos sistemas, desarrollados a menudo en centros universitarios en colaboración con las grandes empresas de informática, que llevan a cabo en la actualidad una auténtica búsqueda competitiva de *materia gris* para nutrir sus programas de inteligencia artificial.

Nombres exóticos y otros indicativos figuran en la todavía corta lista de sistemas expertos ya existentes en el mercado. Uno de los más conocidos, por ejemplo, el Internist —desarrollado en la universidad de Pittsburg—, indica su función de diagnóstico médico, mientras el Dendral, realizado en la universidad de Stanford, está relacionado con el mundo de la química, y el Deviser, del Jet Propulsion Laboratory, se refiere a la ayuda en el cálculo de trayectorias para los vuelos planetarios.

En total se calcula que no hay más de 200 sistemas expertos en estos momentos en el mundo, y muchos son muy específicos y no tienen aplicación general. Sin embargo, sus partidarios afirman que

funcionan, y citan el ejemplo de un sistema de ayuda oncológica que reunió el conocimiento de siete expertos y que ha dado únicamente un 5% de error en el diagnóstico del cáncer en 10.000 casos tratados.

"Un sistema experto pretende reunir el conocimiento fruto de la experiencia de los mejores expertos en un tema concreto y hacerlo accesible a todo el mundo a través de programas de ordenador", explica Mario Guerrero, consultor de Sperry en España. Saturnino Martín Vicente, de la facultad de Informática de Madrid, concreta más: "Un sistema experto es un programa de ordenador inteligente que utiliza procedimientos de deducción y conocimiento para resolver problemas complejos o difíciles que hasta ahora sólo podía hacer el ser humano".

El sentido común

La dificultad que han encontrado los especialistas en IA se centra en la forma de plasmar el conocimiento, algo mucho más difícil de lo que podría parecer a primera vista. La ingenuidad de los que creyeron que era algo relativamente fácil llevó en los años setenta al fracaso de los primeros experi-

mentos de inteligencia artificial que intentaron la traducción automática de un idioma a otro. Encontraron que la codificación del conocimiento difícilmente englobaba la del sentido común humano, una mezcla de conocimiento y experiencia propios y transmitidos que es muy difícil de definir, de concretar y sobre todo de plasmar en un papel.

A partir de ahí se replanteó la forma de enfocar el problema, y se ha venido avanzando pausadamente —tanto en sistemas expertos como en robótica— en la visión y el tratamiento del lenguaje natural (ordenadores que hablan y escuchan).

Para tener las herramientas para esta codificación se ha creado lo que ya es una nueva ciencia, la ingeniería del conocimiento, que se basa en la lógica formal y que se relaciona tanto con las matemáticas como con la filosofía. Para hoy está prevista en Madrid la celebración de un simposio sobre IA —con la presencia de una de las máximas autoridades en el tema, Edward Feigenbaum— y el próximo 4 de noviembre comenzará también en Madrid un simposio internacional sobre la ingeniería del conocimiento.

Sin embargo, un sistema exper-

to, por ahora, es únicamente una ayuda al especialista, que es el que debe tomar la decisión final. De hecho, un sistema experto no da una solución, sino varias, explica en qué se basa cada una de ellas y calcula la tasa de error probable. No puede aprender de sus propios errores, aunque no se descarta que lo logre. El sistema experto se puede ir perfeccionando a medida que se adquiere experiencia en su uso, lo que de hecho se hace continuamente; pero éste perfeccionamiento lo debe hacer el programador, corrigiendo la base de conocimientos del sistema.

Los directivos de Sperry explican que les ha costado mucho que este centro —el único que la empresa norteamericana va a poner en Europa— se haga en España. Las condiciones que impone el PEIN, junto a su propio interés en traer a España tecnología de punta, lo consiguieron. Sperry ha entrado en el campo de la inteligencia artificial hace relativamente poco. Su centro en Estados Unidos, que empezó a funcionar en 1983, todavía no está a pleno rendimiento, aunque ya trabaja sobre 26 sistemas expertos y lleva un ritmo rápido. Santos Alonso, director comercial de Sperry, SA, señala que se trata de una verdadera transferencia de tecnología. El director será español, Carlos Fernández Esteban, y para 1988 se espera que cuente con 17 personas. La dotación del centro será de 1.800 millones en cuatro años, y se prevé la colaboración con cuatro universidades españolas, todavía por determinar, para actitividades de investigación y desarrollo que puedan interesar a empresas concretas.

La dotación de *hardware* se basa en el Explorer, una máquina diseñada para IA que comercializa Sperry en colaboración con Texas Instruments, y el *software* es el Knowledge Engineering Environment (KEE), un paso más en los lenguajes de inteligencia artificial después del LISP, que ayuda a la realización de sistemas expertos.

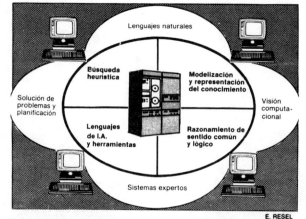

En el centro del esquema figuran los elementos básicos de la inteligencia artificial. Rodeando el núcleo, las áreas de desarrollo de IA, basadas en estos elementos.

Indudablemente, las plantas son elementos decorativos muy importantes, porque sus colores y sus formas son agradables a la vista, además de que su presencia le da vida y calor a cualquier ambiente. Pero es fundamental saber escoger el tipo de planta que va bien con nuestros muebles, la iluminación

CASA

interior y la función y el color de las habitaciones de nuestra casa o apartamento. En otras palabras, tienes que conocer cuál especie de planta se daría bien en la atmósfera calurosa y super-iluminada de la cocina, cuál en la semi-oscuridad de la sala de estar, y cuál en el dormitorio. ¿Captas la idea...? Te recomendamos que, para no fallar, recurras a plantas de interior que sean muy fuertes, ya que son las que no necesitan cuidados minuciosos que te esclavizarán.

Para que tengas una idea... las plantas de hojas de color verde uniforme prefieren la sombra (¡regias para la sala de estar y los dormitorios!) y hasta la ausencia total de luz. Las de hojas coloreadas, por el contrario, necesitan mucha luz, porque si no la tienen... ¡se mueren! Como tú sabes, los cactus y las plantas grasas (las de hojas muy gruesas) soportarán el sol directo de una ventana, porque ellas tienen la capacidad de almacenar mucha agua. En caso de que seas una fanática de las flores o tu apartamento tenga una decoración moderna (de líneas sencillas, muebles modulares y elementos de metal) decora con violetas africanas, begonias (éstas tienen colores brillantes), camelias, orquídeas o tus flores favoritas.

De más está decirte que el cuidado de las plantas es esencial para que éstas se encuentren saludables y bellas. De manera que debes tener a mano vitaminas, fertilizantes, tierra e insecticidas. Las plantas de interiores por lo general se riegan dos veces a la semana (una si viven en aire acondicionado central) y para evitar que se "asfixien" a causa del polvo o la grasa del ambiente, sus hojas deben limpiarse una vez por semana con una esponja húmeda. Además, las hojas marchitas y secas deben retirarse semanalmente. Si notas que sus raíces crecen demasiado, trasplántalas para tiestos más grandes y, sobre todo... ¡préstales atención! Te lo agradecerán embelleciendo tu casa.

PLANTAS

Las plantas y las flores cumplen una mayor función decorativa cuando la habitación en que se van a colocar está pintada de blanco o de un tono neutro que requiere un toque de color. En la cocina, por ejemplo, es imprescindible la presencia de las plantas. Pero recuerda que éstas deben ser de fuerte constitución para que resistan la atmósfera cargada y calurosa de esta pieza. El aloe, las distintas variedades de cactus y las plantas pertenecientes a la familia de las _Bromiliáceas_ (éstas son célebres por sus cualidades ornamentales y su fortaleza) son las perfectas para darle vida a una cocina-comedor.

COLOCALAS EN LUGARES ESTRATEGICOS

Publicaciones del Fondo de Cultura Económica

Román Piña Chan
CHICHEN ITZA. LA CIUDAD DE LOS BRUJOS DEL AGUA

Este libro habla de un pueblo y de una ciudad. La ciudad de los brujos del agua: Chichén Itzá. Mediante la reconstrucción de la historia de esa ciudad, Román Piña Chan adelanta hipótesis que seguramente habrán de revolucionar nuestras ideas sobre las influencias que ejercieron entre sí las culturas de Tula y de Chichén Itzá. Según el autor, ni la historia ni la arqueología apoyan la opinión generalizada de que los toltecas de Tula influyeron sobre Chichén Itzá; más bien sucedió lo contrario: fueron los itzáes quienes influyeron tardíamente en los toltecas.

Oskar Lange
ECONOMIA POLITICA

El propósito fundamental del autor es mostrar cómo pueden establecerse las leyes que determinan el desarrollo de la moderna sociedad económica y de qué manera pueden ser utilizadas para someter el fenómeno a la voluntad humana. Lange considera que la economía es el principal instrumento para lograr, mediante la planificación, el máximo beneficio posible para los pueblos: de ahí su contexto marcadamente social y profundamente humano, que reviste un especial interés para Hispanoamérica, dados sus añejos problemas de subdesarrollo y su posición particular frente a la política de coexistencia pacífica.

Claude Morin
MICHOACAN EN LA NUEVA ESPAÑA DEL SIGLO XVIII

El estudio de Claude Morin —inédito aún en su original francés; el autor es canadiense— tiene como escenario el "antiguo Michoacán, región centro occidental de México, tierra de la plata y cuna de la Indepencia del país, por lo menos en su primera versión". De entrada, el autor declara su instrumental y su perspectiva: el horizonte teórico del materialismo histórico; a partir de esta fundamentación metodológica, Morin procede a desplegar su obra. Cada vez, y esta obra lo ratifica, nuestra visión del pasado colonial mexicano resulta un campo fértil para entender variados mecanismos de la historia de nuestro país así como de Hispanoamérica.

Toros

DEPORTES

¿Será cierto?

Se llevaron vacas bravas a Estados Unidos

* Personas que recientemente estuvieron en California nos dieron la noticia * Ya hay seis ganaderías bravas en ese Estado norteamericano *

Por Ricardo TORRES

Hace tiempo publicamos que de muy buen fuente nos había llegado noticia de que en Estados Unidos había ya ganaderías de reses bravas y que en una de ellas se tenía una punta de vacas bravas mexicanas, cosa que nos hizo parar la oreja porque de todos es sabido que está o estaba prohibida la exportación de hembras de ganado de lidia.

En aquella ocasión pedimos a los directivos de la Asociación Nacional de Criadores de Toros de Lidia se hiciera una investigación al respecto y hasta la fecha no hemos sabido que se haya hecho cosa alguna.

Recordemos también que hace varios años se descubrió una exportación fraudulenta de vacas bravas de Torrecilla a Venezuela y en aquella ocasión se llegó al grado de mandar una comisión formada por varios ganaderos para que, en caso de encontrarlas, se diera muerte a esas vacas, cosa que al parecer sucedió y hasta se habló de que se habían traído los cueros de las reses sacrificadas para mayor prueba.

El pasado viernes desayunamos con un taurino de reconocido prestigio que recientemente había estado de visita en Estados Unidos, concretamente en el estado de California, y nos recibió con la noticia de que ya había seis ganaderías bravas en aquellas tierras, siendo la última de reciente formación con VACAS MEXICANAS que, según

le dijeron personas de su amistad y de suma confianza, habían sido llevadas recientemente con permisos debidamente registrados por los gobiernos de ambos países.

Comentamos el incidente con un ganadero amigo nuestro, quien nos señaló que andábamos atrasados de noticias, pues desde hace tiempo se andaba moviendo el agua para tratar de conseguir los permisos necesarios para sacar vacas bravas de nuestras ganaderías. Todo ello con la bendición y el apoyo de la Asociación Nacional de Criadores de Toros de Lidia, A.C., que preside el buen amigo Chacho Barroso.

Nada de lo anterior lo podemos asegurar pero una vez más sacamos a colación ese ya muy trillado refrán de que "cuando el río suena es que agua lleva".

Una vez más le pedimos a los directivos de la Asociación de Criadores de Toros de Lidia sean tan amables de investigar como está la cosa y que nos lo hagan saber para que ustedes, amables lectores, estén enterados de ese tipo de cosas que de una u otra forma dañan nuestra fiesta brava, pese a que llenan de dinero las bolsas de unos cuantos aprovechados.

Como final diremos que las vacas que nos dijeron pastan en Estados Unidos y que fueron llevadas no hace mucho tiempo, eran de una ganadería norteña, de poca monta, propiedad de un Sr. Arce, padre del novillero Manolo Arce.

INFORMACIÓN PARA EL CONSUMIDOR

Los Diamantes

¿Quiere usted saber cuáles son las características que determinan el valor y la calidad de un diamante? Si va a adquirir una de estas gemas debe saber a qué atenerse, para no dejarse confundir. Las cualidades principales son cuatro: talla, color, pureza y peso en quilates.

Talla: mucha gente confunde la talla con la forma de un diamante. La talla es una de las características más importantes a la hora de determinar su valor y calidad. La forma es una mera cuestión de gustos y no afecta el valor del diamante. Una buena talla produce más brillos y destellos. Y ésa es precisamente la labor de un tallador experto: conseguir que el diamante refleje el máximo de luz.

Color: el mejor diamante es el *incoloro* (sin ningún color). La ausencia de color permite a la luz atravesar el diamante limpiamente y transformarse en un perfecto arcoiris, como en un prisma. La escala de colores del diamante va desde el totalmente incoloro, o blanco excepcional, al color. Las diferencias entre los tonos son muy sutiles.

Pureza: Durante el proceso de cristalización de los diamantes, la naturaleza fue dejando minúsculas huellas en la gran mayoría. Estas características naturales se llaman *inclusiones* (comúnmente, grietas o fisuras) y no afectan para nada la belleza ni la durabilidad de la gema. Un diamante que carece de inclusiones, sean internas o externas, es considerado de la calidad más alta, ya que nada impide a la luz atravesarlo limpiamente. Si observamos un diamante con una lupa de 10 aumentos y no tiene ninguna inclusión, podemos clasificarlo como "internamente perfecto".

Peso en quilates: el tamaño de un diamante se divide en quilates. Un quilate se divide en 100 puntos, de manera que un diamante de 75 puntos pesa 0.75 quilates. Para determinar el valor de un diamante se considera factor primordial su tamaño. Sin embargo, dos diamantes de igual tamaño pueden tener dos valores totalmente diferentes; todo dependerá de su calidad. Los diamantes de calidad excepcional se pueden encontrar en distintos tamaños. Estos que mostramos en el cuadro de arriba son los más frecuentes.

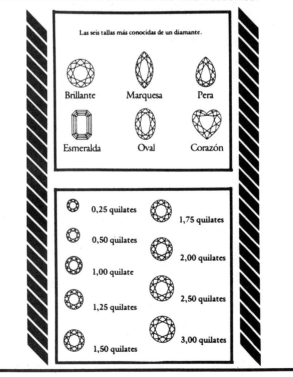

Las seis tallas más conocidas de un diamante.

Brillante · Marquesa · Pera · Esmeralda · Oval · Corazón

0,25 quilates · 0,50 quilates · 1,00 quilate · 1,25 quilates · 1,50 quilates · 1,75 quilates · 2,00 quilates · 2,50 quilates · 3,00 quilates

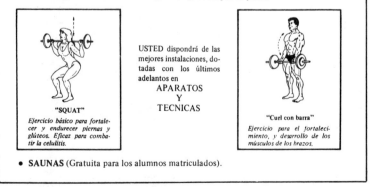

SALUD

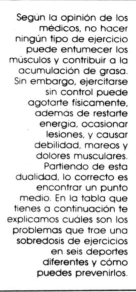

Ejercicio—Correcto o incorrecto

Según la opinión de los médicos, no hacer ningún tipo de ejercicio puede entumecer los músculos y contribuir a la acumulación de grasa. Sin embargo, ejercitarse sin control puede agotarte físicamente, además de restarte energía, ocasionar lesiones, y causar debilidad, mareos y dolores musculares. Partiendo de esta dualidad, lo correcto es encontrar un punto medio. En la tabla que tienes a continuación te explicamos cuáles son los problemas que trae una sobredosis de ejercicios en seis deportes diferentes y cómo puedes prevenirlos.

NATACION	JOGGING	DANZA AEROBICA	BICICLETA	TENIS	LEVANTAMIENTO DE PESAS
● Los estilos de natación que exigen brazadas muy fuertes o nadar demasiado rápido pueden lesionar e inflamar los músculos de los hombros, el cuello y la espalda. ● Nadar excesivamente contribuye a que los músculos del cuello y de la espalda se desarrollen demasiado. ● Los productos químicos del agua pueden producir infecciones en los oídos y en los ojos.	● Correr o trotar sobre una superficie muy dura produce lesiones en los tobillos, las rodillas, la parte baja de la espalda, y callosidades y ampollas en los pies. ● Hacer inadecuadamente los ejercicios de calentamiento y correr demasiado aprisa, causa molestias y dolores muy fuertes en los músculos, además de cortar la respiración y provocar problemas en la menstruación.	● Hacer movimientos demasiado bruscos o rápidos puede tensar y lastimar los músculos. ● Los saltos muy exagerados sobre superficies muy duras lesionan las articulaciones y producen muchos dolores en los tobillos, las rodillas, las caderas y la espalda. ● La danza aeróbica, por la fricción sobre los pies, puede causar molestas callosidades y ampollas dolorosas.	● La inclinación del cuerpo para alcanzar los manubrios de la bicicleta se refleja en fuertes dolores y tensión en el cuello y en la espalda. ● Estar sentadas por muchísimo tiempo sobre la silla de la bicicleta produce dolores en el *derrière*. ● Andar en bicicleta sobre superficies irregulares y bajo un sol radiante, puede ocasionar una deshidratación muy fuerte en el organismo.	● En el tenis se practican movimientos violentos que pueden resultar en torceduras de tobillos y desgarraduras en los ligamentos. ● Usar una raqueta muy pequeña produce inflamación en los músculos de la muñeca. ● Esforzarse mucho para pegarle a la pelota causa estiramiento muscular. ● Jugar tenis bajo el sol en la temporada de mucho calor produce dolor de cabeza y fatiga.	● El uso incorrecto de las pesas (usar unas muy pesadas, levantarlas antes de los ejercicios de calentamiento y no llevar el ritmo recomendado) puede resultar en una lesión de los músculos. ● Pasar drásticamente de un ejercicio con pesas a otro, sin hacer un ejercicio de estiramiento, causa mareos. ● El exceso de peso afecta el corazón y la flexibilidad de los músculos.
● Antes de nadar, hay que calentar y estirar los músculos con ejercicios, y nadar despacio durante los primeros 10 minutos. ● Si notas que los músculos se desarrollan mucho, debes reducir la rutina de natación. ● Es imprescindible usar *goggles* (una especie de anteojos submarinos) y tapones en los oídos para evitar las irritaciones que causa el cloro de la piscina.	● Se debe trotar sobre superficies blandas, como la hierba o pistas de goma; evitar el asfalto y el cemento, y usar tenis que tengan un buen acolchonamiento. ● Antes de trotar, hay que hacer ejercicios de calentamiento y luego comenzar a correr muy lentamente. ● Si la menstruación se altera, se debe suspender el ejercicio y consultar al ginecólogo inmediatamente.	● Es esencial practicar ejercicios de calentamiento antes de la danza aeróbica y usar zapatillas especiales para este tipo de ejercicio. ● Si no se puede seguir el ritmo de la clase, se debe tomar un descanso y continuar después practicando el ejercicio. ● Es indispensable usar medias para que el pie no tenga fricción con las zapatillas, y evitar las ampollas y las callosidades.	● Es necesario ajustar los manubrios de la bicicleta lo más hacia arriba posible. Así la espalda no tendrá que flexionarse mucho. ● Se debe sustituir la silla regular por una más acolchonada. ● Antes de andar en *bici*, hay que hacer ejercicios de calentamiento, pedaleando despacio y después con rapidez. Si el recorrido es largo, hay que llevar agua en una botella plástica.	● Para practicar este deporte, hay que usar zapatos tenis que ajusten cómodamente. ● Evitar los problemas en las muñecas usando una raqueta de mango largo, que no tenga las cuerdas muy tensas. ● Realizar ejercicios de calentamiento. ● Proteger las manos con cinta adhesiva para evitar las callosidades. ● Practicar este ejercicio moderadamente durante la temporada de calor.	● Antes de usar las pesas, se deben conocer todas las indicaciones e instrucciones del equipo. También hay que conocer el peso adecuado que debe usarse, pero tomando en cuenta los músculos que se desean desarrollar más. ● Descansar y hacer ejercicios de estiramiento entre una sesión y otra de levantamiento de pesas y complementar el programa con ejercicios aeróbicos.

PERSONALIDAD

CASAL ES EL nombre de un artista, un cantante, compositor, arreglista y productor. Casal es música estética. Casal es español. Casal es EMI Capitol.

Se nos ha preguntado en ocasiones cuál es el común denominador en la carrera de Casal. Al final, hemos tenido que abandonar cualquier tipo de fórmula y refugiarnos en el artista. No había más remedio.

Se puede decir que Casal es un cantante porque sólo se precisa el escucha, ya que él posee una técnica elevada, un poder de afinación superior a la media habitual: es una voz con gusto, dúctil, llamativa, con un arco iris de posibilidades. Pero no se le puede llamar sólo cantante.

Se puede decir que Casal es un compositor porque ha escrito casi todas las letras de sus canciones, porque posee una intuición especial, una rara inteligencia musical entre lo popular y lo selecto: combina las dos ecuaciones con sorprendente ductilidad, no es un compositor de élite. Puede serlo; sin embargo, no es un compositor estrictamente popular o de canción comercial. Su canción "Op-art" para Goma de Mascar fue un lujo en un mundo comercial.

Se puede decir que Casal es un músico porque combina la habilidad de componer armonía y aparearla con el único objeto de la percusión. Toca la batería y es amigo de los instrumentos electrónicos, y es capaz de sorprender con el sonido de una extraña guitarra japonesa que vigila como una reliquia.

Se puede decir, también, que Casal es un productor porque ya había acometido la aventura antes con Goma de Mascar y, últimamente, con Obús, un grupo juvenil de heavy metal. Tiene idea de producto final, paciencia y comprensión.

Se puede decir que Casal es pintor, diseñador y mucho más, porque se trata de un artista que ha tenido que pintar y diseñar. Entonces, ¿qué definición podríamos tomar? Sólo una para salir del atolladero: artista.

Casal no es músico o, mejor dicho, no sabe música, pero esto no supone una frustración. En el mejor de los casos le encanta depender del equipo que habitualmente trabaja con él y con el cual se entiende perfectamente.

Se sabe que este artista compone mentalmente incluyendo las armonías, melodías, incluso los "gimmicks" instrumentales, de tal manera que el problema se plantea cuando tiene que explicar a los demás las cosas que se van escribiendo o ejecutando. En la grabación de su segundo LP., donde se grabó el hit "Embrujada", estuvo como productor Julián Ruiz, con el cual Casal está unido por una gran amistad que luego se refleja en el estudio, donde simplemente con miradas o frases sueltas, pueden entenderse perfectamente.

El corte del sencillo "Embrujada" se realizó en Town House, Londres, y la gente que trabajó en él se refirió al tema como "New spanish sound", o sea, "El nuevo sonido español", para ellos esta canción era un clarísimo 'hit'.

En el mismo acetato se grabó otro 'hit' potencial intitulado "African chic", el cual, cuando se escuche en México, será sin duda un éxito.

La tecnología, el perfeccionismo, la estética y el profesionalismo, son dosis importantes en su fórmula de trabajo. "Siempre me ciño" —dice Casal— "a las primeras ideas que van surgiendo en mi mente pues considero que son más válidas que lo que el resto de la fórmula pueda aportar". De ahí que utilice los medios tecnológicos en función de sus ideas, nunca en sentido contrario.

Casal ha comentado: "cuando tengo que explicar a los músicos cada una de las partes que han de interpretarse surge la paranoia. Todo esto supone no limitarse, ya que si fuera instrumentista acabaría componiendo a expensas de mis posibilidades. De cualquier forma, me encantaría tocarlo todo; tan sólo es por no sufrir tanto a lo largo de todo el proceso".

En la grabación del álbum "Etiqueta negra" se utilizaron, por ejemplo, todo tipo de instrumentos nuevos, tales como las percusiones electrónicas "Simmons", "Roland" y "Lynn", unas programadas básicamente y otras disparadas por timbales acústicos: el "bass line", utilizado como secuenciador de medios graves; el bajo "stick" de diez cuerdas, que emite dos octavas más graves que el normal; el "emulator", especie de melotrón electrónico, y los sintetizadores "PPG", "Jupiter 8", "Prophet". . . en fin, estaban todos.

El LP. fue grabado digitalmente en los estudios Audiofilm de Madrid, y procesado también en digital en los famosos estudios Abbey Road de Londres.

El productor del disco fue Julián Ruiz. "Me gusta mucho trabajar con Julián", comentó Casal; "veo su cara reflejada en el cristal del estudio y ya sé si le está gustando lo que hacemos o no. Nuestros gustos musicales son muy semejantes: Peter Gabriel, Johnny Warman, Malcolm McLaren, Quincy Jones. . . Me gusta trabajar con un productor, me siento más seguro y me quito de encima gran parte de la responsabilidad. Por el contrario, cuando trabajo como productor para otros artistas, me siento totalmente padre, me preocupo hasta la exageración".

"Etiqueta negra" es el segundo LP. de Casal y es, sin duda, la confirmación absoluta de la categoría de un artista. "Poker para un perdedor" es el nuevo sencillo también incluido en este LP. y hay temas para todos los gustos y tendencias como la balada más atrevida y elaborada "Un minuto más", el exorcismo de miedo en el clímax sobrecogedor de "Los pájaros". Este disco salió en 1983.

Y Casal es ahora un artista que se promocionará con fuerza en México.

MUSICA ESTETICA

TELEGUÍA

Lunes
MAÑANA—TARDE JUN 20

LA PROXIMA SEMANA DON PEDRO VARGAS
TERMINA DE RECORDAR SU VIDA... NO DEJE
DE ADQUIRIR SU EJEMPLAR DE TELE GUIA

¿CUALES SON LAS ACTIVIDADES DE JUAN
FERRARA EN PUERTO RICO?... SEPALO
LEYENDO LA PROXIMA SEMANA TELE GUIA

Lunes
JUN 20   TARDE

Lunes 20 San Silverio

Lunes

7.00 🄫 HOY MISMO. Noticiario.

[MAÑANA] 🄭 7. A.M. Noticiario.

8.00 🄬 TELESECUNDARIA.

🄮 DIVULGACION UNIVERSITA-RIA. Cátedra Universitaria. Justicia y Sociedad; 9.00: Educación Para la Salud; 10.00: Productividad y Administración; 11.00: Apoyo Académico; 11.30: La Prueba Confesional; 12.00: Divulgación y Cultura.

10.00 🄪 CORTE Y CONFECCION. Clases.

10.30 🄪 LA MUELA DEL JUICIO. Educativo. La Amistad. Cuáles son los elementos que influyen para que los humanos hagan mistades, qué afinidad debe existir entre los seres humanos.

11.00 🄫 TODOS PARA TODOS. Consejos

🄪 TEMAS DE PRIMARIA. Ier. grado. Lecturas Interpretación de Textos.

11.30 🄬 ALBRICIAS. Informativo.

🄪 HISTORIA BAJO LAS ARENAS. Documental. El Emperador que Llegó de Africa.

12.00 🄪 EL MARAVILLOSO MUNDO [TARDE] DE LA CIENCIA. Documental. Hacia el Mañana.

12.30 🄫 CLUB DEL HOGAR. Variedades, humorismo.

🄮 SECUNDARIA INTENSIVA PARA ADULTOS. Matemáticas I.

1.00 🄳 INTRODUCCION A LA UNIVERSIDAD. Cátedra Universitaria.

Biotecnología; 1.30: La Universidad También es Deporte; 2.00: Alimentación y Desarrollo; 2.30: Historia Novohispana; 3.00: Sicología Ahora.

2.00 🄫 24 HORAS. Noticiario.

🄮 MUSICA.

🄭 PRIMERA EDICION. Noticias.

2.30 🄫 PELICULA.
El Rey del Barrio. (Comedia). 1949. Germán Valdés, "Tin Tan"; Silvia Pinal. Ladrón que se hace pasar por ferrocarrilero, vive en una vecindad con su hijo y trata de ayudar a una vecina para que no caiga en la mala vida.

🄪 PARTIDOS POLITICOS. Propaganda política. P.D.M.

2.45 🄪 DE PESOS Y CENTAVOS. Orientación.

3.00 🄮 SEÑORITA COMETA. Comedia.

🄪 ENLACE. Noticiario.

🄭 OCIO Y CULTURA. Literatura, cine, danza, ópera, deportes, entrevistas. Sally de Perete.

3.30 🄬 APRENDAMOS JUNTOS. Alfabetización.

🄮 LOS HIJOS DE LOS PICAPIEDRA. Dibujos animados.

🄳 LA TORMENTA. Telenovela histórica. Repetición. Capítulo 56. Emiliano Zapata es torturado cruelmente por insurrecto, amarrado de cara al sol y sin gota de agua.

🄪 HOMBRES, MUJERES Y ANIMALES. Reportajes.

🄭 LOS DIAS FELICES. Dibujos animados. Las aventuras de tres simpáticos muchachos con su perro

en el espacio. La Gran Muralla de Ming-Fu.

4.00 🄬 PELICULA.
La Venenosa. (Aventuras). 1949. Armando Calvo, Gloria Marín. La vida de todos los artistas de un circo y una bella clarividente que resulta faltal para una banda de ladrones.

🄮 LA CARRERA ESPACIAL DE YOGUI. Dibujos animados.

🄳 AVENTURA DEL PENSAMIENTO. Documental. Los campesinos de Kafa Hari.

🄪 LA MUELA DEL JUICIO. (Repetición de las 10.30)

🄭 EL REY ARTURO. Dibujos animados. Los Caballeros de la Mesa Cuadrada y su lealtad a su atontado rey.

4.30 🄫 LA PANTERA ROSA. Dibujos animados.

🄮 EL HOMBRE ARAÑA. Dibujos animados.

🄪 TEMAS DE PRIMARIA. Ier. grado. (Repetición de las 11.00 A.M.)

🄭 LA PRINCESA SALLY. Dibujos animados. El Duende del Viento Norte.

5.00 🄫 AMOR AJENO. Telenovela. Capítulo 41.—Pablo promete a Charly que dará la ayuda necesaria para que Susana v.va. Oscar exige dinero a Linda, prometiendo que ahora sí entregará las dos cartas comprometedoras que tiene de ella. Susana sólo piensa en reunirse con su hijita, a la que cree muerta. El doctor Serrano llama a unos especialistas para que vayan a verla.

🄮 METEORO ROBIN HOOD. Dibujos animados.

🄳 EL TESORO DEL SABER. La Forma Alegre de Aprender. Capítulo 56: A.B.N. y A.R.N.

🄪 INSTANTANEAS MUNDIALES. Documental. Grecia.

🄭 CANDY. Dibujos animados.

5.30 🄫 BIANCA VIDAL. Telenovela. Capítulo 146.—Bianca va a buscar a Mónica al sanatorio y allí se encuentra con el doctor Mauricio, su ex compañero de Prepa. Nana María cuenta a José Miguel que Bianca se sacrificará nuevamente con tal de saber el paradero del niño. La foto de Rodolfito sale en todos los periódicos de la tarde, pero Chenta no lo ha leído todavía. Bianca promete a Mónica olvidarse de José Miguel para siempre.

🄮 ADIOS JOSEFINA. Dibujos animados. El Secreto de la Ballena.

🄳 ¿QUE HACES? ¿QUIEN ERES? Orientación Vocacional. Luis, Lucero y Fernando presentan concursantes e invitados en las secciones: ¿Qué profesión tiene?, ¿Qué hubieras querido ser?, ¡Un día en la vida, Tu tiempo es oro y Datos, datos y más datos.

🄪 LAS BATALLAS DEL SIGLO. Documental. Verdún. (Segunda parte).

🄭 LA CASA DE LOS MUCHACHOS. Polémica.

Lunes
TARDE   JUN 20

Lunes
JUN 20 TARDE-NOCHE

Horario estelar

	6:00	6:30	7:00	7:30	8:00	8:30
2	Chispita	Busca Paraíso	XETU	Chiquilladas	Chespirito	
4	Cuando Regrese Mamá. Película				Las grandes peleas	
5	S. Amigos	Picapiedra	Flash Gordon	Popeye	Increíble	
8	Qué haces	Tú a alguien	Contrapunto		México Cultura	
11	Ferias	Desastres	Primaria	Aprendamos	Enlace	Cómo Vivir
13	Ser mujer	Sangre y Arena	Los Médicos		Teatro Universal	

CABLEVISION

7	Tuned in...	Over easy	News	B. Miller	Entertainment	You asked...
10	Square Pegs	Small & Frye	Alice movie	One day	Cagney & Lancey	
16	Música		Rosa de leios		Disneylandia	
20	Deportes de todo el mundo traídos directamente por satélite					
23	El Mariachi Desconocido. Película				24 horas	

Horario estelar
Vea la programación para más detalles

	9:00	9:30	10:00	10:30	11:00	11:30	
Inc/Hijos van	El maleficio	24 horas			México en la Cultura		2
Beisbol grandes ligas							4
Magnum		Profesionales			Hawaii 5-0		5
Noche a noche		Gdes. Autores			Garibaldi. Película		8
La Pareja Humana			Escándalo en la Costa Azul. Película				11
Siete días		Crónica de los Años 20			Programa Esp.		13

CABLEVISION

Incredible		Movie T.B.A.					7
News	Tonight show		Late ninght		News		10
Amores Juveniles. Película				Música			16
Deportes de todo el mundo traídos directamente por satélite.							20
Cuánto Vale tu Hijo. Película			El Centauro Pancho Villa. Película				23

6.00 2 CHISPITA. Telenovela.
Capítulo 153.—Lucía no puede conocer a Bertha, pero Alejandro la invita a cenar. Lola llega poco después, met'che como siempre y también es invitada a cenar. Olga recuerda a J. Carlos que falta poco para su boda y Juan Carlos y Braulio se reconcilian.
4 PELICULA.
Cuando Regrese Mamá. (Melodrama). 1959. Rafael Bertrand, María Duval. Seis hermanos tratan de que dos vecinos se casen para que así los adopten.
5 SUPER AMIGOS. Dibujos animados.
11 FIESTA DE MEXICO. La Triste Fiesta de Santiago Apóstol. En el pueblo Tzotzil de la sierra Chiapaneca, se lleva a cabo esta fiesta pagano religiosa.
13 EL OFICIO DE SER MUJER. Reportajes. Entrevistas. "Hasta la Cocina". Conductora: Nadia Piamonte.

6.30 2 EN BUSCA DEL PARAISO. Telenovela.
Capítulo 154.—Obsesionado con la idea de quiénes pueden ser los padres de Alberto, Antonio pide a Enrique pregunte a Gustavo dónde puede verlo para tratar algo muy delicado respecto a Patricia. Sofía critica a Patricia su instinto maternal. Esta acepta tenerlo y asegura que Leonardo no es su hijo. Sabino y Natalia van a la academia, y Leonardo se avergüenza de que sean sus padres. Estos aseguran a Alberto que no es hijo de Antonio.
5 TRAVESURAS DE LOS PICAPIEDRA. Dibujos animados. Pebbles, Campeona de Futbol.
8 TU... A ALGUIEN LE IMPORTAS. Dramatización de problemas. Orientación sobre el comportamiento juvenil. Conductores: Jaime Alejo Castillo y Ana Cristina Fernández. Producción: Salvador Ortiz. Dirección: Ricardo Franco.
11 GRANDES DESASTRES. Documental.
13 SANGRE Y ARENA. Telenovela. De Vicente Blanco Ibáñez. Con: Luis Miranda, Ana Lilia Tovar y María Fernanda.

7.00 2 XE TU. SUEÑO POSIBLE. Concurso. René Casados y Marcela Páez. El artista invitado, debe escoger entre los tres concursantes. al que mejor conteste y haga sus preguntas.
5 FLASH GORDON. Dibujos animados. Planeta en Peligro.

8 CONTRAPUNTO. Periodístico. Jacobo Zabludovsky.
11 PRIMARIA INTENSIVA PARA ADULTOS. Comunicación. Contemos hasta 100. Sumemos hasta 100.
13 LOS MEDICOS. Melodrama. Mi Médico, mi Amigo.

7.30 2 CHIQUILLADAS. Cómico infantil. Genny Hoffman, Pituka y Petaka, Chuchito, Carlitos Espejel, Mago Rody, Pili, Carina, Alejandro Escajadillo. Secciones: 24 Horitas, Zulanita la Huerfanita, Carlinfias, Números musicales, Héctor Carrito. Realización y libreto: César González.
5 POPEYE. Dibujos animados. El Carnaval.
11 APRENDAMOS JUNTOS. Alfabetización.

8.00 2 CHESPIRITO. Comedia. Roberto G. Bolaños, Florinda Meza, María Antonieta de las Nieves, Edgar Vivar, Angelines Fernández, Horacio Gómez, Raúl "Chato" Padilla, Rubén Aguirre. Secciones: Doctor Chapatín; El Flaco; Los Chifladitos; El Chavo; El Chapulín Colorado. Producción y dirección: Carmen Ochoa.
4 LAS GRANDES PELEAS DE LOS SETENTAS. El boxeo en Estados Unidos. MUHAMMAD ALI vs. JOHN CONTEH.
5 MUNDO MAGICO. INCREIBLE Reportajes insólitos de Estados Unidos. Frank Takerton y Cathy Lee Crosby.
8 MEXICO EN LA CULTURA. La Magia del Baile. Capítulo 4.
11 ENLACE. Noticiario. Sergio de Alba, Beatriz Pagés, Alejandra Marentes, Enrique Velasco.
13 LA SOGA. Teleteatro. Con Jaime Garza, Blanca Sánchez, Ernesto Rendón.

8.30 11 COMO VIVIR MEJOR. Consejos. Aspectos Legales.

9.00 2 ¡INCREIBLE!. Reportajes de cinco minutos.
4 BEISBOL DE LAS GRANDES LIGAS. Desde Estados Unidos. El partido de la semana. Equipos por confirmar.
5 MAGNUM. Policiaca. Detective privado que se dedica a resolver difíciles casos, en las islas de Hawaii. La Sexta Posición.
8 NOCHE A NOCHE EN EL 8. Variedades, entrevistas, eventos culturales, poesía, deportes. Conductor: Félix Cortés Camarillo.
11 LA PAREJA HUMANA. Entrevistas. James R. Fortson.
13 SIETE DIAS. Noticiario.

9.05 2 CUANDO LOS HIJOS SE VAN. Telenovela.
Capítulo 68.—Damián felicita a Ignacio cuando éste le dice que va a casarse, en ese momento llega Julio. Se quedan asombrados cuando Ignacio les dice que su novia es ciega. Teresa asegura a Alvaro que tiene miedo de hablar con Damián porque sabe que va a herirlo, pero lo hará.

9.35 2 EL MALEFICIO. Telenovela. Capítulo 97.—Beatriz está celosa porque Enrique regaló a Nora el collar el día de su cumpleaños; y él afirma que no podría amar a una mujer alcohólica en potencia. Felipe dice por teléfono a Enrique, ya habló con los hombres que vigilan a Ricardo y él le ordena lo informe en cuanto acorralen, pues quiere estar presente.

10.00 5 LOS PROFESIONALES. Policiaca. Tres policías ingleses utilizan nuevos métodos para cumplir con su cometido. El Atentado.
8 LOS GRANDES AUTORES. Teleteatro. Los Misterios de París. Capítulo 5: Los Castigos. Flor de María es rescatada. Sarah confiesa a Rodolfo que la jovencita María es su hija, y se casan para darle su nombre.
13 CRONICA DE LOS AÑOS VEINTE. Drama.

10.05 2 24 HORAS. Noticias.

10.30 11 PELICULA. Escándalo en la Costa Azul. (Comedia). Danny Kaye, Gene Tierney. Grupos y turistas y sus escapadas a las costas de la Riviera, que les proporciona diversión y romances.

11.00 5 HAWAII 5-0. Policiaca. El Protegido de la Cortina de Bambú.
8 PELICULA. Garibaldi. (Biográfica). Renzo Ricci, Paolo Stoppa. Vida del ilustre soldado y estadista italiano del siglo pasado.
13 PROGRAMA ESPECIAL.

11.05 2 MEXICO EN LA CULTURA. Programa especial. Arsénico y encaje. Obra de teatro, con Jacqueline Andere. Anfitrión: Miguel Sabido.

11.30 13 CORAZON INDOMITO. Comedia. Las vidas paralelas de un buscador de peligro, un boxeador y un doble de cine.

12.00 2 PELICULA.
1/2 NOCHE Juntos Otra vez. (Comedia). 1944. Irenne Dunne, Charles Boyer. La fidelidad a su marido muerto, la lleva a rechazar el amor que le ofrece un escultor.
5 EN CONTACTO DIRECTO.

12.30 13 ULTIMA EDICION. Noticias.

FICCIÓN DE LA SEMANA

ROSAMUNDA

Estaba amaneciendo, al fin, El departamento de tercera clase olía a cansancio, a tabaco y a botas de soldado. Ahora se salía de la noche como de un gran túnel y se podía ver a la gente acurrucada, dormidos hombres y mujeres en sus asientos duros. Era aquel un incómodo vagóntranvía, con el pasillo atestado de cestas y maletas. Por las ventanillas se veía el campo y la raya plateada de mar.

Rosamunda se despertó. Todavía se hizo una ilusión placentera al ver la luz entre sus pestañas semicerradas. Luego comprobó que se cabeza colgaba hacía atrás, apoyada en el respaldo del asiento y que tenía la boca seca de llevarla abierta. Se rehízo, enderezándose. Le dolía el cuello —su largo cuello marchito—. Echó una mirada a su alrededor y se sintió aliviada al ver que dormían sus compañeros de viaje. Sintió ganas de estirar las piernas entumecidas —el tren traqueteaba, pitaba—. Salió con grandes precauciones, para no despertar, para no molestar, "con pasos de hada" —pensó—, hasta la plataforma.

El día era glorioso. Apenas se notaba el frío del amanecer. Se veía el mar entre naranjos. Ella se quedó como hipnotizada por el profundo verde de los árboles, por el claro horizonte de agua.

—"Los odiados, odiados naranjos. . . Las odiadas palmeras. . . El maravilloso mar. . ."

—¿Qué decía usted?

A su lado estaba un soldadillo. Un muchachito pálido. Parecía bien educado. Se parecía a su hijo. A un hijo suyo que se había muerto. No al que vivía; al que vivía, no, de ninguna manera.

—No sé si será usted capaz de entenderme —dijo, con cierta altivez—. Estaba recordando unos versos míos. Pero si usted quiere, no tengo inconveniente en recitar. . .

El muchacho estaba asombrado. Veía a una mujer ya mayor, flaca, con profundas ojeras. El cabello oxigenado, el traje de color verde, muy viejo. Los pies calzados en unas viejas zapatillas de baile. . ., sí, unas asombrosas zapatillas de baile, color de plata, y en el pelo una cinta plateada también, atada con un lacito. . . Hacía mucho que él la observaba.

—¿Qué decide usted? —preguntó Rosamunda, impaciente—. ¿Le gusta o no oir recitar?

—Sí, a mí. . .

El muchacho no se reía porque le daba pena mirarla. Quizá más tarde se reiría. Además, él tenía interés porque era joven, curioso. Había visto pocas cosas en su vida y deseaba conocer más. Aquello era una aventura. Miró a Rosamunda y la vio soñadora. Entornaba los ojos azules. Miraba el mar.

—¡Qué difícil es la vida!

Aquella mujer era asombrosa. Ahora había dicho esto con los ojos llenos de lágrimas.

—Si usted supiera, joven. . . Si usted supiera lo que este amanecer significa para mí, me disculparía. Este correr hacia el Sur. Otra vez hacia el Sur. . . Otra vez a mi casa. Otra vez a sentir ese ahogo de mi patio cerrado, de la incomprensión de mi esposo. . . No se sonría usted, hijo mío; usted no sabe nada de lo que puede ser la vida de una mujer como yo. Este tormento infinito. . . Usted dirá que por qué le cuento todo esto, por qué tengo ganas de hacer confidencias, yo, que soy de naturaleza reservada. . . Pues, porque ahora mismo, al hablarle, me he dado cuenta de que tiene usted corazón y sentimiento y porque esto es mi confesión. Porque, después de usted, me espera, como quien dice, la tumba. . . El no poder hablar ya a ningún ser humano. . . a ningún ser humano que me entienda.

Se calló, cansada quizá, por un momento. El tren corría, corría. . . El aire se iba haciendo cálido, dorado. Amenazaba un día terrible de calor.

—Voy a empezar a usted mi historia, pues creo que le interesa. . . Sí. Figúrese usted una joven rubia, de grandes ojos azules, una joven apasionada por el arte. . . De nombre, Rosamunda. . . Rosamunda, ¿ha oído?. . . Digo que si ha oído mi nombre y qué le parece.

El soldado se ruborizó ante el tono imperioso.

—Me parece bien. . . bien.

—Rosamunda. . . —continuó ella, un poco vacilante.

—Su verdadero nombre era Felisa; pero, no se sabe por qué, lo aborrecía. En su interior siempre había sido Rosamunda, desde los tiempos de su adolescencia. Aquel Rosamunda se había convertido en la fórmula mágica que la salvaba de la estrechez de su casa, de la monotonía de sus horas; aquel Rosamunda convirtió al novio zafio y colorado en un príncipe de leyenda. Rosamunda era para ella un nombre amado, de calidades exquisitas. . . Pero, ¿para qué explicar al joven tantas cosas?

—Rosamunda tenía un gran talento dramático. Llegó a actuar con éxito brillante. Además, era poetisa. Tuvo ya cierta fama desde su juventud. . . Imagínese, casi una niña, halagada, mimada por la vida, y, de pronto, una catástrofe. . . El amor. . . ¿Le he dicho a usted que ella era famosa? Tenía dieciséis años apenas, pero la rodeaban por todas partes los admiradores. En uno de los recitales de poesía, vio al hombre que causó su ruina. A. . . A mi marido, pues Rosamunda, como usted comprenderá, soy yo. Me casé sin saber lo que hacía, con un hombre brutal, sórdido y celoso. Me tuvo encerrada años y años. ¡Yo!. . . Aquella mariposa de oro que era yo. . . ¿Entiende?

(Sí, se había casado, sino a los dieciséis años, a los veintitrés; pero ¡al fin y al cabo!. . . Y era verdad que le había conocido un día que recitó versos suyos en casa de una amiga. El era carnicero. Pero, a este muchacho, ¿se le podían contar las cosas así? Lo cierto era aquel sufrimiento suyo, de tantos años. No había podido ni recitar un solo verso, ni aludir a sus pasados éxitos —éxitos quizás inventados, ya que no se acordaba bien; pero. . .—. Su mismo hijo solía decirle que se volvería loca de pensar y llorar tanto. Era peor esto que las palizas y los gritos de él cuando llegaba borracho. No tuvo a nadie más que al hijo aquél, porque las hijas fueron descaradas y necias, y se reían de ella, y el otro hijo, igual que su marido, había intentado hasta encerrarla.)

—Tuve un hijo único. Un solo hijo. ¿Se da cuenta? Le puse Florisel. . . Crecía delgadito, pálido, así como usted. Por eso quizá le cuento a usted estas cosas. Yo le contaba mi magnífica vida anterior. Sólo él sabía que conservaba un traje de gasa, todos mis collares. . . Y él me escuchaba, me escuchaba. . . como usted ahora, embobado.

Rosamunda sonrió. Sí, el joven la escuchaba absorto.

—Este hijo se me murió. Yo no lo pude resistir. . . El era lo único que me ataba a aquella casa. Tuve un arranque, cogí mis maletas y me volví a la gran ciudad de mi juventud y de mis éxitos. . . ¡Ay! He pasado unos días maravillosos y amargos. Fui acogida con entusiasmo, aclamada de nuevo por el público, de nuevo adorada. . . ¿Comprende mi tragedia? Porque mi marido, al enterarse de esto, empezó a

escribirme cartas tristes y desgarradoras: no podía vivir sin mí. No puede, el pobre. Además es el padre de Florisel, y el recuerdo del hijo perdido estaba en el fondo de todos mis triunfos, amargándome.

El muchacho veía animarse por momentos a aquella figura flaca y estrafalaria que era la mujer. Habló mucho. Evocó un hotel fantástico, el lujo derrochado en el teatro el día de su "reaparición"; evocó ovaciones delirantes y su propia figura, una figura de "sílfide cansada", recibiéndolas.

—Y, sin embargo, ahora vuelvo a mi deber. . . Repartí mi fortuna entre los pobres y vuelvo al lado de mi marido como quien va a un sepulcro.

Rosamunda volvió a quedarse triste. Sus pendientes eran largos, baratos; la brisa los hacía ondular. . . Se sintió desdichada, muy "Gran dama". . . Había olvidado aquellos terribles días sin pan en la ciudad grande. Las burlas de sus amistades ante su traje de gasa, sus abalorios y sus proyectos fantásticos. Había olvidado aquel largo comedor con mesas de pino cepillado, donde había comido el pan de los pobres entre mendigos de broncas toses. Sus llantos, su terror en el absoluto desamparo de tantas horas en que hasta los insultos de su marido había echado de menos. Sus besos a aquella carta del marido en que, en su estilo tosco y autoritario a la vez, recordando al hijo muerto, le pedía perdón y la perdonaba.

El soldado se quedó mirándola. ¡Qué tipo más raro, Dios mío! No cabí duda de que estaba loca la pobre. . . Ahora le sonreía. . . Le faltaban dos dientes.

El tren se iba deteniendo en una estación del camino. Era la hora del desayuno, de la fonda de la estación venía un olor apetitoso. . . Rosamunda miraba hacia los vendedores de rosquillas.

—¿Me permite usted convidarla, señora?

En la mente del soldadito empezaba a insinuarse una divertida historia. ¿Y si contara a sus amigos que había encontrado en el tren una mujer estupenda y que. . .?

—¿Convidarme? Muy bien, joven. . . Quizá sea la última persona que me convide. . . Y no me trate con tanto respeto, por favor. Puede usted llamarme Rosamunda. . . no he de enfadarme por eso.

Por Carmen Laforet

TELEVISIÓN

IMPOSIBLE COMPRAR NUEVAS VIDEOCASSETTERAS

* 600% de incremento en el precio
* Un cassette cuesta 12,000 pesos
* En Alemania las regalan con el café

El mercado del video casero sigue su marcha ascendente en el mundo industrializado, aunque a pasos menos acelerados de lo que previeron los optimistas hace algunos años.

En México se ha detenido la expansión del mercado, que pudo calificarse como explosiva de 1980 a principios de 1982. Las causas son de sobra conocidas. Una videocassettera de $400 dólares costaba antes $10,000 pesos, mientras que hoy el precio es de $60.000 pesos, un incremento de 600% en menos de un año.

Además, no es ningún secreto que la mayoría de las videocassetteras y videodisqueras

Con las videocassetteras, llegó a los hogares el gran mundo del espectáculo. Las superproducciones como "All That Jazz", antes vedadas a los televidentes, pueden ahora ser vistas cuantas veces se desee, a cualquier hora.

que se encuentran en territorio mexicano, pasaron las fronteras por "canales inadecuados", evadiendo los controles aduaneros.

A pesar de que es ya difícil que un residente mexicano adquiera una videocassettera y de que es imposible saber el número de estos aparatos que se encuentran en el país, sí parece cierto que hay un mercado fuerte, posiblemente tan importante por "más que el de algunos países industrializados, como Italia, aunque mucho mejor que el de Alemania o Japón.

Por ello es posible esperar que en los próximos años lleguen al país las más nuevas ediciones de videocassettes y videodiscos, a pesar de los precios tan altos. Pero es seguro que ya serán muy pocos los que puedan tener su propia colección de películas. Más bien los videofanáticos recurrirán más a clubes o a compañías especializadas en la renta de cintas.

El precio de un videocassette puede ser ya terriblemente alto en pesos. "Poltergeist", la película de terror, fue uno de los grandes éxitos del 82, y se vendió a $79.95 dólares en Estados Unidos, casi $12,000 pesos, a los que habrá que sumarles el 20% de IVA.

La situación no debe considerarse del todo trágica, pues a cambio de que las devaluaciones han reducido nuestro poder adquisitivo en el extranjero, los precios de aparatos y cintas siguen bajando en el extranjero, y seguramente no pasarán más de dos o tres años antes de que sean de nuevo accesibles al público nacional.

El ejemplo más ilustrativo es el caso alemán, donde las tiendas venden tan barato, que los productores japoneses se han llegado a molestar por ello. Ya es posible en Alemania comprar en menos de mil marcos aparatos que hace un par de años valían el doble. El caso de las cafeterías Tchibo es hasta cómico.

En el pasado, Tchibo hacía promociones con libros y discos de larga duración, ofreciéndolos a precios sujetos a grandes descuentos a cambio del consumo de café. Inclusive llegó a tener una promoción con bicicletas a un precio tan bajo, que una cadena de tiendas de bicicletas decidió devolver el golpe vendiendo café a precios más bajos que Tchibo. Ahora, las cafeterías están ofreciendo a precios ridículos 40,000 videocassetteras. Lo curioso está en que el negocio no está en vender los aparatos electrónicos, sino el café.

La clave del asunto es que los japoneses produjeron demasiadas videocassetteras y debieron importar en 82 más de siete millones de ellas a Europa, únicamente en el primer semestre del año. Actualmente en Alemania casi cualquier hogar tiene una videocassettera.

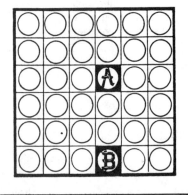

SICOLOGÍA

Dra. Joyce Brothers

Cualquiera de estos casos puede ser el suyo. Infórmese leyendo esta sección y las soluciones que ofrece esta famosa sicóloga

siempre levantada, mirando por detrás de la cortina de la ventana. Me molesta mucho esta impertinencia. ¿Qué debo hacer?"

Desde luego, tiene usted una vecina muy entrometida. Y si tanto le molesta que ella la vigile por detrás de la cortina, sencillamente salúdela muy normalmente cada vez que se repita la ocasión. Al notar una actitud tan natural de parte suya, quizá deje de supervisar su vida y se dedique más a la de ella.

MADRE DEMASIADO ABARCADORA

"Llevo varios años de casada y tengo 2 niños. Por razones económicas, mi madre ha venido a vivir con nosotros luego de enviudar. Ni a mi marido ni a mí nos molestó en un principio. Al contrario, nos sentíamos felices de poderle dar calor y, a la vez, de tener alguien en casa que mucho representara para nuestros niños. Sin embargo, según han pasado los meses, la situación ha cambiado. Por ser muy dominante, mi madre me sigue viendo como "su niña" y pretende dirigir mi vida como cuando realmente era niña. Quiero poner final a esta situación cuanto antes, pero no sé qué hacer."

Ya usted ha dado el primer paso en la solución del problema que tiene: darse cuenta de que tiene que ponerle final. ¿Cómo exactamente? Valiéndose de una

firmeza absoluta cada vez que su madre desee imponer su voluntad sobre la suya, para así demostrarle que usted es toda una persona adulta. No quiero con ello decir que deba usted asumir una actitud agresiva. Sencillamente firme. Hable abiertamente con ella sobre el tema y, si aun así persistiera en su comportamiento dominante, no dude en buscar ayuda profesional, ya sea un sacerdote o sicólogo. Si nada de ello pareciera funcionar, tendrá que estudiar muy bien la economía familiar, para que ella viva sola.

UNA VECINA IMPERTINENTE

"Tengo 50 años. Soy divorciada y algunas veces salgo acompañada de buenos amigos con quienes generalmente regreso a casa tarde en la noche. Cada vez que esto ocurre, mi vecina, una señora algo mayor que yo, está

¿TIENE MI MARIDO OTRA . . . ?

"Aunque tengo un marido cariñoso y de muchos detalles conmigo, últimamente he comenzado a dudar de su fidelidad. No sólo lo noto algo frío, sino que muchas son las ocasiones en que me pone excusas de trabajo para llegar a horas inacostumbradas. ¿Cree usted que él tenga otra?"

Si las excusas de trabajo son verdaderas, su marido tiene una recarga de trabajo. Y, por lo tanto, se siente lleno de presiones, que le impiden ser el mismo hombre cariñoso que generalmente es. En su caso, trataría de comprobar muy delicadamente (llamándolo a la oficina en esas horas que antes no acostumbraba trabajar, por ejemplo) si sus excusas profesionales son válidas. De serlo, como estoy casi segura que lo es, no tendría que preocuparse por "otra".

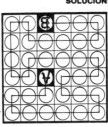

OPINIÓN

La lectura, ese proceso mágico

POR JEAN-MARIE JAVRON

*Ninguna máquina es capaz de reproducir la
portentosa complejidad de esta secuencia
de fenómenos que ocurre entre ojos y cerebro.*

*U*n señor toma el tranvía después de comprar el diario y ponérselo bajo el brazo. Media hora más tarde desciende con el mismo diario bajo el mismo brazo.

Pero ya no es el mismo diario, ahora es un montón de hojas impresas que el señor abandona en un banco de plaza.

Al leer estas líneas del libro *Historias de cronopios y de famas,* del escritor argentino Julio Cortázar, no habrá pensado el lector que realizaba una proeza extraordinaria. Con todo, durante unos cuantos segundos, hacía practicar a su cerebro ejercicios gimnásticos tan complejos que ningún científico ha logrado describirlos satisfactoriamente. En verdad, tratar de entender lo que sucede cuando leemos pone en juego a disciplinas científicas como la oftalmología, la pedagogía, la neurología, la lingüística, la psicología, la cibernética, la informática y otras más.

Nuestro trabajo, nuestros actos como ciudadanos, las actividades que realizamos en nuestras horas de ocio; casi todo se fundamenta en la palabra impresa. Hasta salir a dar una caminata nos hace leer anuncios publicitarios, los nombres de los comercios, los de las calles. Pero la lectura, tal como ahora la practicamos, no llegó a difundirse hasta hace relativamente poco. Los antiguos griegos y romanos se valían de lectores profesionales, quienes les leían en voz alta, y en los inicios de la Edad Media los monjes seguían haciendo lo mismo. Como en aquella época se acostumbraba escribir juntando las palabras una tras otra, a menudo en forma abreviada, sin espacios que las separaran y sin puntuación, había que recurrir a los servicios de un lector profesional a fin de captar el sentido del texto. Trate el lector de seguir todo un libro escrito así: UNSEÑORTOMAELTRANVIADESPUESD ECOMPRARELDIARIOYPONERSELOBA JOELBRAZOMEDIAHORAMASTARDED ESCIENDECONELMISMODIARIOBAJO ELMISMOBRAZO.

Según el lingüista francés Lionel Bellenger, no fue sino hasta alrededor del año 1000 de nuestra era cuando la lectura se hizo más visual que oral, gracias a que había mejores manuscritos. La invención de la imprenta, hacia 1440, incrementó más la legibilidad; pero hasta el siglo XIX siguió siendo privilegio de una pequeñísima minoría. En Hispanoamérica, la lectura empezó a generalizarse en la segunda mitad del siglo XIX, cuando algunos países establecieron la enseñanza primaria obligatoria y gratuita.

Sin embargo, anacrónicamente, la lectura se enseña demasiado a menudo en forma oral, sílaba por sílaba, como hace 1200 años, en la época de Carlomagno; incluso muchos adultos no logran romper el hábito de pronunciar lo que van leyendo. En tanto que una persona promedio puede leer cerca de 500 palabras por minuto, y un consumado lector es capaz de leer hasta 1000, las personas que necesitan pronunciar cada palabra alcanzan apenas una velocidad de 100 a 150.

Lectura a saltos. Poco antes de 1900, el oftalmólogo Émile Javal descubrió que, cuando leemos, nuestros ojos no se desplazan regularmente de izquierda a derecha a lo largo de una línea impresa, sino más bien a saltos fulgurantes. Sin darnos cuenta, con los ojos dividimos cada línea en seis o siete partes de unas diez letras cada una, y los hacemos saltar de un segmento al siguiente en el increíble lapso de cuatro millonésimas de segundo.

Basta sólo un cuarto o un tercio de segundo para identificar cada grupo de letras. ¿Qué hacemos con cada una de las letras? ¡Nada! Ni siquiera las miramos. Al leer el fragmento de Cortázar trascrito,

no sumamos t+r+a+n+v+í+a, pues reconocimos inmediatamente la forma de la palabra "tranvía". Las palabras que no nos son familiares son las únicas que leemos letra por letra. En efecto, en 1843 el notario público Leclair descubrió que si se cortan las palabras por la mitad horizontalmente es suficiente ver la parte superior para reconocer su significado.

¿Cómo entiende el cerebro lo que leemos? La retina, la sensible membrana del ojo humano, compuesta de 500 millones de células receptoras, identifica las palabras casi instantáneamente. Trasmite en seguida estas imágenes por medio de impulsos eléctricos al cerebro, que consta a su vez de miles de millones de células nerviosas, llamadas neuronas. Con su asombrosamente intrincado sistema de circuitos, y su "voraz apetito" de velocidad, el cerebro registra de manera directa las imágenes de las palabras en grupos de dos o tres.

Es más: gracias al enorme cúmulo de información que se archiva en las neuronas, nuestro cerebro es capaz, con gran frecuencia, de prever la conclusión de una frase cuando los ojos acaban de captar el inicio. El filósofo francés del siglo XVII René Descartes escribió: "Al ver un sombrero desde nuestra ventana, deducimos que un hombre pasa por la calle". De igual modo, nos explican hoy los lingüistas, expresiones cortas como "y", "para", "así", "pues", "en efecto", obran como postes indicadores que nos advierten qué viene después, y aceleran notablemente nuestro avance en la lectura.

Capacidad ilimitada. Al cerebro se le compara a menudo con la computadora. Pero la computadora no hace sino aquello para lo que está programada, en tanto que la capacidad del cerebro para improvisar es en verdad ilimitada. Por otra parte, la computadora, a diferencia del cerebro humano, tiene que descifrar las palabras letra por letra. Tomemos la siguiente frase como ejemplo de la clase de acertijos que el cerebro es capaz de resolver: "En aquel banco me esperaban varias personas".

En español, *banco* puede entenderse como mueble de varios asientos, o bien como el establecimiento donde cambiamos los cheques por dinero en efectivo. Es probable que el 50 por ciento de los lectores interprete *banco* en el sentido de mueble, y que el otro 50 por ciento tenga la imagen de un edificio o local con ventanillas y cajeros que cuentan dinero. Pero si añadimos que se trata del "lugar donde siempre me cambian los cheques", nuestras neuronas captan el significado exacto de "banco" en una fracción de segundo. Entender lo que leemos significa coordinar constantemente el texto con lo que podemos encontrar en nuestra memoria.

Todavía sabemos muy poco en cuanto al funcionamiento de la memoria, si bien podemos distinguir dos clases de memoria. Lo que los hombres de ciencia denominan "memoria a corto plazo" es lamentablemente débil. Por ejemplo: somos incapaces de recordar más de unas 15 palabras durante más de 20 segundos, luego de haberlas leído. Por esta razón olvidamos a veces el principio de una frase antes de haber llegado a su término, sobre todo si tenemos que volver la página a mitad de la frase.

Por otra parte, nuestra "memoria a largo plazo" es algo que nos deja verdaderamente perplejos. Al leer un texto, esta memoria nos ayuda a filtrarlo; a rechazar lo que nos parece inútil; a simplificar, para almacenarlo, aquello que se relaciona con nuestras preocupaciones personales, a compararlo con lo que ya sabemos, a alterarlo o pasarlo por alto si tropieza con bloqueos del inconsciente. Esta inmensa tarea de separar, mezclar, deducir, asimilar y archivar es algo que nuestra memoria a largo plazo ejecuta con rapidez inconcebible, a

tiempo que seguimos con los ojos las líneas del texto y que nuestro cerebro se anticipa a lo que vamos a leer a continuación.

En el extremo final de esa complejísima cadena de operaciones, por lo común sólo retenemos el sentido general de lo leído, pero meses después, y aún años después, el más leve incidente puede evocar lo que leímos alguna vez. El semiólogo Roland Barthes observó que un escrito, al hacer que entren en juego todos los recursos de la inteligencia, "hace de un lector, no un consumidor, sino un productor".

Imágenes verbales. Muchas personas "ven", literalmente, lo que leen. Michel Denis, investigador del Centro Nacional de Investigaciones Científicas, de Francia, ha hecho experimentos respecto a las imágenes que visualizamos al leer. "Lo que es notable", dice, "es que la frase resulta siempre *menos* descriptiva que lo que ve el lector". Por ejemplo, al leer: "El águila se lanzó en picada sobre el hombre", la mayoría de nosotros veremos al águila lanzándose con las garras extendidas, y tal vez al hombre que se protege con los brazos. La frase no dice nada de esto.

Tan misteriosa aptitud para descubrir la realidad tras unos pequeños símbolos impresos no tiene nada que ver, necesariamente, con la inteligencia. Constituye una aptitud, como la de ser capaz de correr velozmente, y los lectores que más visualizan son dueños de la mejor memoria. También se ha demostrado con experimentos que quienes leen con rapidez diez veces mayor que la del lector promedio recuerdan lo leído dos veces más.

Quienes leen con rapidez son también, por lo general, lectores voraces. De Balzac, el famoso novelista francés del siglo XIX, se decía que "devoraba" los libros, y al parecer leía a prodigiosa velocidad. El presidente norteamericano John Kennedy, digería documentos de Estado con vertiginosa rapidez, y al ocupar la Casa Blanca instó a sus colaboradores a aprender la técnica de la lectura rápida. Actualmente tales técnicas se pueden ad-

quirir con facilidad, y aunque no hagan un Balzac o un Kennedy de cada uno de nosotros, sí pueden, bien aplicadas, mejorar en forma considerable nuestra velocidad de lectura.

Pero incluso sin haber estudiado ninguna técnica, todos solemos leer más rápidamente de lo que hablamos. Mientras que un locutor de radio o de televisión habla a razón de 9000 palabras por hora, el individuo promedio es capaz de leer a una velocidad tres veces mayor. Así pues, 20 minutos de noticias trasmitidas por televisión representan apenas el equivalente de la información contenida en tres columnas de un periódico. Ya esto por sí solo bastaría para explicarnos cómo la radio, el cine y la televisión no han logrado sustituir a los libros. En realidad, jamás se habían publicado tantos libros como en los años trascurridos desde que la televisión entró en los hogares. Sólo en México y Argentina, el número de libros publicados aumentó de 25 millones en 1965 a 171 millones en 1983.

El poder de la lectura. "Al abrirnos el camino hacia el hallazgo de nuevos conocimientos y experiencias humanas", afirma Elisabeth Badinter, filósofa e historiadora, "la lectura es una forma de vivir más plenamente y con mayores satisfacciones".

Podríamos añadir que tal vida más rica pertenece a cada individuo. "Cuando mis alumnos me comentan sobre algún programa de televisión", observa una profesora de segunda enseñanza, "advierto que todos emplean esencialmente las mismas palabras para expresar las mismas opiniones. Pero jamás he conocido a dos estudiantes que lean un libro de igual manera".

François Richaudeau, especialista en comunicación, opina: "La invención de la imprenta nos permitió escapar de la tiranía de la palabra hablada, y ha reforzado el libre albedrío y el sentido crítico. Todas las grandes conquistas del pensamiento moderno han sido fruto de estos dos privilegios".

LÍNEA DIRECTA

Comuníquese
con otros por correo

Nombre: María A. Bello.
Dirección: Armillita No. 2333, Fracc. Higuerillas, Guadalajara, Jalisco, MEXICO.
Edad: 22 años.
Signo zodiacal: Virgo.
Estudios: Secretariado.
Pasatiempos: Leer, escuchar música, coleccionar postales, disfrutar la naturaleza, y tener amistades alrededor del mundo.

Nombre: Araceli Bojórquez.
Dirección: Calle 5 de Mayo No. 7, Vicente Riva Palacio, Texcoco, C.P. 56200, MEXICO.
Edad: 20 años.
Signo zodiacal: Leo.
Trabajo: Oficinista.
Pasatiempos: Leer la revista TU, oír música, y tener amigos y amigas por todo el mundo.

Nombre: Julio H. Guevara.
Dirección: Calle Hipólito Unanue No. 238, La Rinconada, Juliaca Puno, PERU.
Edad: 23 años.
Signo zodiacal: Géminis.
Pasatiempos: Intercambiar estampillas, postales, ideas, billetes y monedas, y tener amistades por todo el mundo.

Nombre: Enrique Vázquez.
Dirección: Apartado 1337, Mazatlán, Sinaloa, C.P. 82000, MEXICO.
Edad: 26 años.
Signo zodiacal: Tauro.
Estudios: Medicina.
Pasatiempos: La fotografía, leer, escuchar música, jugar ajedrez, y tener nuevas amistades por todos los países.

Nombre: Ricardo Díaz.
Dirección: 110 E. Cypress Street, Monrrovia, California 91016, ESTADOS UNIDOS.
Edad: 19 años.
Estudios: Escuela Superior y Música.
Pasatiempos: Pasear, leer, e intercambiar correspondencia.

Nombre: Leonardo Blacio.
Dirección: Calle Sucre No. 3-64 y 15 de Octubre, Santa Rosa, El Oro, ECUADOR.
Edad: 23 años.
Trabajo: Maestro.
Pasatiempos: Escuchar música, ir al cine, escribir, leer poemas, coleccionar postales, estampillas, etiquetas de ropa y recortes de Marilyn Monroe, y mantener correspondencia con jóvenes de todas partes del mundo.

Nombre: Sonia Cruzado.
Dirección: 434 S. 5 Street, Apt 5, Brooklyn, New York 11211, ESTADOS UNIDOS.
Edad: 18 años.
Signo zodiacal: Sagitario.
Estudios: Escuela Superior.
Pasatiempos: Coleccionar calcomanías y postales, tener amigos por todo el mundo, escuchar música, especialmente la de Duran Duran, Phil Collins, Culture Club, y Tears for Fears.

Nombre: Ruth García.
Dirección: Floresta, Mz. 62, Villa 14, Guayaquil, ECUADOR.
Edad: 20 años.
Signo zodiacal: Piscis.
Pasatiempos: Leer, intercambiar correspondencia, escuchar música, y estudiar sobre Historia.

Nombre: Ana Ruth Agüero.
Dirección: Residencial El Encanto, Calle Blancos No. 241, San José, COSTA RICA.
Edad: 19 años.
Signo zodiacal: Sagitario.
Pasatiempos: Coleccionar monedas y estampillas, leer, hacer nuevas amistades, y patinar.

Nombre: Leticia E. López.
Dirección: Apartado 6-3946, El Dorado, Panamá, PANAMA.
Edad: 19 años.
Signo zodiacal: Capricornio.
Estudios: Dibujo Publicitario.
Pasatiempos: Bailar, escuchar música de todo tipo, coleccionar estampillas, e intercambiar correspondencia con jóvenes.

Nombre: Luis A. Hernández.
Dirección: 3918 Beverly Blvd. No. 401, Los Angeles, California 90004, ESTADOS UNIDOS.
Edad: 19 años.
Estudios: Computadoras.
Pasatiempos: Practicar baloncesto, y coleccionar fotografías.

Nombre: Luis M. Nunes
Dirección: Calle Fermin Toro No. 30-2, La Matica, Los Teques, Edo. Miranda, C.P. 1202, VENEZUELA.
Edad: 18 años.
Estudios: Arte.
Pasatiempos: Coleccionar estampillas, llaveros, y postales.

Nombre: Laura Gil Hurtado.
Dirección: Santiago Tapia No. 250, Morelia, Michoacán, C.P. 58000, MEXICO.
Edad: 18 años.
Signo zodiacal: Libra.
Estudios: Contabilidad.
Pasatiempos: Recibir mucha correspondencia, escuchar música, y coleccionar estampillas, billetes y fotografías.

Nombre: Mayra Menendez.
Dirección: Calle 3, No. A 36-75, Zona 7, Guatemala, GUATEMALA.
Edad: 25 años.
Signo zodiacal: Tauro.
Estudios: Turismo y Secretariado Bilingüe.
Pasatiempos: Coleccionar estampillas, fotografías de grupos juveniles, autógrafos y frascos de perfumes en miniatura; escuchar música, bailar, pintar, y conocer gente de diferentes países.

Nombre: María Y. García.
Dirección: Calle 47, No. 72-183, Apt. 201, Medellín, Antioquia, COLOMBIA.
Edad: 22 años.
Signo zodiacal: Aries.
Pasatiempos: Ir al cine, escuchar música, practicar deportes, y recibir correspondencia.

UNIT **Ejercicios**

Exercise A. *Plantas*

1. Match each paragraph with its topic.

_____ **a.** 1
_____ **b.** 2
_____ **c.** 3
_____ **d.** boxed paragraph

A. plants in the kitchen
B. selecting appropriate plants
C. advantages of using plants
D. caring for plants

2. Identify each of the following (discussed in the opening paragraph): (a) two reasons for decorating with plants; (b) three decorating concerns when choosing a plant; (c) three rooms for which plants are appropriate.

3. Match these types of plants with their preferred light conditions.

_____ **a.** dark-leaf plants
_____ **b.** thick-leaf plants
_____ **c.** colored-leaf plants

A. direct sun
B. shade
C. sunny

4. According to the article, what are three characteristics of style in modern interior decorating? Why are begonias, camelias, and similar plants appropriate for rooms decorated in a modern style?

5. What supplies are required in order to give proper care to houseplants, according to the article?

6. Identify four activities that are part of keeping houseplants healthy.

7. Why does the writer say that plants are **imprescindible** in a kitchen? What special considerations must be kept in mind when using plants in a kitchen?

8. Write a one-sentence summary of the main idea contained in this article.

9. The subtitle only reinforces one aspect of the article: the value of plants as a decorating device. Improve the subtitle by incorporating the second major aspect of the article: proper care for houseplants.

10. Are there other reasons for using houseplants in interior decoration? Are there disadvantages not mentioned by the writer? Can you think of other information that might have been included in an article like this one?

Exercise B. *Publicaciones del Fondo de Cultura Económica*

1. What evidence is there that this publisher is located in Mexico?
2. Consider the review of **Chichén Itzá.**
   a. Recall the bookstore directory you worked with in Unit 7. To what category of books is this work best assigned?
   b. According to the review, what two ancient Mexican cultures receive important treatment in the work?
   c. What is the usual theory about the relationship of the two?
   d. What is Piña Chan's revolutionary hypothesis?
3. Consider the review of **Economía política.**
   a. According to Lange, what is the primary purpose of the application economic theory?
   b. In the section following the colon, what is the referent of **su** in **su contexto?**
   c. Is it the same as the referent in **su posición?**
   d. Why does the reviewer think this work has special relevance to Latin America?
4. Consider the review of the book on **Michoacan.** (Note the misspelling of **independencia.)**
   a. What is the author's theoretical and methodological perspective?
   b. What claim about the historical role of Michoacán is implicit in the phrase **cuna de la Independencia?**
   c. According to the reviewer, what is the value of studying the Mexican colonial past?
5. a. How many of these books have you heard of?
   b. Which ones are the most closely related to your own work or courses?
   c. You have probably read at least one of the works listed here, or a similar work, in English. Write a short review of that book in Spanish, modeled on the reviews given here.

Exercise C. *Los diamantes*

1. What is the best English equivalent for **talla?** _____
   For **quilate?** _____
2. Define each of the four principal factors in determining the quality of a diamond. _____
3. Of the four factors, which is the most important? _____
4. Is it possible to have a half-carat diamond of higher quality than a three-carat diamond? _____
5. How are color, cut, and purity related to light?

   _____

Exercise D. *Ejercicio—Correcto e incorrecto*

1. According to the introductory paragraph, what are two negative results of too little physical exercise?

2. What are four negative results of too much exercise?

3. Describe the organization of this passage.

4. What body parts are most likely to be damaged by excessive swimming? By excessive jogging or aerobic dance?

5. What time-of-day and weather considerations are relevant to both bicyling and tennis?

6. What two kinds of important preliminary exercises are necessary for safe weightlifting?

7. Which sports require special attention to equipment?

8. What is the best Spanish equivalent for *jogging*, based on the usage you observe in the chart?

9. According to the information in the chart, which two types of exercise described are best done together?

10. Do you engage in any of these activities? Is the advice given in the article sound, based on your own experience? Would you add anything to the information given here?

Exercise E. *Teleguía*

1. What time of day is covered by the chart? _____

2. What program is shown at 8:00 P.M. on channel 8? _____

   What is the topic on this week's program? _____

3. At 6:30 on channel 2, a soap opera (**telenovela**) called **En busca del paraíso** is shown. Which chapter is scheduled for this week? _____

   How many different characters will appear in the episode? _____

4. How many different **telenovelas** are shown on Monday evening? _____

5. On which noncable channel, and at what time, can you see a program popular in the United States? _____

6. Give the best English equivalent for **dibujos animados.** _____

7. Examine the ads that appear with the listings. Would you say that the advertisers are appealing primarily to men or to women? Why?

8. Identify at least two educational programs shown on Mondays during the day. Why do you suppose that there are so many?

9. What are the age limits for children at the Camp Rancho Abajo? _____

How many branches of Estética Monique are listed in its ad? _____

10. How does this television schedule compare to the one you are familiar with? What are the principal diferences and similarities you notice?

Exercise F. *Dra. Joyce Brothers*

1. Make all necessary changes to convert the letters from female writers to male ones.
2. Underline the roots in the following words:

   a. enviudar   c. comportamiento

   b. entrometida   d. inacostumbradas

3. Identify the referent for each of the three examples of **su** or **sus** in Dr. Brothers' last answer.
4. Would you have given the questioners different advice? Have you or someone you know had similar problems? How were they solved?

Exercise G. *Un estudio revela cinco tipos de comportamiento del comprador de libros*

This passage is full of detailed information and lends itself well to skimming. This exercise helps you practice skimming skills.

1. Identify five reasons why people buy books, according to the study reported in this article.

2. Put these factors that relate to book purchasing into the order of their importance to buyers.

   _____ a. author

   _____ b. author, title and press

   _____ c. title

   _____ d. topic

   _____ e. author and title

3. What percentage of purchasers take other factors into account when buying a book? _____ If "other factors" were included in the categories given above, where would it rank on the list? _____

4. Using the information contained in paragraph 4, match the reader's age to the preferred types of reading material. (You'll have to make some deductions.)

               I. young   II. middle-aged   III. older

   _____ a. poetry   _____ f. the classics

   _____ b. encyclopedias   _____ g. fantasy

   _____ c. science fiction   _____ h. self-help books

   _____ d. technical manuals   _____ i historical novels

   _____ e. historical nonfiction _____ j. travel guides

5. Using the information provided in paragraph 6, identify which of the following are positive factors to potential book buyers.

   a. discounts and special offers

   b. knowledgeable sales clerks

   c. shrink-wrapping on books

   d. large selection

   e. security tags and cameras

6. What single factor best accounts for the high consumption of books by young people?

7. What two factors make the family a basic training ground for reading?

8. Compare the description of the five reasons for purchasing books listed in the last paragraph with those given in the first. What new information is included in the last paragraph?

9. Think about the last book you bought that was not a textbook. Which of the reasons identified by the study motivated your own book purchase?

10. Do the study results agree with your own experience? For example, do you generally pay more attention to author, title, or topic when buying a book? What other factors do you commonly consider?

11. Are your reading tastes typical of your age group, as identified in the study? How do they differ? Do you regularly read any types of books not mentioned in the article?

12. In what way might the study have differed if the subjects surveyed had been from the United States instead of Spain?

Exercise H. *Se cumple el segundo centenario del nacimiento del mayor del los hermanos Grimm.*

1. In what year did this article first appear? _____

2. What is the usual English title of the Grimm brothers' most famous work?

   _____

3. What are the English titles of the stories known in Spanish as **Caperucita roja** and **La cenicienta.** _____

4. What was the source of the stories collected by the Grimm brothers?

   _____

5. Match the years in the list below with the activities given on the right to form a chronology of the life of Jacob Grimm.

_____	a. 1785	A.	invited to live in Berlin
_____	b. 1802	B.	death
_____	c. 1805	C.	signed a document that led to his exile
_____	d. 1812	D.	entered Marburg University
_____	e. 1829	E.	publication of the first volume of tales
_____	f. 1837	F.	was appointed librarian at Göttingen
_____	g. 1840	G.	traveled to Paris
_____	h. 1863	H.	birth

6. What circumstances led to the signing of the **Manifiesto de los siete?**

7. At what age did Wilhelm Grimm die? _____ And Jacob? _____

8. Jacob Grimm is known among scholars for his analysis of historical change in the Germanic language family. (Perhaps you've heard of Grimm's Law—it's the same Grimm!) Besides taking an interest in language and popular tales, he also studied for a career in **derecho.** Use your dictionary to help you identify the best English equivalent for this field.

9. Did you read Grimm's fairy tales as a child? Which ones were your favorites? Did you realize that they were folk tales collected over 150 years ago? Before reading this article, did you know anything about the lives of the Grimm brothers?

Exercise I. *Llega la inteligencia artificial*

In answering these questions, identify the paragraph that contains each answer.

1. What event prompted the publication of this article?

2. Underline the article's definition of **inteligencia artificial (IA).**

3. What are the two most significant commercial uses for **IA?**

4. Underline the best definition provided for **sistema experto.**

5. What types of expert systems are currently in use in the United States?

6. What were the first experimental attempts to apply **IA?** Why did they fail?

7. What is the current focus of research in the field of **IA?**

8. What is **ingeniería del conocimiento?**

9. What advantages will Spain gain from this new center?

10. What is the Sperry Company's history in the field of **IA?**

Exercise J. *Se llevaron vacas bravas a Estados Unidos*

This report is written in a casual journalistic style. Watch for examples of stylistic writing, including the use of idioms, irony, and exaggeration.

1. Which of the following best classifies the category of this article?
   a. a report
   b. an exposé
   c. an editorial
   d. a society/gossip item

2. Underline all phrases that suggest that the topic of this article has been dealt with by the writer in earlier articles.

3. What person is referred to by the **-mos** verb forms used in the article?

4. What specific problem is addressed in the article?

5. What new information about the problem is presented here?

6. Identify the paragraph in which the writer's opinion about the issue is made most explicit.

7. Provide nonidiomatic (literal) Spanish equivalents for these expressions used in the article.

   a. parar la oreja

   b. andábamos atrasados de noticias

   c. se andaba moviendo el agua para tratar

8. What is a possible English metaphorical expression that corresponds in meaning to the Spanish proverb **(refrán) cuando el río suena es que agua lleva** (in paragraph 6)?

9. Underline the two sentences in the article that account for the writer's use of the phrase **está o estaba** in paragraph 1.

10. On the basis of the information provided in this article, do you think it is likely that there are breeding farms for Mexican fighting bulls located in the US? Do you agree with the reporter that such farms should not be legal? Do you agree with his reasons?

Exercise K. *Casal*

Your interst in this article will depend on your musical background. Exercise K assumes that your purpose is to read it for general—not detailed—comprehension.

1. Which of the following statements is the best summary of the main idea of this passage?
   a. Casal, while not, strictly speaking, a musician, is an important figure in the popular music world.
   b. Casal is a musical artist with many talents and is sure to receive greater public attention.
   c. Many recent songs by Casal deserve to be authentic hits.

2. Identify all the individuals or groups who were probably interviewed for this article. How many of them are actually quoted?

3. Provide good translation equivalents for the following false cognates, as used in their contexts in this article.

    a. batería _____

    b. equipo _____

    c. sencillo _____

    d. corte _____

4. What kinds of musical work has Casal been involved in? (Identify each one by the number of the paragraph in which it is described.)

5. Categorize each of these paragraphs on the basis of its primary content and main idea.

           I. Fact   II. Opinion

    _____ a. 10   _____ c. 15

    _____ b. 11   _____ d. 18

6. What is meant by **Casal es un músico** in paragraph 5? What is meant by **Casal no es un músico** in paragraph 8? How can both statements be true?

7. Reread paragraph 17. Do you think you would like the music of Casal? Why or why not?

Exercise L. *Imposible comprar nuevas videocassetteras*

1. Identify the paragraphs that relate directly to the subtitles with stars, which appear at the head of the article.

    _____ **a.** 600% de incremento en el precio

    _____ **b.** Un cassette cuesta 12,000 pesos

    _____ **c.** En Alemania las regalan con el café

2. Indentify the paragraphs that explain why

    _____ **a.** the VCR explosion was over in Mexico by 1982

    _____ **b.** Mexican consumers are unlikely likely to collect videocassettes

    _____ **c.** videocassette players are so inexpensive in Germany

3. What is meant by **canales inadecuadas** (paragraph 3)?

4. What two reasons are given for the difficulty of knowing the size of the VCR market in Mexico?

5. Reread paragraph 9 and make sure you know how the Tchibo coffee promotion works. Why do you think **los productores japoneses se han llegado a molestar por ello** (paragraph 8)?

Exercise M. *La lectura, ese proceso mágico*

Information Questions. These questions are about facts presented in the article about reading. They are in the order in which the answers appear in the article.

1. According to the author, what disciplines contribute to our understanding of the reading process?
2. Why was a professional reader required in medieval times?
3. According to this writer, when was printing invented?
4. What caused the skill of reading to generalize in Hispanic America after 1850?
5. What discovery did Leclair make in 1843?
6. What are **neuronas**?
7. What is the function of words such as **y, para, así, pues** and so on?
8. What are the limits for short-term memory? (That is, how many words can you keep in short-term memory and for how long?)
9. Identify five functions of long-term memory for reading.
10. Which has greater detail: visual images or written images?
11. How many words can an average person read per hour?
12. True or false? Television has reduced the number of books being published.

Interpretation. The questions ask for your reactions and interpretations. Reread the article before you respond.

1. The authors claims that "Casi todo se fundamenta en la palabra impresa." (paragraph 4) Do you agree?
2. What does the author mean by each of the following statements?
   a. Entender lo que leemos significa coordinar constantemente el texto con lo que podemos encontrar en nuestra memoria. (paragraph 12)
   b. un escrito, al hacer que entren en juego todos los recursos de la inteligencia, "hace de un lector, no un consumidor, sino un productor." (paragraph 15)
   c. "la lectura es una forma de vivir más plenamente y con mayores satisfacciones." (paragraph 20)
3. In the **banco** example in paragraphs 11 and 12, are there other possible interpretations for **banco** besides those the author gives? What additional phrases could be added to the sentence to clarify which meaning is meant?
4. Think of another example to illustrate Denis' claim that "la frase resulta siempre menos descriptiva que lo que ve el lector" in paragraph 16.

5. Do you think the author of this article would approve of the *Reading strategy?* Why or why not?

Exercise N. *Rosamunda*

This short story is by one of Spain's best known post-Civil War writers, Carmen Laforet. It is well within your reading skills. The story is accompanied by three sets of questions: one to help you check your comprehension of the action of the story; one to help you focus on style; and one to guide you as you react to the author's work. Do not begin the exercises until you have worked with the story enough to undestand its basic organization. Then do the questions in order. When you number the paragraphs, note the use of the dash (—) to mark direct quotes. Count each occasion of the dash as a new paragraph. You will have 33 paragraphs altogether.

Action

1. Where does the story take place? _____
Underline all the evidence in the first paragraph that indicates that the setting is a vehicle.

2. What time of day is it when the story begins? _____
Underline all phrases in the first paragraph related to time of day.

3. List the characters in the story and identify the paragraph in which each one is first introduced.

4. How many of these descriptive adjectives could apply to the soldier, according to the information provided in the story?

    a. young   e. artistic   i. adventuresome

    b. handsome   f. educated   j. slender

    c. pale   g. naive

    d. sickly   h. curious

5. Describe Rosamunda, using single words from the narrator's or soldier's point of view.

6. **Rosamunda** is modified by **aquel** in paragraph 20. What masculine sinpglular noun does the word **Rosamunda** represent in that paragraph?

_____

7. How many children does Rosamunda say she had?   _____

How many did she really have? _____

8. How old was Rosamunda when she got married? _____

How old does she say she was? _____

9. Rosamunda describes herself as a poet (paragraph 21), with many adventures, an adoring public (paragraph 25), and a fortune (paragraph 27). What paragraph contains evidence that none of these self-descriptions are true?

10. Reread paragraphs 25 through 28. Why does Rosamunda say she's going back to her husband? Why do you think she's really going back?

Study Guide to Style

1. Reread the story, noting the way in which the author uses both dialogue and narrative to develop a picture of the characters. Then identify the point of view taken in each of the following paragraphs.

   I. Rosamunda   II. the soldier   III. narrator

   _____ a. 1   _____ d. 6   _____ g. 22

   _____ b. 2   _____ e. 8   _____ h. 29

   _____ c. 3   _____ f. 15   _____ i. 32

2. Laforet uses a great many references to physical sensations such as sight, sound, touch, and smell in defining setting and character. Many of these details serve a dual purpose, one physical and one spiritual or psychological. One of the most arresting images of this type is found in the opening paragraph: **se salía de la noche como de un gran túnel,** which is a metaphorical description, but one directly related to the story's setting in a train. Reread the story, paying special attention to details of this kind and the way they are used to signal changes in the progression of the relationship between the two characters.

3. Another of Laforet's stylistic characteristisc is the use of foreshadowing: she often mentions an image that returns later with greater importance. To see an example, reread paragraph 6 and paragraphs 22 and 23. Note how the early hints about Rosamunda's different reactions to her two sons prepares the reader for her reaction to one son's death.

4. Reread paragraphs 14 and 27. What does Rosamunda mean when she refers to her future as a **tumba** and a **sepulcro?**

5. Reread paragraph 20, which explains why Rosamunda took a new first name, and then the last paragraph. What do think is the meaning of the author's deliberate stylistic decision to use the "call me Rosamunda" ending?

Reacting to the Story

1. Have you ever known anyone like Rosamunda? Do you think she's a sympathetic character? Do you like her? Do you think the author does?

2. Many people have observed that travelers often tell strangers the intimate details of their personal lives. Has something like that ever happened to you? Do you think that explanation accounts for Rosamunda's behavior or do you think she's the sort of person who talks about herself in that way to anyone?

3. The soldier thinks Rosamunda is crazy (paragraph 29). Do you agree? Why or why not?

4. In spite of her delusions, the soldier is strongly attracted to Rosamunda. Why? What is it about his personality that makes him find her appealing? Why does she find him so attractive? What is the basis for the relationship between them? What do you think will happen after the story ends? (Be sure to use details of the story to support your opinions.)

5. One characteristic of successful creative writing, as the reviewer of **Gringo viejo** pointed out in an earlier unit, is the way it makes us think about great universal truths. What human realities is Laforet dealing with in "Rosamunda"?

MAPA DE LA PENÍNSULA IBÉRICA

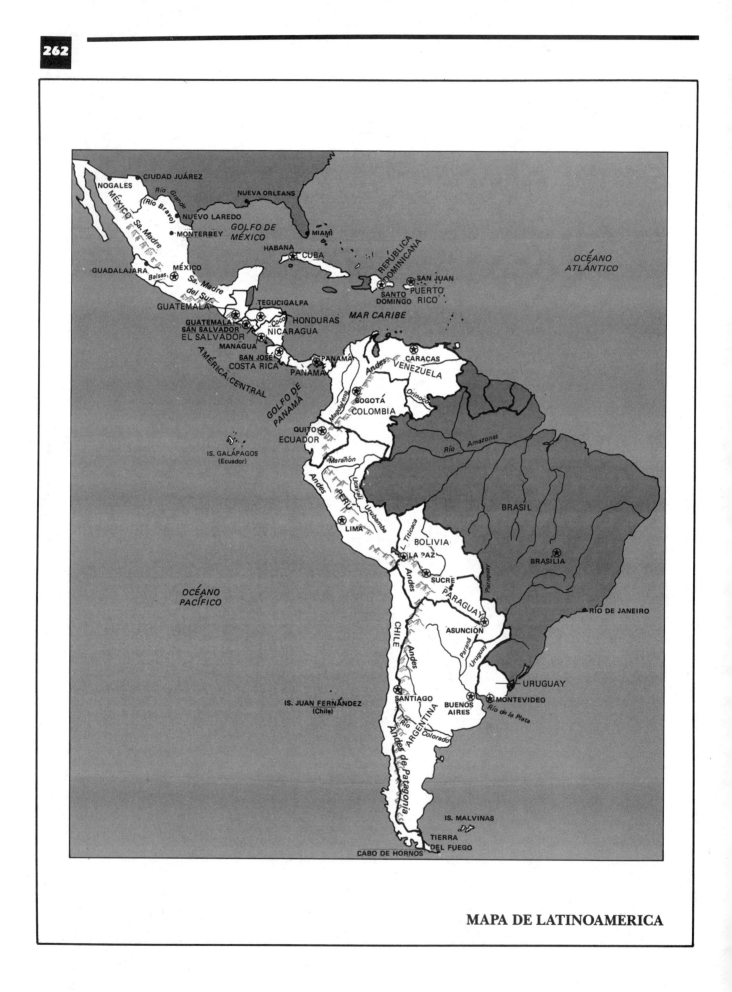

MAPA DE LATINOAMERICA

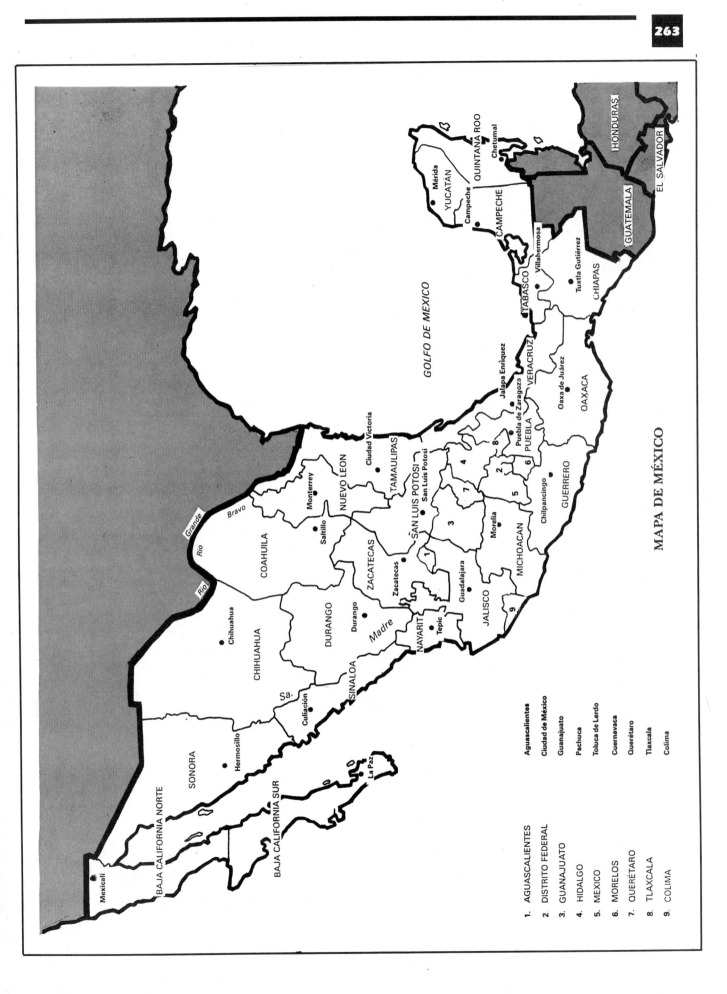

MAPA DE MÉXICO

GOLFO DE MÉXICO

HONDURAS

EL SALVADOR

GUATEMALA

QUINTANA ROO

Chetumal

Mérida

YUCATÁN

CAMPECHE

Campeche

TABASCO

Villahermosa

CHIAPAS

Tuxtla Gutiérrez

VERACRUZ

Jalapa Enríquez

Puebla de Zaragoza

PUEBLA

Oaxa de Juárez

OAXACA

GUERRERO

Chilpancingo

Ciudad Victoria

TAMAULIPAS

NUEVO LEON

Monterrey

SAN LUIS POTOSI

San Luis Potosi

Morelia

MICHOACAN

Saltillo

COAHUILA

ZACATECAS

Zacatecas

Guadalajara

JALISCO

Grande

Bravo

Rio

Rio

Chihuahua

DURANGO

Durango

Madre

NAYARIT

Tepic

CHIHUAHUA

Sa.

Culiacán

SINALOA

SONORA

Hermosillo

La Paz

BAJA CALIFORNIA NORTE

BAJA CALIFORNIA SUR

Mexicali

1. AGUASCALIENTES   Aguascalientes
2. DISTRITO FEDERAL   Ciudad de México
3. GUANAJUATO   Guanajuato
4. HIDALGO   Pachuca
5. MEXICO   Toluca de Lerdo
6. MORELOS   Cuernavaca
7. QUERÉTARO   Querétaro
8. TLAXCALA   Tlaxcala
9. COLIMA   Colima

263

APPENDIX
Grammar Guides for Readers of Spanish

I. *Reader's Guide to Adjective Agreement*

1. Spanish adjectives agree with nouns in number. If plural, they add **-s** if they end in a vowel and *-es* if they end in a consonant.
2. Spanish adjectives agree with nouns in gender. If the adjective ends in **-o**, it changes the **-o** to **-a** in the feminine. If it ends in **-e** or a consonant, there is usually no change at all. If it ends in a consonant and refers to nationality (e.g., **español**) or an occupation (e.g., **profesor**), it may add **-a** in the feminine.
3. Most native (not borrowed) Spanish words end in a vowel, usually **o, a,** or **e,** or in one of these consonants: **s, n, d, l, r** (or less frequently, **m, z.**)

II. *Reader's Guide to Gender*

1. All Spanish nouns are either *masculine* or *feminine.*
2. The gender of a noun is reflected in the definite and indefinite articles used with it: **el** and **un** for masculine nouns and **la** and **una** for feminine ones. Plural nouns take **los/unos** and **las/unas.**
3. Most nouns referring to humans (and some nouns naming domestic animals) belong to the class that reflects the sex of the individual referred to by the noun, e.g. **hombre** *(man)* is masculine and **mujer** *(woman)* is feminine: **gato** refers to a male cat and **gata** to a female one.
4. For other nouns, gender must simply be learned. There is no particular reason why **árbol** *(tree),* for example, is masculine while **pared** *(wall)* is feminine.
5. Fortunately, there are some clues to gender. Most nouns ending in **a** are feminine and most nouns ending in **-o** are masculine. Other feminine endings include **-dad/-tad, -cion,** and **-z.** Generally masculine endings include **-or, -e** and **-ma** (in very close cognates such as **programa, sistema,** and **problema.)** All these patterns have some common exceptions: e.g. **el día** *(day),* **la mano** *(hand),* **el lápiz** *(pencil),* and **la tarde** *(afternoon).*
6. Adjectives take the gender of the nouns they modify. For adjectives that end in **-o** in the masculine singular, the **-o** changes to **-a** when modifying a feminine noun. Compare **problema serio** with **dificultad seria.** Most adjectives that end in **-e** or a consonant do not change in the feminine, although all adjectives add **-s** (or **-es**) when they modify plural nouns.
7. Both nouns and adjectives of nationality that end in a consonant and those adjectives that end in **-dor** add **-a** in the feminine: e.g. **(hombre) francés** *(French [man])* but **(mujer) francesa** *(French [woman])* and **trabajador** *(worker/ hardworking)* but **trabajadora** *female worker/ hardworking).*

III. *Reader's Guide to the Use of* **Ser** *and* **Estar**

1. **Ser** and **estar** are both translated into English as "to be," but they are not used in the same way. In fact, there are no sentences in which both verbs could occur and have identical meanings.
2. **Ser** is a verb of identification. It is used to define and categorize. Therefore, it is used in sentences of equation, such as **Esa mujer es mi madre, Soy estudiante,** and **Esto es un libro. Ser** is used in identity statements: occupations, nationalities, and the substance or material something is made of. **La mesa es de madera.** (The table is *[made of]* wood.)
3. **Ser** is also used for telling time: **son las dos** *(it's two o'clock).*
4. **Estar** is a verb of location. **Estar** is always used to express simple location: **Ella está en su oficina, Las mesas están dentro del edificio, estoy aquí**
5. **Estar** is also used to describe the state or condition of a noun. States and conditions are often represented by adjectives. What is important is that the state or condition is somehow different from the way the entity is characteristically or naturally identified. Examples of such sentences are **El profesor está furioso** (he's not normally that mad), **El presidente está muerto** (a person is by definition alive—being dead is a new state), **Estás muy bonita hoy** (you are prettier than usual today).

6. The only situation in which both **ser** and **estar** may occur is with adjectives, but the meanings of the resulting sentences are very different. In a sentence like **Las manzanas todavía están verdes**, the apples are assumed to be naturally or characteristically some other color. When those apples are green, they're in an unripe state and **estar** is used. In **Las manzanas son verdes,** on the other hand, the sentence refers to some kind of apples that the speaker classifies as characteristically green. They are naturally green apples, not red apples.

IV. Reader's Guide to Spanish Prepositions

1. The major difference between the use of prepositions in English and Spanish is that English permits prepositions to occur as adverbs (for example, "He's going *in*," "Turn the radio *up*") or with nouns preceding them (as in "What's this *for*?"). Spanish never allows constructions of these kinds. Whenever you see a preposition in Spanish, you can expect to find the noun it is linked to following it.

2. Prepositions always give information about the relation of the referent of some noun (the object of the preposition) to the rest of the sentence. Sometimes this relationship is abstract: what the noun refers to may be the possessor of something, for example. Sometimes the relationship is concrete and physical: "The book is *under* the table." Most prepositions have concrete (physical or spatial) functions as well as less literal (abstract) ones.

3. **En** means both *in* and *on*. It always follows certain verbs, including the common verbs **entrar** *(enter)* and **consistir** *(consist [of])*, whenever a closely associated noun is mentioned: **El señor entra en la casa** and **esta ensalada consiste en frutas y vegetales frescas.**

4. **A** can be the equivalent of *to, toward, in, into,* and *on*. It also has a special (nonprepositional) use as the marker of human direct object nouns (the personal **a**). When used before a masculine singular definite article (**el**), **a** contracts with the article to become **al**, as in **Veo al señor** (but **Veo a la señora**).

5. **Para** is used for some of the functions of *for*. **Para** indicates that the noun it introduces is the goal or destination of the verb action, as in **Voy para el parque** *I'm going to the park)*. In this sense, it is often the equivalent of *toward*.

6. **De** can function as *of, about,* and *from*. It is the marker of possession, used whenever the noun possessor is mentioned (**Este carro es de Juan**). It is obligatory with certain verbs, such as **depender** when an associated noun is mentioned: **Dependemos de ellos** *(We depend on them)*. When **de** precedes the masculine singular article, it contracts to form **del**.

7. **Con** *(with)* has special forms when it combines with certain pronouns: **conmigo** *(with me)*, **contigo** *(with you)*, and **consigo** *(with himself/herself/itself)*. This last form is rare.

8. **Por** has a great many uses, including *by, for, through, during, in exchange for, for the sake of, because of,* and *around*.

9. The most common prepositions of physical relationship are the following: **debajo de** *underneath;* **encima de** *on top of;* **fuera de** *outside of;* **dentro de** *inside of;* **en frente de** *in front of;* **detrás de** *in back of, behind;* **lejos de** *far from;* **cerca de** *near to;* **delante de** *in front of;* **al lado de** *beside;* **ante** *before*.

ANSWER KEY

UNIT 1

A. 1. *Dallas* 2. sections 2 and 51 3. Ultramar 4. the belief that the North would not fight; the hope of foreign aid; the expectation of a military victory 5. Probably both!

B. 1. e 2. b 3. c 4. a 5. d

C. Since every dictionary is different, no "correct" answers can be provided here. If you are in a Spanish class, check your answers with those of a classmate who has the same dictionary.

D. 1. D, H 2. B, I 3. C, A, J, J 4. G, K 5. G, M 6. b 7. c 8. a 9. d 10. the Ohio one; the Madrid one

E. 1. a. cloudy; high 45, low 35 b. raining; high 52, low 46 c. showers; in the 40s d. partly cloudy; high in the 80s e. raining and hot 2. a. sunny and hot b. cool c. overcast and rainy d. clear in the morning, partly cloudy in the afternoon

UNIT 2

A. 1. These numbers have fewer digits. 2. #-##-## and #-#### 3. yellow 4. The business listings have more drawings, use a variety of typefaces and layouts, and are organized by category. 5. The heads serve as an index to the categories on the page. They are in alphabetical order. They are repeated at the beginning of each section on the page itself. 6. abbreviation for **teléfonos** 7. adhesive tape; ribbon for gift wrapping; a belt has a shape like a ribbon 8. the name of the author and the title of the book 9. *El terrorismo en España* and *Antología de tradiciones* 10. table of contents 11. the advertisements for **Cueve Andaluza, Farmacia Santa Catalina,** and **Foto Sistema** 12. a. **Foto Sistema** ad b. **Cueva Andaluza** ad c. **Farmacia** ad 13. Madrid; Valencia; Barcelona 14. The subscription form might be found in a magazine or newspaper. The business card is probably from the person named on it.

B. 1. **Paloma Esnal Elorrieta** 2. False. (If he were her brother's son, **Serrador** would be his *first* surname.) 3. Check with your instructor if you need help. 4. a. first names: **María Dolores**; first surname: **Cardozo**; second surname: **Castrejón** b. first names: **María de la Luz**; first surname: **Cardenas**; second surname: **Alvarez** c. first name: **Agustín**; first surname: **Cardenas**; second surname: **Castaneda** d. first names: **María Félix**; first surname: **Millán**; husband's name: **de Cardoso** e. first names: **Olga Leticia**; first surname: **Santana**; husband's name: **de Campos** f. first names: **María Luz**; first surname: **Castro**; husband's name: **de Canovas** g. first name: **Nilza**; first surname: **Castellanos**; husband's name: **de Cano** h. first name: **Erasmo**; first surname: **Cano**; second surname: **del Angel** i. first name: **Constantino**; first surname: **Campos**; second surname: **Pacheco** j. first names: **María del Carmen**; first surname: **Yahuoca**; husband's name: **vda. de Cano** 5. True.

C. 1. Spain: ### ## ## 2. Mexico: #-#### or #-##-## 3. Colombia: ## ## ## All these formats may be found in the same country; others also exist.

D. 1. any of the people on the list whose first surname is López 2. Juan Manuel González 3. Eduardo Ortiz González or Juan J. López González 4. Elizabeth L. Jiménez D. 5. Juan Carlos Aznorez or Manuel Luis Pedreira 6. Pascual Espósito Cabello 7. Magariños Cervantes (home of Augustina Villarino) 8. 10 de junio (where Miguel Angel Vázquez Caña lives)

E. If possible, check your answers with classmates using the same dictionary.

F. 1. a. **ñapa**: feminine noun. Did your dictionary tell you that this is a word used only in the Americas? Note how few Spanish words begin with **ñ**. b. **dechado**: adjective. If you had trouble finding **dechado**, be sure that you look after all the words that begin with **dec-**. c. **callar**: verb d. **carnal**: adjective 2. a. **carácter** (masculine noun), b. **carnal** (adjective), c. **carpintero** (masculine noun), d. **caro** (adjective), e. **carrera** (feminine noun), f. **carro** (feminine noun), g. **cartón** (masculine noun) 3. a. **anejo**: attached (adjective)/**añejo**: old (adjective) b. **ola**: wave (feminine noun)/**olla**: kettle (feminine noun) c. **marchar**: to march (verb)/**marcar**: to mark (verb). The entries in your dictionary no doubt contain more information than is given here. Be sure to read the entire entry when you look up a word. 4. **Ll**, like **ch**, is treated as a completely separate letter in the Spanish alphabet. Therefore, **galón** comes before **gallo** since the letter **ll** follows the letter **l** in the alphabet. On the other hand, for determining alphabetical order, **rr** is treated in the same way as any other combination of consonants. Therefore, **garra** comes before **garza** since **r** comes before **z** in the alphabet. 5. a. **cal**, b. **calar**, c. **calibre**, d. **calmar**, e. **calzar**, f. **calloso**, g. **cámara**. You should have circled **cal** and **cámara**.

G. 1. b. *Historia de Uruguay* (Most of the titles in the list include references to Uruguay or to history.) 2. *Diario de sesiones...* or *Estado Mayor del Ejército* 3. Put single last names first. Alphabetize double last names as if they were single words. Ignore **de** when it comes between two names. 4. If you had trouble locating the names, review and try again. Check your answers with your classmates or your instructor. 5. Ramón García Collazo comes before García Cordero, Manuel. María García-Conde comes before García-Hoz Rosales, Víctor. Alfredo Garchitorena Díaz comes before Gardogui, Miguel.

H. 1. use of section titles and page numbers ·2. greater use of different typefaces; more information about individual sections; sections not listed in page order 3. It is probably from some source that pays greater attention to visual cues for reading, for example, a popular magazine. (You may also have recognized the title!) 4. The contents are divided into sections. Titles in larger type correspond to more general sections; smaller type is used for smaller units, e.g. individual articles.   5. pages where different sections begin; organized by section rather than by page order

I.   1. Calle 1 Nº 187.   2. Carrera 41 No. 44-34 Oficina 204; Bogotá, Medellín, and Cali. (Look for these large cities on a map of Colombia.)   3. M. Schurmann Pacheco and M. L. Coolighan Sanguinetti   4. "Un anillo que descubre la verdad"; Julio Lucas Jaimes ("Aventuras nocturnas")   5. St. Catherine's church is probably on Sombrerería Street, right across from the pharmacy of the same name.   6. **Foto Sistema** offers photo developing in 1 hour; it also provides quality and service.   7. weekly   8. The camera is reviewed on p. 66 *Mecánica Popular.*   9. the fiftieth anniversary of the first Dominican airmail stamp   10. The list of stamp collectors is from the **filatelia** section of the magazine—one of the **secciones fijas**. Remember, each reader brings different background knowledge and vocabulary to every reading task! If **filatelia** is not a familiar cognate to you, you may need to check it in your dictionary.

UNIT 3

A.   statement 3

B.   Here are the words and how many times their Spanish equivalents occur in the Camay ad: Camay: 10 occurences (Six of them occur in the drawings.);   skin: 10;   free: 4 (There's a coupon for a free offer.);   clean: 2;   water: 0;   body: 0 (The ad is for face soap.)   How well did you predict them?

C.   Here are the content words (stems) used more than once in the ad, listed in order of frequency. Do not be concerned if you overlooked one or two occurences. Marking repetitions accurately requires that you be really careful!   **Camay:** 10 (There are six on the boxes in the drawings.); **piel(es):** 10; **gratis:** 4; **personalizado:** 3; **normal:** 3; **grasiento(a):** 3; **seco(a):** 3; **cuidado:** 2; **hermosa:** 2; **fórmula(s):** 2; **ayuda:** 2; **tiene:** 2 (Did you also notice **contiene?**); **suave:** 2; **uno:** 2

D.   1. Here are the content words that a student can probably recognize or guess by the second week of Spanish study. (They are listed in the order in which they appear in the ad.) **Gratis, personalizado, es, programa, dividirse, tipo, normal, estas, contiene, cosmética, reducir, humedecedor, natural, suave, intensos, emolientes, válido, tres, fórmula(s), necesita, uno.** You may have recognized or guessed more words than this. If you are in a class, you might enjoy comparing your own list with those of other students.   2. You may consider several other words to be easier to recognize than the ones on this list. Each person's mental list will vary from every other.   3. Three bars of soap appear together in the ad (twice). The written material contains three indented sentences that all start the same way: **Camay para piel.** There are references to **tres fórmulas.** Be sure that you have located all these features in the ad.

E.   1. a, c, d   2. b, c, a   3. c, b, a   4. b   5. False

F.   1. feminine   2. masculine   3. feminine   4. masculine   5. masculine   6. feminine   If you had trouble with this exercise, you may need to review the *Reader's Guide to Gender* in the Appendix. Your grammar text or your instructor can also help you.

G.   Items 3, 6, and 9 are least likely to be mentioned in personal ads.

H.   1. c   2. a   3. f   4. b   5. d   6. Ariel Alfaro from Chiapas

I.   1. These are verbs you probably already know or should be able to guess: **escribir, importar, desear, relacionar,** and **tener.**   2. and   3. Did you pay enough attention to context in your guessing? For example, the verb **enviar** is hard to guess all alone but almost every occurence of it is followed by the word **foto.** What would an advertiser in the personals probably want a respondent to do with a **foto?**   4. Here are the meanings of all the verbs in the list. The number following each represents the number of times it occurs in the ads.

a. to write (18)
b. to exchange (7)
c. to be important (12)
d. to want (desire) (26)
e. to send (6)
f. to begin (initiate) (7)
g. to answer (4)
h. to know someone (9)
i. to relate to (8)
j. to have (14)

J.   1. d   2. e   3. a   4. c   5. b

K.   1. Horóscopo   2. Daniel Fernández   3. lion, crab, fish   4. Sagitario, Escorpión, Acuario   5. September/October, March/April   6. Hasta el 18   7. days of the month

L.   1. c   2. a. Sagitario, Virgo, Géminis, Escorpión   b. Aries, Leo, Tauro, Libra, Escorpión, Piscis   c. Sagitario, Tauro, Virgo, Géminis, Libra, Acuario   d. Leo, Capricornio, Acuario, Cancer   e. Capricornio, Géminis, Cancer   (Did you notice that even if you did not know what **viajes** meant, you could still complete the exercise correctly?)   3. Your own sign probably deals with at least two of the fields in the list. Check your answers with a classmate who has the same sign.

M.   a. **iniciar** to start, to begin, to initiate   b. **prestar** to lend   c. **favorecer** to favor   d. **aprovechar** to take advantage of   e. **significar** to mean   f. **tener** to have   g. **preparar** to prepare   h. **intensificar** to intensify   i. **observar** to observe   j. **desarrollar** to develop

N.   1. Sicología   2. c   3. d   4. similar vocabulary and typefaces in paired sentences

O.   In doing Exercise O, you may find that you are not sure why **ser** or **estar** is used in a particular case. If so, you may need to review these verbs. Use the *Reader's Guide* in the Appendix or consult your textbook or your instructor.

P.   1. c   2. d   3. a   4. e   5. b   6. h   7. i   8. g   9. j   10. f

UNIT 4

A. 1. ticket (public transportation) 2. receipt (for telephone service) 3. ad (street flyer) for clothing sale 4. ad (street flyer) for English lessons 5. receipt/bill for goods (paper supplies) 6. receipt/bill for service (food) 7. receipt/bill for service (refrigerator repair) 8. ad (street flyer) for copy center 9. ad for legal services 10. ticket (museum)

B. 1. a, b, c, d 2. c 3. item 1 (ticket for public transportation) 4. items 1 and 6

C. 1. four thousand, three hundred and fifty **pesetas** per month 2. **Precio** is the item price; **importe** is the total price for all items at that price. 3. 150 **pesos** total IVA (60 **pesos** plus 90 **pesos**) 4. 260 5. The Valencia Cathedral ticket gives weights in thousands of kilograms.

D. 1. Sevilla 2. 17:00 3. 8 4. yes 5. 027 6. 413 to Valencia and 885 to Alicante 7. 3 (flight numbers 287, 777, and 629)

E. 1. Hotel-Balneario Vallfogona 2. Provincia de Tarragona 3. Viajes CEMO 4. Hotel-Balneario 5. Any of those listed under the title **Especialmente recomendadas para:** 6. 27,950 **pesetas** 7. They refer to the days in the program of activities.

F. 1. 12 2. Metro stop Alonso Martínez 3. c 4. True

G. 1. True 2. True 3. c If you had trouble with this exercise, look at the paragraphs again before going on.

H. 1. 100 km. 2. True 3. True 4. True 5. True

I. There are many prepositional phrases you might have chosen. Your instructor can help you check the particular ones you selected. The *Reader's Guide to Spanish Prepositions* in the Appendix may also be helpful.

J. 1. b 2. c 3. c 4. a

K. 1. allowance 2. baggage compartment 3. seat 4. weight 5. inches 6. baggage

L. 1. b, d 2. fishing 3. 315 miles/507 kilometers 4. Each route will be different. You may compare yours with those of some classmates. 5. ARIPO is item 31 on the list of interesting places given on the map. 6. Artesanías e Industrias Populares del Estado de Oaxaca 7. 4:00 P.M. 8. e, a, d, c, b 9. fur Check your dictionary for other possible translation equivalents for **piel.** 10. e, c, d, b, a 11. c 12. all kinds of toys

UNIT 5

A. 1. Spain; the addresses in the ads 2. c; the job title 3. e, b, d, c, a 4. Each list may be different.

B. 1. Did you remember to pay attention to titles, format cues, and repetitions? 2. Remember that some words that look familiar do not mean what you expect them to. a. **ofrece:** offers (It's an **-er** verb form.) b. **requiere:** requires (An **-ir** verb form.)

c. **empresa:** company; business d. **dirección:** management (Did you notice how many different translation equivalents this word has? The one that you can guess on the basis of its familiarity is not appropriate for this context.) e. **jefe:** chief (Your dictionary may have given you only formal equivalents for **jefe.** In informal contexts, the best English equivalent is "boss.") f. **secretaria:** secretary (In reading related entries, did you find **secretaría,** a word whose meaning differs from that of **secretaria** in a subtle way?) g. **delegado:** agent ("Delegate" is not really the best equivalent for this particular context. Sometimes, you have to THINK of good equivalents on your own—your dictionary does not know the context!) h. **precisa:** needs (Did you notice the similar contexts for **busca, solicita, necesita,** and **precisa?** Your ability to guess two of these allows you to predict the other two with a high degree of confidence!) 3. Were your extra words helpful in understanding more of the passage?

C. 1. c, d, b, a 2. exhibition representative (TEST) 3. store clerk (Bédaux) 4. sales representative (importer) 5. sales agent (Dinkal, S.A.) 6. sales agent, store clerk (Dinkal, S.A. and Bédaux)

D. 1. correspondence courses 2. coupons 3. job-related drawings or photos

E. 1. Mecánico de Automóviles, Electricidad del Automóvil, Jefe Taller Automóviles 2. Jardinería 3. Educación Preescolar and Puericultura 4. (93) 245 33 06 5. Centro de Enseñanza a Distancia 6. Afinación de Motores 7. dinero y prestigio 8. Argentina 9. 1953 10. No; there's a free pamphlet. 11. age (edad) 12. Electrónica, Mecánica, Electricidad

F. 1. c 2. b 3. a 4. a 5. b

G. 1, 2, 4, 5, 7

H. 1. Mecánica Automotriz y Diesel, Electricidad Práctica, Inglés Práctico 2. Cada día su uso es más vital para los hogares y la industria. 3. Puestos en bancos, hoteles, oficinas comercios, etc. 4. Audio Electrónica y Comunicaciones

I. 1. a. carta b. ensalada c. leche d. papel e. ponche f. tabaco 2. a container 3. noun 4. noun 5. feminine

J. 1. noun 2. **-Eza** makes an abstract noun out of an adjective. 3. a. **belleza:** beauty; b. **simpleza:** simplicity; c. **dureza:** harshness

K. 1. -ero 2. -ería

L. 1. a. to eat breakfast b. to rest c. to lose hope, to despair d. to take apart e. to unfasten f. to remove 2. It negates a verb's meaning. 3. Each list will vary. 4. Compare your new words with those of other students.

M. 1.

el guarda/fangos	a. guards	b. mud
el salva/vidas	a. saves	b. lives
el abre/latas	a. opens	b. cans
el para/caídas,	a. stops	b. falls
el toca/discos	a. plays	b. records
el lava/platos	a. washes	b. plates
el para/brisas	a. stops	b. breezes
el par/aguas	a. stops	b. waters

(The **a** in **para** is dropped.)

2. masculine
3. False
4. life preserver, can opener, dishwasher, record player, and windshield

N. 1. comercio mundial, inflación en la CEE, trabajadores de los astilleros, reformas económicas húngaras, exportaciones de acero, Andorra, trabajadores de Astano, extradición de Ruíz-Mateos 2. Did you look up any words? Were your predictions about likely vocabulary correct? 3. When you have finished the exercise, you may wish to compare your questions to those of other readers. 4. the two reports about the **astilleros** 5. CEE 6. d

O. 1. Comunidad Económica Europea; European Economic Community (the Common Market) 2. No. (Do you know where Andorra is located?) 3. 6.5%; oil prices 4. dock workers/stevedores; they do not want to join the compensation program 5. A limit of 7.6% of the US market is assigned to the Common Market countries. 6. a West German businessman accused of financial irregularities in Spain; Spain wants to extradite him for trial 7. 2500 8. Comisión Económica para América Latina; a meeting of experts; the General Agreement on Tariffs and Customs Duties 9. private stock investment; they are not socialist

P. 1. a, b, c, e, g, h, i, j 2. the last two on Viernes 6 3. Japan has recently begun to open factories in Spain. 4. good 5. no 6. a price war; to bring the pricing structure under control 7. 119 **pesetas** to the Canadian dollar 8. Spain and Portugal 9. pescar, pesquera, pesquero 10. **Renta** can mean "income".

UNIT 6

A. 1. Manuel Llano Gorostiza; photo, repeated use of name 2. a prize 3. 58 4. San Salvador del Valle in Vizcaya 5. wine

B. Your version of the paragraph should look like this one:

Premio nacional de Gastronomía
De Manuel Llano Gorostiza, sus amigos (dicen) que (es) la persona que más (sabe) del vino de Rioja; que lo (sabe) todo. Manuel Llano Gorostiza, 58 años, natural de una población minera, San Salvador del Valle, en Vizcaya, premio nacional de Gastronomía este año, (es) mucho más modesto, dentro de su habitual modestia, y (asegura) que su único mérito (es) "insertar el vino dentro de la cultura, porque yo (tengo) muy claro que (existe) una cultura del vino". En 1971 el nombre de Llano Gorostiza (comienza a adquerir) relevancia como consecuencia de un libro que hoy día (continúa siendo) un manual sobre el vino de Rioja. (Fue) un compromiso increíble, pero (acabé escribiéndolo) (Los vinos de Rioja)". Desde entonces (no ha parado) de escribir ni de dar conferencias.

C. 1. a sentence of equivalence 2. y 3. Llano Gorostiza 4. yo 5. There is a quote. 6. porque

D. 1. The parts of the article are (a) the photo of a salad; (b) the title; (c) the subtitle, which states the purpose—to provide practical suggestions for appetizing and refreshing summer salads; (d) three paragraphs of prose; (e) a recipe with a title, a list of ingredients, and a set of instructions. 2. ensalada(s), plato, ingredientes, pescado; meses calurosos 3. topic: salads; pur-

pose: to explain why salads are healthful and to teach the reader how to make one 4. main idea: Salad is a delicious, nutritious meal, especially for summer. (Note that this idea is stated in an "X is Y" sentence. The first and last paragraphs repeat the content of the title and subtitle. 5. (1) Salads are an essential summer meal because they use the nutritious raw produce of the garden; (2) Salads are good summer meals because they are light and cool; (3) Salads may be made infinitely variable through the use of different ingredients. 6. a. 3 b. 1 c. 2 7. a. 3 b. 2 c. 1 d. 0 e. 3 f. 2 g. 1 h. 1 i. 2 j. 0 8. Look carefully at this list before continuing. Note that the verb cores suggest something about the flow of subjects in the paragraphs, and the verb meanings alone provide information about probable topics. Verb cores in subtitle: ofrecemos, hacer; paragraph 1: son, aportan, se encuentran, se prestan, podremos improvisar, aprovechar, terminar, sobró, utilizar, se iba a echar a perder, son, admiten, puede ser; paragraph 2: gustan, digerir, es, preparar, se pueden convertir, añadimos; paragraph 3: podríamos comer, aburrirnos, daríamos, puede resultar, elegimos, protestan, se quedan, comen, podemos agregar: recipe: ponga, mezcle, remoje, incorpore, espolvoree, sirva

E. 1. Changes in type mark each part. 2. pechuga *(breast)* 3. hueso *(bone)* 4. libra, taza 5. nouns

F. 1. sazonar, dorarlas, dejarlas, cocinar, picarla, preparar, calentando, espese, agregarle, batiendo, lograr, agregarle, cubrir, servirlas, son, es, se le llama (Note the way in which the attached object pronouns help you keep track of what is being worked on in the recipe. Remember to use each word you look up to help you guess the meanings of other ones.) 2. dorarlas... para dejarlas cocidas; batiendo fuertemente para lograr; calentando... hasta que... espese 3. trocitos (trozo); cucharadita (cucharada); papitas (papa) 4. double boiler

G. 1. a. 2 b. 1 c. 4 d. 3 e. 5 2. three 3. They are not part of the recipe; they are to be added when the dish is served.

H. se les cortan, se pone a hervir, esté, se cuela, se calienta, se le pone, esté, se le añade, se deja hervir, se le incorpora, se le da, se sirve

I. 1. espárragos; mantequilla; mantequilla (con harina); mantequilla (con harina y leche); mantequilla (con harina y caldo y espárragos) 2. ya que esté bien cocido se cuela; cuando esté bien disuelta se le añade

J. 1. cortar, incorporar, colocar, vaciar, adornar, servir 2. 1 can of asparagus tips, 1/2 kg. of boiled and shelled shrimp, one cup of mayonnaise, 1 head of Romaine lettuce, 1 red and 1 green pepper, artichoke hearts, 2 hard-boiled eggs 3. a. 5 b. 3 c. 1 d. 6 e. 2 f. 4

K. Compare meals with your classmates. How much did you spend?

L. 2. The best meanings for the original contexts are the following: a. compromiso *(engagement* [In the article, the best translation equivalent would be *responsibility.*]) b. conferencia *(lecture)* c. crudos *(raw)* d. restos *(leftovers)* e. estación *(season)* f. jamón *(ham)* Compare your results with those of classmates using other dictionaries to see how much variation you find.

M. 1. a. **comienza a adquirir** and **continúa siendo** The first part of this sentence is about the Llano Gorostiza's name and the second part is about his book. b. The two parts have a cause and effect relationship. **Como consequencia** is somewhat like **porque** because it says one sentence is the result of the other. c. He wrote the book; then, he became famous. The actual order of the events has been reversed by the use of **como consequencia**. d. *as a result* or *consequently* 2. a. ya (que) *(as soon as)* b. cuando *(when)* c. en seguida *(immediately)* d. después *(later; after)* e. luego *(then; next)* f. hasta (que) *(until)* g. para (que) *(in order that; so that)*

N. 1. a. rice b. arroz 2. b 3. c 4. and 5. because they contain the body of the article (new information) and they are the longest

O. 1. a. 5 b. 3 c. 1 d. 4 e. 6 2. a. origin and use (paragraph 5) b. 16% (paragraph 3) c. Valencia (paragraph 1) d. requires half the cooking time of regular rice (paragraph 4) e. **naturistas** and **macribióticos** (paragraph 4) 3. three types: round grain (in both precooked and regular varieties); long grain (also precooked and regular); and whole grain

P. 1. a. 4 and 7 b. 4 c. 0 d. 1 e. 0 2. b

UNIT 7

Exercise, page 142: 1. a, c, e, f, h, i 2. b, c, e 3. g, h 4. a, b, c, d, e 5. a, b, c, e, h, i 6. f, h

A. 1. 10:00 P.M. 2. Noon 3. 7:00 A.M. You can't leave between midnight and 7.

B. 1. Each of the subsections is clearly identified by its format cues. 2. five 3. Here is the quickest route: Go along San Agustín to the Plaza de las Cortes and turn onto San Jerónimo. Take San Jerónimo to the Plaza Puerta del Sol. Cross the Plaza and go up Preciados. The store will be on your left. 4. amabilidad y profesionalidad; servicios especiales; seguridad; La Carta de Compra 5. a, b, d, e

C. 1. 11 2. B 3. You will have an opportunity later to see if you were right about this one!

D. 1. b 2. 4 (floors 2, 3, 4, and 5) 3. floors S2, S3 and 1 4. a. 3 b. 7 c. 3 d. S2 and S3 e. 3 5. S2

E. 1. a photo of a single speaker; the titles, which seem more like single lecture topics than conference topics 2. secretario general de la Asociación de Escritores y Artistas; secretario del Ateneo de Madrid 3. secretario general *(of an arts organization)*, poeta, crítico, ensayista, and novelista 4. to celebrate a centennial 5. centenario

F. 1. autor (The Spanish word **autor** can be used to refer to the producer of any artistic work, such as the series of drawings referred to here.) 2. llegar a la verdadera identidad del objeto o el sujeto reflejado 3. Inventiva 82, the exhibition (The writer assumes the reader will take that name as the subject of the verbs in the first sentence if no other noun is mentioned.) 4. feminine singular 5. b 6. exposición 7. If a direct object pronoun is used, it is standing in place of the noun to which it refers. Both the noun and the pronoun cannot occur in the same sentence unless the noun is in a prepositional phrase. (**Le,** used in

Spain, refers to direct objects who are male humans. In most other regions of the Spanish-speaking world, **lo** is used for that purpose and **le** is used only as an indirect object pronoun.) 8. The sentence that begins **El es.** 9. Sanz Magallón 10. different styles; Sanz Magallón's drawings are **ocres, difusos,** with **niebla, misterio,** and **soledad;** Pérez-Serrano is able to represent la **verdadera identidad** of his subjects.

G. 1. no 2. private education; economic perspectives; young people's associations; Spanish financing 3. secondary school 4. two 5. whether the author wrote before 1800 or after 6. the translation (six copies); the original (also six copies); a résumé; the criteria of selection 7. almost 3200 years old 8. ancient 9. The exhibit includes blueprints and scale drawings. 10. The photo pictures the potter (**alfarero**) earning a living (**gana la vida**) as a street musician. 11. the readers 12. Holland, the US, Czechoslovakia, Spain 13. anything on the order of "You're in luck. . . " 14. afortunadamente; tiene buena suerte 15. decorations and music 16. Sevilla has parades and seems to be more crowded. 17. exposición and (se) exponen 18. exposición (both are nouns) 19. José María Carreras 20. directing 21. the time of the concert 22. tierra batida (clay courts) 23. Spain's most distinguished tennis players

H. 1. a. 4 b. 1 c. 3 d. 2 2. d is least likely 3. possible answers: direct comparisons with other movies, information about rating

I. 1. a. 4 b. 2 c. 1 d. 3 2. 2 3. probably no more than two for **regular** (a false cognate) 4. How closely does your summary of the *Legend* review resemble this one—in meaning, at least, if not in style! *Legend* is another in the continuing stream of fantasy movies that appeal more to kids than to adults. Its cast of imaginary creatures and its otherworldly atmosphere are visually rich, but its message—if any—is obscured by its superficial trappings. Adults can do better—both as directors and viewers.

J. 1. llover a cántaros *(to be raining pitchers)* 2. estar en ayunas *(to be fasting or on a fast)* 3. estar entre la espada y la pared *(to be between the sword and the wall)* 4. matar dos pájaros con un solo tiro *(to kill two birds with one shot)*

K. 1. to go looking for trouble *(lit.* to look for three legs on a cat) 2. to jilt *(lit.* to give him squash) 3. to butt in (where you don't belong) *(lit.* to stick your spoon in) 4. to go through a lot; to suffer *(lit.* to sweat a fat drop) 5. to sleep on something *(lit.* consult with the pillow) 6. to make a big fuss (about something) *(lit.* shout it to heaven) 7. to remain unmarried *(lit.* to stay to dress the saints) 8. to not like someone *(lit.* to not stand to see even a picture of someone)

L. 1. 2, historia 2. 2, sociología *or* política 3. 3, economía *or* 1 diccionarios 4. B, literatura clásica y moderna 5. 3, ciencias naturales 6. B, religiones 7. 1, geografía 8. 2, bellas artes 9. B, libros de bolsillo en español 10. S2, textos escolares *or* 3 pedagogía

M. 1. the opening and closing sentences 2. los fanáticos del esteticismo decadente, los fanáticos de las narraciones breves, los cinéfilos, y los adictos a la revista 3. the readers of the review 4. Not really. He refers to this issue as **menos deslabazada de lo habitual.** 5. Forsyth 6. eight 7. The style is **menos pegada.** 8. absorbing stories (stories you want to "gobble up") 9. Not really, but he thinks they are a way to pasar un rato agradable. 10. *Caballos hacia la noche* and *La revolución permanente* 11. la imaginación; el sentido estético de la narración 12. un trabajo excepcional sobre . . . Porcel 13. sociólogo, historiador y periodista 14. la política 15. su síntesis 16. Yes. Su aportación al conocimiento del tema y su valoración político-social son sumamente estimables.

N. 1. a. *Suicidio en México;* b. Mariano Aguirre; c. 189 pages 2. the third paragraph 3. 1 and 2 4. a. 4 b. 1 c. 3 d. 2 5. The sentence which begins **La tesis literaria de Fuentes es . . .** 6. Bierce 7. protagonista 8. no

O. 1. bases, fundaciones 2. what is actually known about Bierce; hints in his works; rumors about his encounter with Villa 3. a, c, d; If you selected other answers, read the paragraph again, looking for the connectors (**primero, segundo,** and **tercero**) that introduce the three ideas. 4. trama 5. el amor, la relación del ser humano con la historia y la búsqueda de la propia identidad, y el sentido de la vida al confrontarse con un contexto extraño

P. 1. Fuentes does something **magistralmente;** the novel has three **gran méritos;** the novel is referred to as **una gran novela** 2. Sample summary: Carlos Fuentes' recent novel *Gringo viejo* is a fictional account of the last days of Ambrose Bierce, an American writer who went to Mexico in 1913 and was never heard from again. Using this device as a foundation, Fuentes comments on everything from the history of the Mexican revolution to the consequences of cultural encounters. Primarily, though *Gringo viejo* is a masterful treatment of some of the great themes in literature. Written in Fuentes' richly innovative style, it is an important addition to the existing literature of American contacts with Mexican reality.

UNIT 8

A. 1. oponente; b. 2. . . . hacerles sentir lo mismo. 3. las personas atrás de usted 4. the reader; decisión 5. Oberve la reacción de su amiga y si nota que algo la detiene o que no se siente cómoda en la situación, ése es el momento de hablar acerca de lo que lo (le) preocupa. 6. saber; estar 7. los empleados 8. algo 9. dueño

B. 1. a. Dr. William H. Frey II b. two c. sentimental tears and those produced by physical irritations d. watching a movie and cutting up onions e. Emotional tears contained more proteins. 2. biochemical (eliminates dangerous substances from the body) physiological (induces relaxation) 3. accumulation of toxic substances; tension; general aches and pains; pessimistic view of one's problems 4. False 5. Crying is often thought to reveal immaturity and weakness. 6. a. use of somewhat technical terms from biochemistry b. health care theme, use of research findings c. use of objective language in detailed account of experiment d. use of exclamatory style and direct address in the **tú** form 7. esperamos que cambies tu opinión

C. 1. El Mercurio de Santiago de Chile 2. Fransisco Javier Bernal, un profesor español 3. Los Domingos de ABC 4. El Día del Libro y el aniversario de la muerte de Cervantes 5. semántico y eufónico

D. 1. a. I b. I c. I d. II e. I f. I g. I h. I i. II j. II k. II l. II m. II n. II o. II p. I q. I r. I 2. euphonic;

semantic 3. Each group of lists will be different. The semantic lists tend to have some words in common (as the introduction reminds us) and tend to include many abstract nouns. As you work through the lists, be sure to pay attention to the effect of each group as a whole. For example, Antonio Gala's list has a different effect from the one by Federico Carlos Sainz de Robles, even though they share many words. 4. Your own reactions may not be the same as those of your classmates. Compare them to see why. Did you notice a common thread in the words associated with the dawn: **crepúsculo, alborear, azul, rubor, gallear.** 5. The variations of accent are certainly an interesting element in this list. Perhaps you can see a relationship among the words **antaño, hogaño, melancolía,** and **nocturno,** but, in general, this list seems to have been chosen with less attention to meaning than to sound.

E. 1. meaning 2. They are all very difficult to translate with single words.; Camilo-José Cela 3. If you know something about Spanish history, particularly the colonization of the New World, and you think about the relation of each word to the first and the last on the list, you could probably see the theme. 4. political; perhaps reactions of pride or brotherhood

F. 1. He says they are all beautiful. 2. Each person's psychological and environmental circumstances will alter his or her preferences and interpretations for words. 3. changes in meaning. 4. The associations we have for **rosa** are partly a result of our awareness of the ways poets have used it (in other words, its contexts). 5. It changes and expresses all of human experience.

G. 1. three: the interviewer, Fanny (an employee), and Borges himself 2. He has an **agotamiento físico** and is under doctor's orders to rest (paragraph 1); he is weak, with a **falta de aliento** (paragraph 3.) 3. near the **ventana del sexto piso de su modesto apartamento en el centro de Buenos Aires** (paragraph 1) 4. a. 9 b. 5 c. 7 d. 4 e. 9 f. 10 g. 7 h. 2 5. a. - "No soy creyente." (paragraph 9) b. - "No entiendo la política." (paragraph 2) (other quotes are possible as well) c. + "Hay, en este país, algunas circunstancias favorables. . ." (paragraph 7) d. - "No veo solución a los problemas. . ." (paragraph 2) e. - ". . .entre dos países que fomentan violencia, Estados Unidos y la Unión Soviética." (paragraph 8) f. - "Fue un período diabólico. . ." (paragraph 5) g. + "Estoy continuamente pensando en versos." (paragraph 10)

H. 1. **Luces** refers to the inner thoughts that Borges expresses—his personal philosophy that brightens a difficult existence. **Tarde** has two possible meanings in Spanish: *afternoon* (the time of the interview and a time of lowered light) and *late.* (The lateness could be both a reference to how long the political situation of Argentina has been difficult and to the fact that Borges is at the end of his life.) Note how difficult it would be to find an English word that could convey all these ideas at once. 2. The author uses the references to movement of the eyes to remind his readers that Borges is blind and also to allude to his vibrancy, even in the midst of general weakness. 3. These references serve to give the reader a sense of Borges' physical presence, to remind us of his blindness, and to suggest something of the alertness of his mind. 4. **Oscuro** refers to the physical darkness of the room, to the poet's blindness, and to the (metaphorical) darkness of Argentina's recent history. 5. a. She is a devoted servant, of lower-class background, who does housework. She can be strong willed in carrying out her duties. 6. The image of an operator and an arranger able to communicate in spite of blindness serves at a surface level to give us insight into the relationship between Borges and Fanny. Experienced users of Spanish can pick up deeper semantic associations from **ordenador** as well. In particular, it has some specialized military uses which are referred to again in the **gest**c **militar** phrase.   7. The author uses the quotes to give us an idea of Fanny's attitudes and personality—in particular, her respect for Borges. They also suggest subservience.   8. Fanny's peasant straightforwardness (referred to in an exaggerated way as **brutalidad**) is identified as her primary characteristic and then made into a metaphor that includes associations of earthiness, truth, and health. (An injection is usually for medical reasons— remember, Borges is ill.)   9. Borges himself tells us that the wolf's head is a physical thing. He uses it for a Halloween mask and it has a terrible smell. However, the references to disguise and the phrase ''man is a wolf (to other) men'' suggests its metaphorical meaning, as a symbol of man's inhumanity or animal nature. This inhumanity is a direct reference to the brutality of the military government. Note the way Borges links his unmasking (he isn't really a wolf, he's a man) and the announcement of the election of a democratic government (the inhuman(e) government has been replaced by a human(e) one.) This linkage depends solely on the metaphorial meaning of the wolf's head, and not at all on the physical one.   10. The last image of the article is one of light in a darkening room, a further reminder of Borges' external blindness. It is also a return to the earlier references to his internal light and to his identity as a writer who illuminates. Did you remember to make a connection to the use of **luminoso** in the subtitle?

I.   Your answers to these questions depend largely on your personal perspectives on the issues Borges raises. You may find it useful to compare your conclusions to those reached by other readers.

J.   You may want to compare your answers with those of other readers.

UNIT 9

Since most of the exercises in this unit call for opinion or evaluation, there may be important differences in the answers that different readers produce. If your answers differ substantially from those given here, check to be sure that you can support them using material contained in the readings.

A.   1. a. B   b. E   c. D   d. C   e. A   f. F   g. H   h. G
2. a. II.   b. I.   c. II.   d. II.   e. I.   f. I.   g. II.   h. I.   3. The three easiest articles are E, B, and H because they deal with familiar issues or events. The next group includes F and A, which, although they may be about stories that are less familiar to US readers, are nevertheless about topics (a drought in Brazil and the burglary of a museum) that probably do not require a great deal of special background. Note that the robbery article is the first on this topic; a later article might be more difficult because it would assume that readers had been following the story. The most difficult articles are G and D, because they deal with economic issues of local Mexican concern, and C, which is about a person who is not well-known outside Mexico. Your particular order may vary depending on your own familiarity with the individual stories or events.

B.   1. 9   2. 10   3. 2 and 3   4. 6   5. 4   6. 11   7. 8   8. 13
9. 1   10. 14

C.   1. a. F   b. O   c. F   d. O   e. O   2. the first nine   3. b
4. no   5. the fact that Texas already has a Mexican flag, which was taken in the decisive battle for independence (the Battle of San Jacinto)   6. that the battle of the Alamo is a sensitive topic for Mexicans, since it reminds them of the loss of half their territory (in the Mexican-American War of 1846-1848)   7. He probably agrees with the Houston journalist and does not want to send the flag back. (Note also the use of the word *obstinados* to refer to the Texans who won't give up the issue.)   8. You have to interpret the article. How much weight will you give to the argument made by the Houston editorialist?

D.   1. a. paragraph 4 b. 1 and 2 c. 5 d. 3 e. 9 f. 6 g. 7 and 8   2. no hay ninguna movilidad intelectual en Europa; los profesores importantes de Europa se quedan en los Estados Unidos; no hay contacto intelectual entre los países europeos   3. no puede haber desarrollo científico y technológico europeo; no se puede tener conciencia política europea; no es posible reformar los sistemas universitarios (Did you notice the use of repeated negatives?)   4. Academia Europea de las Ciencias, de las Letras y de las Artes   5. los grandes estudiosos y artistas de todos los campos que hayan hecho contribución original   6. para evitar que la **Academia** de convierta en un geriátrico   7. encontrarse, conocerse, trabajar juntas, hacer proyectos avanzados, (*work on*) las tareas más esforzadas y difíciles   8. in order to insure that the members feel a sense of service and responsibility to Europe   9. They should have offices, meeting rooms, places to receive guests, and an efficient secretary.   10. the sentence beginning **Su objetivo. . .** (paragraph 9)

E.   Some likely responses are given below. For more examples, look at those of your classmates.   1. They might become so infatuated with opportunities in the US that even such a law would not dissuade them; keeping scholars home still doesn't solve the problem of lack of contact across national boundaries.
2. Entities with government funding tend to lose track of their relationships to the real world. The purpose of this institution is to work on serious European economic and cultural problems; it needs to have close connections to the practical aspects of those problems. Anything that is linked to the government can be affected by changes in administration. Its membership might be controlled by political interests. Besides, the whole purpose of the **Academia** is to avoid the nationalism and localism that is embodied in governments.   3. Members will be selected because they are willing to undertake a resonsibility that obligates them to consider themselves citizens of Europe. Any creative, successful person is likely to be interested in many fields and to have the capacity to learn quickly and make connections between his or her own field and others.   4. European intellectuals, especially philosophers and artists, have always received more respect and been more involved in finding solutions to national and international problems than has been the case in the US. In any case, some specific problems mentioned here include improving mutual scientific and technological development, creating a competitive intellectual environment for Europeans, and producing a suitable pool of experts who can serve as consultants to industry or universities.

F.   1. the war between Iran and Iraq   2. Consejo Nacional de Resistencia de Irán   3. May 7, 1985, at a place to be announced later   4. 11   5. Although the most obvious purpose is (c), and (a) is also accomplished, the bulk of the written material suggests that the real purpose is (b). Continue your analysis to be sure.

G. 1. reprimir al pueblo iraní y perpetrar la opresión *(opinion)* 2. reaccionario, anti-humano, inestable *(Each of these reflects an opinion.)* 3. The first two consequences (the numbers of casualties and homeless) are supported by specific figures whose validity could be verified. The third (destruction of the national heritage and economy) may be valid, but no examples are given here to support it. 4. conseguir la paz 5. only the fourth, which concerns a cease-fire

H. Here are some examples; you may have selected others. Compare your results with those of other readers. **Definir puntos claves:** The street flyer uses format and special typefaces to highlight important ideas. **Dar pocas ideas fundamentales:** Note the repetition of the words **paz** and **protesta** and the claims about the nature of the Iranian government. **Apoyar los conceptos sobre el sentimiento:** Note the use of **amantes de la paz** and examples that provoke emotional reactions. **Aportar experiencias propias:** The writers make references to **nuestra patria** and incude a list of organizational activities.

I. 1. The pronouns refer to politicians. 2. cuarenta horas; sin decir absolutamente nada 3. The chart was developed by a group of Polish students. 4. Código universal del discurso político-burocrático para políticos principiantes 5. Choose a phrase from each column, in order. According to the students, the resulting combinations will sound like typical political speeches—and won't make any sense at all! 6. (politicians) **los profesionales de la casa pública**

J. 1. a. E b. C c. F d. A e. B f. D 2. a. B, D b. C c. G, I d. J e. A, F f. E, H 3. a. next b. on the other hand c. nevertheless d. in addition e. therefore f. likewise g. that is to say h. in the same way i. however j. in summary, therefore k. for example l. finally 4. a. d, f, h b. g c. b, c, i, d. k e. a, l f. e, j

K. 1. **Sin embargo** and **pese** both serve to contrast the information that follows them with that contained in the previous three paragraphs. **Además** adds further information to the quoted material. 2. **En cambio** contrasts the intellectual climate in the US (following information) with that in Europe (preceding information). **Por ejemplo** illustrates the kind of location that would be appropriate for the new **Academia**. 3. Como consecuencia, no puede haber... De igual manera, no se puede tener... Además, no es posible... En cambio, lo que se puede hacer... Por lo tanto, la iniciativa... 4. a. contrastive b. additive c. contrastive d. additive e. additive f. additive

L. 1. several years as a visiting professor at Berkeley 2. the number of machines in use 3. whether or not there are children 4. During Carter's administration, it was difficult to get research funds, professors' salaries failed to keep pace with inflation, and students were abandoning engineering. During the Reagan administration, all these trends were reversed. 5. defense spending and military buildup 6. Deterrence and keeping pace with the Soviets is essential. The arms would never be used anyway. The prosperity is not really a result of military spending but of the normal expansion of the US economy. 7. Automobile workers became conservative in order to retain their job security, high salaries, and pensions. University professors became conservative because they could earn more money as consultants to government and the defense industry. Engineering students became conservative because they foresee an improved economic future under the new emphasis on defense. 8. They use their money for machines, not for humanitarian in-

terests or pursuits. 9. The military expansion of the US and the Soviet Union with its preoccupation with high technology threatens disaster to all other nations. 10. Does your summary resemble this one? Americans are excessively preoccupied with the benefits of the technological explosion and fail to understand the potentially negative consequences of the premises on which it is based.

UNIT 10

A. 1. a. C b. B c. D d. A 2. (a) sus colores y formas son agradables; su presencia da vida y calor al ambiente (b) si va con los muebles, la iluminación y la función o color de las habitaciones (c) cocina, sala y dormitorio 3. a. C b. A c. B 4. líneas sencillas, muebles modulares y elementos de metal; they add color because they are flowering plants 5. vitaminas, fertilizantes, tierra, insecticidas 6. watering, dusting, removing dead leaves, repotting 7. They add needed color; they must be strong enough to stand the heat and atmosphere of cooking. 8. Sample: Las plantas tienen una función muy importante en la decoración si se selecionan bien y se cuidan. 9. Sample: Colócalas y cuíadalas bien—¡y te corresponderán! 10. Compare your answers with those of other readers.

B. 1. Many books concern Mexican topics. 2. archeology or history; the itzás and the toltecs; that the toltecs influenced the Itzás; that the influence went in the reverse direction 3. lograr el máximo beneficio para los pueblos; Lange; no, the second *su* refers to Hispanoamérica; because of his views on economics 4. historical materialism; that Michoacán had a key role in the early struggle for Mexican independence from Spain; it illuminates the historical process, not just of Mexico but of Hispanic America generally 5. Compare your answers with those of other readers.

C. 1. cut; carat 2. Cut and color are self-explanatory. Purity refers to the presence of cracks in the crystal, and weight to the size of the stone. 3. size 4. yes (Everything depends on purity and color.) 5. They enhance or diminish the capacity of the stone to reflect light.

D. 1. muscle weakness and fat accumulation 2. exhaustion; lack of energy; injuries; general physical complaints such as weakness, dizziness, and muscle aches 3. Six types of exercises are listed with the problems that accompany incorrect exercise in one part of a chart and correct ways to exercise in the other section. 4. shoulders, neck and back; ankles, knees, and back 5. You shouldn't overdo them when it is extrememly hot or sunny. 6. warmup and stretching exercises 7. all of them: swimming (goggles); jogging and aerobic dance (proper shoes); bicycling (size and adjustment of the seat and handlebars); tennis (proper racquet and shoes); weightlifting (weights in the proper size) 8. **trotar** 9. weightlifting and aerobic exercise 10. Compare your answers with those of other readers.

E. 1. evening prime time (6:00 to midnight) 2. "Mexico en la cultura"; La magia del baile 3. 154; nine 4. five: "Chispita," "En busca del paraíso," "Sangre y arena," "Cuando los hijos se van," "El maleficio" 5. Several answers are correct, including "Magnum" at 9:00 on channel 5 and "Great Boxing Matches of the Seventies" at 8:00 on channel 4. 6. cartoons 7. women, because most of them advertise products or services of interest to women 8. There are several, including school courses such as first-grade reading on channel 11 at 11:00 (repeated at 4:30), intensive high school courses for adults (mathematics at 12:30

on channel 11), university courses beginning at 8:00 A.M. on channel 8 and continuing until noon, and a literacy show at 3:30 on 4. Mexican television serves a large population of undereducated citizens.   9. 6 to 14 years of age; four   10. Compare your answers to those of other readers.

F. 1. Letter one: change casada, "su nino," and niña to masculine forms. You will also want to change **marido** to **esposa** or **mujer**, in accordance with Spanish usage. Letter two: divorciado, acompañado   Letter three: una esposa cariñosa, la noto algo fría, ella tenga otro   2. a. viuda b. comportar c. meter (entrometer) d. costumbre (acostumbrar)   3. su marido: your; su caso: your; sus excusas: his   4. Answers will vary; compare them with other readers'.

G. 1. professional obligation; personal desire; influence of cover or publicity; as a gift; on special occasions   2. a. 5 b. 3 c. 1 d. 4 e. 2   3. 20%; second in importance   4. a. I. b. II. c. I. d. II. e. III. f. I. g. I. h. II. i. I. j. II. 5. a, b, d   6. the fact that they are in school   7. family tradition and the desire of parents to keep up with their children 8. a definition of **intención propia**; inclusion of the term **impulso** to explain the influence of book jackets; **recurso** is added to reason number 4   9 - 12. Compare your answers to those of other readers.

H. 1. 1985   2. *Grimm's Fairy Tales*   3. "Little Red Riding Hood" and "Cinderella"   4. oral tradition   5. a. H b. D c. G d. E e. F f. C g. A h. B   6. The unilateral abolition of the Constitution of 1833 by the new governor of Hanover. 7. 73; 78   8. **Derecho** refers to law, as a field of study. An individual law is a **ley**. (**Leyes** is also sometimes used to refer to the study of law.) The other meanings of **derecho** should give you some insight into why it has this specialized usage.   9. You might like to know that Grimm's fairy tales are readily available in Spanish and are very easy to read, especially since you already know the plots!

I. 1. the agreement to open a private research center dedicated to IA (paragraph 2)   2. ese campo de la informática que trata de acercarse al modo de razonar humano (paragraph 1)   3. expert systems and robotics (paragraph 3)   4. un programa de ordenador inteligente que utiliza procedimientos de deducción y conocimiento para resolver problemas complejos o difíciles que hasta ahora sólo podía hacer el ser humano (paragraph 6) 5. Several are mentioned in paragraphs 1 and 4.   6. machine translation of languages; they failed because of the difficulty in codifying what is known as "common sense" (paragraph 7) 7. producing computers that hear and speak (paragraph 8) 8. a logic-based attempt to arrive at an adequate codification of human knowledge (paragraph 9)   9. transfer of technology, new jobs, collaboration between business and universities (paragraph 11)   10. very recent entry, now working on 26 expert systems (paragraph 11)

J. 1. exposé   2. Hace tiempo publicamos (paragraph 1); En aquella ocasión (paragraph 2); una vez más le pedimos (paragraph 7)   3. the writer (This is the editorial *we*, common in journalistic writing.)   4. the export—legal or illegal—of Mexican animals bred for bullfighting   5. that six breeding farms had been recently established in California with Mexican animals exported with government permission   6. 7   7. a. escuchar; b. no sabíamos las noticias más recientes; c. se trataba   8. Where there's smoke, there's fire.   9. con permisos debidamente registrados por los gobiernos de ambos países (paragraph 4); Todo ello con la bendición y el apoyo de la Asociación Nacional de Criadores de Toros de Lidia (paragraph 5) (If government per-

mission was given, then what was formerly illegal —estaba— must have been declared acceptable. The writer wants to know why.)   10. Remember that two people can reach the same conclusion but use different reasoning. Bullfighting is a controversial topic for many people in the US, and their reasons for opposing it are not the same as those of this writer whose concern has to do primarily with economic and quality considerations.   When reading, you must be sure to distinguish what a writer says from the writer's opinions and, finally, from your own reactions to what you read.

K. 1. b   2. Casal, Julián Ruíz, and (perhaps) the group which worked on his production of "Embrujada" (paragraph 10); only Casal is quoted   3. a. drums b. team c. single d. cut 4. commercial jingles (paragraph 4); popular (paragraph 4); electronic (paragraph 5); heavy metal (paragraph 6); experimental (paragraph 15)   5. a. I. b. I. c. II. d. I. e. II.   6. The first probably refers to his overall musical talent, while the second refers specifically to the ability to read music; the two phrases distinguish having a skill from knowing a fact.   7. Perhaps other readers will have different reactions.

L. 1. 2, 6, 9   2. 2, 6, 10   3. VCRs are brought into the country illegally   4. It is impossible to know how many VCRs are already there and it's still difficult for consumers to get them. 5. The market is so flooded that the machines are devalued.

M. Information: 1. oftalmología, pedagogía, neurología, lingüística, psicología, cibernética informática (y más) 2. Words were joined without spaces or punctuation; words were also abbreviated.   3. about 1440   4. free obligatory education   5. the discovery that readers can recognize words if only parts of them are present   6. nerve cells that receive electrical impulses   7. They serve as signposts for what follows and speed reading.   8. fewer than 15 words for 20 seconds 9. separar, mezclar, deducir, asimilar, archivar   10. visual images   11. about 27000   12. false   **Interpretation:** Each reader's examples and answers are likely to vary somewhat from others. Comparison with other students and discussion with your instructor will help you amplify your interpretations.

N. Action: 1. in a train; tercera clase, asiento duro, ventanillas, pasillo atestado de cestas y maletas   2. dawn; amaneciendo, se salía de la noche, gente dormida   3. Rosamunda (paragraph 2); the soldier (paragraph 6)   4. a, c, f (paragraph 6), h (paragraph 11), j (paragraph 23)   5. Did you find all of these: mayor, flaca, red-haired (all in paragraph 8), blue-eyed (11), asombrosa (13)?   6. nombre   7. 1; two sons and more than one daughter (paragraph 22)   8. 23; 16 (paragraph 22) 9. 28   10. She says she's going back because he needs her; the story (see paragraph 28) suggests that she's going back because she is broke and lonely and has no where else to go.   **Style:** 1. a. III. b. I. c. III. d. I. e. II. f. III. g. I. h. II. i. II.   2. Did you notice the ways in which the details of the physical journey parallel the inner or psychic journey of the two characters?   3. - 5. These questions can be further explored in discussion with other readers.   **Reacting to the Story:** All these questions require you to think about the relationships between the characters and relate it to your own life. They also ask you to evaluate the relationship between what the author says and what she probably means. Discussion with others may change or enhance your understanding of the story. Laforet's short stories and even her best known novel **Nada** are all written in a fairly straightforward style and well repay the time you might spend reading them. Your instructor or librarian can lead you to other serious writers whose works would be of interest to you. Enjoy them!

PHOTO CREDITS

Stuart Cohen 9, 10, 29, 30, 70, 72, 89, 103, 106, 134, 136, 143, 155, 165, 213, 219

PERMISSIONS

p. 3: TV listing from *Cableviews Magazine*, April 5-11, 1986.

p.4: Reprinted from Cleveland State University course schedule, Fall 1986.

p. 5: Book list reprinted with permission from *Speedimpex USA, Inc. 1985-1986 Catalogue of books from Spain and Latin America.*

p. 6: Excerpt reprinted from *The Hidden Civil War: The Story of Copperheads* by Wood Gray, Viking Press, Compass Books Edition, 1964, with permission by the publisher.

"When a Man Hath No Freedom to Fight for at Home" by George Gordon, Lord Byron, reprinted from *Norton Anthology of Poetry*, Shorter Edition, W.W. Norton and Company, 1970. Reprinted with permission by the publisher.

p. 11: Excerpt reprinted from the "Intel Compatibility Guide", [Intel iAPX286 Programmer's Reference Manual] in *PC Tech Journal* 2:6.132, December 1984. Used with permission by the Intel Corporation.

p. 14: Weather page reprinted from *Cleveland Plain Dealer*, April 16, 1986.

p. 15: Reprinted from *ABC*, Num. 23.801, 20 julio 1982.

p. 19: Reprinted from telephone directory listing, Cuernavaca, Mexico.

p. 20: Reprinted from yellow pages telephone directory listing, Barranquilla, Colombia.

p. 21: Item 3 reprinted from *El terrorismo en España* by Alejandro Muñoz Alonso (Barcelona: Planeta/Instituto de Estudios Economicos, 1982), with permission by the publisher.

Item 4 reprinted from *Historia del Uruguay* by Mauricio Schurmann Pacheco and Maria Luisa Coolighan Sanguinetti (Montevideo: Monteverde, 1971), with permission by the publisher.

Item 5 reprinted from *Antología de tradiciones y leyendas bolivianas* by Antonio Paredes Candia (La Paz: Los Amigos del Libro, 1974), with permission by the publisher.

p. 23: Subscription form reprinted with permission from *El País*.

pp. 26-27: Reprinted from *ABC*, 20 julio 1982.

p. 32: Reprinted from *Mécanica Popular*, Vol. 37, No. 7, julio 1984, with permission by Popular Mechanics, International Editions, copyright © by the Hearst Corporation.

p. 36: Reprinted from *Historia del Uruguay*, with permission by the publisher, Monteverde.

p. 37: Reprinted from *El Terrorismo en España*, with permission by the publisher, Planeta/Instituto de Estudios Economicos.

p. 39: "Contenido" reprinted from *Mécanica Popular*, Vol. 37, No. 7, julio 1984. Reprinted with permission by Popular Mechanics, International Editions, copyright © by the Hearst Corporation.

pp. 49-51: "Club de la Amistad" reprinted from *Rutas de Pasión*, Issue 599, 6 junio 1983, with permission by the publisher, Editorial Mex-Ameris, S.A.

p. 56: "Horoscopo" by Daniel Fernández, reprinted from *Buenhogar*, Vol. 21, No. 4, February 12, 1986. Reprinted with permission by Good Housekeeping, International Editions, copyright © by the Hearst Corporation.

pp. 60-61: Article "Hombre y Mujer: Cuando de trabajo se trata" reprinted from *Vanidades Continental*, Vol. 25, No. 8, September 3, 1985, with permission by the publisher, Editorial América, S.A. Photographs reproduced with permission by the photographer, George Chinsee.

p. 83: Charts reprinted with permission from Librería Patria, S.A.

p. 111: News briefs reprinted from *El País*, Año III, No. 133, 7 enero 1985, with permission by the publisher.

p. 112: Reprinted from *El País*, Año II, No. 84, 9 diciembre 1985, with permission by the publisher.

p. 117: "Premio nacional de Gastronomía" reprinted from *El País*, Año II, No. 84, 31 diciembre 1984, with permission by the publisher.

p. 122: "Ensalada: nutritiva, refrescante" reprinted from *Padre e Hijos*, Año 4, No. 48, julio 1984, with permission by the publisher, Antermex, S.A.

p. 125: "Pechugas a la potrerillos" by Fabiola Morera de Moré, reprinted from *Vanidades Continental*, Año 25, No. 18, September 3, 1985. Used with permission by the publisher, Editorial América, S.A.

p. 127: Recipes reprinted from *Cocina y reposteria práctica* (8th edition) by Concepción Hernández F. De Rodriguez. Reprinted with permission by the author.

p. 129: "Las Super Recetas" by Berta Zavala, reprinted from *Tele-guía*, No. 1610, 16-23 junio 1983, with permission by the publisher.

p. 137: "El arroz" by Carmen Casas, reprinted with permission from *Cocina y Hogar*.

pp. 138-39: Cartoons by Sixto Valencia, reprinted from *Cocina Popular*, Año 1, No. 10, with permission by the publisher, Grupo Vertice, S.A. de C.V.

pp. 148-49: "Para enterarse" reprinted from *El Alcázar fin de semana*, No. 182, abril 1982, with permission by the publisher.

p. 156: Guide to movies reprinted from *Guía del Ocio*, Año X, No. 524, 1985, with permission by the publisher.

pp. 158-59: "Estrenos que siguen en cartel" and movie poster, reprinted with permission from *Guía del Ocio*, Año X, No. 524, 1985.

p. 161: "Critica" by Fernando Mendez, reprinted with permission from *Guía del Ocio*, Año X., No. 524, 1985.

p. 167: Reviews reprinted from *Los Domingos de ABC*, No. 729, 25 abril 1982, with permission by the publisher.

p. 169: "Suicidio en México" by Mariano Aquirre, reprinted from *El País*, Año III, 4 noviembre 1985, with permission by the publisher.

p. 171: Poem reprinted by permission of Herederos de Juan Ramón Jiménez.

pp. 174-76, 178: Photo and excerpts from "Es asertiva" by Jane Clark, reprinted from *Buenhogar*, Año 21, No. 9, 20 abril 1986. Reprinted with permission by Good Housekeeping, International Editions, the Hearst Corporation.

p. 179: Article ¡No controles tus lágrimas! A veces. . . llorar es bueno" by Alfonso P. Farfante, reprinted from *Tú*, Año 7, No. 2, with permission by the publisher, Editorial América, S.A. Photograph reproduced with permission by Jahreszeiten Verlag.

p. 183-88: "Las diez palabras más bellas del español" by Francisco Javier Bernal, reprinted from *Los domingos de ABC*, 25 abril 1982. Used with permission by the publisher.

p. 193: "Jorge Luis Borges vive enfermo los días difíciles de su pueblo" by Carlos Ares, reprinted from *El País*, Año III, No. 129, 11 noviembre 1985, with permission by the publisher.

p. 197: Poem "Elogio de la sombra" by Jorge Luis Borges, reprinted from *Elogio de la sombra* (Buenos Aires: Emecé Editores, S.A., 1969), with permission by the publisher. Special permission granted by the estate of Jorge Luis Borges.

p. 202: "Los texanos quieren, aunque sea prestada, la bandera perdida en el Alamo" by Gerardo Galarza, reprinted from *Proceso*, No. 475, 9 diciembre 1985. Used with permission by the publisher.

p. 205: "Una Academia para Europa" by Francesco Alberoni, reprinted from *El País*, Año III, No. 126, 21 octubre 1985. Reprinted with permission by the author.

pp. 210-11: "Método revolucionario para montar un discurso político" reprinted from *El Alcázar fin de semana*, No. 182, abril 1982, with permission by the publisher.

p. 216: Cartoon reprinted from *El País*, Año III, No. 132, 2 diciembre 1985, with permission by the artist, M%áximo.

p. 217: "Los jóvenes y sus máquinas" by Gabriel Jackson, reprinted from *El País*, Año III, No. 85, 7 enero 1985, with permission by the author.

p. 223: "Vive leyendo" cartoon by Mena, reprinted from *Novedades*, Hispamerican Books, Inc., abril/junio 1985, with permission by the publisher.

p. 225: Top photo reproduced from "Sicología" by Dra. Joyce Brothers, in *Buenhogar*, Año 21, No. 9, 23 abril 1986, with permission by Good Housekeeping, International Editions, the Hearst Corporation.

Middle photo reprinted from "Llega la inteligencia artificial" by Malén Ruíz de Elvira, in *El País*, Año III, No. 128, 4 noviembre 1985, with permission by the publisher.

Bottom photo reproduced from "Imposible comprar nuevas videocassetteras" by Gabriel Martinez, in *Tele-guía*, No. 1610, 1983, with permission by the publisher.

p. 226: "Un estudio revela cinco tipos de comportamiento del comprador de libros" by Bel Carrasco, reprinted from *El País*, Año III, No. 85, 7 enero 1985. Reprinted with permission by the publisher.

p. 227: "Se cumple el segundo centenario del nacimiento del mayor de los hermanos Grimm" by Francesco Arroyo, reprinted from *El País*, Año III, No. 85, 7 enero 1985. Used with permission by the publisher.

p. 228: "Llega la inteligencia artificial" by Málen Ruíz de Elvira, reprinted from *El País*, Año III, No. 128, 4 noviembre 1985, with permission by the publisher.

p. 229: Article "Plantas" reprinted from *Tú*, Año 7, No. 2, febrero 1986, with permission by the publisher, Editorial América, S.A. Photograph reproduced with permission by Mondadori Press.

p. 230: Reprinted from *La gaceta* (Fondo de Cultura Economica), septiembre 1980, with permission by the publisher.

p. 231: "Se llevaron vacas bravas a Esatdos Unidos" by Ricardo Torres, reprinted from *Ovaciones*, Año XXXVII, No. 12,623, 3 julio 1984. Used with permission by the publisher.

"Los diamantes" reprinted from *Buenhogar*, Año 21, No. 9, 23 abril 1986. Reprinted with permission by Good Housekeeping, International Editions, the Hearst Corporation.

p. 233: Article reprinted from *Tú*, Año 7, No. 2, febrero 1986, with permission by the publisher, Editorial América, S.A.

pp. 234-35: "Casal, música estética" reprinted from *Sonido*, Año VIII, No. 7, julio 1984. Used with permission by the publisher, Corporación Editorial, S.A. de C.V.

pp. 236-37: Reprinted from *Tele-guía*, No. 1610, 20 junio 1984, with permission by the publisher.

pp. 238-39: "Rosamunda" by Carmen Laforet, reprinted from *Novelas* (Barcelona: Editorial Planeta, 1957), with permission by the publisher.

p. 240: "Imposible comprar nuevas videocassetteras" by Gabriel Martinez, reprinted from Tele-guía, No. 1610, 1983, with permission by the publisher.

p. 240-41: "Pasatiempos" reprinted from *Tú*, Año 7, No. 2, febrero 1986. Used with permission by the Hector Ronzoni.

p. 241: "Sicología" by Dra. Joyce Brothers, reprinted from *Buenhogar*, Año 21, No. 9, 23 abril 1986. Used with permission by Good Housekeeping, International Editions, the Hearst Corpoartion.

pp. 242-43: "La lectura, ese proceso mágico" by Jean-Marie Javron, reprinted from *Selecciones del Reader's Digest*. Reprinted with permission from the April 1984 *Selection du Reader's Digest*. © 1984 by Reader's Digest World Services S.A.

p. 244: "Línea directa" reprinted from *Tū*, Año 7, No. 2, febrero 1986, with permission by the publisher, Editorial América, S.A.